The Age of Migration

The Age of Migration

International Population Movements in the Modern World

Second edition

STEPHEN CASTLES
MARK J. MILLER

THE GUILFORD PRESS
New York   London

Published in the United States of America by
The Guilford Press
A Division of Guilford Publications, Inc.
72 Spring Street, New York, NY 10012
http://www.guilford.com

Printed in Hong Kong

This book is printed on acid-free paper.

Last digit is print number: 9 8 7 6 5 4 3 2

Library of Congress Cataloging-in-Publication Data
Castles, Stephen.
  The age of migration : international population movements in the
modern world / Stephen Castles and Mark J. Miller. — 2nd ed.
    p. cm.
  Includes bibliographical references and index.
  ISBN 1-57230-381-6. — ISBN 1-57230-382-4 (pbk.)
   1. Emigration and immigration.   I. Miller, Mark J.   II. Title.
JV6032.C37 1998
325'.09'04—dc21   98-16000
                                                       CIP

Contents

List of Maps, Tables and Exhibits

Maps

Tables

Exhibits

Preface to the Second Edition

The Age of Migration was originally published in 1993, with the aim of providing an accessible overview of global migrations and their consequences for society. In the meantime, international migration has become a major theme of public interest, and a number of excellent comparative works on the topic have been published. None the less, we feel that *The Age of Migration* still provides a unique perspective, and that its analysis and conclusions have stood the test of time. This second edition updates the work by providing more recent data, describing new developments in migration and minority formation, and providing a more detailed treatment of certain key topics.

The second edition has been substantially rewritten and changed somewhat in structure compared with the original work. Additions, corrections and changes are to be found throughout the text. Chapter 2 has been extended, especially the first part on migration theory. The second part of Chapter 4, which deals with migration to highly-developed countries since the mid-1970s, has been thoroughly revised and updated. Chapter 6 of the original version has been expanded and split in two, in response to greater availability of information on emerging areas of migration: Eastern Europe, the Arab region, Africa and Latin America are examined in the new Chapter 5, while the Asia-Pacific region is the focus of Chapter 6. The old Chapter 5, which compares the migratory process in two very different countries, Germany and Australia, is now Chapter 8, to link it better to the discussion of the long-term impact of immigration on society and politics in Chapters 9 and 10.

We considered adding a statistical appendix, but refrained, since such figures rapidly become outdated, and are in any case now readily available through the Internet, as well as from the sources given elsewhere in the book. A number of the most relevant Internet sources are listed under 'Further Reading'.

In this new Preface, we want briefly to draw attention to some of the major developments since we wrote the original work. These topics are dealt with in more detail in the book. The most obvious trend is the growing politicisation of international migration issues. The first half of the 1990s saw anti-immigration movements in many countries, which sometimes led to racist violence against minorities. Governments too became concerned about their ability to control migration and to manage cultural diversity. These tendencies precipitated some major changes: the 1993 'asylum compromise' in Germany meant abandoning a fundamental tenet of Germany's Basic Law; the change to France's Nationality Code in the same year represented the watering down of the long-standing principle of integration through citizenship; while cuts to welfare rights of legal immigrants in the USA in 1996 questioned the tradition of assimilation of immigrants which is part of the 'American Creed'. On the other hand, several European states have changed their nationality laws to make it easier for immigrants and their children to become citizens.

The politicisation of migration affected new areas too: the 1995 Flor Contemplacion case, in which a Filipino maid was executed for murder in Singapore, led to heated public debates in the Philippines which have been echoed in other labour-exporting countries. What does it mean for national identity if a country is forced to export its most valuable good – its people – for economic reasons? How can a labour-exporting country protect its citizens overseas when most of the power in the global labour market lies with the labour-importing countries? Many people in poorer countries are beginning to question the strategy of development based on migrant remittances and to demand a search for alternatives. New immigration countries, like Italy, Japan and Malaysia, have begun to worry about the consequences of immigration for their societies. The most common responses are increasing restrictiveness through deportation campaigns, border controls and measures to prevent permanent settlement. Many governments still follow a strategy of denial: by tacitly tolerating illegal immigration, and ignoring the likelihood of settlement, they avoid facing up to difficult decisions.

One consequence of the politicisation of international migration has been attempts at international cooperation. In Western Europe, the Schengen Agreement and a range of other multilateral measures have had some effect in reducing immigration. At the beginning of the 1990s, Western Europe was gripped by fears of uncontrollable mass migrations from the east and the south. There have indeed been significant movements, but the predicted mass influx of impoverished people did not take place. However, it is not clear if this was because of multilateral efforts, border control measures, stabilisation of the situation in Eastern Europe, or because migrants lacked the social networks and cultural capital required for migration. Probably all these factors played a part.

Debate on international migration has occurred in other regions, especially in economic fora such as the Asia-Pacific Economic Co-operation (APEC), the North American Free Trade Area and the Latin American Southern Common Market (MERCOSUR). However, no effective mechanisms have been devised even for monitoring migrations in these regions, let alone for regulating them.

There is still no global agency responsible for observing international migration and coordinating responses. The United Nations (UN) has played only a limited role, partly due to problems of demarcation between such agencies as the International Labour Organisation (ILO), the United Nations High Commission for Refugees (UNHCR) and the UN Population Division. The UN's main initiative on migration – the 1990 Convention on the Rights of All Migrant Workers and their Families – has been ratified by only a handful of countries. There are many other international instruments on migrant workers, going back to the ILO Convention of 1949, and including declarations and agreements by the Council of Europe, the European Union (EU) and a range of other bodies. These have had an important role in setting standards for the rights and treatment of migrants, but remain unenforceable and are ignored by many governments. The world is still a long way from a universal system of rights for migrants.

The 1990s have seen the emergence of new types of migration and the entry of ever more countries into the international migration arena. Labour markets for both skilled and unskilled work are being rapidly globalised. The mobility of highly-skilled personnel, usually on a temporary basis, is encouraged by most governments. Lower-skilled workers are often not officially welcomed, even where there is strong employer demand; the result is increased illegal migration, often organised by labour recruiters or migration brokers (the so-called 'migration industry'). One of the most significant quantitative developments is the rapid growth of labour migration to the fast-growing economies of Asia. Africa has also had large new labour migrations, such as the inflows into post-apartheid South Africa. In Latin America, both intra-regional flows and migration to North America have continued to grow. Despite the recent restrictiveness in Western Europe, political, economic and demographic factors are leading some countries to consider new forms of labour recruitment.

A surprising development is the expansion of domestic service both in developed countries where it had almost disappeared, and in fast-growing economies (like Hong Kong or Singapore), where immigrant servants allow local women to take up new employment opportunities.

The Filipino, Sri Lankan or Colombian maid has become an almost ubiquitous emblem of prosperity from Toronto to Tokyo, from Rome to Riyadh. The rebirth of domestic service is part of two broader interconnected trends: the increasing polarisation of labour markets on the basis of skill, and the growing feminisation of international migration.

Global refugee flows seem to have declined somewhat following the rapid expansion of the late 1980s and early 1990s, but large-scale involuntary movements continue around such trouble spots as Afghanistan and Burma, while the whole of Asia fears the potential for mass flows if conflicts erupt in North Korea, Indonesia or China. There have been return flows of refugees where political stability has improved – for example in Mozambique and Central America – but also massive new refugee movements, of which the most dramatic was that of 1995–7 involving the central Africa countries of Rwanda, Burundi, Zaire and Tanzania. Large-scale movements still continue within and between the successor states of the former Soviet Union. Motivations are both political and economic, but the essential cause is the fundamental dislocation brought about by the end of communism. Mass movements of asylum seekers from parts of the former Yugoslavia to Western Europe were a feature of the early 1990s. Now return movements are being initiated by receiving governments.

As for incorporation of new minorities into society, the last few years have seen heated debates, but little progress in finding viable solutions. There is growing awareness that permanent exclusion of immigrants (and their descendants) from citizenship leads to dangerous political and social divisions. Yet the fundamental controversy on assimilation versus multiculturalism is far from being resolved. In some countries there has been a trend away from multiculturalism, with a renaming or watering down of multicultural policies in Canada, Australia, the Netherlands and Sweden. Yet the social forces which led to multilingualism and cultural pluralism still exist, so that a return to assimilationism seems improbable. Other countries have officially rejected multicultural policies, but have sometimes tacitly introduced them in such areas as education or social welfare. Certainly, public discussion of multiculturalism has grown in countries such as the USA, France and Germany. But there is also growing realisation that multiculturalism may not just mean allowing colourful folkloric practices, but also accepting the possibility of cultural and institutional change. Many people (including political leaders) find this too unsettling to contemplate.

International migration has become a major force of social transformation in the modern world. Where migration flows are large, they affect the whole of both the sending and receiving societies. Migrants develop transnational identities which question traditional notions of distinct national belonging. The age of migration is just beginning.

Finally, the authors wish to acknowledge the many valuable criticisms of the original book made by reviewers and colleagues, although it has not been possible to respond to all of them in the new edition. We thank Colleen Mitchell and Lyndal Manton (University of Wollongong) and Mary McGlynn (University of Delaware) for help in preparing the revised text. Most of the maps have been redrawn to improve clarity by David Martin of Cadmart Drafting, Wollongong. Thanks also to our publisher Steven Kennedy for his continued support.

STEPHEN CASTLES
MARK J. MILLER

Acknowledgements to the First Edition

The idea for this book took shape at a conference on Minority Language Rights and Minority Education sponsored by the Western Societies Program of Cornell University in 1988. A conference on East–West migration sponsored by the European Culture Research Centre of the European University Institute in Florence in 1991 again enabled the authors to meet to discuss the project. We would like to thank our publisher, Steven Kennedy, for his advice and encouragement, as well as his patience throughout the project, and John Solomos and Fred Halliday for their constructive and helpful comments.

Stephen Castles wishes to thank Ellie Vasta of the Department of Sociology, University of Wollongong, for reading the whole manuscript and providing many useful suggestions, as well as giving a great deal of support and encouragement. Jock Collins of the University of Technology, Sydney, also read parts of the work and made valuable comments. Colleen Mitchell of the Centre for Multicultural Studies (CMS), University of Wollongong, edited the manuscript and helped prepare the bibliography. Kim McCall of CMS worked on the tables, prepared the final manuscript and gave administrative support throughout. Thanks also to my colleagues at CMS who put up with my preoccupation with this task and provided useful ideas.

Mark Miller wishes to thank Gloria Parisi, Mary McGlynn, Aaron C. Miller and Debjani Bagchi, in particular, for the assistance they provided during the preparation of the manuscript. He also wishes to thank the clerical staff of the Department of Political Science and International Relations at the University of Delaware and that of the Center for Migration Studies in Staten Island, New York, for their unflagging assistance. A leave of absence granted by the University of Delaware in Autumn 1991 greatly facilitated completion of this book. The maps were drawn by David Martin of Cadmart Drafting, Wollongong.

STEPHEN CASTLES
MARK J. MILLER

List of Abbreviations

AAE	*Amicale des Algériens en Europe*
ABS	Australian Bureau of Statistics
ALP	Australian Labour Party
ANC	African National Congress
APEC	Asia-Pacific Economic Cooperation
BfA	*Bundesanstalt für Arbeit* (Federal Labour Office)
BIMPR	Bureau of Immigration, Multicultural and Population Research
BIR	Bureau of Immigration Research
CDU	Christian Democratic Union
CGT	*Confédération Générale du Travail*
CIA	Central Intelligence Agency
CMS	Centre for Multicultural Studies
CSIMCED	The Commision for the Study of International Migration and Cooperative Economic Development
CSL	*Confédération des Syndicats Libres*
DIMA	Department of Immigration and Multicultural Affairs
EC	European Community
ECOWAS	Economic Community of West African States
ECSC	European Convention on Security and Cooperation in Europe
EFTA	European Free Trade Association
EU	Eurpean Union
EVW	European Voluntary Worker
FAS	*Fonds d'Action Sociale* (Social Action Fund)
GATT	General Agreement on Tariffs and Trade
HCI	*Haut Conseil a l'Intégration* (High Council for Integration)
HLMs	*habitations à loyers modestes* (public housing societies)
IFOR	Implementation Force in Bosnia following the 1995 Dayton Agreement
INS	Immigration and Naturalization Service
IOM	International Organisation for Migration
IRCA	Immigration Reform and Control Act

KDP	Kurdish Democratic Party
KPP	Kurdish Workers Party
MERCOSUR	Latin American Southern Common Market
NAFTA	North American Free Trade Agreement
NATO	North Atlantic Treaty Organisation
NICs	newly industrialising countries
OCW	overseas contract worker
ONI	Office National d'Immigration (National Immigration Office)
OPEC	Organisation of Petroleum Exporting Countries
PCF	French Communist Party
PRD	Party of the Democratic Revolution
PUK	Patriotic Union of Kurdistan
RSA	Republic of South Africa
SAC	Special Assistance Category
SGI	*Société Générale d'Immigration*
SHP	Special Humanitarian Programme
SPD	Social Democratic Party
UN	United Nations
UNHCR	United Nations High Commisions for Refugees
WTO	World Trade Organisation
ZEP	*zones d'éducation prioritaire* (educational priority zones)

1 Introduction

The end of the Cold War has ushered in a period marked by enormous change and uncertainty. States have imploded and entire regions verge on anarchy and ruin. Yet, at the same time, democratic institutions, liberal economic strategies and regional integration have become globally ascendant, although still challenged. The ambivalent nature of the period can be seen in the juxtaposition of global human rights norms with episodes of horrific savagery involving mass killings and expulsions of entire populations.

For some observers, the late twentieth-century world is in the throes of systemic transformation. The global order based on sovereign national states is giving way to something new. However, the contours of the emerging new order are unclear. Hope and optimism coexist with gloom and despair. Other observers doubt that fundamental change can or will occur. The nation-state system has been questioned since its inception and still endures despite the growth in the power of global markets, multilateralism and regional integration. National states command the loyalties of most human beings and millions have fought and died for them in recent memory.

These contradictory trends and notions comprise the backdrop to an unfolding drama which has riveted the attention of peoples and leaders: the emergence of international migration as a force for social transformation. While movements of people across borders have shaped states and societies since time immemorial, what is distinctive in recent years is their global scope, their centrality to domestic and international politics and their enormous economic and social consequences. Migration processes may become so entrenched and resistant to governmental control that new political forms will emerge. This would not necessarily entail the disappearance of national states; indeed, that prospect appears quite remote. However, novel forms of interdependence, transnational society and bilateral and regional co-operation are rapidly transforming the lives of millions of people and inextricably weaving together the fates of states and societies.

Growing numbers of dual nationals in many societies are a harbinger of the future. In 1996, for instance, Mexico prepared to change its

1

constitution to allow Mexicans living abroad to cast absentee ballots and to become citizens of another state without losing their rights as Mexicans (*New York Times*, 10 December 1996). Of the estimated 6.3 million Mexicans resident in the USA, about half are legally resident and potentially eligible for US citizenship. Of the over 600 000 Mexicans admitted to the USA as immigrants in the 1970s, only 19 per cent had naturalised as of the end of fiscal year 1994 (US Department of Justice, 1994: 134). By changing its constitution, Mexico in effect would be encouraging Mexicans in the USA to become US citizens and to participate in US politics. The emigrant voice in Mexico's politics would also increase.

For the most part, the growth of transnational society and politics is a beneficial process, but is neither inevitably nor inherently so. Indeed, international migration is frequently a cause and effect of various forms of conflict. One of the most distinctive features of late twentieth-century migration was its growing saliency to discussions of national and regional security. Migration has figured prominently in post-Cold War discussions of a new security agenda. Major events since the 1980s underscore why this is so.

In May 1992, the Los Angeles riots shocked the American nation. At first they were widely portrayed as black–white race riots: a rerun of the ghetto insurrections of the mid-1960s. But a closer look showed that the 1992 riots had a new character. Few of the businesses destroyed by arson and looting were white-owned: about half belonged to Koreans, and around a third to Latinos (mainly Mexican Americans and Cubans). Most of the looters were black, but there was a sizeable share of whites. Moreover one-third of those killed were Latinos, and so were about one-third of the 13 000 people arrested in the week of mayhem. About 1200 of those arrested were illegal immigrants. The white against black violence of the Rodney King (a black motorist beaten up by the police) case may have precipitated the disturbances, but other ethnic and social divisions played a major part. An article in New York's radical Voice spoke of 'the first multicultural riots' (Kwong, 1992), while another writer referred to 'the nation's first multi-ethnic riot' (Rutten, 1992).

In that same year, Europe was alarmed by an series of neo-Nazi onslaughts on refugee hostels in Germany. The attacks were marked by extreme violence, the apparent inability of the police to prevent them, and by the incapacity of the political parties to get a grip on the root causes. Many of the attacks were in the former German Democratic Republic, where the collapse of the communist regime had left high unemployment, poor environmental conditions and disintegrating social institutions. Undermanned police forces were overwhelmed and ill-prepared (Ireland, 1997). Young Germans seemed to be flocking to extreme-right organisations as the only groups able to fill the void in their lives. But there were disturbing reminders of the past: the neo-Nazis used the symbols and methods of the 1930s, while the main target among the refugees – Eastern European gypsies – was one of the groups to which Hitler had applied his 'final solution'. Many Europeans feared the beginning of a new period of instability in Germany, although violence against aliens was commonplace in post-Cold War Europe and extremist anti-immigrant parties fared less well in Germany than elsewhere.

Throughout the early 1990s, the world watched helplessly while Yugoslavia disintegrated into warring fragments. Shelling of civilians, concentration camps and 'ethnic cleansing' became instruments of politics, as elites claiming to represent distinct historical peoples struggled to create new states. Millions of people sought refuge from the war in nearby countries, which were reluctant to receive them, because they added to the already insoluble problems of the European refugee crisis.

All these events were linked to growing international migration and to the problems of living together in one society for culturally and socially diverse ethnic groups. These developments in turn are related to fundamental economic, social and political transformations in this post-modern and post-Cold War epoch. Developments included upheavals in the former Soviet Bloc; the crumbling of apartheid in South Africa; wars, famines and crises throughout Africa; rapid growth and development in Asia; a shift from dictatorships to unstable and debt-plagued democracies in Latin America; and growing economic and political integration in Western Europe. All these upheavals have one thing in common: they have been linked in various ways with mass population movements. It therefore seems fitting to predict that the closing years of the twentieth century and the beginning of the twenty-first will be an age of migration.

Millions of people are seeking work, a new home or simply a safe place to live outside their countries of birth. For many less developed countries, emigration is one aspect of the social crisis which accompanies integration into the world market and modernisation. Population growth and the 'green revolution' in rural areas lead to massive surplus populations. People move to burgeoning cities, where employment opportunities are inadequate and social conditions miserable.

Massive urbanisation outstrips the creation of jobs in the early stages of industrialisation. Some of the previous rural–urban migrants embark on a second migration, seeking to improve their lives by moving to highly developed countries.

The movements take many forms: people migrate as manual workers, highly qualified specialists, entrepreneurs, refugees or as family members of previous migrants. Whether the initial intention is temporary or permanent movement, many migrants become settlers. Migratory networks develop, linking areas of origin and destination, and helping to bring about major changes in both. Migrations can change demographic, economic and social structures, and bring a new cultural diversity, which often brings into question national identity.

This book is about contemporary international migrations, and the way they are changing societies. The perspective is international: large-scale movements of people arise from the accelerating process of global integration. Migrations are not an isolated phenomenon: movements of commodities and capital almost always give rise to movements of people. Global cultural interchange, facilitated by improved transport and the proliferation of print and electronic media, also leads to migration. International migration is not an invention of the late twentieth century, or even of modernity in its twin guises of capitalism and colonialism. Migrations have been part of human history from the earliest times. However, international migration has grown in volume and significance since 1945, and most particularly since the mid-1980s. Migration seems likely to go on growing into the new millennium, and may be one of the most important factors in global change.

There are several reasons for this assumption: growing inequalities in wealth between the North and South are likely to impel increasing numbers of people to move in search of better living standards; political, ecological and demographic pressures may force many people to seek refuge outside their own countries; increasing political or ethnic conflict in a number of regions could lead to mass flights; and the creation of new free trade areas will cause movements of labour, whether or not this is intended by the governments concerned. One corollary is the virtual certainty that states around the world will be increasingly affected by international migration, either as receiving societies, lands of emigration, or both.

No one knows exactly how many international migrants there are worldwide. The head of the International Organisation for Migration (IOM) ventured an estimate of 120 million persons in 1994, including all types of migrants whether undocumented or not (Purcell, 1995).

However, there are great unknowns, such as the number of illegal immigrants. Credible statistics concerning international migration are lacking in many regions of the world. There were over 15 million refugees and asylum seekers in need of protection and assistance as of December 1995 (US Committee for Refugees, 1996). This total can be compared to a figure well over 23 million in 1993, suggesting that population movements are neither inexorable nor unidirectional. Successful repatriation policies and the end of conflict in certain areas resulted in a decrease in numbers. However, concurrently, the number of people who were in refugee-like situations, but who were not officially recognised as refugees or asylum seekers, grew rapidly in the 1990s as did the number of internally displaced persons (estimated at over 20 million people worldwide in 1995).

The estimate of 120 million recent international migrants is equivalent to less than 2 per cent of the world's population. The vast majority of human beings reside in their countries of birth. Taking up residence abroad is the exception, not the rule. Yet the impact of migration is much greater than the small percentage suggests. People tend to move not individually, but in groups. Their departure may have considerable consequences for social and economic relationships in the area of origin. In the country of immigration, settlement is closely linked to employment opportunities, and is almost always concentrated in industrial and urban areas, where the impact on receiving communities is considerable. Migration thus affects not only the migrants themselves, but the sending and receiving societies as a whole. There can be a few people in either industrial countries or less developed countries today who do not have personal experience of migration and its effects. For example, some 30 million of the recent immigrants are foreign workers. They are believed to remit over $67 billion annually to their homelands. If accurate, this figure would place labour second only to oil in world trade (Martin, 1992).

Contemporary migrations: an overview

International migration is part of a transnational revolution that is reshaping societies and politics around the globe. It has affected the world's regions in different ways. Areas such as the USA, Canada, Australia, New Zealand or Argentina are considered 'classical countries of immigration'. Their populations consist mainly of European immigrants and their descendants. The aboriginal populations have been partially destroyed and dispossessed; today the survivors have a marginal and discriminated existence. In the last 20 years the USA, Canada, Australia and New Zealand have experienced large-scale immigration from new source areas, particularly from Asia, as well as from Latin America in the case of USA.

A growing number of new immigration countries have emerged. Virtually all of Northern and western Europe was affected by labour migration between 1945 and the early 1970s. Even Southern European states like Greece, Italy and Spain, which for a long times were zones of emigration, have become immigration areas. Several Central and Eastern European states, particularly Hungary, Poland and the Czech Republic, are becoming immigration lands.

The Middle East is affected by complex population movements. Turkey is both a country of emigration and immigration. In the 1960s and 1970s millions of Turks went to work in Western Europe. When labour recruitment stopped, family reunion and refugee movements took over, while workers started to go on to the oil states of the Persian Gulf. Turkey has also been a haven for ethnic Turks and Muslims encountering persecution in Eastern Europe, as well as for Iranian and Kurdish refugees. To its south, Syria has been a major recipient of Palestinian refugees, as has Lebanon. Israel is a state whose raison d'être is the gathering-in of Jews from around the world. Jordan serves as a refuge for Palestinian refugees and hosts many other immigrants as well. The oil-rich Gulf Arab states, particularly Saudi Arabia and Kuwait, became major magnets to immigrants from the Arab world and Asia following the oil-price explosion of the 1970s. Iran became the world's principal haven for refugees. Millions of Afghans, Iraqi Kurds and Shi'ites and later Azeris found refuge, amounting to a total of 5 million by 1993 (Rajaee, 1996).

In Africa, colonialism and white settlement led to the establishment of migrant labour systems for plantations and mines. The largest international recruitment system was set up by South Africa, and continues to function in a modified form in the post-apartheid era. One of the key problems faced by the post-apartheid government was prevention of illegal immigration from throughout Africa. West Africans from former French colonies still go in search of work to the former colonial power. Algeria had mass emigration to France until recently, but also has a significant refugee population from the Western Sahara. The Sudan, which is one of the world's poorest nations despite its enormous resources, houses a huge population of refugees. Indeed, throughout Africa there were over 5 million refugees in 1995. Many

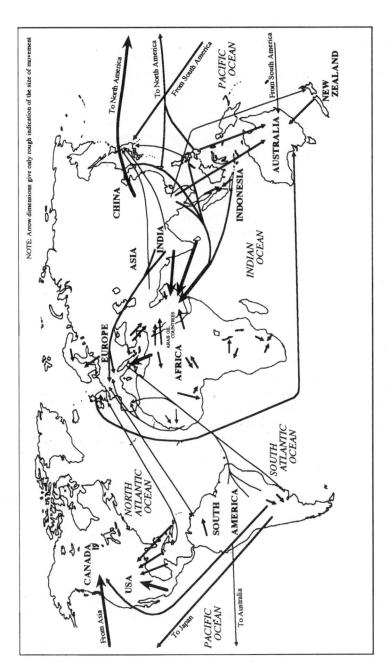

MAP 1.1   Global migratory movements from 1973

African states, such as Nigeria and the Ivory Coast, also receive foreign workers, both legal and illegal.

In Asia, large-scale international migrations have also become frequent. Pakistan has millions of Afghan refugees. India has received immigrants from Bangladesh, Sri Lanka and Nepal. To the north, in the area of the ex-Soviet Union, the potential for migration unleashed by the momentous changes of recent years seems enormous. In East and South-east Asia, the emerging industrial powers, Japan, Hong Kong, Taiwan and Singapore, have all joined the ranks of immigration lands. Malaysia receives hundreds of thousands of foreign workers, many of whom arrive illegally. Outflows of refugees from Indo-China have greatly affected Thailand, Malaysia, Hong Kong and other states. Large proportions of the population of some of the smaller Pacific Islands have migrated to New Zealand or the USA.

Virtually all Latin American countries experience movements of refugees or foreign workers. Venezuela, Brazil, the Dominican Republic and Argentina are major poles of immigration. Many countries are simultaneously countries of emigration and immigration. Dominican emigrants journey northward to the East Coast of the USA while Haitians traditionally are employed during the Dominican Republic's sugar cane harvest. Large-scale labour migration (often illegal) across the long border between Mexico and the USA is of great economic and political significance. There have been mass labour migrations from Jamaica and other Caribbean countries to the USA, while refugees from Cuba and Haiti continue to arrive and settle in the USA.

Comparing migration movements around the world, it is possible to identify certain general tendencies, which are likely to play a major role in the next 20 years.

1. The first might be referred to as the *globalisation of migration*, the tendency for more and more countries to be affected by migratory movements at the same time. Moreover, the diversity of the areas of origin is also increasing, so that most immigration countries have entrants from a broad spectrum of economic, social and cultural backgrounds.

2. The second tendency is the *acceleration of migration*, the fact that migrations are growing in volume in all major regions at the present time. Clearly this quantitative growth increases both the urgency and the difficulties of government policies. However, as indicated by the decrease in the global refugee total since 1993, international migration is not an inexorable process. Governmental

policies can prevent or reduce international migration and repatriation is a possibility.

3. The third tendency is the *differentiation of migration*: most countries do not simply have one type of immigration, such as labour migration, refugee or permanent settlement, but a whole range of types at once. Typically, migratory chains which start with one type of movement often continue with other forms, despite (or often just because of) governments efforts to stop or control the movement. This differentiation presents a major obstacle to national and international policy measures.

4. The fourth tendency is the *feminisation of migration*: women play an increasing role in all regions and all types of migration. In the past most labour migrations and many refugee movements were male dominated, and women were often dealt with under the category of family reunion. Since the 1960s, women have played a major role in labour migration. Today women workers from the majority in movements as diverse as those of Cape Verdians to Italy, Filipinos to the Middle East and Thais to Japan. Some refugee movements, including those from the former Yugoslavia, are marked by a majority of women.

5. The fifth tendency is the growing *politicisation of migration*. Domestic politics, bilateral and regional relationships and national security policies of states around the world are increasingly affected by international migration.

Migration and international politics

Until recently, international migration was generally not seen by governments as a central political issue. Rather migrants were divided up into categories, such as permanent settlers, foreign workers or refugees, and dealt with by a variety of special agencies, such as immigration departments, labour offices, aliens police, welfare authorities and education ministries. It was only in the late 1980s that international migration began to be accorded high-level and systematic attention. For example, as the EU countries removed their internal boundaries, they became increasingly concerned about strengthening external boundaries, to prevent an influx from the south and the east. By the 1990s, the successful mobilisation of extreme-right groups over immigration and supposed threats to national identity helped bring these issues to the centre of the political stage. Three examples of recent political upheavals are discussed in Exhibits 1.1, 1.2 and 1.3 to give an idea of the complex ramifications of migratory movements.

Starting with the 1985 Schengen Agreement between Germany, France and the Benelux countries, there was a series of conferences and treaties between western European countries designed to improve control of migration. In North America and Australia, public debates took place on the volume of immigration and its changing character. Government commissions of inquiry were set up, and new legislation was enacted. In 1991, the so-called G-7 Group, the leaders of the seven major industrial democracies, declared that '[international] migration has made and can make a valuable contribution to economic and social development [and that] . . . there is now a growing concern about worldwide migratory pressures, which are due to a variety of political, social and economic factors'. This declaration constituted a watershed (Martin, 1992: 171). Against the backdrop of the enormous changes associated with the end of the Cold War period, and the grouping efforts to inaugurate a 'New World Order', the significance of international migration as a major determinant of global politics was finally coming into focus.

Ethnic diversity, racism and multiculturalism

Regulation of international migration is one of the two central issues arising from the mass population movements of the current epoch. The other is the effects of growing ethnic diversity on the societies of immigration countries. Settlers are often distinct from the receiving populations: they may come from different types of societies (for example, agrarian-rural rather than urban-industrial) with different traditions, religions and political institutions. They often speak a different language and follow different cultural practices. They may be visibly different, through physical appearance (skin colour, features, hair type and so on) or style of dress. Some migrant groups become concentrated in certain types of work (generally of low social status) and live segregated in low-income residential areas. The position of immigrants is often marked by a specific legal status: that of the foreigner or non-citizen. The differences are frequently summed up in the concepts of 'ethnicity' or 'race'. In many cases, immigration complicates existing conflicts or divisions in societies with long-standing ethnic minorities.

EXHIBIT 1.1

The Gulf War

After the oil-price lead of 1973, the oil-rich states of the Persian Gulf recruited masses of foreign workers from both Arab and Asian countries for construction and industrialisation. At first most were men; later many female domestic servants were recruited from the Philippines and Sri Lanka. Resentments over the status accorded to various categories of aliens in Kuwait became a major factor in Iraq–Kuwait tensions. At the beginning of the Gulf Crisis in 1990 there were 1.1 million foreigners in Iraq, of whom 900 000 were Egyptians and 100 000 Sudanese. Kuwait had 1.5 million foreigners: two-thirds of the total population. The main countries of origin were Jordan/Palestine (510 000 people), Egypt (215 000), India (172 000), Sri Lanka (100 000), Pakistan (90 000) and Bangladesh (75 000).

The Iraqi occupation of Kuwait and the subsequent war led to mass departures of foreign workers. Most Egyptians left Iraq, hundreds of thousands of Palestinians and other migrants fled Kuwait, and perhaps a million Yemenis were forced out of Saudi Arabia when their government sided with Iraq. An estimated 5 million persons were displaced, resulting in enormous losses in remittances and income for states from South-east Asia to North Africa.

The Gulf War suggested, as perhaps never before, the centrality of migration in contemporary international relations. Migrants were viewed as potentially subversive – a fifth column – by the major Arab protagonists, and became scapegoats for domestic and international tensions. Hundreds of migrants were killed in the outbreaks of violence. The political realignments occasioned by the conflict had major repercussions upon society and politics in the Arab region and beyond. For example, emigration had long served as a safety-value for Palestinian Arabs in the Israeli-occupied West Bank and Gaza Strip. The War foreclosed the possibility of emigration to the Gulf, further exacerbating tensions in the Gaza Strip. Hundreds of thousands of Palestinians forced out of Kuwait found refuge in the Kingdom of Jordan. The new influx of Palestinian refugees threatened to compound Jordan's severe economic and political difficulties.

EXHIBIT 1.2

Eastern Europe and the collapse of the Berlin Wall

Migration played an important part in the political transformation of Central and Eastern Europe. The Hungarian government, under the pressure of a wave of would-be emigrants to the west, dismantled the border barriers with Austria in the late 1989. This destroyed a major symbol of the Cold War and created the first opportunity for emigration for East Germans since the construction of the Berlin wall in 1961. Tens of thousands rushed to depart. The steady haemorrhage to the West helped to create a political crisis in the German Democratic Republic, forcing a change in leadership. In a final gambit to maintain control, the new government opened the Wall, enabling East Germans to travel freely to West Germany. The communist regime quickly collapsed and Germany was reunited in 1990. Large-scale migration continued: at least 1 million East Germans moved West from the opening of the wall to the end of 1991.

The collapse of East Germany had a 'domino effect' upon other communist regimes. The political transformation of the region enabled hundreds of thousands to emigrate. During 1989 alone, some 1.2 million people left the former Warsaw Pact area. Most were ethnic minorities welcomed as citizens elsewhere: ethnic Germans who had the right to enter the Federal Republic, ethnic Greeks going to Greece, or Jews who automatically become citizens according to the Israeli Law of Return. The mass arrival of Soviet Jews in Israel was viewed with alarm by Arabs who feared that one result would be further dispossession of the Palestinians.

The spectre of uncontrolled mass emigration from Eastern Europe became a public issue in the West. Before long, Italy deployed troops to prevent an influx of Albanian asylum seekers, while Austria used its army to keep out Romanian gypsies. For Western European leaders, the initial euphoria prompted by the destruction of the barriers to movement was quickly succeeded by a nostalgia for the ease of migration control of an earlier epoch.

The disintegration of the USSR led to the creation of a plethora of successor states. Some of the 25 million or so ethnic Russians living outside the Russian Republic suddenly confronted the possibility of losing their citizenship. Economic crisis and the potential for interethnic violence attendant on the reshaping of the former Warsaw Bloc area made emigration a preferred option for many. But the great mass of Eastern Europeans did not see the welcome mat rolled out for them. Even in Germany and Israel, there was resentment over the massive arrival of newcomers from the ex-USSR and Warsaw Bloc states.

The social meaning of ethnic diversity depends to a large extent on the significance attached to it by the populations and states of the receiving countries. The classical immigration countries have generally seen immigrants as permanent settlers who were to be assimilated or integrated. However not all potential immigrants have been seen as suitable: the USA, Canada and Australia all had policies to keep out non-Europeans and even some categories of Europeans until the 1960s. Countries which emphasised temporary labour recruitment – Western European countries in the 1960s and early 1970s, more recently the Gulf oil states and some of the fast-growing Asian economies – have tried to prevent family reunion and permanent settlement. Despite the emergence of permanent settler populations, such countries have declared themselves not to be countries of immigration, and have denied citizenship and other rights to settlers. Between these two extremes are a wealth of variations, which will be discussed in later chapters.

Culturally distinct settler groups almost always maintain their languages and some elements of their homeland cultures, at least for a few generations. Where governments have recognised permanent settlement, there has been a tendency to move from politics to individual assimilation to acceptance of some degree of cultural difference. The result has been granting of minority cultural and political rights, as embodied in the polices of multiculturalism intro-duced in Canada, Australia and Sweden since the 1970s. Governments which reject the idea of permanent settlement also oppose pluralism, which they see as a threat to national unity and identity . In such cases immigrants tend to turn into marginalised ethnic minorities. In other cases (France, for example), governments may accept the reality of settlement, but demand individual cultural assimilation as the price for granting of rights of citizenship.

Whatever the policies of the governments, immigration may lead to strong reactions from some sections of the population. Immigration often takes place at the same time as economic restructuring and far-reaching social change. People whose conditions of life are already changing in an unpredictable way often see the newcomers as the cause of insecurity. One of the dominant images in the highly developed countries today is that of masses of people flowing in from the poor south and the turbulent east, taking away jobs, pushing up housing prices and overloading social services. Migrations and minorities are seen as a danger to living standards, life styles and social cohesion. Extreme-right parties have grown and flourished through anti-immi-

---

EXHIBIT 1.3

Ethnic cleansing and conflict in Central Africa

Events in the former Yugoslavia and Central Africa in the 1990s made ethnic cleansing a principal problem of post-Cold War world order. In densely populated Rwanda, periodic strife between the Hutu majority and the Tutsi minority had created a Rwandan Tutsi diaspora. Rwanda Tutsi exiles launched a campaign to overthrow the Hutu-dominated Rwandan government from Ugandan territory with the support of the Ugandan government. Advances by the rebels led to negotiations, but then in 1994 the Rwandan President's aircraft was destroyed by a rocket, killing him and the fragile accord.

The killing of the Hutu President served as the pretext for a campaign of violence by a Hutu-dominated faction targeted against the Tutsi minority and moderate Hutus. Hundreds of thousands were hacked to death in a frenzy of violence as the Tutsi-dominated rebel forces advanced. The collapse of governmental forces and their Hutu extremist allies led millions of Rwandan Hutus to flee to Tanzania and Zaire. Many of the perpetrators of the mass killings fled with them.

The governments of Tanzania and Zaire and international relief agencies scrambled to cope with the influxes. Eventually, Tanzania would force many of the Rwandan refugees to repatriate. Some returning refugees were killed. In Zaire, the government threatened to expel the Rwandan refugees *en masse* but may have lacked the capacity to do so. International agencies and governments around the world pleaded against forcible return of the Rwandan refugees.

$\longrightarrow$

---

grant campaigns. Racism is a threat, not only to immigrants themselves, but also to democratic institutions and social order. Analysis of the causes and effects of racism must therefore take a central place in any discussion of international migration and its effects on society.

International migration does not always create diversity. Some migrants such as Britons in Australia or Austrians in Germany, are virtually indistinguishable from the receiving population. Other groups, like Western Europeans in North America, are quickly assimilated. 'Professional transients' – that is, highly-skilled personnel who move temporarily within specialised labour markets – are rarely seen as presenting an integration problem. But these are the exceptions; in most instances, international migration increases diversity within a society. This presents a number of problems for the state. The most obvious concerns social policy: social services and education may have

→

By 1996, military intervention by Western states, including the USA and France in coordination with the UN, was contemplated in the midst of a deteriorating situation which threatened the lives of the Rwandan refugees in Zaire. However, an ethnic Tutsi militia from Eastern Zaire and other anti-government insurgents moved against the Rwandan Hutu militants entrenched in the refugee camps. This enabled many of the Rwandan Hutus to repatriate to an uncertain future while tens of thousands of other Hutu refugees fled deeper into Zaire to elude the insurgents.

In 1997, the beleaguered Zairian government began to arm Rwandan Hutu refugees as part of a broader effort, involving the use of foreign mercenaries, to quell the anti-governmental insurgency in Eastern Zaire. But the Mbotu dictatorship, which had long been supported by Western governments, soon collapsed. The insurgency was reportedly backed by Uganda and the new Tutsi-dominated government of Rwanda. There were also signs of a spillover of Hutu-Tutsi strife to Burundi, where Hutus and Tutsi comprise the bulk of the population.

The Central African crisis of the 1990s was as emblematic of world affairs in the post-Cold War period as the North American Free Trade Agreement (NAFTA) or the APEC. Ethnic violence led to mass movements of people and an emigrant-led insurgency toppled two governments and threatened several others. Mass refugee flows destabilised an entire region, and the UN and major Western powers contemplated the use of military force to protect refugees and prevent further escalation of the violence.

to be planned and delivered in new ways to correspond to different life situations and cultural practices.

More serious is the new challenge to national identity. The nation-state, as it has developed since the eighteenth century, is premised on the idea of cultural as well as political unity. In many countries, ethnic homogeneity, defined in terms of common language, culture, traditions and history, has been seen as the basis of the nation-state. This unity has often been fictitious – a construction of the ruling elite – but it has provided powerful national myths. Immigration and ethnic diversity threaten such ideas of the nation, because they create a people without common ethnic origins. The classical countries of immigration have been able to cope with this situation most easily, since absorption of immigrants has been part of their myth of nation building. But countries which place common culture at the heart of their nation-building process have found it very difficult to resolve the contradiction.

One of the central ways in which the link between the people and the state is expressed is through the rules governing citizenship and naturalisation. States which readily grant citizenship to immigrants, without requiring common ethnicity or cultural assimilation, seem most able to cope with ethnic diversity. On the other hand, states which link citizenship to cultural belonging tend to have exclusionary policies which marginalise and disadvantage immigrants.

It is one of the central themes of this book that continuing international population movements will increase the ethnic diversity of more and more countries. This has already called into question prevailing notions of the nation-state and citizenship. New approaches seem most likely to develop out of the multicultural models evolved in certain countries of immigration. But countries must adapt foreign models to meet their own circumstances and needs. Debates over how best to do so will shape the politics of many countries in coming decades.

Aims and structure of the book

The first goal of this book is describe and explain contemporary international migration. We set out to show the enormous complexity of the phenomenon, and to communicate both the variations and the common factors in international population movements as they affect more and more parts of the world.

The second goal is to explain how migrant settlement is bringing about increased ethnic diversity in many societies, and how this is related to broader social, cultural and political developments. Understanding these changes is the precondition for political action to deal with problems and conflicts linked to migration and ethnic diversity.

The third goal is to link the two discourses, by showing the complex interaction between migration and growing ethnic diversity. There are large bodies of empirical and theoretical work on both themes. However, the two are often inadequately linked. There is a tendency towards specialisation both in academic circles and among policy-makers. Many of the research institutes which deal with migration are distinct from those concerned with ethnic relations. For instance, the International Sociological Association has separate research committees for 'ethnic, race and minority relations' and for 'sociology of migration'. Similarly, many governments have one ministry or agency to deal with immigration, and another to deal with ethnic or race relations.

Immigration and ethnic relations are closely interrelated in a variety of ways. The linkages can best be understood by analysing the migratory process in its totality. It is an ambitious (some would say elusive) undertaking to try to do this on a global level in one short book. Hence accounts of the various migratory movements must inevitably be concise, but a global view of international migration is the precondition for understanding each specific flow. The central aim of this book is therefore to provide an introduction to the subject of international migration and the emergence of multicultural societies, which will help readers to put more detailed accounts of specific migratory processes in context.

The book is structured as follows: Chapter 2 examines some of the theories and concepts used to explain migration and formation of ethnic minorities, and emphasises the need to study the migratory process as a whole. Chapter 3 describes the history of international migration up to 1945. There is some discussion of the role of migration in the emergence of European nation-states, but the main focus is the migrations brought about by capitalism and colonialism, in the process of creating a world market.

Chapter 4 is concerned with migration to industrial countries since 1945. It shows the patterns of labour migration which developed during the post-war boom and discusses the differences and similarities between permanent, post-colonial and guestworker migration systems. The major changes in migratory patterns after the oil shock of 1973 are examined. Finally the increasing volume and complexity of migrations in the late 1980s and early 1990s are discussed.

Chapters 5 and 6 look at some of the new areas of migration, showing how major political, social and economic changes are leading to mass population movements. Chapter 5 is concerned with the Middle East, Eastern Europe, Africa and Latin America, while Chapter 6 deals with Asia. These areas are major sources of migrants to highly-developed countries, and it is from here that the 'next waves' are likely to come. But movements within these regions are of growing importance, particularly where the emergence of new industrial countries is leading to economic and demographic imbalances.

Chapter 7 considers the economic position of immigrants in highly-developed countries, looking at labour market segmentation, the role played by immigrants in economic crisis and why employment of migrants can continue despite high unemployment. The recent history of foreign worker employment in the French motor construction and building industries is used as an example.

Chapter 8 presents a comparative study of the migratory process in two countries which appear at first sight to have had almost diametrically opposed experiences of immigration: Australia and Germany. The aim is to show both parallels and differences, and to discuss the factors which determine them. Chapter 9 goes on to examine the position of immigrants within the societies of some of the other highly-developed immigration countries, looking at such factors as legal status, social policy, formation of ethnic communities, racism, citizenship and national identity. It discusses the reasons for the different policies and attitudes in the various countries, as well as there possible consequences.

Chapter 10 examines some of the key political effects of increasing ethnic diversity, looking both at the involvement of minorities in politics and at the way mainstream politics are changing in reaction to migrant settlement. Perspectives for the emergence of multicultural societies are discussed. Chapter 11 sums up the arguments of the book and presents some conclusions on the future of international migration, and what it is likely to mean for individual societies and for the global community as a whole.

2 The Migratory Process and the Formation of Ethnic Minorities

International migration is hardly ever a simple individual action in which a person decides to move in search of better life-chances, pulls up his or her roots in the place of origin and quickly becomes assimilated in the new country. Much more often migration and settlement is a long-drawn-out process, which will be played out for the rest of the migrant's life, and affect subsequent generations too.[1] It is a collective action, arising out of social change and affecting the whole society in both sending and receiving areas. Moreover, the experience of migration and of living in another country often leads to modification of the original plans, so that migrants' intentions at the time of departure are poor predictors of actual behaviour. Similarly, no government has ever set out to build an ethnically diverse society through immigration, yet labour recruitment policies often lead to the formation of ethnic minorities, with far-reaching consequences for social relations, public policies, national identity and international relations.

The aim of the chapter is to link two bodies of theory which are often dealt with separately: theories on migration and settlement, and theories on ethnic minorities and their position in society. It will start by looking at the concept of the migratory process, and then go on to examine theories of ethnicity and racism. These will be discussed in relation to concepts of gender, class, nation, state and citizenship. This chapter provides a theoretical framework for understanding the more descriptive accounts of migration, settlement and minority formation in later chapters. However, the reader may prefer to read those first and come back to the theory later.

Explaining migration and settlement

Research on migration and ethnic relations is intrinsically interdisciplinary: sociology, political science, history, economics, geography,

19

demography, psychology and law are all relevant. These disciplines look at different aspects of population mobility, and a full understanding requires contributions from all of them. Within each social-scientific discipline, there is a variety of approaches, based on differences in theory and methods. For instance, researchers who base their work on quantitative analysis of large data-sets (such as censuses or representative surveys) will ask different questions and get different results from those who do qualitative studies of small groups. Those who examine the role of migrant labour within the world economy using historical and institutional approaches will again get different findings. All these methods have their place, as long as they lay no claim to be the only correct one.

Representatives of all the various social-scientific paradigms have devised theories of migration (see Massey *et al.*, 1993, 1994). A detailed survey is not possible here, but a useful distinction may be made between three of the main approaches used in contemporary debates: neo-classical economic equilibrium theory, the historical-structuralist approach and migration systems theory (Hugo, 1993: 7–12).

The *neo-classical economic equilibrium perspective* has its antecedents in the earliest systematic theory on migration: that of the nineteenth-century geographer Ravenstein, who formulated statistical laws of migration (Ravenstein, 1885, 1889). These were general statements unconnected with any actual migratory movement (Cohen, 1987: 34–5; Zolberg, 1989: 403–5). This tradition remains alive in the work of many demographers, geographers and economists (for example, Jackson, 1969). Such 'general theories' emphasise tendencies of people to move from densely to sparsely populated areas, or from low- to high-income areas, or link migrations to fluctuations in the business cycle. These approaches are often known as 'push–pull' theories, because they perceive the causes of migration to lie in a combination of 'push factors', impelling people to leave the areas of origin, and 'pull factors', attracting them to certain receiving countries. 'Push factors' include demographic growth, low living standards, lack of economic opportunities and political repression, while 'pull factors' are demand for labour, availability of land, good economic opportunities and political freedoms.

This theory is essentially individualistic and ahistorical. It emphasises the individual decision to migrate, based on rational comparison of the relative costs and benefits of remaining in the area of origin or moving to various alternative destinations. Constraining factors, such as government restrictions on emigration or immigration, are mainly dealt with as distortions of the rational market, which should be removed. Clearly the model has much in common with neo-classical economics. For example, Borjas (1989, 1990) puts forward the model of an immigration market:

> Neo-classical theory assumes that individuals maximise utility: individuals 'search' for the country of residence that maximises their well-being . . . The search is constrained by the individual's financial resources, by the immigration regulations imposed by competing host countries and by the emigration regulations of the source country. In the immigration market the various pieces of information are exchanged and the various options are compared. In a sense, competing host countries make 'migration offers' from which individuals compare and choose. The information gathered in this marketplace leads many individuals to conclude that it is 'profitable' to remain in their birthplace . . . Conversely, other individuals conclude that they are better off in some other country. The immigration market nonrandomly sorts these individuals across host countries. (Borjas, 1989: 461)

Borjas claims that 'this approach leads to a clear – and empirically testable – categorisation of the types of immigrant flows that arise in a world where individuals search for the "best" country' (Borjas, 1989: 461). On this basis, one would expect the most disadvantaged people to move from poor countries to richer areas. The mere existence of economic disparities between various areas should be sufficient to generate migrant flows. In the long run, such flows should help to equalise wages and conditions in underdeveloped and developed regions, leading towards economic equilibrium.

Such theories have been criticised as simplistic and incapable of explaining actual movements or predicting future ones (see Sassen, 1988; Boyd, 1989; Portes and Rumbaut, 1990). Empirical study shows that it is rarely the poorest people from the least-developed countries who move to the richest countries; more frequently the migrants are people of intermediate social status from areas which are undergoing economic and social change. Similarly the push–pull model predicts movements from densely populated areas to more sparsely peopled regions, yet in fact countries of immigration like the Netherlands and Germany are amongst the world's more densely populated. Finally the push–pull model cannot explain why a certain group of migrants goes to one country rather than another: for example, why have most

Algerians migrated to France and not Germany, while the opposite applies to Turks?

An alternative economic approach is provided by the 'new economics of labour migration' put forward by Stark (1991) and others. Stark argues that markets rarely function in the ideal way suggested by the neo-classicists. Migration cannot simply be explained by income differences between two countries, but also by factors such as chances of secure employment, availability of capital for entrepreneurial activity, and the need to manage risk over long periods. For instance, as Massey *et al.* (1987) point out, Mexican farmers may migrate to the USA although they have sufficient land, because they lack the capital to make it productive.

The neo-classical model tends to treat the role of the state as an aberration which disrupts the 'normal' functioning of the market. Borjas, for instance, suggests that the US government should 'deregulate the immigration market' by selling visas to the highest bidder (Borjas, 1990: 225–8). But examination of historical and contemporary migrations (see Chapters 3, 4, 5 and 6 below) shows that states (particularly of the receiving countries) play a major role in initiating, shaping and controlling movements. The most common reason to permit entry is the need for workers – with states sometimes taking on the role of labour recruiter on behalf of employers – but demographic or humanitarian considerations may also be important. Immigration as part of nation building has played a major role in new world countries such as the USA, Canada, Argentina, Brazil and Australia. Policies on refugees and asylum seekers are major determinants of contemporary population movements.

Thus the idea of individual migrants who make free choices which not only 'maximise their well-being' but also lead to an 'equilibrium in the marketplace' (Borjas, 1989: 482) is so far from historical reality that it has little explanatory value. It seems better, as Zolberg suggests, to analyse labour migration 'as a movement of workers propelled by the dynamics of the transnational capitalist economy, which simultaneously determines both the "push" and the "pull"' (Zolberg, 1989: 407). This implies that migrations are collective phenomena, which should be examined as sub-systems of an increasingly global economic and political system.

An alternative explanation of international migration was provided from the 1970s by what came to be called the *historical-structural approach*. This has its intellectual roots in Marxist political economy, and stresses the unequal distribution of economic and political power in the world economy. Migration is seen mainly as a way of mobilising cheap labour for capital. It perpetuates uneven development, exploiting the resources of poor countries to make the rich even richer (Castles and Kosack, 1985; Cohen, 1987; Sassen, 1988). Historical-structuralist analysts criticise the neo-classical perspective because its assumption of free choice for individuals is unrealistic (Hugo, 1993). Rather, inequalities in resources and power between different countries, combined with the entry policies of potential immigration countries, put great constraints on migrants' choices (Zolberg, 1989).

While the 'push–pull' theories tended to focus on mainly voluntary migrations of individuals, like that from Europe to the USA before 1914, historical-structuralist accounts looked at mass recruitment of labour by capital, whether for the factories of Germany, for the agribusiness of California or for infrastructure projects like Australia's Snowy Mountain Hydro-Electric Scheme. The availability of labour was both a legacy of colonialism and the result of war and regional inequalities within Europe. For world systems theories, labour migration was one of the main ways in which links of domination were forged between the core economies of capitalism and its underdeveloped periphery. Migration was as important as military hegemony and control of world trade and investment in keeping the Third World dependent on the First.

But the historical-structuralist approach was in turn criticised by many migration scholars: if the logic of capital and the interests of Western states were so dominant, how could the frequent break-down of migration policies be explained, such as the unplanned shift from labour migration to permanent settlement in certain countries? Both the neo-classical perspective and the historical-structuralist approach seemed too one-sided to analyse adequately the great complexity of contemporary migrations. The neo-classical approach neglected historical causes of movements, and down-played the role of the state, while the historical-functional approach often saw the interests of capital as all-determining, and paid inadequate attention to the motivations and actions of the individuals and groups involved.

Out of such critiques emerged a new approach, *migration systems theory,* which is increasingly influential in comparative research. Migration systems theory (like the historical-structural perspective) emphasises international relations, political economy, collective action and institutional factors. A migration system is constituted by two or more countries which exchange migrants with each other. The tendency is to analyse regional migration systems, such as the South Pacific,

West Africa or the Southern Cone of Latin America (Kritz, Lin and Zlotnik, 1992). However, distant regions may be interlinked, such as the migration system embracing the Caribbean, Western Europe and North America; or that linking North and West Africa with France. The migration systems approach means examining both ends of the flow and studying all the linkages between the places concerned. These linkages can be categorised as 'state-to-state relations and comparisons, mass culture connections and family and social networks' (Fawcett and Arnold, 1987: 456–7).

Migration systems theory suggests that migratory movements generally arise from the existence of prior links between sending and receiving countries based on colonisation, political influence, trade, investment or cultural ties. Thus migration from Mexico to the USA originated in the south-westward expansion of the USA in the nineteenth century and the deliberate recruitment of Mexican workers by US employers in the twentieth century (Portes and Rumbaut, 1990: 224–30). The migration from the Dominican Republic to the USA was initiated by the US military occupation of the 1960s. Similarly both the Korean and the Vietnamese migrations to America were the long-term consequence of US military involvement (Sassen, 1988: 6–9). The migrations from India, Pakistan and Bangladesh to Britain are linked to the British colonial presence on the Indian sub-continent. Similarly Caribbean migrants have tended to move to their respective former colonial power: for example, from Jamaica to Britain, Martinique to France and Surinam to the Netherlands. The Algerian migration to France (and not to Germany) is explained by the French colonial presence in Algeria, while the Turkish presence in Germany is the result of direct labour recruitment by Germany in the 1960s and early 1970s.

The migrations systems approach implies that any migratory movement can be seen as the result of interacting macro- and micro-structures. Macro-structures refer to large-scale institutional factors, while micro-structures embrace the networks, practices and beliefs of the migrants themselves. The macro-structures include the political economy of the world market, interstate relationships, and the laws, structures and practices established by the states of sending and receiving countries to control migration settlement. The evolution of production, distribution and exchange within an increasingly integrated world economy over the last five centuries has clearly been a major determinant of migrations (and not merely of labour migration but also of nation-building migrations and refugee flows: see Portes and Böröcz, 1989: 626).

The role of international relations and of the states of both sending and receiving areas in organising or facilitating movements is also significant (Dohse, 1981; Böhning, 1984; Cohen, 1987; Fawcett, 1989; Mitchell, 1989; Manfrass, 1992). Industrial states guard their borders and admit workers or refugees as exceptions, rather than the rule, so 'it is necessary to account for the wall they have erected as well as for the small doors they have provided in it' (Zolberg, 1989: 408).

The micro-structures are the informal social networks developed by the migrants themselves, in order to cope with migration and settlement. Earlier literature used the concept of 'chain migration' to refer to the phenomenon (for example, Price, 1963: 108–10). Today many authors emphasise the role of information and 'cultural capital' (knowledge of other countries, capabilities for organising travel, finding work and adapting to a new environment) in starting and sustaining migratory movements. Informal networks include personal relationships, family and household patterns, friendship and community ties, and mutual help in economic and social matters. Such links provide vital resources for individuals and groups, and may be referred to as 'social capital' (Bourdieu and Wacquant, 1992: 119).

Informal networks bind 'migrants and nonmigrants together in a complex web of social roles and interpersonal relationships' (Boyd, 1989: 639). These bonds are double-sided: they link migrants with nonmigrants in their areas of origin, but also connect settlers with the receiving populations in relationships of cooperation, competition and conflict. Such networks are dynamic cultural responses, which encourage ethnic community formation and are conducive to the maintenance of transnational family and group ties.

The family and community are crucial in migration networks. Research on Asian migration has shown that migration decisions are usually made not by individuals but by families (Hugo, 1994). In situations of rapid change, a family may decide to send one or more members to work in another region or country, in order to maximise income and survival chances. In many cases, migration decisions are made by the elders (especially the men), and younger people and women are expected to obey patriarchal authority. The family may decide to send young women to the city or overseas, because the labour of the young men is less dispensable on the farm. Young women are also often seen as more reliable in sending remittances. Such motivations correspond with increasing international demand for female labour as factory workers for precision assembly or as domestic servants, contributing to a growing feminisation of migration.

Family linkages often provide both the financial and the cultural capital which make migration possible. Typically migratory chains are started by an external factor, such as recruitment or military service, or by an initial movement of young (usually male) pioneers. Once a movement is established, the migrants mainly follow 'beaten paths' (Stahl, 1993), and are helped by relatives and friends already in the area of immigration. Networks based on family or on common place of origin help provide shelter, work, assistance in coping with bureaucratic procedures and support in personal difficulties. These social networks make the migratory process safer and more manageable for the migrants and their families. Migratory movements, once started, become self-sustaining social processes.

However, the social networks are complex and often ambivalent in character. Some people (both migrants and non-migrants) become facilitators of migration. A 'migration industry' emerges, consisting of recruitment organisations, lawyers, agents, smugglers and other middle-people (Harris, 1996: 132–6). Such people can be both helpers and exploiters of migrants. Especially in situations of illegal migration or of oversupply of potential migrants, the exploitative role may predominate: many migrants have been swindled out of their savings and found themselves marooned without work or resources in a strange country. The emergence of a migration industry with a strong interest in the continuation of migration has often confounded government efforts to control or stop movements. The migration industry can be seen as a 'maso-structure' which acts in the space between micro- and macro-structures, by linking individual activities to the state and economy.

Migration networks also provide the basis for processes of settlement and community formation in the immigration area. Migrant groups develop their own social and economic infrastructure: places of worship, associations, shops, cafés, professionals like lawyers and doctors, and other services. This is linked to family reunion: as length of stay increases, the original migrants (whether workers or refugees) begin to bring their spouses and children in, or found new families. People start to see their life perspectives in the new country. This process is especially linked to the situation of migrants' children: once they go to school in the new country, learn the language, form peer group relationships and develop bicultural or transcultural identities, it becomes more and more difficult for the parents to return to their homelands.

The links between immigrant community and area of origin may persist over generations. Remittances fall off and visits home may decline in frequency, but familial and cultural links remain. People stay in touch with their area of origin, and may seek marriage partners there. Migration continues along the established chains and may increase dramatically at a time of crisis, as shown in the early 1990s by the mass refugee movement of former Yugoslavs to Germany, where they joined compatriots who had migrated as workers 20 years earlier. Economic relations may start with import of homeland foods and other products to the immigration area, and export of manufactured goods in the other direction, leading to international business networks (Lever-Tracy *et al.,* 1991). Migration can also affect international political relations between sending and receiving countries (Esman, 1992, 1994). Cultural links persist as a two-way connection: the migrants' linguistic and cultural roots are maintained, while influences from the immigration country encourage value-change in the area of origin. In the long run, migrations may lead to international communicative networks, which affect economic relations, social and political institutions, and the culture and national identity of all the countries concerned (Basch, Glick-Schiller and Blanc, 1994).

Macro- and micro-structures are linked at all levels with each other. Together they can be examined as facets of an overarching *migratory process.* This concept sums up the complex sets of factors and interactions which lead to international migration and influence its course. No single cause is ever sufficient to explain why people decide to leave their country and settle in another. It is essential to try to understand all aspects of the migratory process, by asking questions such as the following.

1. What economic, social, demographic, environmental or political factors have changed so much that people feel a need to leave their area of origin?
2. What factors provide opportunities for migrants in the destination area?
3. How do social networks and other links develop between the two areas, providing information, means of travel and the possibility of entry to prospective migrants?
4. What legal, political, economic and social structures and practices exist or emerge to regulate migration and settlement?
5. How do migrants turn into settlers, and why does this lead to discrimination, conflict and racism in some cases, but to pluralist or multicultural societies in others?

6. What is the effect of settlement on the social structure, culture and national identity of the receiving societies?
7. How does emigration change the sending area?
8. To what extent do migrations lead to new linkages between sending and receiving societies?

Although each migratory movement has its specific historical patterns, it is possible to generalise on the way migrations evolve, and to find certain internal dynamics in the process. For example, most migrations start with young, economically active people. They are 'target-earners', who want to save enough in a higher-wage economy to improve conditions at home, by buying land, building a house, setting up a business, or paying for education or dowries. After a period in the receiving country, some of these 'primary migrants' return home, but others prolong their stay, or return and then remigrate. This may be because of relative success: they find living and working conditions in the new country better than in the homeland. But it may also be because of relative failure: migrants find it impossible to save enough to achieve their aims, necessitating a longer sojourn. As time goes on, many erstwhile temporary migrants send for spouses, or find partners in the new country. With the birth of children, settlement takes on a more permanent character, whatever the original intentions. These patterns can be summarised in a four-stage model (see Böhning, 1984).

1. Temporary labour migration of young workers, remittance of earnings and continued orientation to the homeland.
2. Prolonging of stay and the development of social networks based on kinship or common area of origin and the need for mutual help in the new environment.
3. Family reunion, growing consciousness of long-term settlement, increasing orientation towards the receiving country, and emergence of ethnic communities with their own institutions (associations, shops, cafés, agencies, professions).
4. Permanent settlement which, depending on the actions of the government and population of the receiving country, leads either to secure legal status and eventual citizenship, or to political exclusion, socioeconomic marginalisation and the formation of permanent ethnic minorities.

In the post-1945 period this model of the migratory process applies most obviously to the movement from the Mediterranean basin to

Western Europe and Australia, and from Latin America and Asia to North America. A high proportion of these movements was labour migration, followed by family reunion, settlement and community formation. The model also fits the migrations from former colonies to the colonial powers fairly well. It is less appropriate to refugee movement or to temporary migrations of highly skilled personnel. None the less the model has analytical value for these groups too, since both refugee movement and highly skilled migration do often lead to family reunion and community formation.

In any case it is important to realise that distinctions between the various types of migrations, however important for the people concerned, are only relative. Labour migrants, permanent settlers and refugees have varying motivations and move under different conditions. Yet all these types of population movement are symptomatic of modernisation and globalisation. Colonialism, industrialisation and integration into the world economy destroy traditional forms of production and social relations, and lead to reshaping of nations and states. Such fundamental societal changes lead both to economically motivated migration and to politically motivated flight. Sometimes it is difficult to distinguish between the two, as the European asylum-seeker crisis of the early 1990s demonstrated.

The formation of ethnic minorities

The long-term effects of immigration on society emerge in the fourth stage of the migratory process: permanent settlement. Outcomes can be very different, depending on the actions of the state and population of the receiving society. At one extreme, openness to settlement, granting of citizenship and gradual acceptance of cultural diversity may allow the formation of *ethnic communities*, which are seen as part of a multicultural society. At the other extreme, denial of the reality of settlement, refusal of citizenship and rights to settlers, and rejection of cultural diversity may lead to formation of *ethnic minorities*, whose presence is widely regarded as undesirable and divisive. In the first case, immigrants and their descendants are seen as an integral part of a society willing to reshape its culture and identity. In the second, immigrants are excluded and marginalised, so that they live on the fringes of a society which is determined to preserve myths of a static culture and a homogeneous identity. Most countries of immigration fit somewhere between these two extremes.

Critics of immigration portray ethnic minorities as a threat to economic well-being, public order and national identity. Yet these ethnic minorities may in fact be the creation of the very people who fear them. Ethnic minorities may be defined as groups which:

a) have been assigned a subordinate position in society by dominant groups on the basis of socially-constructed markers of phenotype (that is, physical appearance or 'race'), origins or culture;
b) have some degree of collective consciousness (or feeling of being a community) based on a belief in shared language, traditions, religion, history and experiences.

An ethnic minority is therefore a product of both 'other-definition' and of self-definition. *Other-definition* means ascription of undesirable characteristics and assignment to inferior social positions by dominant groups. *Self-definition* refers to the consciousness of group members of belonging together on the basis of shared cultural and social characteristics. The relative strength of other- and self-definition varies. Some minorities are mainly constructed through processes of exclusion (which may be referred to as *racism*) by the majority. Others are mainly constituted on the basis of cultural and historical consciousness (or *ethnic identity*) among their members. The concept of the ethnic minority always implies some degree of marginalisation or exclusion, leading to situations of actual or potential conflict. Ethnicity is rarely a theme of political significance when it is simply a matter of different group cultural practices.

Ethnicity

In popular usage, ethnicity is usually seen as an attribute of minority groups, but most social scientists argue that everybody has ethnicity, defined as a sense of group belonging, based on ideas of common origins, history, culture, experience and values (see Fishman, 1985: 4; A.D. Smith, 1986: 27). These ideas change only slowly, which gives ethnicity durability over generations and even centuries. But that does not mean that ethnic consciousness and culture within a group are homogeneous and static. Cohen and Bains argue that ethnicity, unlike race 'refers to a real process of historical individuation – namely the linguistic and cultural practices through which a sense of collective identity or "roots" is produced and transmitted from generation to generation, *and is changed in the process*' (Cohen and Bains, 1988: 24–5, emphasis in original).

The origins of ethnicity may be explained in various ways. Geertz, for example, sees ethnicity as a 'primordial attachment', which results: 'from being born into a particular religious community, speaking a particular language, or even a dialect of a language and following particular social practices. These congruities of blood, speech, custom and so on, are seen to have an ineffable, and at times, overpowering coerciveness in and of themselves' (Geertz, 1963, quoted from Rex, 1986: 26–7). In this approach, ethnicity is not a matter of choice; it is presocial, almost instinctual, something one is born into.

By contrast, many anthropologists use a concept of 'situational' ethnicity. Members of a specific group decide to 'invoke' ethnicity, as a criterion for self-identification, in a situation where such identification is necessary or useful. This explains the variability of ethnic boundaries and changes in salience at different times. The markers chosen for the boundaries are also variable, generally emphasising cultural characteristics, such as language, shared history, customs, religion, and so on, but sometimes including physical characteristics (Wallman, 1986: 229). In this view there is no essential difference between the drawing of boundaries on the basis of cultural difference or of phenotypical difference (popularly referred to as 'race').[2]

Similarly, some sociologists see ethnic identification or mobilisation as rational behaviour, designed to maximise the power of a group in a situation of market competition. Such theories have their roots in Max Weber's concept of 'social closure', whereby a status group establishes rules and practices to exclude others, in order to gain a competitive advantage (Weber, 1968: 342). For Weber (as for Marx), organisation according to 'affective criteria' (such as religion, ethnic identification or communal consciousness) was in the long run likely to be superseded by organisation according to economic interests (class) or bureaucratic rationality. None the less the instrumental use of these affiliations could be rational if it led to successful mobilisation.

Other sociologists reject the concept of ethnicity altogether, seeing it as 'myth' or 'nostalgia', which cannot survive against the rational forces of economic and social integration in large-scale industrial societies (Steinberg, 1981). Yet it is hard to ignore the growing significance of ethnic mobilisation in highly-developed countries, so that many attempts have been made to show the links between ethnicity and power. Studies of the 'ethnic revival' by the US sociologists Glazer and Moynihan (1975) and Bell (1975) emphasise the instrumental role of ethnic identification: phenotypical and cultural characteristics are used to strengthen group solidarity, in order to struggle more effectively for market advantages, or for increased allocation of resources by the state. Bell sees ethnic mobilisation as a substitute for the declining power of class identification in advanced industrial societies. For Bell, the decision to organise on ethnic lines seems to be an almost arbitrary 'strategic choice'. This does not imply that markers, such as skin colour, language, religion, shared history and customs are not real, but rather that the decision to use them to define an ethnic group is not predetermined.

Whether ethnicity is 'primordial', 'situational' or 'instrumental' need not concern us further here. The point is that ethnicity leads to · identification with a specific group, but its visible markers – phenotype, language, culture, customs, religion, behaviour – may also be used as criteria for exclusion by other groups. Ethnicity only takes on social and political meaning when it is linked to processes of boundary drawing between dominant groups and minorities. Becoming an ethnic minority is not an automatic result of immigration, but rather the consequence of specific mechanisms of marginalisation, which affect different groups in different ways.

Racism

As will be shown in later chapters, racism towards certain groups is to be found in all the countries examined. Racism may be defined as the process whereby social groups categorise other groups as different or inferior, on the basis of phenotypical or cultural markers. This process involves the use of economic, social or political power, and generally has the purpose of legitimating exploitation or exclusion of the group so defined.

Racism means making (and acting upon) predictions about people's character, abilities or behaviour on the basis of socially constructed markers of difference. The power of the dominant group is sustained by developing structures (such as laws, policies and administrative practices) that exclude or discriminate against the dominated group. This aspect of racism is generally known as institutional or structural racism. Racist attitudes and discriminatory behaviour on the part of members of the dominant group are referred to as informal racism.

Many social scientists now use the term 'racialisation' to refer to public discourses which imply that a range of social or political problems are a 'natural' consequence of certain ascribed physical or cultural characteristics of minority groups. Racialisation can be used to apply to the social construction of a specific group as a problem, or in the wider sense of the 'racialisation of politics' or the 'racialisation of urban space'.

In some countries, notably Germany and France, there is reluctance to speak of racism. Euphemisms such as 'hostility to foreigners', 'ethnocentrism' or 'xenophobia' are used. But the debate over the label seems sterile: it is more important to understand the phenomenon and its causes. Racism operates in different ways according to the specific history of a society and the interests of the dominant group. In many cases, supposed biological differences are not the only markers: culture, religion, language or other factors are taken as indicative of phenotypical differences. For instance, anti-Muslim racism in Europe is based on cultural symbols which, however, are linked to phenotypical markers (such as Arab or African features).

The historical explanation for racism in Western Europe and in post-colonial settler societies lies in traditions, ideologies and cultural practices, which have developed through ethnic conflicts associated with nation building and colonial expansion (compare Miles, 1989). The reasons for the recent increase in racism lie in fundamental economic and social changes which question the optimistic view of progress embodied in Western modernism. Since the early 1970s, economic restructuring and increasing international cultural interchange have been experienced by many sections of the populations of developed countries as a direct threat to their livelihood, social conditions and identity. Since these changes have coincided with the arrival of new ethnic minorities, the tendency has been to perceive the newcomers as the cause of the threatening changes: an interpretation eagerly encouraged by the extreme right, but also by many mainstream politicians.

Moreover, the very changes which threaten disadvantaged sections of the population have also weakened the labour movement and working-class cultures, which might otherwise have provided some measure of protection. The decline of working-class parties and trade unions, and the erosion of local communicative networks have created the social space for racism to become more virulent (Wieviorka, 1991; 1995; Vasta and Castles, 1996).[3]

Ethnicity, class, gender and life-cycle

Racial and ethnic divisions are only one aspect of social differentiation. Others include social class, gender and position in the life-cycle. None of these distinctions is reducible to any other, yet they constantly cross-cut and interact, affecting life chances, life styles, culture and social consciousness. Immigrant groups and ethnic minorities are just as heterogeneous as the rest of the population. The migrant is a gendered subject, embedded in a wide range of social relationships.

In the early stages of post-1945 international labour mobility, the vital nexus appeared to be that between migration and class, and considerations of gender, racism and ethnic identity were often neglected. Migration was analysed in terms of the interests of various sectors of labour and capital (Castles and Kosack, 1985) or of the incorporation of different types of workers into segmented labour markets (Piore, 1979). International migration continues to be an important factor helping to shape labour market patterns and class relations (see Chapter 7). However, there has been a growing awareness of the crucial links between class, ethnicity and gender.

Even in the early stages, the role of women in maintaining families and reproducing workers in the country of origin was crucial to the economic benefits of labour migration. Moreover a large proportion of migrant workers was female. As Phizacklea (1983: 5) pointed out, it was particularly easy to ascribe inferiority to women migrant workers, just because their primary roles in patriarchal societies were defined as wife and mother, dependent on a male breadwinner. They could therefore be paid lower wages and controlled more easily than men.

Developments since the 1970s have made one-sided emphasis on the link between migration and class all the more inadequate. Restructuring and unemployment have made normal employment situations more the exception than the rule for some minorities. Workforce participation rates – very high in the period of primary migration – are now often below average. Very high rates of unemployment among ethnic minority youth may mean that 'they are not the unemployed, but the never employed' (Sivanandan, 1982: 49). Many members of ethnic minorities have experienced racism from some white workers and therefore find it hard to define their political consciousness in class terms.

Migrant women's work experience often remains distinct from that of men. They tend to be overrepresented in the least desirable occupations, such as repetitive factory work and lower-skilled positions in the personal and community services sectors. However, there has been some mobility into white-collar jobs in recent years, partly as a result of the decline of manufacturing. Professional employment is often linked to traditional caring roles. Minority women have experienced casualisation of employment and increasing unemployment (which often does not appear in the statistics due to their status as 'dependents'). Complex patterns of division of labour on ethnic and gender lines have developed (Waldinger *et al.,* 1990). In a study of the fashion industry in European countries, Phizacklea (1990: 72–93) argues that this industry has been able to survive, despite the new global division of labour, through the development of 'subcontracting webs': large retail companies are able to put pressure for lower prices on small firms controlled by male ethnic entrepreneurs, whose market position is constrained by racial discrimination. These in turn are able to use both patriarchal power relations and the vulnerable legal position of women immigrants to enforce extremely low wages and poor working conditions in sweatshops and outwork. Collins *et al.* (1995: 180–1) present a similar picture of the links between racialisation and gender in ethnic small business in Australia.

Some writers treat racism and sexism as mere by-products of class domination. According to Wallerstein (1991: 33–5), by 'ethnicising' the workforce, capitalists can pay workers differentially and at the same time gain mass support for this hierarchy. Similarly, sexism reinforces exploitation by forcing women to do unpaid work in the household, or to take low wages outside it. This comes close to the classical Marxist argument that class domination has primacy over other forms of domination. This approach has been criticised by such scholars as Anthias and Yuval-Davis (1983) and Brah (1991), who see the 'the primacy of class' as a form of functionalism, which reduces racial and gender oppression to mere mechanisms of ruling-class manipulation. They argue that racism and sexism have always played a part within labour movements, as well as in the wider society. Racism, sexism and class domination are three specific forms of 'social normalisation and exclusion' which are intrinsic to capitalism and modernity, and which have developed in close relationship to each other (Balibar, 1991: 49).

Racism and sexism both involve predicting social behaviour on the basis of allegedly fixed biological or cultural characteristics. According to Essed, racism and sexism 'narrowly intertwine and combine under certain conditions into one, hybrid phenomenon. Therefore it is useful to speak of *gendered racism* to refer to the racist oppression of Black women as structured by racist and ethnicist perceptions of gender roles' (Essed, 1991: 31, emphasis in original). Balibar (1991: 49) argues that 'racism always presupposes sexism'. The type of social order which subordinates women is also likely to racialise ethnic minorities.

Anthias and Yuval-Davis (1989) analyse links between gender relations and the construction of the nation and the ethnic community. Women are not only the biological reproducers of an ethnic group, but also the 'cultural carriers' who have the key role in passing on the language and cultural symbols to the young (see also Vasta, 1990, 1992). In nationalist discourses women serve as the symbolic embodiment of national unity and distinctiveness. They nurture and support the (male) warrior-citizens. In defeat and suffering, the nation is portrayed as a woman in danger. Such symbolism legitimates the political inferiority of women: they embody the nation, while the men represent it politically and militarily (Lutz, Phoenix and Yuval-Davis 1995).

The role of gender in ethnic closure is evident in immigration rules which still often treat men as the principal immigrants while women and children are mere 'dependents'. Britain has used gender-specific measures to limit the growth of the black population. In the 1970s, women from the Indian sub-continent coming to join husbands or fiancés were subjected to 'virginity tests' at Heathrow Airport. The authorities also sought to prevent Afro-Caribbean and Asian women from bringing in husbands, on the grounds that the 'natural place of residence' of the family was the abode of the husband (Klug, 1989: 27–9). In many countries, women who enter as dependents do not have an entitlement to residence in their own right and may face deportation if they get divorced.

The stages of the life-cycle – childhood, youth, maturity, middle age, old age – are also important determinants of economic and social positions, culture and consciousness. There is often a gulf between the experiences of the migrant generation and those of their children, who have grown up and gone to school in the new country. Ethnic minority youth become aware of the contradiction between the prevailing ideologies of equal opportunity and the reality of discrimination and racism in their daily lives. This can lead to the emergence of counter-cultures and political radicalisation. In turn, ethnic minority youth are perceived as a 'social time-bomb' or a threat to public order, which has to be contained through social control institutions such as the police, schools and welfare bureaucracies (see Chapter 9).

Culture, identity and community

Culture has become a central theme in debates on the new ethnic minorities. First, as already outlined, cultural difference serves as a marker for ethnic boundaries. Second, ethnic cultures play a central role in community formation: when ethnic groups cluster together, they establish their own neighbourhoods, marked by distinctive use of private and public spaces. Third, ethnic neighbourhoods are perceived by some members of the majority group as confirmation of their fears of a 'foreign take-over'. Ethnic communities are seen as a threat to the dominant culture and national identity. Fourth, dominant groups may see migrant cultures as primordial, static and regressive. Linguistic and cultural maintenance is taken as proof of inability to come to terms with an advanced industrial society. Those who do not assimilate 'have only themselves to blame' for their marginalised position.

For ethnic minorities, culture plays a key role as a source of identity and as a focus for resistance to exclusion and discrimination. Reference to the culture of origin helps people maintain self-esteem in a situation where their capabilities and experience are undermined. But a static, primordial culture cannot fulfil this task, for it does not provide orientation in a hostile environment. The dynamic nature of culture lies in its capacity to link a group's history and traditions with the actual situation in the migratory process. Migrant or minority cultures are constantly recreated on the basis of the needs and experience of the group and its interaction with the actual social environment (Schierup and Ålund, 1987; Vasta *et al.,* 1992). An apparent regression, for instance to religious fundamentalism, may be precisely the result of a form of modernisation which has been experienced as discriminatory, exploitative and destructive of identity.

It is therefore necessary to understand the development of ethnic cultures, the stabilisation of personal and group identities, and the formation of ethnic communities as facets of a single process. This process is not self-contained: it depends on constant interaction with the state and the various institutions and groups in the country of immigration, as well as with the society of the country of origin. Immigrants and their descendants do not have a static, closed and homogeneous ethnic identity, but instead dynamic multiple identities, influenced by a variety of cultural, social and other factors.

The concept of national culture and identity has become highly questionable. Increasing global economic and cultural integration is leading to a simultaneous homogenisation and fragmentation of culture. As multinational companies take over and repackage the artefacts of local cultures it becomes possible to consume all types of cultural products everywhere, but at the same time these lose their meaning as symbols of group identity. National or ethnic cultures shed their distinctiveness and become just another celebration of the cultural dominance of the international industrial apparatus. Hence the constant search for new sub-cultures, styles and sources of identity, particularly on the part of youth (compare Castles *et al.*, 1992b: 139–41). As Fishman points out:

> Characteristic of postmodern ethnicity is the stance of simultaneously transcending ethnicity as a complete self-contained system, but of retaining it as a selectively preferred, evolving, participatory system. This leads to a kind of self-correction from within and from without, which extreme nationalism and racism do not permit. (Fishman, 1985: 11)

Fishman uses the term 'mainstream ethnicity' to refer to the dominant ethnic consciousness in a society (for example, American ethnicity in the USA) and 'sidestream ethnicities' to refer to the consciousness of minority groups. He emphasises that the two are not mutually exclusive, are constantly changing and are linked in complex and contradictory ways (Fishman, 1985: 490–517).

Gilroy sees the focus of this recreation of culture in the social movements of local communities, as well as in youth sub-cultures. He argues that legacies of anti-colonial struggles have been reshaped in Britain in the reproduction of classes and 'races' which become youth culture:

> The institutions they create: temples, churches, clubs, cafés and blues dances confound any Eurocentric idea of where the line dividing politics and culture should fall. The distinction between public and private spheres cuts across the life of their households and communities in a similar manner. Traditional solidarity mediates and adapts the institutions of the British political system against which it is defined. (Gilroy, 1987: 37)

Culture is becoming increasingly politicised in all countries of immigration. As ideas of racial superiority lose their ideological strength, exclusionary practices against minorities increasingly focus on issues of cultural difference. At the same time, the politics of minority resistance crystallise more and more around cultural symbols. Yet these symbols are only partially based on imported forms of ethnicity. Their main power as definers of community and identity comes from the incorporation of new experiences of ethnic minority groups in the immigration country.

State, nation and citizenship

Large-scale migrations and growing diversity may have important effects on political institutions and national identity. In the contemporary world, the nation-state (of which there are some 200) is the predominant form of political organisation. It derives its legitimacy from the claim of representing the aspirations of its people (or citizens). This implies two further claims: that there is an underlying cultural consensus which allows agreement on the values or interests of the people, and that there is a democratic process for the will of the citizens to be expressed. Such claims are often empty slogans, for most countries are marked by heterogeneity, based on ethnicity, class and other cleavages. Only a minority of countries consistently use democratic mechanisms to resolve value and interest conflicts. None the less, the democratic nation-state has become a global norm.

Immigration of culturally diverse people presents nation-states with a dilemma: incorporation of the newcomers as citizens may undermine myths of cultural homogeneity; but failure to incorporate them may lead to divided societies, marked by severe inequality and conflict. This problem arises from the character of the nation-state, as it developed in Western Europe and North America in the context of modernisation, industrialisation and colonialism. Pre-modern states based their authority on the absolute power of a monarch over a specific territory. Within this area, all people were subjects of the monarch (rather than citizens). There was no concept of a national culture which transcended the gulf between aristocratic rulers and peasants. The modern nation-state, by contrast, implies a close link between cultural belonging and political identity.

A *state*, according to Seton-Watson (1977: 1), 'is a legal and political organisation, with the power to require obedience and loyalty from its citizens'. The state regulates political, economic and social relations in a bounded territory. Most modern nation-states are formally defined by a constitution and laws, according to which all power derives from the people (or nation). It is therefore vital to define who belongs to the people. Membership is marked by the status of citizenship, which lays down rights and duties. Non-citizens are excluded from at least some of these. Citizenship is the essential link between state and nation, and obtaining citizenship is of central importance for newcomers to a country.

Seton-Watson describes a nation as 'a community of people, whose members are bound together by a sense of solidarity, a common culture, a national consciousness' (Seton-Watson, 1977: 1). Such essentially subjective phenomena are difficult to measure. Moreover, it is not clear how a nation differs from an ethnic group, which is defined in a very similar way (see above). Anderson provides an answer with his definition of the nation: 'it is an imagined political community – and imagined as both inherently limited and sovereign' (Anderson, 1983: 15). This concept points to the political character of the nation and its links with a specific territory: an ethnic group that attains sovereignty over a bounded territory becomes a nation and establishes a nation-state. As A.D. Smith (1991: 14) puts it: 'A nation can . . . be defined as a named human population sharing an historic territory, common myths and historical memories, a mass, public culture, a common economy and common legal rights and duties for all members.'

Anderson (1983) regards the nation-state as a modern phenomenon, whose birthdate is that of the US Constitution of 1787. Gellner (1983) argues that nations could not exist in pre-modern societies, owing to the cultural gap between elites and peasants, while modern industrial societies require cultural homogeneity to function, and therefore generate the ideologies needed to create nations. However, both Seton-Watson (1977) and A.D. Smith (1986) argue that the nation is of much greater antiquity, going back to the ancient civilisations of East Asia, the Middle East and Europe. All these authors seem to agree that the nation is essentially a belief system, based on collective cultural ties and sentiments. These convey a sense of identity and belonging, which may be referred to as national consciousness.

Specific to the modern nation-state is the linking of national consciousness with the principle of democracy: every person classified as a member of the national community has an equal right to participate in the formulation of the political will. This linking of nationality and citizenship is deeply contradictory. In liberal theory, all citizens are meant to be free and equal persons who are treated as homogeneous within the political sphere. This requires a separation between a person's political rights and obligations, and their membership of specific groups, based on ethnicity, religion, social class or regional location. The political sphere is one of universalism, which means abstraction from cultural particularity and difference. Difference is to be restricted to the 'non-public identity' (Rawls, 1985: 232–41).

This conflicts with the reality of nation-state formation, however in which being a citizen depends on membership in a certain national community, usually based on the dominant ethnic group of the territory concerned. Thus a citizen is always also a member of a nation, a national. Nationalist ideologies demand that ethnic group, nation and state should be facets of the same community and have the same boundaries: every ethnic group should constitute itself as a nation and should have its own state, with all the appropriate trappings: flag, army, Olympic team and postage stamps. In fact such congruence has rarely been achieved: nationalism has always been an ideology trying to achieve such a condition, rather than an actual state of affairs.

The construction of nation-states has involved the spatial extension of state power, and the territorial incorporation of hitherto distinct ethnic groups. These may or may not coalesce into a single nation over time. Attempts to consolidate the nation-state can mean exclusion, assimilation or even genocide for minority groups. It is possible to keep relatively small groups in situations of permanent subjugation and exclusion from the 'imagined community'. This has applied for instance, to Jews and gypsies in various European countries, to indigenous peoples in settler colonies and to the descendants of slaves and contract workers in some areas of European colonisation. Political domination and cultural exclusion is much more difficult if the subjugated nation retains a territorial base, like the Scots, Welsh and Irish in the United Kingdom, or the Basques in Spain.

The experience of 'historical minorities' has helped to mould structures and attitudes, which affect the conditions for new immigrant groups. The pervasive fear of 'ghettoes' or 'ethnic enclaves' indicates that minorities seem most threatening when they concentrate in distinct areas. For nationalists, an ethnic group is a potential nation which does not (yet) control any territory, or have its own state. Most modern states have made conscious efforts to achieve cultural and political integration of minorities. Mechanisms include citizenship itself, centralised political institutions, the propagation of national languages, universal education systems and creation of national institutions like the army or an established church (Schnapper, 1991, 1994). The problem is similar in character everywhere, whether the minorities are 'old' or 'new': how can a nation be defined, if not in terms of a shared (and single) ethnic identity? How are core values and acceptable behavioural forms to be laid down, if there is a plurality of cultures and traditions?

Coping with diversity has become even more difficult in the era of globalisation. In the nation-states of the nineteenth and early twentieth centuries, politics, the economy, social relations and culture were all organised within the same boundaries. Even movements for change, such as the labour movement or left-wing parties, based their strategies on the nation-state. Globalisation has destabilised this model. The dynamics of economic life now transcend borders, and have become increasingly uncontrollable for national governments. De-industriali-sation of the older industrial nations has led to profound social changes. The nation-state is still the basic unit for defence, public order and welfare, but its room for autonomous action is severely reduced. No government can pursue policies which ignore the impera-tives of global markets. The nexus between power and national boundaries is declining.

The states of immigration countries have had to devise a range of policies and institutions to respond to the problems which arise through increased ethnic diversity. These relate to certain central issues: defining who is a citizen, how newcomers can become citizens and what citizenship means. In principle the nation-state only permits a single membership, but immigrants and their descendants have a relationship to more than one state. They may be citizens of two states, or they may be a citizen of one state but live in another. These situations may lead to 'divided loyalties' and undermine the cultural homogeneity which is the nationalist ideal. Thus large-scale settlement inevitably leads to a debate on citizenship.

Citizenship designates the equality of rights of all citizens within a political community, as well as a corresponding set of institutions guaranteeing these rights (Bauböck, 1991: 28). However, formal equal-ity rarely leads to equality in practice. For instance, citizenship has always meant something different for men than for women, because the concept of the citizen has been premised on the male family-father, who represents his woman and children (Anthias and Yuval-Davis, 1989). The citizen has generally been defined in terms of the cultures, values and interests of the majority ethnic group. Finally, the citizen has usually been explicitly or implicitly conceived in class terms, so that gaining real participatory rights for members of the working class has been one of the central historical tasks of the labour movement. The history of citizenship has therefore been one of conflicts over the real content of the category in terms of civil, political and social rights (Marshall, 1964).

The first concern for immigrants, however, is not the exact content of citizenship, but how they can obtain it, in order to achieve a legal status formally equal to that of other residents. Access has varied considerably in different countries, depending on the prevailing concept of the nation. We can distinguish the following ideal-types of citizenship.

1. The imperial model: definition of belonging to the nation in terms of being a subject of the same power or ruler. This is a notion which predates the French and American revolutions. It allowed the integration of the various peoples of multi-ethnic empires (the British, the Austro-Hungarian, the Ottoman). This model remained formally in operation in Britain until the Nationality Act of 1981, which created a modern type of citizenship for the first time. It also had some validity for the former Soviet Union. The concept almost always has an ideological character, in that it helps to veil the actual dominance of a particular ethnic group or nationality over the other subject peoples.

2. The folk or ethnic model: definition of belonging to the nation in terms of ethnicity (common descent, language and culture), which means exclusion of minorities from citizenship and from the community of the nation. (Germany has come close to this model in both the past and the present.)

3. The republican model: definition of the nation as a political community, based on a constitution, laws and citizenship, with the possibility of admitting newcomers to the community, providing they adhere to the political rules and are willing to adopt the national culture. This assimilationist approach dates back to the French and American revolutions. France is the most obvious current example.

4. The multicultural model: definition of the nation as a political community, based on a constitution, laws and citizenship, with the possibility of admitting newcomers to the community providing they adhere to the political rules, while at the same time accepting cultural difference and the formation of ethnic communities. This pluralist or multicultural approach is relatively new. It has gained most ground in Australia, Canada and Sweden, but is also influential in the Netherlands, USA, Britain and other countries.

The applicability of these models to specific countries will be discussed in more detail in Chapter 9. In fact, the models are neither universally accepted nor static even within a single country. For example, Gordon has argued that three main variants can be found in the USA: 'Anglo-conformity' (that is, the attempt to assimilate minorities completely so that they conformed with existing institutions and values); the 'melting pot', in which the folk ways of various groups were mixed and fused together into a new American type; and 'cultural pluralism', in which ethnic groups maintained their own cultures and languages as distinct communities within an embracing commonwealth (Gordon, 1978: 181–208).

The distinction between citizens and non-citizens is becoming less clear-cut. Immigrants who have been legally resident in a country for many years can often obtain a special status, tantamount to 'quasi-citizenship'. This may confer such rights as: secure residence status; rights to work, seek employment and run a business; entitlements to social security benefits and health services; access to education and training; and limited political rights, such as the rights of association and of assembly. In Sweden and the Netherlands, long-term foreign residents have voting rights in local elections. Such arrangements create a new legal status, which is more than that of a foreigner, but less than that of a citizen. Hammar (1990: 15–23) has suggested the term *denizen* for people 'who are foreign citizens with a legal and permanent resident status'. Hammar estimated that some 7.5 million persons – more than half of the foreign resident population of Western Europe – were denizens by 1987 (Hammar, 1990). Many of the denizens were actually born in their countries of residence.

A further element in the emergence of quasi-citizenship is the development of international human rights standards, as laid down by bodies like the UN, the ILO and the World Trade Organisation (WTO). A whole range of civil and social rights are legally guaranteed for citizens and non-citizens alike in the states which adopt these international norms (Soysal, 1994). However, the legal protection provided by international conventions can be deficient when states do not incorporate the norms into their national law, despite ratifying the conventions.

The EU provides the furthest-going example for transnational citizenship. The 1991 Maastricht Treaty established the legal notion of Citizenship of the European Union, which embraced the following individual rights:

- freedom of movement and residence in the territory of member states
- the right to vote and to stand for office in local elections and European Parliament elections in the state of residence
- the right to diplomatic protection by diplomats of any EU state in a third country
- the right to petition the European Parliament and the possibility to appeal to an ombudsman (Martiniello, 1994: 31)

However, EU citizens living in another member state do not have the right to vote in elections for the national Parliament of that state. People dependent on social security do not have a right to settle in another member country; and access to public employment is still generally restricted to nationals (Martiniello, 1994: 41). For the time being, it seems more appropriate to treat EU citizenship as a case of quasi-citizenship. The limited character is made even clearer by the fact that an 'EU passport' is legally still a passport of one of the member countries. Most importantly, EU citizenship does nothing at all for the majority of immigrants, who come from outside the EU.

The question is whether democratic states can successfully operate with a population differentiated into full citizens, quasi-citizens and foreigners. The central principle of the democratic state is that all members of civil society should be incorporated into the political community. That means granting full citizenship to all permanent residents. Migrations are likely to continue and there will be increasing numbers of people with affiliations to more than one society. Dual or multiple citizenship will become increasingly common. This corresponds with the multiple identities which are becoming the rule for most people, but particularly for migrants. The consequence is that the meaning of citizenship is likely to change, and that the exclusive link to one nation-state will become more tenuous. This could lead to some form of 'transnational citizenship', as Bauböck (1991, 1994) suggests. But that in turn raises the question of how states will regulate immigration if citizenship becomes more universal.

Conclusion

This chapter has been concerned with some of the theoretical explanations of migration and formation of ethnic minorities. One central argument is that migration and settlement are closely related to other economic, political and cultural linkages being formed between different countries in an accelerating process of globalisation. International migration – in all its different forms – must be seen as an integral part of contemporary world developments. It is likely to grow in volume in the years ahead, because of the strong pressures for continuing global integration.

A second argument is that the migratory process has certain internal dynamics based on the social networks which are at its core. These internal dynamics can lead to developments not initially intended either by the migrants themselves or by the states concerned. The most common outcome of a migratory movement, whatever its initial character, is settlement of a large proportion of the migrants, and formation of ethnic communities or minorities in the new country. Thus the emergence of societies which are more ethnically and culturally diverse must be seen as an inevitable result of initial decisions to recruit foreign workers, or to permit immigration.

_ The third argument concerned the nature of ethnic minorities and the process by which they are formed. Most minorities are formed by a combination of other-definition and self-definition. Other-definition refers to various forms of exclusion and discrimination (or racism). Self-definition has a dual character. It includes assertion and recreation of ethnic identity, centred upon pre-migration cultural symbols and practices. It also includes political mobilisation against exclusion and discrimination, using cultural symbols and practices in an instrumental way. When settlement and ethnic minority formation take place at times of economic and social crisis, they can become highly politicised. Issues of culture, identity and community can take on great significance, not only for immigrants, but also for the receiving society as a whole.

The fourth argument focuses on the significance of post-1945 immigration for the nation-state. It seems likely that increasing ethnic diversity will contribute to changes in central political institutions, such as citizenship, and may affect the very nature of the nation-state. Such effects will be even more profound if mass migration continues, as seems likely.

These theoretical conclusions help to explain the growing political salience of issues connected with migration and ethnic minorities. The migratory movements of the last 50 years have led to irreversible changes in many countries. Continuing migrations will cause new transformations, both in the societies already affected and in further countries now entering the international migration arena.

The more descriptive accounts which follow will provide a basis for further discussion of these ideas. Chapters 3, 4, 5 and 6 are mainly concerned with the early stages of the migratory process, showing how initial movements give rise to migratory chains and long-term settlement. Chapters 7, 8, 9 and 10 are concerned mainly with the later stages of the migratory process. They discuss the ways in which settlement and minority formation affect the economies, societies and political systems of immigration countries.

3 International Migration before 1945

The post-1945 migrations may be new in scale and scope, but population movements in response to demographic growth, climatic change and the development of production and trade have always been part of human history. Warfare, conquest, formation of nations and the emergence of states and empires have all led to migrations, both voluntary and forced. The enslavement and deportation of conquered people was a frequent early form of labour migration. From the end of the Middle Ages, the development of European states and their colonisation of the rest of the world gave a new impetus to international migrations of many different kinds.

In Western Europe, 'migration was a long-standing and important facet of social life and the political economy' from about 1650 onwards, playing a vital role in modernisation and industrialisation (Moch, 1995: 126; see also Moch, 1992). The centrality of migration is not adequately reflected in prevailing views on the past: as Gérard Noiriel (1988: 15–67) has pointed out, the history of immigration has been a 'blind spot' of historical research in France. This applies equally to other European countries. Denial of the role of immigrants in nation building has been crucial to the creation of myths of national homogeneity. This was obviously impossible in classical countries of immigration such as the USA. It is only in very recent times that French, German and British historians have started serious investigation of the significance of immigration. Exhibit 3.1 provides an illustration of the significance of migration in early processes of nation building.

Individual liberty is portrayed as one of the great moral achievements of capitalism, in contrast with earlier societies where liberty was restricted by traditional bondage and servitude. Neo-classical theorists portray the capitalist economy as being based on free markets, including the labour market, where employers and workers encounter each other as free legal subjects, with equal rights to make contracts. International migration is portrayed as a market in which workers make the free choice to move to the area where they will receive the highest income (compare Borjas, 1990: 9–18). But this harmonious picture often fails to match reality. As Cohen (1987) has shown, capitalism has made use of both free and 'unfree' workers in every phase of its development. Labour migrants have frequently been unfree workers, either because they are taken by force to the place where their labour is needed, or because they are denied rights enjoyed by other workers, and cannot therefore compete under equal conditions. Even where migration is voluntary and unregulated, institutional and informal discrimination may limit the real freedom and equality of the workers concerned.

Since economic power is usually linked to political power, mobilisation of labour often has an element of coercion, sometimes involving violence, military force and bureaucratic control. Examples are the slave economy of the Americas; indentured colonial labour in Asia, Africa and the Americas; mineworkers in southern Africa in the nineteenth and twentieth centuries; foreign workers in Germany and France before the Second World War; forced labourers in the Nazi war economy; 'guestworkers' in post-1945 Europe, and 'illegals' denied the protection of law in many countries today.

One important theme is not dealt with here because it requires more intensive treatment than is possible in the present work: the devastating effects of international migration on the indigenous peoples of colonised countries. European conquest of Africa, Asia, America and Oceania led either to the domination and exploitation of native peoples or to genocide, both physical and cultural. Nation building – particularly in the Americas and Oceania – was based on the importation of new populations. Thus immigration contributed to the exclusion and marginalisation of aboriginal peoples. One starting-point for the construction of new national identities was the idealisation of the destruction of indigenous societies: images such as 'how the West was won' or the struggle of Australian pioneers against the Aborigines became powerful myths. The roots of racist stereotypes – today directed against new immigrant groups – often lie in historical treatment of colonised peoples. Nowadays there is increasing realisation that appropriate models for intergroup relations have to address the needs of indigenous populations, as well as those of immigrant groups.

Colonialism

European colonialism gave rise to various types of migration. One was the large outward movement from Europe, first to Africa and Asia,

EXHIBIT 3.1

Migration and nation in French history

Ancient Gaul encompassed much of the area of modern-day France. At the collapse of the Western Roman Empire in the fifth century AD, Gaul was inhabited by a crazy-quilt of culturally and politically diverse peoples, including Roman citizens and soldiers, slaves, settled Germanic tribes and more recent arrivals. There were multiple centres of political power. Celts from the West of Britain moved across the English Channel to what is now Brittany, to escape the invading Saxons. These Celts fought with the embryonic Frankish state, from which the mediaeval French kingdom would emerge.

Norse raiders wreaked havoc upon the Frankish territory and, from 900 AD, they settled in the area now called Normandy. The expansion of the Frankish state and its steady incorporation of adjacent lands and peoples was a long process, and French identity and consciousness emerged slowly. Life for most inhabitants of mediaeval France was encapsulated by the village and its environs, but there was awareness of the exterior world. To the inhabitants of the Frankish state, the people of Brittany, Normandy or Languedoc were foreigners.

But there were also newcomers: traders and artists from Italy, mercenaries, itinerant clergy, scholars and musicians, Muslim slaves from North Africa, the Eastern Mediterranean and Spain, as well as Jews and gypsies. Jews lived interspersed with the rest of the population and most appear to have spoken the local language. During the Crusades, Jews became scapegoats and victims of violence and persecution. Enforced residential segregation – ghettoes – became commonplace. In 1306, the French king, Philip the Fair, ordered the expulsion of the Jews, who by that time numbered about 100 000, allowing him to seize Jewish possessions. But in 1715 economic considerations led King Louis X to reopen the doors of the French kingdom to Jews. It was only with the French Revolution of 1789 that Jews gained legal equality with the Christian population as

then to the Americas, and later to Oceania. Europeans migrated, either permanently or temporarily, as sailors, soldiers, farmers, traders, priests and administrators. Some of them had already migrated within Europe: Lucassen (1995) has shown that around half the soldiers and sailors of the Dutch East India Company in the seventeenth and eighteenth centuries were not Dutch but 'transmigrants', mainly from poor areas of Germany. The mortality of these migrant workers through shipwreck, warfare and tropical illnesses was very high, but service in the colonies was often the only chance to escape from poverty. Such overseas migrations helped to bring about major

⟶

citizens. However, some people continued to regard Jews as foreigners to the French nation. Even today, the propaganda of the *Front National* (FN) has marked anti-semitic overtones.

The gypsies, also called the Rom or the Tzigane, are the descendants of a people who emigrated from the area of present-day India. Travelling in groups of 50 to 100, they spread throughout the kingdom, hawking their wares. There were soon manifestations of hostility towards them. French cities such as Angers banned them in 1498, followed soon after by King François I's edict prohibiting them from entering his kingdom. The gypsies returned and became part of French society, but they were never fully accepted by some people. Like the Jews, they were singled out for extermination by the Nazis during the Second World War. The roots of twentieth-century genocide were deeply etched in the history of immigration to European countries. Jews and gypsies have been perhaps the most enduring targets of European racism.

The fifteenth century was a turning point at which early modern states emerged. This is the dawn of the Age of Discovery in which Europeans circumnavigated the globe, beginning a long process which eventually brought the world under European domination. By the eighteenth century, the 'divine right of kings' was being questioned. The ideas that gave rise to the 1789 French Revolution included the principle of popular sovereignty, the concept of the nation-state and the idea that every human being belongs to a state. These ideas are particularly significant for our theme: international migration would be meaningless in a world not organised into nation-states. One of the key attributes of sovereignty is the idea, now universally accepted, that states have the authority to regulate movement into and out of the territory of the state. Illegal immigration has become such a politically volatile issue today partly because it is seen as violating one of the main prerogatives of sovereign states.

Source: Lequin (1988).

changes in the economic structures and the cultures of both the European sending countries and the colonies.

An important antecedent of modern labour migration is the system of chattel slavery, which formed the basis of commodity production in the plantations and mines of the New World from the late seventeenth century to the mid-nineteenth century. The production of sugar, tobacco, coffee, cotton and gold by slave labour was crucial to the economic and political power of Britain and France – the dominant states of the eighteenth century – and played a major role for Spain, Portugal and the Netherlands as well. By 1770 there were nearly 2½

52

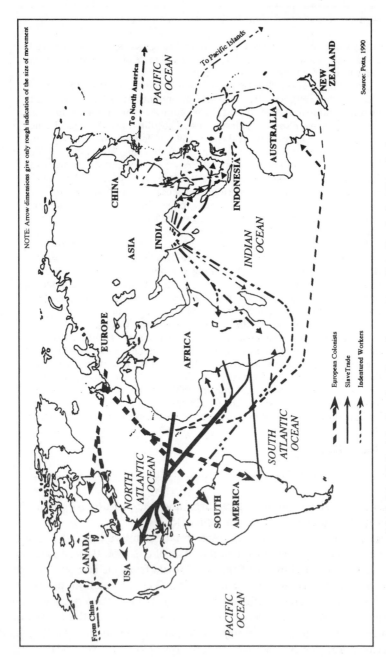

NOTE: Arrow dimensions give only rough indication of the size of movement

Source: Potts, 1990

European Colonists

Slave Trade

Indentured Workers

MAP 3.1 Colonial migrations from the seventeenth to the nineteenth centuries

million slaves in the Americas, producing a third of the total value of European commerce (Blackburn, 1988: 5). The slave system was organised in the famous 'triangular trade': ships laden with manufactured goods, such as guns or household implements, sailed from ports such as Bristol and Liverpool, Bordeaux and Le Havre, to the coasts of West Africa. There Africans were either forcibly abducted or were purchased from local chiefs or traders in return for the goods. Then the ships sailed to the Caribbean or the coasts of North or South America, where the slaves were sold for cash. This was used to purchase the products of the plantations, which were then brought back for sale in Europe.

An estimated 15 million slaves were taken to the Americas before 1850 (Appleyard, 1991: 11). For the women, hard labour in the mines, plantations and households was frequently accompanied by sexual exploitation. The children of slaves remained the chattels of the owners. Slavery was not abolished until 1834 in British colonies, 1863 in Dutch colonies and 1865 in the southern states of the USA (Cohen, 1991: 9). Despite slave rebellions and the abolition of the Atlantic traffic by the great powers in 1815, slavery continued to grow in economic significance. The number of slaves in the Americas doubled from 3 million in 1800 to 6 million in 1860, with corresponding growth in the area of plantation agriculture in the south-western USA, Cuba and Brazil (Blackburn, 1988: 544).

Slavery had existed in many pre-capitalist societies, but the colonial system was new in character. Its motive force was the emergence of global empires, which began to construct a world market, dominated by merchant capital. Slaves were transported great distances by specialised traders, and bought and sold as commodities. Slaves were economic property and were subjected to harsh forms of control to maximise their output. The great majority were exploited in plantations which produced for export, as part of an internationally integrated agricultural and manufacturing system (Fox-Genovese and Genovese, 1983; Blackburn, 1988).

In the latter half of the nineteenth century, slaves were replaced by indentured workers as the main source of plantation labour. Indenture (or the 'coolie system') involved recruitment of large groups of workers, sometimes by force, and their transportation to another area for work. British colonial authorities recruited workers from the Indian sub-continent for the sugar plantations of Trinidad, Guyana and other Caribbean countries. Others were employed in plantations, mines and railway construction in Malaya, East Africa and Fiji. The British also recruited Chinese 'coolies' for Malaya and other colonies. Dutch colonial authorities used Chinese labour on construction projects in the Dutch East Indies. Up to 1 million indentured workers were recruited in Japan, mainly for work in Hawaii, the USA, Brazil and Peru (Shimpo, 1995).

According to Potts (1990: 63–103) indentured workers were used in 40 countries by all the major colonial powers. She estimates that the system involved from 12 to 37 million workers between 1834 and 1941, when indentureship was finally abolished in the Dutch colonies. Indentured workers were bound by strict labour contracts for a period of several years. Wages and conditions were generally very poor, workers were subject to rigid discipline and breaches of contract were severely punished. Indentured workers were often cheaper for their employers than slaves (Cohen, 1991: 9–11). On the other hand, work overseas offered an opportunity to escape poverty and repressive situations, such as the Indian caste system. Many workers remained as free settlers in East Africa, the Caribbean, Fiji and elsewhere, where they could obtain land or set up businesses (Cohen, 1995: 46).

Indenture epitomised the principle of divide and rule, and a number of post-colonial conflicts (for example, hostility against Indians in Africa and Fiji, and against Chinese in South-east Asia) have their roots in such divisions. The Caribbean experience shows the effect of changing colonial labour practices on dominated peoples: the original inhabitants, the Caribs and Arawaks, were wiped out completely by European diseases and violence. With the development of the sugar industry in the eighteenth century, Africans were brought in as slaves. Upon emancipation in the nineteenth century, these generally became small-scale subsistence farmers, and were replaced with indentured workers from India. Upon completion of their indentures, many settled, bringing in dependants. Some remained labourers on large estates, while others became established as a trading class, mediating between the white ruling class and the black majority.

Industrialisation and migration to North America and Australia before 1914

The wealth accumulated in Western Europe through colonial exploitation provided much of the capital which was to unleash the industrial revolutions of the eighteenth and nineteenth centuries. In Britain, profits from the colonies were invested in new forms of manufacture, as well as encouraging commercial farming and speeding up the enclosure of arable land for pasture. The displaced tenant farmers swelled the impoverished urban masses available as labour for the new factories. This emerging class of wage labourers was soon joined by destitute artisans, such as hand-loom weavers, who had lost their livelihood through competition from the new manufactures. Herein lay the basis of the new class which was crucial for the British industrial economy: the 'free proletariat' which was free of traditional bonds, but also of ownership of the means of production.

However, from the outset, unfree labour played an important part. Throughout Europe, draconian poor laws were introduced to control the displaced farmers and artisans, the 'hordes of beggars' who threatened public order. Workhouses and poorhouses were often the first form of manufacture, where the disciplinary instruments of the future factory system were developed and tested. In Britain, 'parish apprentices', orphan children under the care of local authorities, were hired out to factories as cheap unskilled labour. This was a form of forced labour, with severe punishments for insubordination or refusal to work, and not even a hint of free choice.

The peak of the industrial revolution was the main period of British migration to America: between 1800 and 1860, 66 per cent of migrants to the USA were from Britain, and a further 22 per cent were from Germany. From 1800 to 1930, 40 million Europeans migrated permanently overseas, mainly to North and South America and Australia (Decloîtres, 1967: 22). From 1850 to 1914 most migrants came from Ireland, Italy, Spain and Eastern Europe, areas in which industrialisation came later. America offered the dream of becoming an independent farmer or trader in new lands of opportunity. Often this dream was disappointed: the migrants became wage-labourers building roads and railways across the vast expanses of the New World, 'cowboys', gauchos or stockmen on large ranches, or factory workers in the emerging industries of the north-eastern USA. However many settlers did eventually succeed in their dream, becoming farmers, white-collar workers or business people, while others were at least able to see their children achieve education and upward social mobility.

The USA is generally seen as the most important of all immigration countries. An estimated 54 million people entered between 1820 and 1987 (Borjas, 1990: 3). The peak period was 1861 to 1920, during which 30 million people came. Until the 1880s, migration was unregulated: anyone who could afford the ocean passage could come to seek a new life in America. However American employers did organise campaigns to attract potential workers, and a multitude of agencies and shipping companies helped organise movements. Many of the migrants were young single men, hoping to save enough to return home and start a family. But there were also single women, couples and families. Racist campaigns led to exclusionary laws to keep out Chinese and other Asians from the 1880s. For Europeans and Latin Americans, entry remained free until 1920 (Borjas, 1990: 27). The census of that year showed that there were 13.9 million foreign-born people in the USA, making up 13.2 per cent of the total population (Briggs, 1984: 77).

Slavery had been a major source of capital accumulation in the early USA, but the industrial take-off after the Civil War (1861–5) was fuelled by mass immigration from Europe. At the same time the racist 'Jim Crow' system was used to keep the now nominally free African-Americans in the plantations of the southern states, since cheap cotton and other agricultural products were central to industrialisation. The largest immigrant groups from 1860 to 1920 were Irish, Italians and Jews from Eastern Europe, but there were people from just about every other European country, as well as from Mexico. Patterns of settlement were closely linked to the emerging industrial economy. Labour recruitment by canal and railway companies led to settlements of Irish and Italians along the construction routes. Some groups of Irish, Italians and Jews settled in the east coast ports of arrival, where work was available in construction, transport and factories. The same was true of the Chinese on the west coast. Some Central and Eastern European peoples became concentrated in the midwest, where the development of heavy industry at the turn of the century provided work opportunities (Portes and Rumbaut, 1990: 29–32). The American working class thus developed through processes of chain migration which led to patterns of ethnic segmentation.

Canada received many loyalists of British origin after the American Revolution. From the late eighteenth century there was immigration from Britain, France, Germany and other Northern European countries. Many African-Americans came across the long frontier from the USA to escape slavery: by 1860, there were 40 000 black people in Canada. In the nineteenth century, immigration was stimulated by the gold rushes, while rural immigrants were encouraged to settle the vast prairie areas. Between 1871 and 1931, Canada's population increased from 3.6 million to 10.3 million. Immigration from China, Japan and India also began in the late nineteenth century. Chinese came to the west coast, particularly to British Columbia, where they helped build the Canadian Pacific Railway. From 1886 a series of measures was introduced to stop Asian immigration (Kubat, 1987: 229–35). Canada received a large influx from Southern and Eastern Europe over the 1895 to 1914 period. But in 1931, four preferred classes of immigrants were designated: British subjects with adequate financial means from the UK, Ireland and four other domains of the crown; US citizens; dependants of permanent residents of Canada; and agriculturists. Canada discouraged migration from Southern and Eastern Europe, while Asian immigration was prohibited from 1923 to 1947.

For Australia, immigration has been a crucial factor in economic development and nation building ever since British colonisation started in 1788. The Australian colonies were integrated into the British Empire as suppliers of raw materials such as wool, wheat and gold. The imperial state took an active role in providing workers for expansion through convict transportation (another form of unfree labour!) and the encouragement of free settlement. Initially there were large male surpluses, especially in the frontier areas, which were often societies of 'men without women'. But many female convicts were transported, and there were special schemes to bring out single women as domestic servants and as wives for settlers.

When the surplus population of Britain became inadequate for labour needs from the mid-nineteenth century, Britain supported Australian employers in their demand for cheap labour from elsewhere in the Empire: China, India and the South Pacific Islands. The economic interests of Britain came into conflict with the demands of the nascent Australian labour movement. The call for decent wages came to be formulated in racist (and sexist) terms, as the demand for wages 'fit for white men'. Hostility towards Chinese and other Asian workers became violent. The exclusionary boundaries of the emerging Australian nation were drawn on racial lines, and one of the first Acts of the new Federal Parliament in 1901 was the introduction of the White Australia Policy (see de Lepervanche, 1975).

Labour migration within Europe

In Europe, overseas migration and intra-European migration took place side-by-side. Of the 15 million Italians who emigrated between 1876 and 1920, nearly half (6.8 million) went to other European countries (mainly France, Switzerland and Germany: see Cinanni, 1968: 29). As Western Europeans went overseas in the (often vain) attempt to escape proletarianisation, workers from peripheral areas,

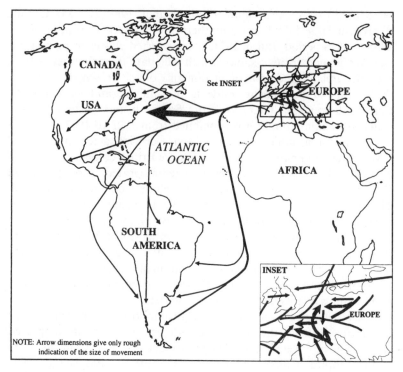

MAP 3.2   Labour migrations connected with industrialisation, 1850–1920

such as Poland, Ireland and Italy, were drawn in as replacement labour for large-scale agriculture and industry.

As the earliest industrial country, Britain was the first to experience large-scale labour immigration. The new factory towns quickly absorbed labour surpluses from the countryside. Atrocious working and living conditions led to poor health, high infant mortality and short life expectancy. Low wage levels forced both women and children to work, with disastrous results for the family. Natural increase was inadequate to meet labour needs, so Britain's closest colony, Ireland, became a labour source. The devastation of Irish peasant agriculture through absentee landlords and enclosures, combined with the ruin of domestic industry through British competition, had led to widespread poverty. The famines of 1822 and 1846–7 triggered off massive migrations to Britain, the USA and Australia.

By 1851 there were over 700 000 Irish in Britain, making up 3 per cent of the population of England and Wales and 7 per cent of the population of Scotland (Jackson, 1963). They were concentrated in the industrial cities, especially in the textile factories and the building trades. Irish 'navvies' (a slang term derived from 'navigators') dug Britain's canals and built her railways. Engels (1962) described the appalling situation of Irish workers, arguing that Irish immigration was a threat to the wages and living conditions of English workers (see also Castles and Kosack, 1973: 16–17). Hostility and discrimination against the Irish was marked right into the twentieth century. This was true of Australia too, where Irish immigration accompanied British settlement from the outset. In both countries it was the active role played by Irish workers in the labour movement which was to finally overcome this split in the working class just in time for its replacement by new divisions after 1945, when black workers came to Britain and Southern Europeans to Australia.

The next major migration to Britain was of 120 000 Jews, who came as refugees from the pogroms of Russia between 1875 and 1914. Most settled initially in the East End of London, where many became workers in the clothing industry. Jewish settlement became the focus of racist campaigns, leading to the first restrictionary legislation on immigration: the Aliens Act of 1905 and the Aliens Restriction Act of 1914 (Foot, 1965; Garrard, 1971). The Jewish experience of social mobility is often given as an example of migrant success. Many of the first generation managed to shift out of wage employment to become small entrepreneurs in the rag trade or the retail sector. They placed strong emphasis on education for their children. Many of the second generation were able to move into business or white-collar employment, paving the way for professional careers by the third generation. Interestingly one of Britain's newer immigrant groups – Bengalis from Bangladesh – now live in the same areas of the East End, often working in the same sweatshops, and worshipping in the same buildings (synagogues converted to mosques). However, they are isolated by racism and violence, and show little sign at present of repeating the Jewish trajectory. It seems that British racism today is more rigid than a century ago.

Irish and Jewish migrant workers cannot be categorised as 'unfree workers'. The Irish were British subjects, with the same formal rights as other workers, while the Jews rapidly became British subjects. The constraints on their labour market freedom were not legal but economic (poverty and lack of resources made them accept inferior jobs and conditions) and social (discrimination and racism restricted their freedom of movement). It is in Germany and France that one finds the first large-scale use of the status of 'foreigner' to restrict workers' rights.

The heavy industries of the Ruhr, which emerged in the mid-nineteenth century, attracted agricultural workers away from the large estates of Eastern Prussia. Conditions in the mines were hard, but still preferable to semi-feudal oppression under the Junkers (large landowners). The workers who moved West were of Polish ethnic background, but had Prussian (and later German) citizenship, since Poland was at that time divided up between Prussia, the Austro-Hungarian Empire and Russia. By 1913, it was estimated that 164 000 of the 410 000 Ruhr miners were of Polish background (Stirn, 1964: 27). The Junkers compensated for the resulting labour shortages by recruiting 'foreign Poles' and Ukrainians as agricultural workers. Often workers were recruited in pairs – a man as cutter and a woman as binder – leading to so-called 'harvest marriages'. However, there was fear that settlement of Poles might weaken German control of the Eastern provinces. In 1885, the Prussian government deported some 40 000 Poles and closed the frontier. The landowners protested at the loss of up to two-thirds of their labour force (Dohse, 1981: 29–32), arguing that it threatened their economic survival.

By 1890, a compromise between political and economic interests emerged in the shape of a system of rigid control. 'Foreign Poles' were recruited as temporary seasonal workers only, not allowed to bring dependants and forced to leave German territory for several months each year. At first they were restricted to agricultural work, but later were permitted to take industrial jobs in Silesia and Thuringia (but not in Western areas such as the Ruhr). Their work contracts provided pay and conditions inferior to those of German workers. Special police sections were established to deal with 'violation of contracts' (that is, workers leaving for better-paid jobs) through forcible return of workers to their employers, imprisonment or deportation. Thus police measures against foreigners were deliberately used as a method to keep wages low and to create a split labour market (Dohse, 1981: 33–83).

Foreign labour played a major role in German industrialisation with Italian, Belgian and Dutch workers alongside the Poles. In 1907, there were 950 000 foreign workers in the German Reich, of whom nearly 300 000 were in agriculture, 500 000 in industry and 86 000 in trade and transport (Dohse, 1981: 50). The authorities did their best to prevent family reunion and permanent settlement. Both in fact took place, but the exact extent is unclear. The system developed to control and exploit foreign labour was a precursor both of forced labour in the Nazi war economy and of the 'guestworker system' in the German Federal Republic from about 1955.

The number of foreigners in France increased rapidly from 381 000 in 1851 (1.1 per cent of total population) to 1 million (2.7 per cent) in 1881, and then more slowly to 1.2 million (3 per cent) in 1911 (Weil, 1991b: Appendix, Table 4). The majority came from neighbouring countries: Italy, Belgium, Germany and Switzerland, and later from Spain and Portugal. Movements were relatively spontaneous, though some recruitment was carried out by farmers' associations and mines (Cross, 1983: Chapter 2). The foreign workers were mainly men who carried out unskilled manual work in agriculture, mines and steelworks (the heavy, unpleasant jobs that French workers were unwilling to take).

The peculiarity of the French case lies in the reasons for the shortage of labour during industrialisation. Birth rates fell sharply after 1860. Peasants, shopkeepers and artisans followed 'Malthusian' birth control practices, which led to small families earlier than anywhere else (Cross, 1983: 5–7). According to Noiriel (1988: 297–312) this *grève des ventres* (belly strike) was motivated by resistance to proletarianisation. Keeping the family small meant that property could be passed on intact from generation to generation, and that there would be sufficient resources to permit a decent education for the children. Unlike Britain and Germany, France therefore saw relatively little overseas emigration during industrialisation. The only important exception was the movement of settlers to Algeria, which France invaded in 1830. Rural–urban migration was also fairly limited. The 'peasant worker' developed: the small farmer who supplemented subsistence agriculture through sporadic work in local industries. Where people did leave the countryside it was often to move straight into the new government jobs that proliferated in the late nineteenth century: straight from the primary to the tertiary sector.

In these circumstances, the shift from small to large-scale enterprises, made necessary by international competition from about the 1880s, could only be made through the employment of foreign workers. Thus labour immigration played a vital role in the emergence of modern industry and the constitution of the working class in France. Immigration was also seen as important for military reasons. The nationality law of 1889 was designed to turn immigrants and their sons into conscripts for the impending conflict with Germany (Schnapper, 1994: 66). From the mid-nineteenth century to the present, the labour market has been regularly fed by foreign immigration, making up, on average, 10–15 per cent of the working class. Noiriel estimates that without immigration the French population today would be only 35 million instead of over 50 million (Noiriel, 1988: 308–18).

The interwar period

At the onset of the First World War, many migrants returned home to participate in military service or munitions production. However, labour shortages soon developed in the combatant countries. The German authorities prevented 'foreign Polish' workers from leaving the country, and recruited labour by force in occupied areas of Russia and Belgium (Dohse, 1981: 77–81). The French government set up recruitment systems for workers from the North African and Indo-Chinese colonies, and from China (about 225 000 in all). They were housed in barracks, paid minimal wages and supervised by former colonial overseers. Workers were also recruited in Portugal, Spain, Italy and Greece for French factories and agriculture (Cross, 1983: 34–42). Britain too recruited colonial workers during the conflict, although in smaller numbers. All the warring countries also made use of the forced labour of prisoners of war.

The period from 1918 to 1945 was one of reduced international labour migrations. This was partly because of economic stagnation and crisis, and partly because of increased hostility towards immigrants in many countries. Migration to Australia, for example, fell to low levels as early as 1891, and did not grow substantially until after 1945. Southern Europeans who came to Australia in the 1920s were treated with suspicion. Immigrant ships were refused permission to land and there were 'anti-Dago' riots in the 1930s. Queensland passed special laws, prohibiting foreigners from owning land, and restricting them to certain industries (de Lepervanche, 1975).

In the USA, 'nativist' groups claimed that Southern and Eastern Europeans were 'unassimilable' and that they presented threats to public order and American values. Congress enacted a series of laws in the 1920s designed to drastically limit entries from any area except north-west Europe (Borjas, 1990: 28–9). This national-origins quota system stopped large-scale immigration to the USA until the 1960s. But the new mass production industries of the Fordist era had a substitute labour force at hand: black workers from the South. The period from about 1914 to the 1950s was that of the 'Great Migration' in which

Afro-Americans fled segregation and exploitation in the southern states for better wages and – they hoped – equal rights in the northeast, midwest and west. Often they simply encountered new forms of segregation in the ghettoes of New York or Chicago, and new forms of discrimination, such as exclusion from the unions of the American Federation of Labor.

Meanwhile, Americanisation campaigns were launched to ensure that immigrants learned English and became loyal US citizens. During the Great Depression, Mexican immigrants were repatriated by local governments and civic organisations, with some cooperation from the Mexican and US governments (Kiser and Kiser, 1979: 33–66). Many of the nearly 500 000 Mexicans who returned home were constrained to leave, while others left because there was no work. In these circumstances, little was done to help Jews fleeing the rise of Hitler. There was no concept of refugee in US law, and it was difficult to build support for admission of Jewish refugees when millions of US citizens were unemployed. Anti-semitism was also a factor, and there was never much of a prospect for large numbers of European Jews to find safe haven before the Second World War.

France was the only Western European country to experience substantial immigration in the inter-war years. The 'demographic deficit' had been exacerbated by war losses: 1.4 million men had been killed and 1.5 million permanently handicapped (Prost, 1966: 538). There was no return to the pre-war free movement policy; instead the government and employers refined the foreign labour systems established during the war. Recruitment agreements were concluded with Poland, Italy and Czechoslovakia. Much of the recruitment was organised by the *Société générale d'immigration* (SGI), a private body set up by farm and mining interests. Foreign workers were controlled through a system of identity cards and work contracts, and were channelled into jobs in farming, construction and heavy industry. However, most foreign workers probably arrived spontaneously outside the recruiting system. The non-communist trade union movement cooperated with immigration, in return for measures designed to protect French workers from displacement and wage cutting (Cross, 1983: 51–63; Weil, 1991b: 24–7).

Just under 2 million foreign workers entered France from 1920 to 1930, about 567 000 of them recruited by the SGI (Cross, 1983: 60). Some 75 per cent of French population growth between 1921 and 1931 is estimated to have been the result of immigration (Decloîtres, 1967: 23). In view of the large female surplus in France, mainly men were recruited, and a fair degree of intermarriage took place. By 1931, there were 2.7 million foreigners in France (6.6 per cent of the total population). The largest group were Italians (808 000), followed by Poles (508 000), Spaniards (352 000) and Belgians (254 000) (Weil, 1991b: Appendix, Table 4). North African migration to France was also developing. Large colonies of Italians and Poles sprang up in the mining and heavy industrial towns of the north and east of France: in some towns foreigners made a third or more of the total population. There were Spanish and Italian agricultural settlements in the south-west.

In the depression of the 1930s, hostility towards foreigners increased, leading to a policy of discrimination in favour of French workers. In 1932 maximum quotas for foreign workers in firms were fixed. This was followed by laws permitting dismissal of foreign workers in sectors where there was unemployment. Many migrants were sacked and deported, and the foreign population dropped by half a million by 1936 (Weil, 1991b: 27–30). Cross concludes that in the 1920s foreign workers 'provided a cheap and flexible workforce necessary for capital accumulation and economic growth; at the same time, aliens allowed the French worker a degree of economic mobility'. In the 1930s, on the other hand, immigration 'attenuated and provided a scapegoat for the economic crisis' (Cross, 1983: 218).

In Germany, the crisis-ridden Weimar Republic had little need of foreign workers: by 1932 their number was down to about 100 000, compared with nearly a million in 1907 (Dohse, 1981: 112). None the less a new system of regulation of foreign labour developed. Its principles were: strict state control of labour recruitment, employment preference for nationals, sanctions against employers of illegal migrants and unrestricted police power to deport unwanted foreigners (Dohse, 1981: 114–17). This system was partly attributable to the influence of the strong labour movement, which wanted measures to protect German workers, but it confirmed the weak legal position of migrant workers. Exhibit 3.2 describes the use of forced foreign labour during the Second World War.

Conclusion

Contemporary migratory movements and policies are often profoundly influenced by historical precedents. This chapter has described the key role of labour migration in colonialism and industrialisation. Labour

---

EXHIBIT 3.2

Forced foreign labour in the Nazi war economy

The Nazi regime recruited enormous numbers of foreign workers – mainly by force – to replace the 11 million German workers conscripted for military service. The occupation of Poland, Germany's traditional labour reserve, was partly motivated by the need for labour. Labour recruitment offices were set up within weeks of the invasion, and the police and army rounded up thousands of young men and women (Dohse, 1981: 121). Forcible recruitment took place in all the countries invaded by Germany, while some voluntary labour was obtained from Italy, Croatia, Spain and other 'friendly or neutral countries'. By the end of the war, there were 7.5 million foreign workers in the Reich, of whom 1.8 million were prisoners of war. It is estimated that a quarter of industrial production was carried out by foreign workers in 1944 (Pfahlmann, 1968: 232). The Nazi war machine would have collapsed far earlier without foreign labour.

The basic principle for treating foreign workers declared by Sauckel, the Plenipotentiary for Labour, was that: 'All the men must be fed, sheltered and treated in such a way as to exploit them to the highest possible extent at the lowest conceivable degree of expenditure' (Homze, 1967: 113). This meant housing workers in barracks under military control, the lowest possible wages (or none at all), appalling social and health conditions, and complete deprivation of civil rights. Poles and Russians were compelled, like the Jews, to wear special badges showing their origin. Many foreign workers died through harsh treatment and cruel punishments. These were systematic; in a speech to employers, Sauckel emphasised the need for strict discipline: 'I don't care about them [the foreign workers] one bit. If they commit the most minor offence at work, report them to the police at once, hang them, shoot them. I don't care. If they are dangerous, they must be liquidated' (Dohse, 1981: 127).

The Nazis took exploitation of rightless migrants to an extreme which can only be compared with slavery, yet its legal core – the sharp division between the status of national and foreigner – was to be found both in earlier and later foreign labour systems.

---

migration has always been a major factor in the construction of a capitalist world market. In the USA, Canada, Australia, Britain, Germany and France (as well as in other countries not discussed here) migrant workers have played a role which varies in character, according to economic, social and political conditions. But in every case the contribution of migration to industrialisation and population building was important and sometimes even decisive.

To what extent does the four-stage model of the migratory process suggested in Chapter 2 apply to the historical examples given? Involuntary movements of slaves and indentured workers do not easily fit the model, for the intentions of the participants played little part. None the less some aspects apply: labour recruitment as the initial impetus, predominance of young males in the early stages, family formation, long-term settlement and emergence of ethnic minorities. Worker migrations to England, Germany and France in the nineteenth and twentieth centuries fit the model well. Their original intention was temporary, but they led to family reunion and settlement. As for migrations to America and Australasia in the nineteenth and early twentieth centuries, it is generally believed that most migrants went with the intention of permanent settlement. But many young men and women went in order to work for a few years and then return home. Some did return, but in the long run the majority remained in the New World, often forming new ethnic communities. Here too, the model seems to fit.

Clearly the study of migrant labour is not the only way of looking at the history of migration. Movements caused by political or religious persecution have always been important, playing a major part in the development of countries as diverse as the USA and Germany. It is often impossible to draw strict lines between the various types of migration. Migrant labour systems have always led to some degree of settlement, just as settler and refugee movement have always been bound up with the political economy of capitalist development.

The period from about 1850 to 1914 was an era of mass migration in Europe and North America. Industrialisation was a cause of both emigration and immigration (sometimes in the same country, as the British case shows). After 1914, war, xenophobia and economic stagnation caused a considerable decline in migration, and the large-scale movements of the preceding period seemed to be the results of a unique and unrepeatable constellation. When rapid and sustained economic growth got under way after the Second World War, the new age of migration was to take the world by surprise.

4 Migration to Highly Developed Countries since 1945

Since the end of the Second World War, international migrations have grown in volume and changed in character. There have been two main phases. In the first, from 1945 to the early 1970s, the chief economic strategy of large-scale capital was concentration of investment and expansion of production in the existing highly developed countries. As a result, large numbers of migrant workers were drawn from less-developed countries into the fast-expanding industrial areas of Western Europe, North America and Australia. The end of this phase was marked by the 'oil crisis' of 1973–4. The ensuing recession gave impetus to a restructuring of the world economy, involving capital investment in new industrial areas, altered patterns of world trade, and introduction of new technologies. The result was a second phase of international migration, starting in the mid-1970s and gaining momentum in the 1980s and 1990s. This phase involved complex new patterns of migration, affecting both old and new receiving countries. This chapter will discuss post-1945 migratory movements to highly developed countries, including Europe, North America and Australia. Labour migration to Japan, which did not become significant until the mid-1980s, will be discussed in Chapter 6, in the context of Asian regional migration.

Migration in the long boom[1]

Between 1945 and the early 1970s, three main types of migration led to the formation of new, ethnically distinct populations in advanced industrial countries:

- migration of workers from the European periphery to Western Europe, often through 'guestworker systems'

67

- migration of 'colonial workers' to the former colonial powers
- permanent migration to North America and Australia, at first from Europe and later from Asia and Latin America

The precise timing of these movements varied: they started later in Germany and ended earlier in Britain, while migration to the USA grew rapidly after the Immigration Act of 1965 and, unlike Western Europe and Australia, did not decline at all in the mid-1970s. These three types, which all led to family reunion and other kinds of chain migration, will be examined here. There were also other types of migration which will not be dealt with here, since they did not contribute decisively to the formation of ethnic minorities:

- mass movements of European refugees at the end of the Second World War[2]
- return migrations of former colonists to their countries of origin as colonies gained their independence.

Foreign workers and 'guestworker' systems

All the highly industrialised countries of Western Europe used temporary labour recruitment at some stage between 1945 and 1973, although this sometimes played a smaller role than spontaneous entries of foreign workers. The rapidly expanding economies were able to utilise the labour reserves of the European periphery: the Mediterranean countries, Ireland and Finland. The reasons for underdevelopment in these countries varied. In some cases it was the result of former colonisation (Ireland, Finland, Algeria). The backwardness of Southern European countries was partly the result of domination by more powerful neighbours, partly the result of wartime devastation.

Immediately after the Second World War, the British government brought in 90 000 mainly male workers from refugee camps and from Italy through the European Voluntary Worker (EVW) scheme. EVWs were tied to designated jobs, had no right to family reunion, and could be deported for indiscipline. The scheme was fairly small and only operated until 1951, because it was easier to make use of colonial workers (see below). A further 100 000 Europeans entered Britain on work permits between 1946 and 1951, and some European migration continued subsequently, though it was not a major flow (Kay and Miles, 1992).

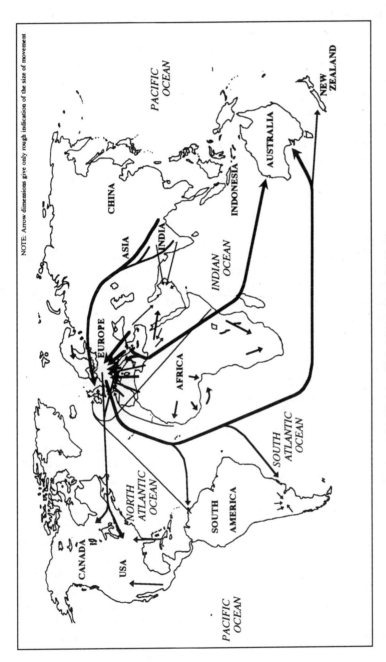

NOTE: Arrow dimensions give only rough indication of the size of movement

MAP 4.1 Global Migrations, 1945–73

Belgium also started recruiting foreign workers immediately after the war. They were mainly Italian men, and were employed in the coal mines and the iron and steel industry. The system operated until 1963, after which foreign work-seekers were allowed to come of their own accord. Many brought in dependants and settled permanently, changing the ethnic composition of Belgium's industrial areas.

France established an *Office National d'Immigration* (ONI) in 1945 to organise recruitment of workers from Southern Europe. Migration was seen as a solution to post-war labour shortages and was expected to be mainly temporary. However, in view of continuing low birth rates, some family settlement was envisaged. ONI also coordinated the employment of up to 150 000 seasonal agricultural workers per year, mainly from Spain. By 1970, 2 million foreign workers and 690 000 dependants had entered France. Many found it easier to come as 'tourists', get a job and then regularise their situation. This applied particularly to Portuguese and Spanish workers escaping their respective dictatorships, who generally lacked passports. By 1968, ONI statistics revealed that 82 per cent of the aliens admitted by the ONI came as 'clandestines'. In any case, ONI had no jurisdiction over French citizens from overseas departments and territories, or from certain former colonies (see below).

Switzerland pursued a policy of large-scale labour import from 1945 to 1974. Foreign workers were recruited abroad by employers, while admission and residence were controlled by the government. Job changing, permanent settlement and family reunion were forbidden. Considerable use was also made of seasonal workers (in agriculture and the tourism industry) and of cross-frontier commuters. Swiss statistics include both these groups as part of the labour force but not of the population: 'guestworkers' *par excellence*. Swiss industry became highly dependent on foreign workers, who made up nearly a third of the labour force by the early 1970s. The need to attract and retain workers, coupled with diplomatic pressure from Italy, led to relaxations on family reunion and permanent stay, so that Switzerland too experienced settlement and the formation of migrant communities.

The examples could be continued: the Netherlands brought in 'guestworkers' in the 1960s and early 1970s, Luxembourg's industries were highly dependent on foreign labour, and Sweden employed workers from Finland and from southern European countries.[3] The key case for understanding the 'guestworker system' was the Federal Republic of Germany (FRG), which set up a highly organised state recruitment apparatus (see Exhibit 4.1).

EXHIBIT 4.1

The German 'guestworker' system

The German Government started recruiting foreign workers in the late 1950s. The Federal Labour Office (*Bundesanstalt für Arbeit*, or BfA) set up recruitment offices in the Mediterranean countries. Employers requiring foreign labour paid a fee to the BfA, which selected workers, testing occupational skills, providing medical examinations and screening police records. The workers were brought in groups to Germany, where employers had to provide initial accommodation. Recruitment, working conditions and social security were regulated by bilateral agreements between the FRG and the sending countries: first Italy, then Greece, Turkey, Morocco, Portugal, Tunisia and Yugoslavia.

The number of foreign workers in the FRG rose from 95 000 in 1956 to 1.3 million in 1966 and 2.6 million in 1973. This massive migration was the result of rapid industrial expansion and the shift to new methods of mass production, which required large numbers of low-skilled workers. Foreign women workers played a major part, especially in the later years: their labour was in high demand in textiles and clothing, electrical goods and other manufacturing sectors.

German policies conceived migrant workers as temporary labour units, which could be recruited, utilised and sent away again as employers required. To enter and remain in the FRG, a migrant needed a residence permit and a labour permit. These were granted for restricted periods, and were often valid only for specific jobs and areas. Entry of dependants was discouraged. A worker could be deprived of his or her permit for a variety of reasons, leading to deportation.

However, it was impossible to prevent family reunion and settlement. Often officially recruited migrants were able to get employers to request their wives or husbands as workers. Competition with other labour-importing countries for labour led to relaxation of restrictions on entry of dependants in the 1960s. Families became established and children were born. Foreign labour was beginning to lose its mobility and social costs (for housing, education and health care) could no longer be avoided. When the Federal government stopped labour recruitment in November 1973, the motivation was not only the looming 'oil crisis', but also the belated realisation that permanent immigration was taking place.

In the FRG we see in the most developed form all the principles – but also the contradictions – of temporary foreign labour recruitment systems. These include the belief in temporary sojourn, the restriction of labour market and civil rights, the recruitment of single workers (men at first, but with increasing numbers of women as time went on), the inability to prevent family reunion completely, the gradual move towards longer stay, the inexorable pressures for settlement and community formation. The FRG took the system furthest, but its central element – the legal distinction between the status of citizen and of foreigner as a criterion for determining political and social rights – was to be found throughout Europe (see Hammar, 1985a).

Multinational and bilateral agreements were also used to facilitate labour migration. Free movement of workers within the European Community (EC), which came into force in 1968, was relevant mainly for Italian workers going to Germany, while the Nordic Labour Market affected Finns going to Sweden. The EC arrangements were the first step towards creating a 'European labour market', which was to become a reality in 1993. However, in the 1960s and early 1970s labour movement within the Community was actually declining, owing to gradual equalisation of wages and living standards within the EC,

TABLE 4.1   Minority population in the main Western European countries of immigration, 1950–75 (thousands)

Country	1950	1960	1970	1975	Per cent of total population 1975
Belgium	354	444	716	835	8.5
France	2 128	2 663	3 339	4 196	7.9
Germany (FRG)	548	686	2 977	4 090	6.6
Great Britain	1 573	2 205	3 968	4 153	7.8
Netherlands	77	101	236	370	2.6
Sweden	124	191	411	410	5.0
Switzerland	279	585	983	1 012	16.0

Notes: Figures for all countries except Great Britain are for foreign residents. They exclude naturalised persons and immigrants from the Dutch and French colonies. Great Britain data are Census figures for 1951, 1961 and 1971 and estimates for 1975. The 1951 and 1961 data are for overseas-born persons, and exclude children born to immigrants in Great Britain. The 1971 and 1975 figures include children born in Great Britain, with both parents born abroad.
Source: Castles, Booth and Wallace (1984): 87–8 (where detailed sources are given).

while migration from outside the Community was increasing. Table 4.1 shows the development of minority populations arising from migration in selected Western European countries up to 1975.

Colonial workers

Migration from former colonies was important for Britain, France and the Netherlands. Britain had a net inflow of about 350 000 from Ireland, its traditional labour reserve, between 1946 and 1959. Irish workers provided manual labour for industry and construction, and many brought in their families and settled permanently. Irish residents in Britain enjoyed all civil rights, including the right to vote. Immigration of workers from the New Commonwealth (former British colonies in the Caribbean, the Indian sub-continent and Africa) started after 1945 and grew during the 1950s. Some workers came as a result of recruitment by London Transport, but most migrated spontaneously in response to labour demand. By 1951, there were 218 000 people of New Commonwealth origin,[4] a figure which increased to 541 000 in 1961. Entry of workers from the New Commonwealth almost stopped after 1962, partly owing to the introduction of severe restrictions through the Commonwealth Immigrants Act of 1962, and partly as the result of the early onset of economic stagnation in Britain.

However, most of the Commonwealth immigrants had come to stay, and family reunion continued, until it in turn was restricted by the 1971 Immigration Act. The population of New Commonwealth origin increased to 1.2 million in 1971 and 1.5 million in 1981. Most Afro-Caribbean and Asian immigrants and their children in Britain enjoyed formal citizenship (although this no longer applies to those admitted since the 1981 Nationality Act). Their minority status was not defined by being foreign, but by widespread institutional and informal discrimination. Most black and Asian workers found unskilled manual jobs in industry and the services, and a high degree of residential segregation emerged in the inner cities. Educational and social disadvantage became a further obstacle to mobility out of initial low-status positions. By the 1970s, the emergence of ethnic minorities was inescapable.

France experienced large-scale spontaneous immigration from its former colonies, as well as from Southern Europe. By 1970 there were over 600 000 Algerians, 140 000 Moroccans and 90 000 Tunisians. Many black workers were also coming in from the former West African colonies of Senegal, Mali and Mauritania. Some of these migrants came before independence when they were still French citizens. Others came later through preferential migration arrangements, or illegally. Migration from Algeria was regulated by bilateral agreements which accorded Algerian migrants a unique status. Moroccans and Tunisians, by contrast, were admitted through ONI. Many people also came from the overseas departments and territories such as Guadeloupe, Martinique and Réunion. They were French citizens, so there were no migration statistics, though estimates put their number at 250 000 to 300 000 in 1972. All these migrations were initially male-dominated, but with increasing proportions of women as the movement matured. Non-European immigrants in France were relegated to the bottom of the labour market, often working in highly exploitative conditions. Housing was frequently segregated, and very poor in quality; indeed, shanty towns (known as *bidonvilles*) appeared in France in the 1960s. Extreme-right groups began to subject non-European immigrants to a campaign of racial violence: 32 North Africans were murdered in 1973.

The Netherlands had two main inflows from former colonies. Between 1945 and the early 1960s up to 300 000 'repatriates' from the former Dutch East Indies (now Indonesia) entered the Netherlands. Although most had been born overseas and many were of mixed Dutch and Indonesian parentage, they were Dutch citizens. The official policy of assimilation appears to have worked well in this case, and there is little evidence of racism or discrimination against this group.[5] After 1965, increasing numbers of black workers came to the Netherlands from the Caribbean territory of Surinam. A peak was reached in the two years leading up to independence in 1975, at which time Surinamese (except those already living in the Netherlands) lost their Dutch citizenship. By the late 1970s there were estimated to be 160 000 Surinamese in the Netherlands.

Permanent migration to North America and Australia

Large-scale migration to the USA developed later than in Western Europe, owing to the restrictive legislation enacted in the 1920s. Intakes averaged 250 000 persons annually in the 1951–60 period, and 330 000 annually during 1961–70: a far cry from the average of 880 000 immigrants per year from 1901 to 1910. The 1970 Census showed that the number of overseas-born people had declined to 9.6 million, only 4.7 per cent of the population (Briggs, 1984: 7). The 1965 amendments to the Immigration and Nationality Act were seen as part of the civil rights legislation of the period, designed to remove the discriminatory national-origins quota system. They were not expected or intended to lead to large-scale non-European immigration (Borjas, 1990: 29-33). In fact the amendments created a system of world-wide immigration, in which the most important criterion for admission was kinship with US citizens or residents. The result was a dramatic upsurge in migration from Asia and Latin America.

US employers, particularly in agriculture, also recruited temporary migrant workers, mainly men, in Mexico and the Caribbean. Organised labour was highly critical, arguing that domestic workers would be displaced and wages held down. Government policies varied: at times, systems of temporary labour recruitment, such as the Mexican *bracero* Programme of the 1940s, were introduced. In other periods recruitment was formally prohibited, but tacitly tolerated, leading to the presence of a large number of illegal workers. Significantly, the 1952 amendments to the US immigration rules included the so-called 'Texas Proviso', which was interpreted as barring punishment of employers who hired unauthorised foreign labour.

Canada followed policies of mass immigration after 1945. At first only Europeans were admitted. Most entrants were British, but Eastern and Southern Europeans soon played an increasing role. The largest immigrant streams in the 1950s and 1960s were of Germans, Italians and Dutch. The introduction of a non-discriminatory 'points system' for screening potential migrants after the 1966 White Paper opened the door for non-European migrants. The main source countries in the 1970s were Jamaica, India, Portugal, the Philippines, Greece, Italy and Trinidad (Breton *et al.*, 1990: 14–16). Throughout the period, family entry was encouraged, and immigrants were seen as settlers and future citizens.

Australia initiated a mass immigration programme after 1945, because policy-makers believed that the population of 7.5 million needed to be increased for both economic and strategic reasons.[6] The policy, summed up in the popular slogan 'populate or perish', was one of permanent, family immigration. The initial target was 70 000 migrants per year and a ratio of ten British migrants to every 'foreigner'. However, it proved impossible to attract enough British migrants. The Department of Immigration began recruiting refugees from the Baltic and Slavic countries, who were perceived as both 'racially acceptable' and anti-communist. Gradually the concept of 'acceptable European races' widened to include Northern Europeans and then Southern Europeans. By the 1950s, the largest sources of migrants were

Italy, Greece and Malta. Non-Europeans were not admitted at all, as the White Australia Policy was still in force. Despite the policy of family migration, there was a male surplus among entrants, leading to schemes to encourage single women to come from Britain and elsewhere. It was not until 1975 that women were allowed to migrate as heads of families.

Immigration was widely regarded as the motor of post-war growth: from 1947 to 1973 it provided 50 per cent of labour force growth, giving Australia the highest rate of increase of any OECD country. By the late 1960s, it was becoming hard to attract Southern European migrants, and many were returning to their homelands in response to economic developments there. The response was further liberalisation of family reunions, recruitment in Yugoslavia and Latin America, and some relaxations of the White Australia Policy. By the 1970s Australian manufacturing industry relied heavily on migrant labour and factory jobs were popularly known as 'migrant work'.

Comparative perspectives

One common feature in the migratory movements of the 1945-73 period is the predominance of economic motivations. Foreign worker migrations to Western Europe were caused primarily by economic considerations on the part of migrants, employers and governments. The same is true of temporary worker recruitment for US agriculture. Economic motives played a major part in Australia's post-war migration programme, although population building was also a consideration. The colonial workers who migrated to Britain, France and the Netherlands generally had economic reasons, although for the governments political considerations (such as the desire to maintain links with former colonies) also played a part. Permanent migration to the USA was probably the movement in which economic factors were least dominant. Yet the migrants themselves often had economic motivations, and their labour played a major role in US economic growth. Of course there were also refugee migrations, in which economic motivations were secondary. The overwhelmingly economic motivation for migration was to become less clear-cut in the post-1973 period.

How important was labour migration for the economies of the receiving countries? Some economists have argued that it was crucial to expansion. Migrants replaced local workers, who were able to obtain more highly skilled jobs during the boom. Without the flexibility provided by immigration, bottlenecks in production and inflationary tendencies would have developed. However, other economists have argued that immigration reduced the incentive for rationalisation, keeping low-productivity firms viable and holding back the shift to more capital-intensive forms of production. Such observers also claim that social capital expenditure on housing and social services for immigrants reduced the capital available for productive investment. Overall there is little doubt that the high net immigration countries, like the FRG, Switzerland, France and Australia, had the highest economic growth rates in the 1945–73 period. Countries with relatively low net immigration (like Britain and the USA at this time) had much lower growth rates.[7] Thus the argument that immigration was economically beneficial in this period is convincing.

Another general feature of the 1945–73 period was growing diversity of areas of origin, and increasing cultural difference between migrants and receiving populations. At the beginning of the period, most migrants to all main receiving countries came from various parts of Europe. As time went on, increasing proportions came from Asia, Africa and Latin America. This trend was to become even more marked in the following period.

A comparison of the situation of colonial workers with that of guestworkers is instructive. The differences are obvious: colonial workers were citizens of the former colonial power, or had some preferential entitlement to enter and live there. They usually came spontaneously, often following lines of communication built up in the colonial period. Once they came in, they generally had civil and political rights; most (though by no means all) intended to stay permanently. On the other hand, guestworkers and other foreign workers were non-citizens. Their rights were severely restricted. Most came because they were recruited; some came spontaneously and were able to regularise their situation; others came illegally and worked without documentation. Generally they were seen as temporary workers who were expected to leave after a few years.

There are also similarities, however, especially in the economic and social situations of the two categories. Both became overwhelmingly concentrated in low-skilled manual work, mainly in industry and construction. Both tended to suffer sub-standard housing, poor social conditions and educational disadvantage. Over time, there was a convergence of legal situations, with family reunion and social rights of foreign workers improving, while the colonial migrants lost many of their privileges. Finally, both groups were affected by similar processes of marginalisation, leading to a degree of separation from the rest of the population and an ethnic minority position.

Migrations in the period of global economic restructuring

The ending of organised recruitment of manual workers by industrialised countries in the early 1970s was a reaction to a fundamental restructuring of the world economy. The subsequent period has been marked by:

a) changes in global investment patterns, with increased capital export from developed countries and establishment of manufacturing industries in some previously underdeveloped areas;
b) the micro-electronic revolution, which has reduced the need for manual workers in manufacturing;
c) erosion of traditional skilled manual occupations in highly developed countries;
d) expansion in the services sector, with demand for both highly skilled and low-skilled workers;
e) growing informal sectors in the economies of developed countries;
f) casualisation of employment, growth in part-time work, increasingly insecure conditions of employment;
g) increased differentiation of labour forces on the basis of gender, age and ethnicity, through mechanisms which push many women, young people and members of minorities into casual or informal-sector work, and which force workers with outmoded skills to retire early.

These transformations have had dramatic effects in Africa, Asia and Latin America. In some places, rapid industrialisation and social change have taken place, leading to the emergence of 'newly industrialising countries' (NICs). In the oil-rich Organisation of Petroleum Exporting Countries (OPEC) countries, reinvestment of oil profits after 1973 led to industrialisation and social change. But in large areas of Africa, Latin America and Asia, post-colonial development strategies have failed. Many countries are marked by rapid population growth, overuse and destruction of natural resources, uncontrolled urbanisation, political instability, falling living standards, poverty and even famine. Thus the idea of the 'Third World' as an area with common economic problems and development perspectives has lost its meaning, and has largely been replaced by the idea of a 'South–North divide'. Economic crisis and social change in the South is generating new pressures for migration to the North.

These developments have led to considerable shifts in migratory patterns and to new forms of migration. Main trends include:

a)   decline of labour migration to Western Europe;
b)   family reunion of former foreign workers and colonial workers, and formation of new ethnic minorities;
c)   transition of some Southern European countries from countries of emigration to countries of immigration;
d)   continuation of mainly economically motivated migration to the 'classical immigration countries' of North America and Oceania, but with considerable shifts in the areas of origin and the forms of migration;
e)   new migratory movements (both internal and international) connected with economic and social change in the NICs;
f)   recruitment of foreign labour, mainly from less-developed countries, by oil-rich countries;
g)   development of mass movements of refugees and asylum-seekers, generally moving from South to North, but also (especially after the collapse of the Soviet Bloc) from East to West;[8]
h)   increasing international mobility of highly-qualified personnel, in both temporary and permanent flows.

These movements will be examined in more detail below. The main population flows of the post-1973 period are shown in Map 1.1.

Migrants and minorities in Western Europe

The post-1973 period was one of consolidation and demographic normalisation of immigrant populations in Western Europe. Recruitment of both foreign workers and colonial workers largely ceased. For colonial migrants in Britain, France and the Netherlands, trends to family reunion and permanent settlement continued. At the same time, the settlement process and the emergence of second and third generations, born in Western Europe, led to internal differentiation and the development of community structures and consciousness. By the 1980s, colonial migrants and their descendants had become clearly visible social groups.

Permanent settlement had not been envisaged for the foreign work-ers. When the German government stopped recruitment in 1973 and other governments followed suit, they hoped that the now unwanted 'guests' would go away. In fact some foreign workers did go home, but many stayed. Governments initially tried to prevent family reunion, but with little success. In the end, it was grudgingly accepted as a human right. Foreign populations changed in structure. In the FRG, for instance, the number of foreign men declined slightly between 1974 and 1981, but the number of foreign women increased by 12 per cent, while the number of children aged up to 15 grew by 52 per cent (Castles, Booth and Walace, 1984: 102). Instead of declining, as policy-

TABLE 4.2   Foreign resident population in selected OECD countries (thousands)

Country	1980	1985	1990	1995	Percentage of total population 1995
Austria	283	272	413	724	9.0
Belgium	..	845	905	910	9.0
Denmark	102	117	161	223	4.2
France	3 714*	..	3 597	..	6.3[†]
Germany	4 453	4 379	5 242	7 174	8.8
Ireland	..	79	80	94	2.7
Italy	299	423	781	991	1.7
Luxembourg	94	98	..	138	33.4
Netherlands	521	553	692	728	5.0
Norway	83	102	143	161	3.7
Portugal	..	..	108	168	1.7
Spain	..	242	279	500	1.2
Sweden	422	389	484	532	5.2
Switzerland	893	940	1 100	1 331	18.9
United Kingdom	..	1 731	1 875	2 060	3.4

*Figure for 1982.
[†]Figure for 1990.
Notes: These figures are for foreign population. They therefore exclude naturalised immigrants (particularly important for France, the UK and Sweden). They also exclude immigrants from colonies or former colonies with the citizenship of the immigration country (particularly important for France, the Netherlands and the UK). The figures for the UK in this table are not comparable with the birthplace figures given in Table 4.1. The figures for Germany refer to the area of the old Federal Republic up to 1990, and to the whole of united Germany in 1995.
Sources: OECD (1992), 131; OECD (1997), 29.

makers had expected, the total foreign population of the FRG remained fairly constant at about 4 million in the late 1970s, only to increase again to 4.5 million in the early 1980s and to over 5 million prior to German reunification in 1990. Table 4.2 gives information on the growth of foreign population of some European immigration countries. By 1995 the total foreign population of European OECD countries was 19.4 million, of whom only 6.7 million were EU citizens. There were 2 million North Africans, 2.6 million Turks and 1.4 million people from former Yugoslavia (OECD, 1997: 30). The foreigners who left after 1973 were mainly those from the more developed countries, where there was some prospect of work for returnees. Those who stayed were from less developed areas, in particular Turkey and North Africa. It was above all the non-European groups who experienced socioeconomic exclusion through discrimination and racism, like the former colonial worker groups.

Intra-EC movement did continue after 1973. It was increasingly an individual migration, mainly of skilled workers or highly qualified personnel. By the late 1980s it was becoming customary to treat the EC (from 1993: the EU) as a single labour market, and to see intra-EU mobility as analogous to internal migration within a national economy.

In the second half of the 1980s, there was a resurgence of migration to Western Europe. The main driving force was economic and political problems in the countries of origin. The new migrants came as workers (both legal and illegal) but increasingly also as asylum seekers. Many were from Africa, Asia and Latin America, but in the late 1980s the crises in the Soviet Union and Eastern Europe led to new East–West movements. Panic developed in Western and Southern Europe, with fears of influxes of up to 50 million East–West migrants (Thränhardt, 1996: 228). The German term *Völkerwanderung* conjured up images of modern-day barbarian invasions. As will be shown in Chapter 5, such predictions proved much exaggerated. By the mid-1990s it was clear that there would be no large-scale movements of population from East to West. This was due to several factors: control measures; economic and political stabilisation in Eastern Europe; and the absence of migration networks to facilitate movements. Those who did move were generally members of ethnic minorities who received an official welcome in their ancestral homelands.

By the mid-1990s, immigration flows to Western Europe had stabilised and in some cases declined from the peak levels of 1991–2. A new debate began about the future need for immigrants. Low fertility was leading to demographic decline and an ageing population (Münz, 1996). Germany began to recruit new types of 'guestworkers' from Eastern Europe, often under conditions even more onerous than the old 'guestworker system' (Rudolph, 1996). Yet Eastern Europe offers no long-term demographic reserves: fertility is low and life expectancy is actually declining in some areas due to environmental factors. The high fertility and young underemployed populations of North Africa and Turkey appear in an ambivalent light to many Europeans. On the one hand they are seen as a source of workers for factories and building sites, and of carers for the aged; on the other hand there are fears of being 'swamped' by new influxes. Overall it is clear that immigration is not a solution to the ageing of the population and there is little support for immigration for demographic purposes.

Even within the EU, discrepancies in wages and social costs between countries lead to anomalies. In the post-reunification construction boom in Germany, employers took on workers through sub-contractors in countries like the UK and Portugal, allowing them to pay wages considerably below German rates. The German construction union protested against this 'social dumping', and secured an agreement with employers to pay construction workers improved rates from 1997. None the less, rates and conditions remained inferior to those paid to German workers under collective agreements (*Migration News* 4:1, January 1997).

Southern Europe

Italy, Greece, Spain and Portugal have long histories of emigration. After 1973, they experienced some return migration from former labour-recruiting countries. However, by the 1980s, a major reversal of historical patterns had developed, with the Southern European countries becoming receivers of immigrants from Africa and Asia. The causes were economic development and declining demographic growth in Southern Europe. In Italy, for instance, the total fertility rate[9] had fallen to 1.3 by the late 1980s (as low as Germany).

In Italy, the legal foreign population grew from 299 000 in 1980 to 781 000 in 1990 and 991 000 in 1995 (OECD, 1992; 1997: 218). This figure is unreliable, however, because of lack of data on illegal immigrants. In 1996, some 500 000 persons are estimated to have entered illegally (*New York Times*, 16 February 1997). About 250 000 illegal residents applied for regularisation in the 1996 amnesty (OECD,

1997: 122). Some 265 000 legal foreign residents in 1995 were from Africa, but the fastest growth was in Eastern Europeans whose numbers rose from 43 000 in 1990 to 215 000 in 1995. Some groups are predominantly female, especially those from the Philippines and Sri Lanka who are mainly employed in domestic service. Many migrants are employed illegally or are engaged in peddling and other marginal activities.

Other Southern European countries have experienced similar developments. In Spain the official number of foreign residents increased from about 200 000 in 1980 to 500 000 in 1995. Over half came from EU countries, but there were 109 000 from America (mainly Latin America) and 96 000 from Africa (OECD, 1997: 156). In Portugal 168 000 foreigners were legally resident in 1995 (OECD, 1997: 142). As elsewhere in Southern Europe, there are also thought to be many illegal foreign workers. Most immigrants came from former Portuguese colonies such as Cape Verde, Angola, Guinea-Bissau and Brazil (OECD, 1995: 115).

In Greece, the foreign population was officially estimated at around 300 000 (including illegals) in 1995. Most foreigners work illegally; their number is put at 250 000 to 470 000 (6–12 per cent of the labour force). Illegal workers earn about half the normal wages and have no social security entitlements. Low-wage foreign labour plays a crucial role in many industries, such as agriculture, tourism and construction. Many of the immigrants are 'ethnic Greeks' from the former Soviet Union, Albania or Turkey. The former are encouraged to settle and granted citizenship, while those from Albania or Turkey are not. Greece also receives many illegal immigrants from elsewhere in Eastern Europe, Africa and Asia. Of the 764 000 illegal entrants deported between 1991 and 1994, 96 per cent were Albanians, many of whom crossed the border repeatedly (OECD, 1997: 110–13).

All the Southern European countries still have some emigration to other European countries, as well as increasing numbers of immigrants. The intra-EU flows include relatively high income groups such as professionals or people attracted by the life style. Migrations from outside Europe are partly connected with former colonial links (for example, Latin Americans in Spain, people from former African colonies in Portugal). Southern Europe also serves as a transit route for illegal migrants from Africa and Asia on their way to north-western Europe. The role of organised crime in trafficking of migrants expanded rapidly in the post-Cold War period. Illegal migrants are transported by smugglers in fishing vessels from Morocco to southern

Spain, Tunisia to Sicily or Egypt to Greece. Smugglers sometimes throw their passengers overboard to escape apprehension by the authorities (OECD, 1997: 112). On Christmas Day 1996 up to 300 illegal migrants from India, Pakistan and Sri Lanka drowned after a collision between two vessels in rough seas between Sicily and Malta (*Guardian Weekly*, 12 January 1997).

North America and Australia

Migration to the USA continued to grow throughout the 1970s, with intakes averaging 450 000 per year. In the 1980s average annual intakes increased to about 600 000. The 1990 Census counted 19.8 million foreign-born residents, 7.9 per cent of the total population, while an official survey in 1996 put the foreign-born population at 24.6 million, 9.3 per cent of total population (OECD, 1997: 175). In 1993, 75 per cent of legal immigrants went to just seven states: California, New York, Texas, Florida, New Jersey, Illinois and Massachusetts (OECD, 1995: 130–2). No less than a third of the foreign-born people in the USA now live in California, where they make up 22 per cent of the total population.

The 1965 amendments to the Immigration and Nationality Act had unexpected results (see Borjas, 1990: 26–39). US residents of Latin American and Asian origin were able to use family reunion provisions to initiate processes of chain migration, which brought about a major shift in ethnic composition. In the 1951–60 period, Europeans made up 53 per cent of new immigrants, compared with 40 per cent from the Americas and only 8 per cent from Asia. In 1995, Europeans were only 18 per cent of all entrants, while 38 per cent came from the Americas and 37 per cent from Asia. Mexico has been the largest single source country for the USA for many years. In 1995, 12 per cent of all immigrants were Mexican which represents a decline from the early 1990s. Other important source countries in 1995 (35 000-70 000 immigrants each) were China, the Philippines, Vietnam, India, the former Soviet Union and the Dominican Republic (OECD, 1997: 264).

The 1990 Immigration Act was designed to increase the number of immigrants admitted on the basis of skills, but also maintained levels of family reunion and refugee resettlement, leading to an overall increase in intakes. The Act also established new admissions programmes for the groups considered to have been adversely affected by the 1965 amendments (OECD, 1995: 130). A world-wide lottery now distributes

55 000 entry visas annually at random, contingent upon certain basic qualifications. Nationals of the eleven countries which have sent the largest numbers of legal immigrants to the USA are excluded. Applicants simply have to write their names and those of their spouse and children on a piece of paper and mail it together with photographs to the processing centre in the USA.

Much of the Mexican immigration started as temporary (and frequently illegal) labour movement across the southern border. Farmworkers from Mexico (and to a lesser extent from other Central American and Caribbean countries) have long played a crucial role for US agribusiness, which has opposed any measures for effective control, such as sanctions against employers of illegal workers. The number of undocumented residents was officially estimated at 5 million in 1996 (OECD, 1997: 177). The Immigration Reform and Control Act of 1986 (IRCA) introduced a limited amnesty which led to about 3 million applications (over 70 per cent from Mexicans) (Borjas, 1990: 61–74). Most applicants (about 2.7 million) were granted resident alien status, giving the right to bring in dependents, and thus establishing new migration chains. IRCA also imposed sanctions against employers of illegal workers.

However illegal immigration continued and the ease of falsifying identification documents undercut enforcement of employer sanctions. By 1996 public outrage about illegal immigration led to the adoption of a new law which would significantly increase Immigration and Naturalization Service (INS) personnel, reinforce physical barriers to illegal entry and build additional detention facilities. Measures were also introduced to deny welfare benefits to illegal residents. The INS has received the largest budget increase of any Federal Government agency in recent years. Supporters of stronger enforcement measures believe that illegal residence and employment would be even more extensive in their absence, while critics regard greater enforcement as misguided and in some instances as counterproductive and dangerous. A growing number of illegal entrants have perished because heightened border controls led them to attempt more dangerous forms of entry in remote areas.

From 1986 to 1995 about 12 million people were legally admitted to the USA as permanent residents: the highest volume ever. The previous peak period was 1905–14, when 10 million immigrants arrived. The highest annual figures were 1.5 million in 1990 and 1.8 million in 1991. A large proportion of these were Mexican illegal immigrants whose status was legalised under IRCA. Immigration declined somewhat to

904 000 in 1993 and 720 000 in 1995. Entries for 1996–8 are projected at 800 000 per year (OECD, 1997: 173). Clearly immigration remains one of the major forces which shape US society. The volume of entries, the concentration of settlement in certain areas and the changing ethnic composition are all factors likely to bring about considerable social and cultural change.

In Canada, the overall number of entries grew from 89 000 in 1983 to 192 000 in 1989. In 1990, the Canadian Government announced a five-year immigration plan, designed to maintain the principles of family reunion and support for refugees, while at the same time increasing entries of skilled workers. Admissions rose from 214 000 in 1990 to 255 000 in 1993, but then fell to 212 000 in 1995, due to poor economic conditions. Overseas-born persons currently make up 16 per cent of the Canadian population. However, concentrations are much higher in cities like Toronto and Vancouver. Entries from Asia, Africa and the Middle East have grown rapidly, while European migration has declined. In 1995, 53 per cent of immigrants came from Asia and the Pacific, 15 per cent from Africa and the Middle East, 20 per cent from the Caribbean and Latin America, 5 per cent from the USA and only 15 per cent from Europe. Hong Kong, the Philippines and India were the top three source counties (OECD, 1997: 83–6, 260).

In the world recession of the 1970s, immigration to Australia was cut sharply to average levels of only 56 000 per year. The White Australia Policy was finally abolished in 1973, paving the way for Asian immigration as entry levels grew again in the late 1970s and early 1980s. Today nearly one-quarter of Australia's population are immigrants from over 100 countries, making it one of the world's most culturally diverse societies. Recent immigration levels have fluctuated according to economic conditions. They were high in the late 1980s (up to 140 000 per year) and declined again in the recession of the early 1990s (70 000 in the financial year 1993–4). Numbers increased again as the economy recovered, with a peak of 98 000 (including refugees and other humanitarian entrants) in 1995–6. The Liberal-National Coalition Government, which came to power in 1996, cut planned entries to 86 000 for 1996–7. Immigration from Asia is now the largest component of entry, making up 35–45 per cent of total intakes. A large proportion of entrants continue to come from Britain and New Zealand. Recently there has been an upsurge in migration to Australia from Russia, former Yugoslavia and other Eastern European countries.

Refugees and asylum-seekers

The current world refugee crisis began to develop in the mid-1970s, with mass departures from Vietnam, Cambodia and Laos. Soon after, large numbers of refugees had to leave Lebanon and Afghanistan. In Africa, thousands fled from Zaire, Uganda, Namibia and South Africa. In Latin America, the suppression of democracy in countries such as Chile and Argentina led to exoduses. Political, ethnic and religious persecution seemed to be an almost inevitable accompaniment of political and economic change in poor countries. The number of refugees worldwide grew from about 8 million in 1980 to 15 million by 1989.

Who is a refugee? The definition used by the UNHCR is based on the concept of *individual persecution* laid down by the 1951 United Nations Convention relating to the Status of Refugees (see Rogers, 1992: 1116–8). A refugee is defined as a person residing outside his or her country of nationality, who is unable or unwilling to return because of a 'well-founded fear of persecution on account of race, religion, nationality, membership in a particular social group, or political opinion'. This definition does not take account of group persecution, or of people forced to flee by warfare or internal conflicts. Later declarations adopted in Africa and Latin America have sought to widen the definition, but have not gained general acceptance (see also Widgren, 1989).

'The number of people of concern to UNHCR has risen substantially in recent years: 17 million in 1991, 23 million in 1993 and more than 27 million at the beginning of 1995' (UNHCR, 1995: 19–20). The 1995 figure includes 14.5 million actual refugees; 5.4 million internally displaced persons; 4 million former refugees who have now returned to their homelands, and 3.5 million outside their homelands who have not been officially recognised as refugees, but who are considered to be of concern to the UNHCR.

Why has the global refugee crisis become so severe in recent times? Zolberg, Suhrke and Aguayo (1989: 18–29) examine the three major refugee crises of the twentieth century: the first followed the First World War and the second came after 1945. These were mainly European crises, and the international systems set up to deal with them were shaped accordingly. The third (and most serious) refugee crisis began to develop in the 1940s, with the mass refugee movements in the Indian sub-continent and the Middle East, and came to a head in the 1980s. This time it was a global crisis, with its main centres in the less-developed regions.

Zolberg, Suhrke and Aguao (1989: 227–57) argue that the main cause of refugee movements in less-developed areas is not poverty and underdevelopment, but rather the generalised and persistent violence that has resulted from rapid processes of decolonisation and globalisation under conditions determined by the developed countries. The results are weak states, underdeveloped economies and poor social conditions. This has been the context for ethnic conflicts and struggles over the social order, leading to impoverishment and denial of human rights. During the Cold War, local conflicts became internationalised: the USA, the Soviet Union and former colonial powers sent weapons and troops to intervene in wars and revolutionary struggles in Africa, Asia and Latin America. Yet with the end of the Cold War, new conflicts broke out, which generated even greater numbers of refugees, for instance in the former Soviet Union, former Yugoslavia, Burma, Somalia and Rwanda. In addition, accelerated degradation of the natural environment has led to a new category: the environmental refugee, with large numbers of people fleeing pollution, drought, floods and deforestation caused by industrialisation and one-sided development.

Another new phenomenon emerged in the 1980s: asylum seekers, who arrive by air or other means and ask for asylum once in the country. The events of 1989–91 led to an upsurge in movements of asylum seekers from Eastern Europe to the West, but inflows from Africa and Asia also grew. Asylum seekers became the largest entry category in several countries, including Germany, France and Sweden. Many states introduced costly and long-drawn-out procedures to assess whether such claimants are really victims of persecution or simply economically motivated migrants. The number of new asylum seekers in European OECD countries increased from 116 000 in 1981 to a peak of 695 000 in 1992. Germany had the biggest increase with 438 000 new entrants in 1992, compared with 49 000 in 1981 (OECD, 1992: 132; 1995: 195). Indeed, nearly two-thirds of asylum seekers in Western Europe were in Germany. However, in relation to population size, Sweden had the highest rate of asylum-seeker entries (10 asylum seekers per 1000 population in 1992, compared with 5.5 per thousand in Germany: see OECD, 1995: 18).

The disintegration of Yugoslavia and the crises in other parts of Eastern Europe were the main causes of the upsurge: in 1992, 28 per cent of the asylum seekers who entered Germany were from the former

Yugoslavia and 24 per cent were from Romania (OECD, 1995: 89). Europeans made up 71 per cent of asylum seekers in Germany in 1992, although there were also many entrants from Vietnam, Turkey, Algeria and elsewhere. It is widely believed in Western Europe that many asylum seekers are really economic migrants, using claims of persecution as a way of evading immigration restrictions. This has led to popular resentment and extreme-right campaigns and violence against asylum seekers. Italy experienced two sudden influxes of Albanian asylum seekers in 1991. The first group, in March, met with a fairly friendly reception, while the second group, in August, were rounded up, confined in football stadiums and then deported. A third wave followed in 1997 as Albania dissolved into anarchy once again.

Pressure grew for restrictions on asylum-seeker entry. In Germany, after heated political debates, Paragraph 16 of the Basic Law (or constitution) was amended to restrict the right to asylum. The new rules came into force on 1 July 1993 and asylum-seeker entries dropped to 128 000 by 1995. Sweden also tightened up entry rules: the number of new asylum seekers dropped from 84 000 in 1992 to 9000 in 1995 (OECD, 1997: 220). International agreements were introduced to prevent applications in more than one European country. Several countries (France, Belgium, Luxembourg, Spain, Portugal, the Netherlands, Germany, Austria and the United Kingdom) introduced rules to refuse entry to persons whose request for asylum is 'manifestly unfounded'. Procedures for determining refugee status have been speeded up, often by reducing possibilities for appeal.

In fact the great majority of applications are rejected. The success rate was only about 4 per cent in Germany, around 10 per cent in Italy, Belgium and Norway, but reached 28 per cent in France in 1993. However, many rejected applicants stay on, with an uncertain legal status, since there are considerable legal and practical obstacles to deportation. Overall, there is a clear shift towards a restrictive interpretation of the UN Refugee Convention. This deters spurious applicants, but it also makes matters much more difficult for genuine ones (OECD, 1995: 45). By 1995, only 308 000 new asylum seekers entered the European OECD countries (OECD, 1997: 220).

Another major flow following the collapse of the Soviet bloc was of persons of German descent from the former Soviet Union and other Eastern European countries to the FRG, where they had a right to entry and citizenship (377 000 persons in 1989: OECD, 1990: 4). The inflow had declined somewhat by the early 1990s, but was still considerable at about 220 000 per year. Similarly, many Jews left the former Soviet Union for Israel and the USA. Such groups are not considered refugees, yet their migration reflects the intertwining of historical, political and economic factors which makes it so difficult to arrive at a clear definition of who is a refugee.

The USA has been a major refugee-receiving country for many years: over 2 million refugees became permanent residents between 1946 and the late 1980s. The largest refugee flows came from Cuba (473 000) and Vietnam (411 000). Refugee entry is closely linked to foreign policy. Prior to 1980, US authorities regarded virtually anyone fleeing a communist country as a refugee. In 1980, the Refugee Act changed the definition of refugees, bringing it into line with the United Nations Convention on Refugees (Borjas, 1990: 33). The President sets an annual 'ceiling' for refugee admissions, after consultation with the Congress. Actual admissions are usually close to the ceiling. Ceilings were increased from 1986 onwards, with a peak level of 142 000 in 1992. Since then levels have been reduced: in 1995 the ceiling was 112 000, and for 1997 it was 78 000 (OECD, 1997: 173).

In the early 1990s, refugee intakes increased rapidly, reflecting events in Eastern Europe, Central America and the Caribbean. During 1993 and 1994 nearly 300 000 asylum applications were filed, increasing the backlog of pending cases to over 420 000. The number of refugee applications actually approved was 105 137 in 1994. An influx of boat-people from Haiti and Cuba claiming political asylum led to a crisis in US refugee policy. The Clinton Administration again ordered the US Coastguard to turn back Haitian boats, as President Bush had in 1992. This policy contrasted with the welcome previously given to Cuban refugees, although both groups were clearly fleeing from dictatorial regimes as well as from conditions of poverty. In 1994, a US-led group of American nations carried out a military operation to depose the dictatorship and bring about political and economic reform in Haiti. This set a precedent for military intervention to stop mass migration. At the same time, the USA and Cuba made an agreement to stop spontaneous migration, with the USA guaranteeing entry to at least 20 000 Cubans per year (OECD, 1995: 132–3).

Canada too has received large numbers of refugees. The total number declined from 37 000 in 1992 to 20 000 in 1994, and then rose again to 28 000 in 1995 (OECD, 1997: 84). The main countries of origin were Bosnia-Herzegovina, Sri Lanka, Somalia, the USSR, China and Iran. Canada has a lengthy and costly process for determination of refugee status of asylum seekers, with a high acceptance rate (57 per cent in 1992). In 1993, the government introduced measures to prevent abuse of refugee determination procedures, including refusal of work permits to those awaiting determination, heavier fines, search and seizure powers, fingerprinting of applicants and greater carrier liabilities for shipping companies and airlines (OECD, 1995: 76).

Australia began to take in refugees from Indo-China in the late 1970s, which was a major factor in the growth of Asian immigration. Australia sets an annual quota for the Humanitarian Programme as part of its immigration policy. Intakes rose from about 12 000 persons per year in the late 1980s to 15 000 in 1995–6. There are three subcategories: Convention refugees (4665 in 1995–6); the Special Humanitarian Programme (SHP), which allows entry of people who do not satisfy UNHCR criteria, but who have suffered severe human rights violations (3465 in 1995–6), and the Special Assistance Category (SAC), for persons in vulnerable situations, for instance in former Yugoslavia (6870 in 1995–6: Department of Immigration and Multicultural Affairs, or DIMA, 1996). The SAC is for people with links to families or communities in Australia, who are expected to provide settlement support. The number of persons seeking asylum while already in Australia fell from 15 500 in 1990–1 to about 2000 per year by 1996. The earlier peak was due to applications by Chinese nationals following the suppression of the Democracy Movement in 1989. Planned entry levels in the Humanitarian Programme were reduced to 12 000 for 1996–7 (Ruddock, 1996).

Overall refugee movements to highly-developed countries have been small compared with movements between countries of the South. According to the UNHCR, 2.6 million refugees had found asylum in the developed countries of Europe, North America and Oceania by 1995; the largest numbers were in Germany (1 million) and the USA (592 000). By contrast there were 5 million refugees in Asia and 6.8 million in Africa. Iran had 2.2 million refugees and Pakistan 1.1 million, mainly from Afghanistan. Some of the world's least developed areas had huge refugee populations: 1.7 million in Zaire, 88 300 in Tanzania, 727 000 in the Sudan and 553 000 in Guinea (UNHCR, 1995: 248–51). It is still the poorer countries which bear the brunt of the world refugee crisis.

Highly skilled migrants

The internationalisation of production, trade and finance is leading to increasing mobility of highly qualified personnel. Appleyard (1989: 32) has coined the phrase 'professional transients' to refer to executives and professionals sent by their companies to overseas branches or joint ventures, or experts sent overseas by international organisations. As Findlay (1995: 515–21) points out, highly skilled temporary migrants are much sought after, even in countries where there is growing hostility to immigration of less-skilled people. Skilled migrants are not an issue of public concern, since they are perceived as bringing economic benefits for the receiving countries, without creating social burdens. Many countries have introduced special entry regulations to facilitate skilled migration. The EU's common labour market is designed to encourage interchange of qualified personnel.

Highly skilled migration grew rapidly in the 1980s and 1990s, and is a key element of globalisation. Much of the movement is of fairly short-term nature (a few months to one or two years) and involves interchange of personnel between the highly developed economies of Japan, the USA and Western Europe. However, some skilled migration is the result of capital investment by companies from industrialised countries in less-developed areas. The types of worker involved include managers and professionals of all kinds: executives, accountants, information technology experts, medical practitioners, engineers, and research and development staff. Migrant entrepreneurs play a closely related role, and the governments of immigration countries compete to attract their capital and abilities. The international exchange of students is closely linked to the globalisation of skilled labour, and cooperation agreements between universities, like the EUs Erasmus Scheme, are designed to encourage such trends.

According to Findlay (1995: 519–20), skilled migrants move within a 'diversity of migration channels'. Perhaps the most important is provided by the internal labour markets of multinational corporations, which send their managers and experts wherever they are needed. Another channel is the international labour markets in which high-level jobs are advertised. People with scarce skills can go anywhere in response to attractive combinations of income levels and lifestyles. This is one of the factors contributing to the concentration of innovation and control in the 'world cities' which dominate the global economy. A third channel is provided by special recruitment agencies, which may be private enterprises or the personnel sections of governmental or supranational bureaucracies.

The skilled transients may stay only for short periods, but can have a considerable impact on the country where they work. They are agents of modernisation and social transformation, with unpredictable effects on economic relationships and life styles. The presence of corporate managers and experts in less-developed countries can also contribute to the development of migration networks which encourage movements of lower-skilled workers in the opposite direction. Temporary migration of highly-qualified workers can help change the sending society too, by exposing members of its managerial and technical elites to other cultures.

Some migration of qualified personnel is from less-developed to highly-developed countries: the so-called 'brain drain'. For example, public hospitals in Britain are heavily dependent on doctors and nurses from Africa and Asia. In Britain, 85 per cent of work permits issued by the government in the late 1980s went to professional and managerial workers, and about two-thirds of all employed immigrants (including EC nationals) were in these categories (Salt, 1989: 450). The 'brain drain' can represent a serious loss of skilled personnel and training resources for the poorer countries. On the other hand, many of the migrants were unable to find work in their home countries. Their remittances may be seen as a benefit, and many return eventually with additional training and experience, which can facilitate technology transfer (Appleyard, 1989). The IOM runs a 'Return of Qualified Human Resources Program', which helps bring back highly-trained expatriates, either permanently or temporarily, to contribute to the skill needs of their countries of origin.

Migration control and the state

Migration scholars put considerable emphasis on the role of the state in initiating and regulating movements (see Chapter 2 above). There is no doubt that government policies greatly influence international migration. However, there is considerable variation in the effectiveness of official policies (Cornelius, Martin and Hollifield, 1994). One of the most striking impressions which emerges from historical study of migration policies is how often they have failed to achieve their stated goals. For example, the German 'guestworker' policies of the 1960s and 1970s were designed to bring in temporary labour without causing settlement. Yet the result was the emergence of new ethnic minorities. Australia, by contrast, wanted European settlers after 1945, to keep the country white and British. The end result of the post-war immigration programme was just the opposite: a multicultural nation with strong links with Asia. In other cases, there is a contradiction between officially stated aims of migration control and the tacit acceptance of undocumented inflows which meet labour market needs: this applies both to the US relationship with Mexico, and to current policies of several Asian labour-importing countries.

Until the 1970s the policies of Western European governments were mainly concerned with recruitment of labour, while North America and Australia had policies designed to control and facilitate permanent immigration. In both cases the focus shifted in the 1980s to prevention of illegal migration, management of refugee and asylum-seeker movements, and finding the right balance between worker and family migrations. There is some convergence in approaches between countries which have pursued very different policies in the past.

Labour market versus family reunion criteria

Immigration policies are often torn between the competing goals of facilitation of family reunion and responsiveness to labour market needs. In Australia, Canada, the USA and Western Europe, most legal immigration today is based on family reunion criteria. Several Western European countries tried to curtail family immigration after 1974, but found it difficult in view of legal obligations and social realities. French governmental efforts to staunch it, for instance, failed because family immigration rights were established by bilateral labour agreements and France's signature of international instruments such as the European Social Charter.

Even Switzerland with its strictly controlled, labour-market oriented policy experienced a shift to family reunion and long-term stay: by the 1990s over half the foreign residents had 'Settlement Permits' of unlimited duration (OECD, 1997: 164). Since the 1974 recruitment curb, family immigration (which means the entry not only of non-working dependants, but also of men and women eager to join the labour force) has provided a steady inflow of additional foreign workers throughout Western Europe. This inflow and the entry into the labour market of children born to resident aliens has largely compensated for foreign workers returning home.

One aim of the US Immigration Act of 1990 was to increase the number of highly skilled immigrants. The number in employment categories rose from 58 200 in 1990 to 147 000 in 1993, but then declined to 85 000 in 1995 (half of these were in fact dependents accompanying workers). The family immigration categories remained by far the largest, making up two-thirds of all permanent entries in 1994 and 1995. From 1995, a minimum of 675 000 immigrants are to be admitted per year, among them 480 000 family immigrants. But that minimum number can be exceeded to admit immediate relatives of US citizens (children and spouses of US citizens and parents of US citizens aged 21 or older), whose entry is not limited. The number admitted in this category in 1995 was 220 000 (OECD, 1997: 173, 261).

Canada introduced a new Immigration Act in 1993, designed to improve the management of immigration and to increase the entry of highly skilled workers through more stringent tests for work skills and language abilities (OECD, 1995: 75–6). Entries in the skilled-worker and business classes rose from 37 per cent of all entries in 1993 to 47 per cent in 1995, while family class migration fell from 43 per cent to 36 per cent. However, well over half the entrants in the skilled-worker and business classes are actually dependents of the principal applicants (OECD, 1997: 83–4), so family migration remains the main form of entry to Canada. A points system is used to regulate entries in the work-related categories, with points given for education, work-skills and proficiency in one of the Canadian official languages (French and English). Family-based immigration is also the main category in Australia (see Chapter 8).

The significance of family-based immigration in the policies of Western democracies stems from the priority accorded to humanitarian and human rights considerations. It also reflects the power of immigrant-origin minorities in democratic political systems. But family-based immigration also facilitates integration of immigrants. Indeed, one of the most striking features of the US immigration system has been its benign neglect of immigrants. It relies on families and ethnic communities to incorporate them. As a rule, US Federal government-funded services have only been provided to refugees. Hence, in sharp contrast to Western Europe and Australia, the USA lacks specific social policies for immigrants (see Chapter 8).

In September 1996 the US Congress passed a law which removed entitlement to a range of welfare benefits for immigrants. Legal immigrants who are not US citizens were excluded from such programmes as Food Stamps and Supplemental Security Income (*Migration News*, 3:10, October 1996). One result was that many eligible resident aliens applied for citizenship: in fiscal year 1996, some 1.2 million people were naturalised. Some states with large concentrations of resident aliens, like New Jersey, encouraged naturalisation in order to retain Federal benefits.

Illegal migration

Illegal migration is, by definition, a product of the laws made to control migration. Until the late nineteenth century, workers and their families could freely enter the USA, Canada, Australia and most Western European countries. From the 1880s, governments began to impose restrictions on the basis of race or national origin, or according to labour market criteria. Ever since, there has been illegal immigration: some aliens enter clandestinely without going through required immigration procedures. Others enter legally but violate the terms of their entry, by overstaying their permit or working without permission.

Illegal immigration and employment have long been fairly widespread. In 1973, illegal immigrants were thought to make up about 10 per cent of the foreign population of Western Europe. In the USA over 1 million Mexican nationals were repatriated by Operation Wetback in 1954. Attitudes towards illegal migration varied. In France and the USA it was generally viewed as benign as long as there was high demand for unskilled labour. The FRG and Switzerland, with stronger traditions of police control of foreigners, did not openly tolerate illegal entries but, even there, some spontaneous entrants managed to stay on and work. Official views on illegal immigration changed as economic conditions worsened, unemployment increased and anti-immigrant political movements began to attract support.

There was a general tightening up of controls in the 1970s and 1980s. Most states enacted or reinforced sanctions punishing illegal employment of aliens. Penalties included deportation of workers, and fines against employers. The USA did not introduce sanctions against employers of illegal immigrants until the 1986 IRCA. Enactment of employer sanctions was extremely controversial. Many Hispanics opposed them, fearing increased discrimination: a fear confirmed by a 1991 Government Accounting Office report, which concluded that employer sanctions had resulted in significant additional employment discrimination against Hispanics. This points to a general dilemma: immigration control measures generally penalise individual workers, who are fined, imprisoned or deported. Thus far, they have had insufficient effect on the employers who benefit from exploiting the workers. Document fraud has also stymied effective enforcement, particularly in the USA.

Other measures to curb illegal immigration include stricter enforcement of border controls and visa requirements. Many industrial countries have also had legalisation programmes, which offered an amnesty and legal status to illegal migrants, providing they came forward by a certain date and satisfied certain criteria, such as having work. By far the largest legalisation programme was that of the USA pursuant to IRCA in 1986 (see earlier in this chapter). Italy and France probably ranked second and third in numbers of aliens legalised. Other Western democracies that legalised illegal immigrants between 1970 and 1997 include Australia, Austria, Canada, the United Kingdom, Belgium, the Netherlands, Portugal, Spain and Sweden. Not all states, however, took this approach. Germany eschewed legalisation on the grounds that it would serve to attract even more illegal immigrants.

The 'migration industry'

One reason why official migration policies often fail to achieve their objectives is the emergence of the so-called 'migration industry'. This term embraces the many people who earn their livelihood by organising migratory movements as travel agents, labour recruiters, brokers, interpreters, and housing agents. Such people range from lawyers who give advice on immigration law, through to human smugglers who transport migrants illegally across borders (like the 'coyotes' who guide Mexican workers across the Rio Grande, or the Moroccan fishermen who ferry Africans to Spain). Banks become part of the migration industry by setting up special transfer facilities for remittances. Some migration agents are themselves members of a migrant community, helping their compatriots on a voluntary or part-time basis: shopkeepers, priests, teachers and other community leaders often take on such roles. Others are unscrupulous criminals, out to exploit defenceless migrants or asylum seekers by charging them extortionate fees for non-existent jobs. Yet others are police officers or bureaucrats, making money on the side by showing people loopholes in regulations.

The development of the migration industry is an inevitable aspect of the social networks which are part of the migratory process (see Chapter 2). Whatever its initial causes, once a migration gets under way, a variety of needs for special services arise. Even when governments initiate labour recruitment, they never provide all the necessary infra structure. In spontaneous or illegal movements, the need for agents and brokers is all the greater. There is a broad range of entrepreneurial opportunities, which are seized upon by both migrants and non-migrants. The role of the agents and brokers is vital: without them, few migrants would have the information or contacts needed for successful migration.

In time, the migration industry may become the main motive force in a migratory movement. If the government concerned then decide to curtail migration, it could run into difficulties. The agents have an interest in the continuation of migration, and go on organising it, though the form may change (for example, from legal worker recruitment to illegal entry). Harris (1996: 135) characterises migration agents as 'a vast unseen international network underpinning a global labour market; a horde of termites . . . boring through the national fortifications against migration, and changing whole societies'.

Restriction and 'root causes'

Illegal migration to industrial countries increased over the 1974–95 period. Together with the upsurge in refugee and asylum-seeker entries from the mid-1980s, it became a focus for aggressive campaigns from the extreme right. This contributed to the politicisation of migration issues, and helped increase the pressure for migration control. There has been a flurry of international meetings and diplomatic activity concerned with migration issues. Current political initiatives take two forms: one is further tightening of restrictive measures, the other is the attempt to address what is often referred to as the 'root causes' of mass migration: the South–North divide.

Since the early 1990s, most OECD countries have changed laws and entry procedures, introducing such measures as: stricter border controls, visa requirements, penalties for airlines which bring in inadequately documented passengers, identity checks, workplace inspections, techniques for the detection of falsified documents and more severe penalties for those caught infringing regulations. Controls were devised to prevent people obtaining the papers needed to get work, social security benefits, schooling or medical services (for changes in various countries see OECD, 1997: 52–7). To give a few examples: the Netherlands reinforced rules for the detention and deportation of illegal residents, and introduced a new Aliens Employment Act. In Norway a central bureau for the fight against illegal immigration was established to centralise information provided by the police, national and foreign governments, airline companies and embassies. French authorities required employers to notify them prior to hiring a foreign worker in order to verify employment eligibility. The USA and Canada took steps to make it harder for immigrants with low income levels to bring in relatives.

International cooperation between immigration countries plays a major part. From the mid-1980s, the Commission of the European Community repeatedly discussed migration, but failed to come up with a common policy towards entrants from non-Community countries. This meant that interstate cooperation was largely left to *ad hoc* groups. The most important was that established at a meeting in Schengen on June 1985: Germany, France and the Benelux countries signed an agreement on the removal of controls on their common borders and a joint policy on entrants from third countries. The 'Schengen Group' became the focus of efforts to tighten border controls for migrants from the South and East (Callovi, 1992). However, the Schengen Agreement was not implemented until 1995.

The collapse of the Soviet Bloc made regulation of migration even more urgent. The 1991 European Convention on Security and Co-operation in Europe (ECSC) was intended to create a zone in which basic human rights and minimum living standards were respected, so that individuals from this area would have no basis to apply for asylum. The model was Poland, from which so many asylum seekers had come in the 1980s. By the 1990s, it was considered that requests by Poles for asylum could be uniformly denied. Further agreements were made in 1991–2 with a number of Eastern European countries on preventing use of their countries for transit of illegal migrants to Western Europe. These countries also signed the United Nations Refugee Convention and themselves began receiving asylum seekers. The ECSC was supposed to prevent developments which would lead to mass population movements. The war in former Yugoslavia, which produced millions of refugees, questioned the efficacy of the ECSC as a mechanism to ensure security.

The 1991 Maastricht Treaty, which set up the European Union from 1 January 1993, also established European citizenship, giving people moving between member states virtually all citizenship rights, except that to vote in national elections. But the Treaty again failed to establish a common policy on immigrants from non-member states, although it did include measures for cooperation on asylum policy.

On 26 March 1995, the Schengen Agreement finally came into force for those signatory states which had established the necessary procedures: Germany, Belgium, Spain, France, Portugal, Luxembourg and the Netherlands. This meant complete removal of border controls for people moving between these countries. Effectively, the Agreement created a new class of 'Schengen citizens', to be added to the existing categories of EU citizens and non-EU citizens. The UK refused to join

Schengen, insisting on continuing its own strict border controls of people coming from the Continent.

This general climate of restrictiveness led some observers to speak of a 'fortress Europe' building walls to keep out impoverished masses from the South and East. Yet in the international debates on mass migration there has been growing agreement that entry restrictions could have only limited success. The amount of control and surveillance needed to make borders impenetrable is inconsistent with the trend towards increased interchange and communication. This is why sanctions against unauthorised employment have become crucial to control strategies. Some scholars believe that the disparities between economic and social conditions in the South and the North is such that illegal migration is likely to grow whatever the barriers (Cornelius, Martin and Hollifield, 1994). Others are more circumspect and point out that some Western countries have developed a considerable capacity to deter illegal migration over the last quarter of a century (M. J. Miller, 1994; Messina, 1996). None the less, there is an emerging consensus about the need to address the 'root causes' of mass migration by supporting efforts to improve conditions in the countries of origin.

Measures to reduce migration do not just mean development aid, but also foreign and trade policy initiatives, designed to bring about sustainable development, and to improve political stability and human rights. This has long been understood in the USA. Yet during the Reagan presidency from 1980 to 1988, US foreign policy was hostile to the North–South dialogue (M. J. Miller, 1991: 36). US involvement in various insurgencies and civil wars at times exacerbated political instability, generating additional migrants. Ironically US intervention, specifically in Central America, was partly justified by what was termed 'the fear of brown bodies'. In other words, if the USA did not quell insurgencies, they might succeed and the result would be millions of additional refugees from the new regimes: the Cuba scenario.

One indication of a changing approach was the conclusion drawn by a US federal study commission in 1990 that 'development and the availability of new and better jobs at home is the only way to diminish migratory pressures over time' (Commission for the Study of International Migration and Cooperative Economic Development, or CSIMCED, 1990: xiii). But the report also found that development would increase international migration to the USA over the short to medium term. The persistence of illegal migration to the USA despite the legalisation and the imposition of employer sanctions was taken by many as proof that a new strategy of 'abatement' was needed to replace or complement a strategy of deterrence. Such considerations played a major part in the discussions which led up to the NAFTA, between the USA, Mexico and Canada in 1993. NAFTA did in fact spur investment and job creation in Mexico, especially along the border with the USA. But there is no evidence that it has yet had any appreciable effect in reducing the economic and demographic pressures which cause Mexicans to emigrate (see Chapter 5).

In Western Europe too, immigration concerns loomed much more prominently in foreign policy debates than they had in the past. There was concern in Eastern Europe and North Africa that the Single European Market would create greater barriers to external trade, thus keeping out products from less-developed areas. In 1996, the EU established a customs union with Turkey and reached separate agreements with Morocco and Tunisia to remove barriers to trade. As with NAFTA, however, it was far from clear whether the measures would reduce 'unwanted' migration in the long run. It was feared, for instance, that trade liberalisation would endanger many medium-sized Tunisan and Moroccan firms, while barriers to North African agricultural exports to the EU remained.

Three types of international cooperation that might abate migration to Europe have been suggested (Böhning, 1991b: 14–15). The first is trade liberalisation. The problem is that the Western European industries that would be most affected by trade liberalisation, such as agriculture and textiles, are precisely those which have been highly protected. Therefore it would appear that Western European governments possess only a limited capacity to liberalise trade, a conclusion confirmed by the trade dispute between the USA and the EC during the Uruguay Round of the General Agreement on Tariffs and Trade (GATT) negotiations in the early 1990s. The second means of international cooperation is direct foreign investment. But governments exercise little control over investors, who follow considerations of profit. Then there is foreign aid, which could abate international migration if designed to rapidly improve economic and social conditions for people otherwise likely to depart. However, in the past, foreign aid has generally done little to improve average living conditions. If it is to help reduce migration, future aid policy will have to be much more concerned with social and demographic issues. Above all, a halt to military aid is essential.

Conclusion

This overview of international migration to developed countries since 1945 can lay no claim to completeness. Rather we have tried to show some of the main trends, and to link them to various phases in global political economy. Many of the large-scale migrations have been primarily economic in their motivations. Labour recruitment and spontaneous labour migration were particularly significant in the 1945–73 period. In the following years, other types of migration, such as family reunion and refugee and asylum-seeker movements, took on greater importance. Even migrations in which non-economic motivations have been predominant have had significant effects on the labour markets and economies of both sending and receiving areas. But it is equally true that no migration can ever be adequately understood solely on the basis of economic criteria. Economic causes of migration have their roots in processes of social, cultural and political change. And the effect on both sending and receiving societies is always more than just economic: immigration changes demographic and social structures, affects political institutions and helps to reshape cultures.

Again it is worth looking back at the four-stage model of the migratory process put forward in Chapter 2. It works very well as an explanatory model for the transition of Western Europe 'guestworker' migrations into permanent settlement. It also applies fairly well to the movements from colonies and former colonies to Britain, France and the Netherlands. Here too initial labour movements led to settlement and formation of ethnic groups. The model appears less directly applicable to permanent movements to North America and Australia, where family migration and permanent settlement were always the intention of a large proportion of migrants. But the four-stage model has some explanatory value here as well, as will be discussed for Australia in Chapter 8. As for recent refugees and 'professional transients', time will show what forms of settlement and ethnic group formation will emerge.

In the early 1990s, Western Europe was gripped by fears of uncontrolled influxes from the East and South. By 1995 this scenario had receded, due both to changes in sending countries, and the tightening of entry rules and border controls. None the less, the pressure for migration, especially from the South, remains. The current relative slowdown in movements may be a passing phase, like that of the late 1970s, which could pave the way for even greater future movements. Much will depend on government actions, such as allocation of sufficient resources to enforce entry laws. States can and do affect migratory outcomes, and there is reason to believe that control measures have some effect in reducing 'unwanted' migrations. In the long run, however, it is the measures to address the 'root causes' which will really count, and there is a long way to go before these are likely to be effective.

The upsurge in migratory movements in the post-1945 period, and particularly in the 1980s and 1990s, indicates that international migration has become a crucial part of global transformations. It is linked to the internationalisation of production, distribution and investment and, equally important, to the globalisation of culture. Even countries like Japan, which have tried to close themselves off from foreign influences, are finding that participation in the international economy brings migration and cultural change.

The end of the Cold War and the collapse of the Soviet bloc added new dimensions to global restructuring. One was the redirection of investment of the advanced capitalist countries away from the South towards Eastern Europe. Another dimension was the growth of East–West migration, with previously isolated countries entering global migratory flows: Albania is the most dramatic example, with large-scale illegal movements to Italy and Greece since 1989. Even recently a distinguished observer of migration could write in *International Migration Review*'s Special Silver Anniversary edition: 'If the world consisted of Albania on the one hand and Japan on the other, there would be no *International Migration Review* at all' (Zolberg, 1989: 405). Today both those countries have entered the international migration arena. There can be few areas today which are not profoundly affected by the growing global migratory flows.

5 The Next Waves:
The Globalisation of
International Migration

The North–South gap – the differentials in life expectancy, demography, economic structure, social conditions and political stability between the industrial democracies and most of the rest of the world – looms as a major barrier to the creation of a peaceful and prosperous global society. International migration is a major consequence of the North–South gap. However, the world can no longer be simply divided up between rich and poor nations. Long before the end of the Cold War, new poles of financial, manufacturing and technological power had emerged in the oil-rich Arab states and in East Asia. Oil-producing areas outside the Arab region, such as Nigeria, Venezuela and Brunei, have also become important areas of immigration. A wide range of industries attract migrant workers: agriculture, construction, manufacturing, domestic services and more. Eastern Europe takes an intermediate position between the industrial and the less-developed countries. Economic and social dislocation, political unrest and technological backwardness create conditions conducive to emigration.

The focus of this chapter is upon current trends in international migration to, from and within the Eastern European, Arab, African and Latin American regions. The next chapter will deal with the Asia-Pacific region, which is home to more than half the world's people. The next waves of migrants will mainly come from these areas. Much of the international migration will continue to be intra-regional, but many migrants will also desire to go to Western Europe, Australia or North America. Understanding migration within the South is an essential precondition for formulating the future policies of the developed countries.

Eastern Europe

In the early 1990s, a new spectre haunted Western Europe: fears of an influx from the East. There was speculation about mass migration on a scale not seen since the collapse of the Western Roman Empire. The disintegration of the USSR and the rest of the communist bloc was accompanied by mounting economic chaos, massive unemployment and political strife. An OECD report summarised the situation as follows:

> In the current transition phase, the countries of Central and Eastern Europe are going through a period of economic recession characterised by negative GDP growth in 1992 (with the exception of Poland) . . . and a fall in intra-regional trade and exchanges with the former Soviet Union. Employment levels have also fallen. The drop in output is most apparent in Romania and Bulgaria, which have extremely high inflation rates . . . The transition to a market economy is not being made at the same rate in all Central and Eastern European countries and the impact of changes . . . differ . . . from one country to another. (OECD, 1994: 107)

However, it was far from certain that the political turmoil and economic collapse would lead to massive 'unwanted' emigration outside the region. There were several reasons why such fears appeared exaggerated. First, there were obvious limits to the outflows of Jews to Israel, Germans to Germany and Greeks to Greece, although it appears that some non-Jews and non-Germans claimed those ethnicities in order to emigrate. There undoubtedly were many people who wanted to emigrate but who lacked 'privileged' ethnic background.

Second, the Cold War had sealed off these states from the rest of the world. There were significant outflows of refugees from the Warsaw Pact area in 1956, 1968 and during the 1970s. But, by and large, ordinary Russians or Romanians did not have networks that would enable them to find work and establish residence in Western Europe or North America. Third, demographic pressure to emigrate like that in North Africa or in Central America is not found in much of the ex-Warsaw Pact area, save for cases like Romania. Most of the Central European countries have demographic structures that are similar to those of Western Europe. Surveys reveal that most Hungarians, for example, do not expect or wish to emigrate. The government of Hungary is much less concerned about prospects for emigration than it is about 'unwanted' immigration (Tamas, 1997).

In Russia, life expectancy decreased in the 1990s, a macabre barometer of the hardships endured. Yet relatively few ordinary Russians emigrated. Most who did repatriated from Soviet successor states to the Russian Federation. The outflow of Jews to Israel, some 532 000 from 1990 to 1994, constituted the exception, not the rule.

Hungary, Poland and the Czech and Slovak Republics appear unlikely to generate large numbers of emigrants. Instead they are fated by geography to be the most proximate areas of relative affluence and perhaps political stability for the areas to their south and east, which appear more likely to generate large numbers of refugees and would-be emigrants. In the space of a few years, they have become lands of immigration. Over 40 years of Soviet domination left them poorly prepared to cope with the novel situation (Toth, 1992); they had to enact laws and develop institutions to regulate international migration almost overnight.

By the 1990s, Hungary possessed a substantial population of refugees, quasi-refugees and foreign workers, both legal and illegal. Hungary served as an important transit point for migrants wishing to go to Western Europe. Border crossing statistics suggested the intensity of movement. There were 110 million border crossings in 1990 compared to 102 million in 1991 (OECD, 1994: 129). As many aliens travelling through Hungary were turned back at the border, Hungary had to provide for many of the aliens not permitted to enter Austria, at significant cost to the financially constrained Hungarian government (Szoke, 1992). To slow the inflow of aliens using Hungary as a transit route, the government announced new rules: from October of 1991, aliens were required to have the equivalent of US$13 for each day of planned stay in Hungary, in addition to a sum to cover the cost of return to the aliens' country of citizenship. In the first three days after the new regulations took effect, some 46 000 aliens were refused entry (Szoke, 1992).

Hungary, Poland and the Czech and Slovak Republics became an immigration buffer zone for Western Europe. These four states are the most directly affected by instability and economic chaos in Eastern Europe. They regard prospects for their own political stability and economic development as contingent upon developing a capacity to regulate international migration and to prevent mass 'unwanted' entry. The 1991 signature of agreements between Poland and the Schengen Group (France, the FRG, Italy and the Benelux countries) helped establish the groundwork for future cooperation. The agreement granted Poles, Hungarians, Czechs and Slovaks the opportunity for visa-less entry into the Schengen Group states for periods up to three months. The Polish government agreed in return to accept the repatriation of its citizens who violate the terms of their entry (for example,

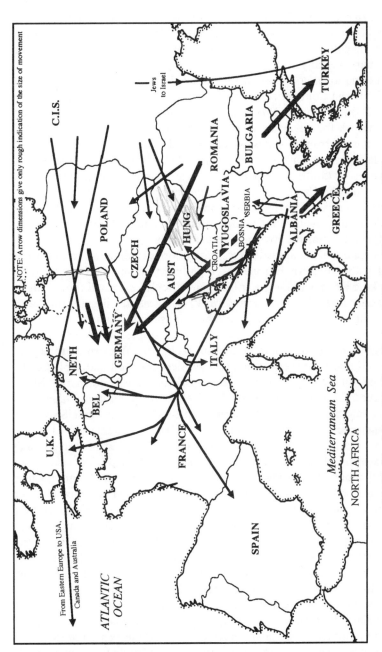

MAP 5.1 Migrations from Eastern to Western Europe since 1989

through illegal work). The Poles also agreed to accept the return of 'third country' nationals who cross Poland and then enter the Schengen area illegally: that is, mainly Russians or Ukrainians who enter Germany illegally.

International cooperation to combat illegal migration was the goal of the Berlin Conference of October 1991, which led to what came to be called the Budapest Process. This became the only pan-European framework for migration control. Subsequent meetings were attended by ministers from 35 states, which testified to the high priority attached to immigration control in the region (UN Economic Conditions for Europe, 1995: 10–11). Germany made economic cooperation with states like the Czech Republic contingent upon cooperation on immigration control. The 1993 change in German asylum law had the effect of deflecting asylum applications to the east and south-east, principally to Poland, Hungary and the Czech Republic.

Despite the Budapest Process, unauthorised migration to and from and within Eastern Europe was significant. While many Poles were working illegally in Dutch or German agriculture, tens of thousands of Russians and Ukrainians found work, also generally illegally, in Polish agriculture and construction. Ukrainians and Russians frequently agreed to work for wages well below those paid to Polish citizens. Large numbers of would-be asylum seekers in Western Europe also entered, many of them Romanian gypsies. Some estimates placed the number of illegally-resident foreign workers from the former USSR in Poland at 70 000 in 1991 (OECD, 1994: 143). In addition Poland was receiving huge influxes of border-crossers from the ex-USSR who would enter for a few days in order to barter and then return home with hard-to-find goods or hard currency. Delays at border crossing points on Poland's eastern frontier lasted for days.

All along the former East West frontier, migrants from Eastern Europe, and from other areas of the world as well, attempt to enter countries like Austria and Germany illegally. The Oder–Neisse river boundary between Poland and Germany has become Western Europe's Rio Grande. Illegal entrants are sometimes flown in by hedgehopping aircraft which are purposely crash-landed and then abandoned. Other migrants are smuggled in by van or lorry. Sophisticated trafficking methods abound. The Czech border with Germany and the Slovenian–Italian border near Trieste also are major entry points.

Italian police have roughed up migrants to discourage illegal entry. Large numbers of Albanians entered Greece in the 1990s. Greek efforts to stymie illegal entry adversely affected the already tense relationship with Albania. Despite ample evidence of extensive illegal entry, authorities did make some headway in bolstering enforcement. Poland, Hungary and the Czech Republic developed embryonic capacities to regulate migration largely through emulation of Western European models.

The situation in the Republic of Bosnia-Herzegovina suggests a possible future pattern for much of the vast area from Poland to the Pacific. The conflict erupted when the Republic declared its independence in 1991 and resulted in the displacement of half of the population. Most of the 2 million displaced were Bosnian Muslims. Of these refugees, just over 1 million went abroad. There were 350 000 Bosnian refugees in Germany, 150 000 in Croatia, 80 000 in Austria and 50 000 in Sweden. Another 650 000 Bosnians became internally displaced persons within the Republic. More than 200 000 people were killed and many more wounded (International Centre for Migration Policy Development, 1996: 7). Despite the enormity of the violence and crimes, relatively few Bosnian refugees found permanent haven in Western Europe. Most stayed in the area of the former Yugoslavia. Those who were admitted to Western Europe mainly were viewed as temporary sojourners.

A key aspect of the 1995 Dayton Agreement to end hostilities in Bosnia involved planned repatriation of the displaced and refugee population. Germany and Switzerland soon afterwards began to plan for repatriation, working in conjunction with the IOM and other international agencies. Despite the deployment of IFOR troops from the USA, France and other countries, and the holding of elections, the situation on the ground was not propitious for refugee return. Some refugees encountered violence when they tried to return to their homes. The economic situation was bleak. Annual per capita income fell to US$500 from US$1900 in 1990. Industrial production was 5–10 per cent of the 1990 level. There had been enormous loss of livestock, machinery and fixed capital in agriculture. Sixty per cent of housing was destroyed; 35–40 per cent of infrastructure was damaged (Internation Centre for Migration Policy Development, 1996: 4). The stakes involved in successful repatriation of the Bosnian refugees were high as suggested in this International Centre for Migration Policy Development report:

> Return must take place but it must take place successfully. The efficient implementation of the return option will bear upon the future of European refugee policies. The current TPS-system (temporary protected status) was largely devised by European Govern-

ments as a parallel track to the regular asylum system, in order to cater for the mass influx of Bosnian war-refugees, who indeed were in need of temporary protection. If this new refugee policy, which demonstrated a clear commitment on the part of the European States to protect the most vulnerable, would imply that the majority continued to stay in the receiving country in spite of peace in their home country, the concept of temporary protection might become problematic. (1996: 1–2)

The fighting in Bosnia resembled conflicts in many areas of the former Warsaw Bloc states, particularly within the former USSR. Millions fled these conflicts and swelled the world's refugee and internally displaced populations. There were also significant movements of temporary foreign workers, especially to Germany, and limited legal emigration. One of the major consequences of emigration from the successor states to the Soviet Union and other Eastern European states was the loss of highly skilled and professional personnel. This was apparent in the extraordinary skills brought to Israel by many Soviet Jews. It was feared that the loss of highly skilled people to Israel, Western Europe and North America could have crippling economic effects and prolong the painful transition period from command to more capitalistic economies (Shevstova, 1992). Prospects for emigration by highly skilled workers are much brighter than for the less skilled as both Western Europe and North America are experiencing shortages of highly skilled workers in the 1990s.

The future of international migration in this area hinges on general economic and political developments. Much depends on whether the new governments can offer their citizens hope of a better life in the future. There is reason to be profoundly pessimistic about long-term prospects for the area's economies and politics, especially if the West were to provide little assistance. There is a long and terrible history of Eastern European governments resorting to forced emigration to resolve the region's complicated ethnic problems (Stola, 1992). But, even in the worst scenarios, mass 'unwanted' migration of East Europeans to Western Europe seems improbable. Even if those uprooted by conflict or economic chaos want to emigrate to the West, it would be quite difficult for most of them to do so. A more reasonable scenario is to expect large-scale population movements between the successor states to the USSR and several Eastern European states.

Most likely, the next waves will be predominantly intra-regional, although there may also be considerable emigration to the South. The mass movement of over 350 000 Bulgarian Turks in 1989 to Turkey was perhaps also a harbinger of the future. Over half of them returned home once the 'repressive policies against them there ceased' (Vasileva, 1992). If human rights are protected, emigration from the area will decrease. By the mid-1990s it had become virtually impossible for Poles to be accorded political asylum in EU member states, although some still attempted to obtain it. One of the goals of the Convention of European Co-operation and Security signed in 1991 was to create a European space from the Atlantic to the Urals in which people would be afforded minimum living standards and human rights. The sooner the spirit of that convention can be translated into practice, the less likely regional instability will be and with it prospects for 'unwanted' mass migration.

The Arab Region[1]

The area from the Atlantic beaches of Morocco to the Western borders of Afghanistan and Pakistan is one of enormous diversity. Within it there are four key migrant labour sub-systems: emigration from the Mediterranean littoral to Western Europe, Arab labour migration to oil-producing states, Arab migration to non-oil producing Arab states, and East and South Asian labour migration to oil-producing states. The first three movements will be dealt with here, while Asian migration to the oil states will be discussed in Chapter 6. There are also large refugee flows, especially to Iran and Turkey, and the special case of mass immigration for settlement in Israel. On the whole, the situation of migrant labour in the Arab region is characterised by extraordinary deprivation of basic rights.

Demographically the Arab region contains extreme contrasts. The swath from Morocco to Turkey is one of the world's most fertile areas. There is enormous population growth and most of the population is young. Areas like Beirut, Gaza and the lower Nile Valley are very densely populated. Population density and the gap between job creation and the entry of new cohorts into the labour market propels emigration. Nearby, however, are lightly populated desert wastelands and zones of rapid economic growth possible only through massive recruitment of foreign labour. The first major forms of international migration within the region in modern times were shaped by European powers that controlled most of the Arab region until the Second World War and even later.

North Africa and Turkey: still Western Europe's labour reservoir?

In 1995, there were over 2 million immigrants from North African countries in European OECD countries (OECD, 1997: 31). This migration is based on the legacy of colonialism, especially for Algeria which was for a long time an integral part of France. The Franco-Algerian nexus illustrates the growing tissue of interdependency that helps generate international migration worldwide and is central to understanding the potential for future migration (M.J. Miller, 1979: 328–41).

During the First World War and thereafter, Algerian Muslims were recruited for employment in metropolitan France. After the Second World War, barriers to emigration to mainland France were removed and Algerians became French citizens. Hundreds of thousands moved to the mainland, especially after the outbreak of the national liberation war in 1954. When Algeria became independent in 1962, persons of Algerian background in France could opt for French or Algerian citizenship. Most chose Algerian, but a significant minority remained French citizens, especially so-called Harkis: Algerian Muslim soldiers who had served with the French army. Following independence, labour emigration to France continued. By 1970, Algerians comprised the largest immigrant community in France, numbering almost 1 million.

Algerians were a predominantly blue-collar workforce concentrated in the most poorly paid, dangerous and physically exhausting work in French industry, particularly construction and motor manufacturing. Independence did little to change this. However, Algerians gained a special legal status which still persists today. Unlike most other foreign workers, Algerians were not admitted to France after 1962 through normal ONI channels. A yearly quota of Algerian labour migrants was determined by Franco-Algerian bilateral labour agreements. The Algerian government divided the quota among various regions, which served to diversify Algerian emigration, and reduce Berber preponderance. Hence the number of Algerian workers in France grew, and many were joined by family members.

Under French law up to 1993, children born in France to parents who themselves were born in France were automatically French citizens. Since most Algerian nationals were born in France, as Algeria was part of France up to 1962, their children if born in France were French citizens, even though the parents were not. Algeria simultaneously regarded many of these children as Algerian citizens (Costa-Lascoux, 1983: 299–320). A long legal controversy between France and

Algeria over the citizenship of this group exemplified the transnational nature of significant segments of both French and Algerian society. The constant flow of workers and dependents across the Mediterranean sustained multiple political, socioeconomic and cultural linkages between the two societies, which in turn created an environment propitious to further emigration. By the early 1970s, however, tensions increased and North Africans became targets of racist attacks in France. This prompted an Algerian government decision to suspend further labour emigration to France in 1973. In all likelihood, this migration would have ended soon anyway, as France stopped most recruitment of foreign labour in 1974.

By the 1980s, Algerians were outnumbered in France by Portuguese migrants. Nevertheless, existence of a sizeable expatriate community continued to critically affect Algeria's economy and society. Entire regions were dependent on wage remittances from Algerians abroad. France continued to function as a safety valve of sorts for a society confronted with mass unemployment and a staggering rate of demographic growth. Family reunification permitted some Algerians to become legally employed in France while others worked illegally. The Algerian community in France participated directly and indirectly in Algerian politics. As in the past, anti-status quo groups found greater freedom of expression and organisation on the mainland than in Algeria itself.[2]

During the Gulf War the Algerian government and the great mass of the population sided with the Iraqis. The war contributed to the growing appeal of Islamic fundamentalism. In the December 1991 elections, the major fundamentalist party came close to winning a majority of seats in the Algerian legislature. In January 1992, the Algerian president resigned and the army intervened to stop a second round of elections that appeared destined to give the fundamentalists a large majority. The French, Italian and Spanish governments feared that Algerian instability would lead to mass emigration. Mainstream political parties in France feared that events in Algeria would increase the appeal of the anti-immigrant NF, and endanger French political stability.

As will be examined in greater detail in Chapter 10, the subsequent civil war in Algeria, which claimed an estimated 60 to 70 000 lives by 1997, did spill over to France in the 1990s. The mass emigration scenario did not materialise, but the interdependency created by decades of trans-Mediterranean migration meant that the Algerian civil war hung like a shadow over France. In the mid-1980s, the noted Algerian sociologist

Ahsene Zahraouis excoriated a group of scholars examining immigration trends in France for not putting Algeria's future at the centre of the analysis. His observation seemed all the more lucid a decade later.

Morocco and Tunisia, by contrast, had been French protectorates. Far fewer Moroccans and Tunisians were uprooted by the arrival of European settlers and land confiscation. Hence emigration to the mainland was less extensive than in the Algerian case. Unlike Algerians, Tunisians and Moroccans were recruited for labour in France through the ONI. Moroccan and Tunisian labour emigration to France became significant only in the 1960s, although as early as 1936 there was a legalisation of Moroccans working illegally in France (Weil, 1991b: 149–50). By 1990, however, the 584 700 Moroccan residents of France nearly equalled the number of its Algerian residents: 619 100 (Bernard, 1993: 61).

The enormous significance of labour emigration to North African societies is shown by the size of wage remittance and other revenue flows from France. Officially recorded revenue transfers nearly quintupled between 1974 and 1981, before slowing somewhat. By 1981, they represented nearly one-third of all transfers received by the three countries. Moroccans and Tunisians seemed to evince a greater propensity to transfer savings than Algerians. In part this was due to the more recent arrival of Tunisians and Moroccans, the ageing of the Algerian workforce and its vulnerability to unemployment, and to the progression of family reunification. But the gap was mainly due to Algerians transferring money and goods back home through means that are not recorded statistically. Simon estimated total transfers resulting from North African emigration to Europe at roughly US$4–5 billion in 1985 (G. Simon, 1990: 29).

Turkey is the other principal source of emigrants from the Arab region to Europe. By 1995, there were 2.6 million Turks in European OECD countries (OECD, 1997: 31). Since 1972, Turkey has been an associate member of the EC, but the EC declined to accept full accession by Turkey in 1989. Immigration concerns were the principal reason behind the EC decision, although other factors, such as human rights violations and the recent history of military intervention in government, also played a role. By the year 2000, Turkey is expected to be the most populous North Atlantic Treaty Organisation (NATO) state after the USA. Turkey has millions of emigrants already established in Western Europe. The village and family networks that have developed since the recruitment era will make it potentially more difficult to prevent migration from Turkey than from many Eastern European countries.

However, countries such as Turkey and Morocco are alarmed that Western Europeans will prefer Eastern European migration to largely Islamic migration from the South. These fears have some basis: it is not unusual to hear French business and governmental officials speak of the desirability of reorienting international migration to the East in order to attenuate integration problems. Significantly Switzerland by 1991 defined both Turkey and Yugoslavia as belonging to the 'Third Circle' of nations from which labour recruitment was not allowed. Central European countries like Poland, Hungary and the Czech and Slovak Republics, on the other hand, were defined to be part of the 'Second Circle' of states from which foreign labour could be recruited.

There was little legal recruitment of foreign workers from the Arab region to the EU lands in the 1990s. Spain, Italy and France admitted large numbers of mainly agricultural workers from North Africa. Most legal immigration involved family reunification and it was far from negligible. Illegal migration from the Arab region to Europe was considerable but far less extensive than widely feared. Migrants from Morocco attempted to evade controls by crossing the Straits of Gibraltar to Spain. Similarly, Tunisian and other Arab migrants sailed to off-shore Italian islands or attempted to land directly on the Italian Peninsula. However, most would-be emigrants from the Arab region could not emigrate illegally and the development of control measures in the EU, such as visa obligations and enforcement of employer sanctions, presumably played a key role in deterring mass migration from the Arab Region. Significant numbers of migrants did elude controls, but they were the exception, not the rule.

Concern over the future of international migration was also a major factor in mounting apprehensions in Mediterranean littoral countries over the consequences of the single European market. The worst of these fears were exaggerated: residents from countries such as Morocco and Turkey would not be forced to repatriate, and better integration of resident alien populations would continue to be a priority. The interdependency woven by decades of international migration meant that Western European and Mediterranean littoral states share a common future that would be jeopardised by short-sighted discriminatory measures aimed essentially at Muslim immigrants. A high degree of trans-Mediterranean tensions over international migration will persist. Only time will tell whether these tensions, which are at the front line of the global North-South divide, will be attenuated through skilful government or exacerbated by the absence thereof.

Arab migration to oil-rich Arab states

Movements, mainly of male workers, from the poorer to the richer Arab states have taken on enormous political significance in this volatile region. Libya has admitted large numbers of migrant workers from neighbouring states, principally Egypt and Tunisia. When Egyptian–Libyan relations soured as Egyptian President Anwar el-Sadat reoriented foreign policy towards the West, large numbers of Egyptians were expelled. Similarly, during periods of Libyan–Tunisian tension, Tunisian migrants were deported. After Yasser Arafat signed the Oslo Accords in 1993 and recognised Israel, thousands of Palestinians were ordered to leave. Many were stranded for months at the Egyptian–Libyan border as Israel refused to accept their 'repatriation' to the area controlled by Palestinian Authority. Since 1990, citizens of the four other Maghreb Union states (Morocco, Tunisia, Mauritania and Algeria) have been able to enter Libya freely.

Libya provides an extreme example of the interconnection between international migration and foreign policy issues. The mass expulsions also testify to the disregard of Libyan authorities for Arab League and ILO standards. As the Moroccan scholar Abdellah Boudahrain has argued, disregard for the rights of migrants is commonplace in the Arab world despite the existence of treaties designed to ensure protection (Boudahrain, 1985: 103–64).

In Iraq, the ruling Ba'ath Party regards freedom of entry, residence and employment for non-Iraqi Arabs as consistent with the ideal of pan-Arab unity and nationhood. However, there have also been Iranian as well as South and South-east Asian migrants in Iraq. The Iraqi government grew increasingly critical of the growing proportion of non-Arab workers employed in nearby states, which it regarded as a threat to the Arab character of the Gulf (Roussillon, 1985: 650–5). By the late 1970s, the number of Asian migrants in Iraq was declining in favour of Arab migrants, while the opposite trend was occurring in the oil-rich Gulf states to the south. The openness of Iraq to migrants from other Arab states helps explain the sympathy felt for Iraq during the Gulf crisis virtually throughout the Arab world.

Estimates of the number of migrants in Iraq are sketchy at best. The Secretary of State for Egyptians Abroad estimated that there were 1.25

million Egyptians working in Iraq in 1983 (Roussillon, 1985: 642). The significance of migration of Arabs to Iraq increased during the long and terrible Iraq–Iran war. In the late 1980s, reports of tensions between Egyptian migrants and the indigenous population became frequent. Moreover, Ba'athist rhetoric against non-Arab migrants intensified.

Arab migration to the oil-rich states of the Arabian Peninsula was even larger. Some areas, like Kuwait, had already had immigrant labour policies under British rule, recruiting workers from British possessions in South Asia, particularly present-day India and Pakistan. Significant East Asian migration to the Gulf also began long before 1975 (Seccombe and Lawless, 1986: 548–74). Those areas under American domination, particularly Saudi Arabia, developed quite different foreign labour policies. In the 1950s and 1960s Westerners and Palestinian refugees often provided the skilled labour required for oil production. In the wake of the 1967 and 1973 Arab-Israeli wars, labour migration skyrocketed as the rising price of oil-financed ambitious development projects. Between 1970 and 1980, oil revenue in the Arab states belonging to OPEC (the Gulf states plus Iraq and Libya) increased from 5 billion to 200 billion dollars. Saudi revenues alone increased from 1 to 100 billion dollars (Fergany, 1985: 587).

From the mid-1960s to mid-1970s, most international migrants to the Gulf states were Arabs, mainly Egyptians, Yemenis, Palestinians, Jordanians, Lebanese and Sudanese. During the 1970s, however, the Gulf monarchies grew increasingly worried about the possible political repercussions. Palestinians, in particular, were viewed as politically subversive. They were involved in efforts to organise strikes in Saudi oil fields and in civil strife in Jordan and Lebanon. Yemenis were implicated in various anti-regime activities (Halliday, 1985: 674). Foreign Arabs were involved in the bloody 1979 attack on Mecca which was subdued only after the intervention of French troops. One result was increased recruitment of workers from South and South-east Asia, who were seen as less likely to get involved in politics, and easier to control (see Chapter 6).

By the mid-1980s, the price of oil had plummeted and some observers, like the Central Intelligence Agency (CIA), concluded that the epoch of massive migration to the Arabian Peninsula had come to an end (J. Miller, 1985). Hundreds of thousands of Arab, South and East Asian workers did lose their jobs and return home. But the conclusion that massive labour migration to the oil-rich states had ended was premature. Migrant labour had become an irreplaceable component of the labour force (Birks, Sinclair and Seccombe 1986: 799–814). Despite government efforts to reduce dependency upon foreign labour, including mass expulsions of illegal aliens, foreigners continued to constitute the bulk of the Kuwait labour force on the eve of the Iraqi invasion. The Gulf crisis of 1990–1, following the Iraqi invasion of Kuwait, led to a massive exodus of migrants from the region (see Exhibit 1.1, above, and Map 5.2). Many migrants, however, stayed on despite the hardships and threats to their lives.

After the 1991 war, the Kuwaiti government announced plans to reduce its dependency on foreign labour, yet Kuwait could not rebuild without massive recourse to migrant labour. In Saudi Arabia, Egyptians began to take the place of politically suspect populations like the Yemenis and Palestinians expelled during the crisis (J. Miller, 1991). There was an increased proportion of South and East Asian workers in the migrant workforces of the Gulf oil-states. Despite the military victory over Iraq, the Gulf monarchies had further eroded their legitimacy in most of the Arab world. This made even their key ally, Egypt, increasingly unattractive as a source of migrant labour.

With a population of over 60 million, Egypt is by far the most populous of Arab states and it has been the most affected by intra-regional labour migration. The evolution of Egyptian labour migration correlated not only with the ups and downs of oil revenues in nearby oil-producing states but also with changes in Egyptian domestic and foreign policies. Dramatic increases in emigration followed the death of President Nasser in 1970 and the waning of the appeal of his mildly socialistic and pan-Arab policies. His successor Sadat proclaimed the *infitah,* or opening towards the West, and more liberal economic policies. Following the 1973 war with Israel, Sadat pursued a decidedly pro-Western foreign policy which included signature of a peace treaty with Israel. Remittance of wages from Egyptians working abroad became a crucial economic concern as entire villages and regions depended on them for consumption and investment (Fadil, 1985).

Emigration greatly affected the fabric of life as peasants, craftsmen and highly-skilled professionals were lured away by wages many times higher than they could expect to earn at home (Singaby, 1985: 523–32). Labour emigration undoubtedly relieved chronic unemployment and underemployment, but it also stripped Egypt of much-needed skilled workers and disrupted, for better or worse, traditional village and family structures. Among the many significant effects of the massive emigration was growing Egyptian dependency upon regional political and economic developments: there were returning waves of migrants

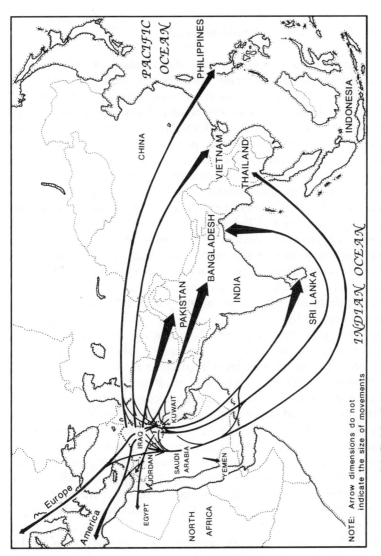

MAP 5.2 Return migration from the Gulf during the 1990–1 Kuwait crisis

NOTE: Arrow dimensions do not
indicate the size of movements

from Libya at the height of Egyptian differences with Colonel Gadaffi, during the oil price drop of the mid-1980s and during the Gulf crisis.

Arab migration to non-oil producing states

Arab migration to non-oil producing states within the Arab region is quantitatively and geopolitically less significant than migration to the oil-producing states, but is none the less important. It is often hard to differentiate between labour and refugee flows. Jordan is a prime example. By the mid-1970s, perhaps 40 per cent of the domestic workforce was employed abroad, primarily in the Gulf (Seccombe, 1986: 378). This outflow prompted replacement migration: the arrival of foreign workers who substituted for Jordanians and Palestinian residents of Jordan who emigrated abroad. However, much of the Jordanian labour that went abroad was skilled. Much of the labour that Jordan receives is skilled as well, but there is also a big inflow of unskilled Egyptians and Syrians. In the 1980s, this inflow is thought to have contributed to growing unemployment amongst Jordanian citizens and resident aliens. Wages in industries heavily affected by foreign workers have also declined (Seccombe, 1986: 384–5). The mass expulsion of Palestinians by Kuwait in 1991 greatly affected Jordan which received most of the influx.

Another important migrant labour pattern involved Palestinian Arab residents of the territories occupied by Israel in the 1967 war. The Israeli labour market was opened up to workers from Gaza and the West Bank. This was part of an Israeli strategy aimed at integrating the occupied territories into the Israeli economy (Aronson, 1990). Most of the workers had to commute daily to work in Israel and were required to leave each evening. Palestinians found jobs primarily in construction, agriculture, hotels and restaurants and domestic services (Semyonov and Lewin-Epstein, 1987). Illegal employment of Palestinians from the territories was fairly widespread (Binur, 1990). In 1984, some 87 000 workers from the occupied territories were employed in Israel, about 36 per cent of the total workforce of the occupied territories.

By 1991, Soviet Jewish immigration was affecting employment opportunities for Arabs. The Israeli government clearly preferred to see Soviet Jews employed in construction or agriculture, rather than Palestinians, yet some of its efforts to employ Soviet Jews met with little or no success. Either the Soviet Jewish immigrants desired different jobs or the pay and working conditions were unsatisfactory. It was difficult to measure the displacement of Palestinians because other factors were also at work. The Gulf War heightened animosities and there was a wave of attacks by Arabs from the occupied territories on Jews in Israel. Israeli authorities introduced more restrictive regulations and admission procedures, aimed at weakening the Intifada, as well as ensuring greater security. A combination of all these elements resulted in a sharp decline in employment of Palestinian workers after 1991. Increasingly, foreign workers from Romania and Thailand were recruited to replace Palestinian Arab labour from the West Bank and Gaza. Concurrently, closure of Gulf state labour markets to Palestinians, which had long served as a safety valve for the population of the occupied territories, has worsened the economic plight of Palestinians in the 1990s. This distress threatened the leadership of the Palestinian Authority and the entire regional peace process.

Refugees and internally displaced persons in the Arab Region

As of 1996, there were some 3.3 million Palestinian refugees scattered around the region and the world. The Palestinian-Israeli peace accords had done very little to alter their plight, although thousands of Palestine Liberation Organisation officials and military or police personnel had been authorised to return to the area of the Palestinian Authority, consisting of parts of the Gaza Strip, Jericho, Hebron and several other urban areas of the West Bank. Negotiations concerning refugees, repatriation, compensation, reparations and access to the territory of the Palestinian Authority loomed as the most difficult aspect of the peace process. Israeli and Palestinian viewpoints and positions differed enormously, starting with enumeration of refugees. With the Palestinian population of the West Bank and Gaza in dire economic straits, with high unemployment compounded by the size of new cohorts coming of working age, prospects appeared bleak or nil for mass repatriation of Palestinian refugees from Lebanon or Syria. The average woman in Gaza had ten children, one of the highest rates of fertility in the world. There were other significant refugee and internally displaced person populations in the region which similarly greatly affected regional politics (see Exhibit 5.1).

Iran became the world's most important haven for refugees by the early 1990s. It succeeded in repatriating large numbers of Afghan refugees and announced that all Afghan refugees must leave in 1997

EXHIBIT 5.1

Kurdish refugees in Middle East regional conflicts

The Kurds constitute an important ethnic minority in Turkey, Iran, Iraq and Syria. The size of the Kurdish population is disputed, but appears to number between 20 and 25 million. About half of all Kurds reside in Turkey where they comprise about one-quarter of the total population. Kurds comprise about one-quarter of Iraq's population, about 12 per cent of Iran's and 10 per cent of Syria's (Gurr and Harf, 1994: 30–2). Kurdish hopes for an independent state were dashed in the wake of the first World War. Since then, Kurdish aspirations for independence or autonomy have fostered conflict.

Kurdish revolts against Iraq's central government have been chronic and frequently have been abetted by Iraq's enemies. Iraqi Kurdish politics has long been dominated by the Barzani family and the Kurdish Democratic Party (KDP). In 1976, the KDP split and a rival party emerged, the Patriotic Union of Kurdistan (PUK) led by Jalal Talabani. In 1975, the Shah of Iran, who had been backing the Kurdish insurgency in Iraq along with Israel, made a deal with the Iraqi government. In return for Iraq renouncing its claim to the Shatt-al-Arab waterway, Iran would close its border and stop aiding the Iraqi Kurdish insurgents. Mustafa Barzani, the legendary KDP leader, stopped fighting and many of his followers fled to Iran. Talabani and the PUK rejected Barzani's decision to stop fighting. Fighting between PUK and KDP forces ensued.

By 1987, PUK forces controlled much of Iraq's Kurdish area. However, Iraqi army forces, using poison gas and indiscriminate bombing of civilian centres, reasserted Iraqi control over much of its northern area by 1988. Tens of thousands of Kurds were killed and millions fled to Turkey and Iran. The Kurdish refugee influx proved to be very expensive for the Turkish government, which received little external aid in coping with the refugees. Meanwhile, a Kurdish insurgency in Turkey was growing. It was led by the Kurdish Workers Party (PKK), a Marxist-Leninist group with important bases of support in Lebanon, where many Kurds worked as foreign labourers, in Europe, amongst Turkish guestworker populations, and in Syria.

In the 1990s, millions of Kurds have been internally displaced by conflicts in Turkey and Iraq. Millions more found refuge in predominantly Kurdish regions of nearby states. In Iraq, Kurdish rebels were crushed by Iraqi troops after the defeat of Iraqi forces in Kuwait in 1991. Millions of Iraqi Kurds fled towards Turkey and Iran to escape retaliation. To prevent another mass influx, Turkey cooperated in a UN-authorised operation to create a protected area in Northern Iraq. The fleeing Iraqi Kurds largely returned home and an autonomous 'federated state' was proclaimed. A parliament was elected and an autonomous administration installed by 1993. However, KDP-PUK hostilities began again. The situation was further complicated by entry into the area by

$\longrightarrow$

$\longrightarrow$

PKK guerillas. Increasingly Turkish forces struck into Northern Iraq to destroy PKK bases. The Turkish government declared its intent to establish a security zone along its border with Iraq.

In 1996, fighting between the KDP and PUK intensified. PUK forces verged on taking control of the protected zone. The KDP appealed to the Iraqi government to intervene. The entry of Iraqi armour turned the tide of battle and PUK forces retreated towards Iran. Many Kurds fled to Iran and were housed in refugee camps near the Iran–Iraq border. The Iraqi military intervention triggered retaliatory strikes by US forces. However, the US-backed Parliament and administration in the protected zone crumbled. Iraqi Kurds fled to Turkey and thousands were promised asylum in the USA. An unknown number of Kurds with ties to the USA were killed by Iraqi agents. By 1997, the covert CIA operation in Northern Iraq appeared to have failed totally.

The stakes involved in Kurdish uprisings and their suppression for regional politics rose steadily. In the 1990s, the USA pursued a so-called dual containment policy against Iraq and Iran. Israel and Turkey began to cooperate extensively in national security matters. Syria, whose Golan Heights area was taken by Israel in 1967 and subsequently annexed, backed the PKK (Kurdish Workers Party), whose training camps in Lebanon's Bekaa Valley were controlled by Syrian troops. The PKK's leader branded the USA, Israel and Germany as enemies of the Kurds and possible targets for PKK guerrillas. Indeed, following a wave of suicide bombings in Israel by Hamas guerrillas in 1996, threats were made by PKK to emulate this tactic in Turkey and Germany (PKK activities in Germany are analysed in Chapter 10). By 1997, the list of PKK enemies had grown and Syria, Iran and Iraq attempted to improve relations to counter the Israel–Turkey axis backed by the USA.

Displacement, eviction, flight, refugee or non-citizen status has been the lot of millions of Kurds in recent decades. Their dispersed and transnational condition is increasingly characteristic of politics around the world. States advance their foreign policy and national security policy goals by mobilising, training and backing refugee populations or by allowing the refugees to pursue their goals autonomously. States will strike against bases and havens used by armed opponents even if this violates the territorial sovereignty of another state. The anti-PKK incursions of the Turkish army into Iraqi territory paralleled Israeli invasions of Lebanon. In both instances, the central government did not control the respective staging areas used by 'foreign' Fatah and PKK guerrillas.

Perhaps most importantly, Kurdish refugee movements led to a multinational military operation aimed at preventing mass outflows. UN-authorised humanitarian intervention in northern Iraq in 1991 was necessitated by Turkey's refusal to become a haven for Iraqi Kurds, as in 1987. Caring for those refugees had cost too much and had further complicated Turkish internal politics and regional relations. Turkey felt vital national security interests were at stake. All around the Middle East, states were coming to similar conclusions.

(US Committee for Refugees, 1996: 111). Meanwhile, hundreds of thousands of Iranian citizens had fled Iran for Turkey, Iraq and the West. Iranian dissidents occasionally attacked targets in Iran from bases in Iraq, and this brought retaliatory strikes. The Iranian government struck against Iranian political opponents abroad. Murders of Iranian opposition leaders in Western Europe severely strained Iran's relations with Germany and France. Iran also received many Azeris fleeing advancing Armenian forces in Azerbaijan. To stem the tide, Iran set up refugee reception centres near its border with Azerbaijan. Iran's refugee policy evolved during the 1990s from one of reception of refugees and integration to more active intervention to prevent inflows or to contain them at the border. The huge cost of caring for refugees played a role in this changing orientation. However, core Iranian interests were at stake in conflicts like that in Azerbaijan as Azeris comprise a major ethnic minority in northern Iran.

Turkey has also received many refugees, including a large flow of Bulgarian Moslems who fled repression in the late 1980s. Turkish citizens of Chechen and Circassian background have given support to insurrectionary movements abroad, principally in the Russian Federation. The Chechen population had been subjugated, slaughtered and dispersed by the Czar and then deported during the Second World War by order of Josef Stalin. The support given by Turkish citizens of Chechen background to the Chechen revolt was typical of the transnational nature of many political conflicts in the late twentieth century. Forced migration in the past was an important grievance for Chechens, Palestinians, Jews, many Turks of Balkan background and others, just as it was a key factor in conflicts in Eastern Europe.

Sub-Saharan Africa

With one-quarter of the world's land mass and a tenth of its population, Africa is the region most affected by refugees. One-third of the world's refugees are found in Africa. Most have fled political and ethnic conflict, but Africa also has environmental refugees, such as the people of Mauritania and Mali, forced by drought to flee their homelands for points south.

Africa includes a large share of the world's poorest states. Migration is often a way to escape crushing poverty, or even death due to starvation or malnourishment. Population statistics leave much to be desired: some of the states have never had a census. The paucity of elementary population information, the frequent absence of identity documents and the ability of some individuals to declare themselves to be nationals of one state when, in fact, they are citizens of another, makes analysis of international migration in sub-Saharan Africa particularly difficult.

Sub-Saharan Africa generates significant outflows of intercontinental migrants, mainly to Western Europe but also to North America and the Middle East. These outflows were traditionally directed primarily to former colonial powers: for example, Zairians emigrating to Belgium, Senegalese to France or Nigerians to the United Kingdom. Many emigrants are college-educated and the loss of scarce human capital though the 'brain drain' has been a long-standing African concern. Intercontinental migration has diversified, however, and increasingly includes poorly educated labour migrants. Sub-Saharan Africans are emigrating in significant numbers to countries such as Spain, Switzerland, Italy, Canada and the USA. But the vast bulk of international migration from sub-Saharan countries stays within the continent.

As in the Arab region, the legacy of colonialism still strongly influences migratory patterns. The European presence shifted the locus of economic activity and trade to coastal areas, producing migrations from the interior that have persisted after independence. The colonial powers carved up the continent into politico-administrative entities (which later became independent states) with little regard for the congruence of ethnic and territorial boundaries. Members of an ethnic group are often citizens of two or more adjoining or nearby states, while many states include members of several ethnic groups. This leads to confusion over legal status or national identity as well as to traditions of movement across international boundaries that are often poorly demarcated and controlled.

The colonial period brought not only European administrators and farmers, but also Syro-Lebanese merchants to West Africa, as well as merchants and workers from the Indian sub-continent to East and Southern Africa. In the post-independence period, these populations generally became privileged but vulnerable minorities. European-origin settler populations often departed *en masse* at independence, with disastrous economic consequences as they had played key roles in agriculture, business and government. The ripple effects of the colonial period were felt long afterwards.

In Kenya, for instance, prime lands were appropriated and allocated to British farmers. When most of the European settlers fled, these lands

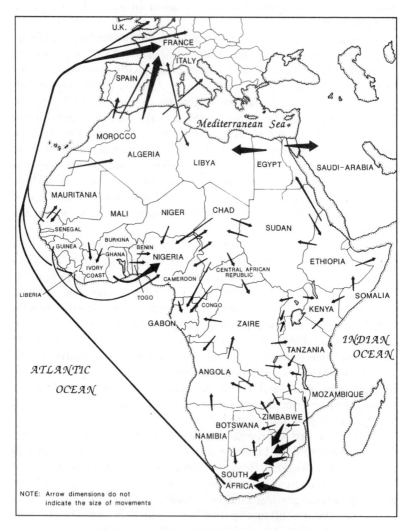

MAP 5.3   Migrations within and from Africa

reverted to the Kenyan government which allocated them to Kikuyus and other ethnic groups then dominant in Kenyan government. By the 1990s, power within Kenyan government had shifted and Kenyan President Moi aided and abetted attacks by pastoralist tribe members like the Masai who laid claim to the lands usurped by the British. Sporadic violence killed 1500 and produced as many as 300 000 internally displaced Kenyans. Donor country pressure upon the Kenyan government led to its grudging approval of a United Nations Development Programme initiative to resettle those displaced. Many lost their lands and were squatters or homeless. Some were able to farm their lands by day but left by night for fear of renewed violence. Many had lost everything and subsisted as day labourers or on charity. Such sequels of colonialism help explain why Africa encompassed 13 of the world's 32 major populations of internally displaced persons in 1995 (US Committee on Refugees, 1996: 6). Sudan alone was estimated to have 4 million internally displaced persons.

In the post-Cold War period, large-scale repatriations of refugees and resettlements of internally-displaced persons have occurred. In the early 1990s, there were an estimated 5.7 million uprooted Mozambicans, including 1.7 million refugees and 4 million internally displaced. By 1996, most had returned home (US Committee for Refugees, 1996: 12). From 1990 to 1996, some 4 million African refugees repatriated, mainly to Ethiopia, Eritrea, Mozambique, Zimbabwe, Namibia, the post-apartheid Republic of South Africa (RSA) and Uganda. In late 1996 and early 1997, tens of thousands of Rwandans also repatriated from Tanzania, when they were ordered to leave by the government. Many returned from Zaire, to escape fighting between insurgents, elements of the Rwandan and Zairian armies and Rwandan Hutu militia and ex-soldiers entrenched in the refugee camps. Some analysts pointed to these large-scale repatriations and resettlements in the post-Cold War era to refute 'chaos theory' which viewed Africa as doomed to political disintegration, mass misery and wholesale uprooting of populations (US Committee on Refugees, 1996: 12). This more upbeat regional appraisal was challenged by unfolding tragedies in Sierra Leone and Liberia in the 1990s as well as by events in Zaire.

Sub-Saharan Africa has witnessed the proclamation of numerous international organisations for the purpose of removing barriers to trade and the free movement of goods, capital and people. Generally these agreements have been poorly implemented or contradicted by policies and practices in member states (Ricca, 1990: 108–34; Segal, 1993: 30). Despite the existence of many zones in which there is

EXHIBIT 5.2

Labour migration to the Republic of South Africa

Foreign worker recruitment to the RSA illustrates the connection between labour migration and broader economic and political dependency characteristic of much of Africa. The roots of this recruitment go back to the colonial period. Most of the workers recruited during the apartheid period from Mozambique, Botswana, Lesotho, Swaziland and Malawi worked in gold mines, with less than 10 per cent in agriculture and other non-mining industries. Lesotho and Swaziland, for example, are landlocked states which border on the RSA (Lesotho is in fact completely surrounded by the RSA). Their populations can barely eke out a living from agriculture. The absence of economic opportunities made employment in RSA mines the only possibility for many, despite the rigours of mine work and the high risk of injury or death.

Recruitment to the RSA was highly organised. Candidates were subjected to a battery of physical and aptitude tests, and many were rejected. The successful ones were transported by air, rail or bus to the mines where they lived in hostels. Virtually only males were hired and most were young. They were given contracts which required them to return home after one or two years of work. Foreign worker policy, during the apartheid era, therefore, did not lead to settlement as expected by the migratory chain theory, because of the strict conditions imposed on the workers.

In 1960, there were about 600 000 foreign workers in the RSA. The number declined to 485 000 in 1975 and 378 000 by 1986 (Ricca, 1990: 226). In 1973, the share of foreigners in the black miner workforce stood at 79 per cent. By 1985, it had been reduced to only 40 per cent. There was a shift away from recruitment of foreign workers from independent but economically dependent states, in favour of increased recruitment from the newly fashioned 'black homelands', which were not recognised by the international community. The change arose partly from the South African regime's fear of being deprived of foreign labour from nearby states as a result of anti-apartheid policies (Ricca, 1990: 226–8).

$\longrightarrow$

nominally freedom of movement by nationals of signatories to these agreements, there is none the less a great deal of illegal migration.

Illegal migration within sub-Saharan Africa is varied and complex. It is often tolerated in periods of good relations and economic prosperity, only to be repressed during economic downturns or periods of international tensions. The mass expulsions from Nigeria in 1983 and 1985 were the most significant in terms of persons uprooted – as many as

$\longrightarrow$

With the renunciation of the apartheid system, a new era is unfolding in the RSA. The 'internalisation' of employment in the mines seems likely to continue. With the former 'homeland' areas faced with crushing poverty and malnourishment, there will be no shortage of potential workers. The future of employment in the mining industry is a vital issue for South Africa and for the region as a whole. The eclipse of apartheid allowed normalisation of long disrupted diplomatic and economic relations between the RSA and its neighbours. A new approach to regional integration and coordination was viewed as critical to the success of post-*apartheid* regulation of international migration.

One of the key problems facing the post-apartheid government of the RSA was unauthorised migration from abroad. There had been considerable illegal migration from neighbouring countries such as Mozambique during the apartheid era. Agriculture was the industry most affected. Security measures, including an electrified fence to deter African National Congress-sponsored guerrilla attacks from bases in nearby states, made illegal entry quite dangerous. With the collapse of apartheid, unauthorised entry is thought to have grown enormously. Africans from as far away as Ghana flocked to the South African 'Eldorado'. Meanwhile substantial repatriations of South African refugees occurred, while South Africans who had been forced to relocate to 'homelands' sought to return home. Widespread unemployment and lawlessness further complicated the picture.

The uneasy partners in the post-apartheid government often had contrasting views on what to do about illegal migration. Governmental action was hampered by a paucity of reliable information concerning the illegally resident population. Certain trade union and African National Congress (ANC) leaders favoured policies which reflected the international solidarity that had been so important during the long struggle against apartheid. Other factions favoured more draconian policies to deter further unauthorised entry and to expel illegal immigrants. Clashes erupted involving unauthorised African immigrants. The overall situation was enormously complex. By 1996, the government had begun a legalisation programme for aliens meeting certain criteria and planned enforcement of employer sanctions. It also continued to recruit foreign labour from nearby states.

2 million – but they are part of a much broader pattern. Many Senegalese have been forced to flee violence in Mauritania, while many Mauritanians had to flee Senegal in 1989 (Fritscher, 1989). In 1991, many Zairians living in Congo were expelled. The director of Congo's Air and Border Police said that three-quarters of the million or so Zairians in Congo would be expelled (Noble, 1991). Tensions over the unregulated arrival of Zairians and other aliens had been building for

some time. Aliens were seen as contributing to rapid population growth in sprawling suburban areas and as overtaxing resources. Zairians were singled out by one specialist as contributing to vice (Loutete-Dangui, 1988: 224–6).

This situation contrasted with the Nigerian case where technically illegal employment of aliens primarily from the Economic Community of West African States (ECOWAS) was looked upon benignly by the Nigerian government during a period of economic expansion. In the mid-1970s, many Ghanaians entered and found work in construction and the services (Andepoju, 1988: 77). A downturn in the economy, coupled with Nigerian governmental instability and deteriorating relations between Nigeria and Ghana prompted a new, stricter policy and mass expulsions.

Taking Africa as a whole, there are reasons for deep pessimism concerning the future of migration. Standards of living have fallen and political instability appears endemic in many areas. On the other hand, there were notable economic success stories in the 1990s, such as Ghana, and an overall continental trend to democratisation (Chazan, 1994). In 1960, there were 300 000 refugees in Africa. By 1970, there were a million. Between then and 1990, the refugee total quintupled but it has hovered near the 5 million mark ever since (Ricca, 1990).

The disproportionally high numbers of refugees and internally displaced persons in Africa is a symptom of the nation-building and state formation process (Zolberg, 1983; Zolberg, Suhrke and Aguao 1989), which can be compared to similar processes in Europe from the sixteenth to the twentieth centuries. There, too, ethnic and religious minorities faced persecution, while war and economic dislocation were rampant. Western European states took centuries to resolve basic issues of national identity and political legitimacy. Sub-Saharan Africa, like much of the former colonised world, has had to confront a broad spectrum of modernisation issues in the decades since independence. This is the underlying cause of the proliferation of refugees and internally displaced persons.

Thus far, however relatively few African refugees have left the continent. In view of the considerable resources – both financial and cultural – needed to move to developed countries, and the considerable barriers erected by potential receiving areas, the likelihood that large numbers of African refugees could leave in the future appears small. Unfortunately, this may help explain why the international community responded so belatedly and inadequately to the mass slaughter in Rwanda and related tragedies in Zaire.

Latin America and the Caribbean: from an immigration to an emigration region

The vast and highly diverse area to the south of the USA is sometimes portrayed as consisting of four principal areas.

1. The Southern Cone comprises Brazil, Argentina, Chile, Uruguay and Paraguay, which are all societies in which a majority of the population is of European origin. This was an area of massive immigrant settlement from Europe. There were also inflows from elsewhere: for example, Brazil received African slaves up to the nineteenth century and Japanese workers from the late nineteenth century until the 1950s.

2. The Andean area to the north and west differs in that Indians and *mestizos* (persons of mixed European-Indian background) comprise the bulk of the population. Immigration from Europe during the nineteenth and twentieth centuries was less significant.

3. Central America where societies are largely comprised of persons of Indian and *mestizo* background, although there are exceptions, such as Costa Rica.

4. The Caribbean, made up predominantly of people of African origin but also people of Asian and European descent.

Quite a number of countries do not fit neatly into these four areas, but the categorisation serves to underscore how immigration since 1492 has differentially affected the area as a whole and how many of these societies were forged by immigration.

De Lattes and de Lattes (1991) estimate that Latin America and the Caribbean received about 21 million immigrants from 1800 to 1970. The single largest migration was the estimated 3 million Italians who went to Argentina. The bulk of immigrants came from Spain, Italy and Portugal, and most of them went to the Southern Cone. States like Argentina and Uruguay encouraged immigration until the interwar period. The economic depression of the 1930s brought significant changes in immigration policies. Apart from the Italian influx from 1947 to 1955, mass immigration from Europe had become a thing of the past by the 1930s (Barlán, 1988: 6–7). A significant exception to this general pattern was Venezuela, which had received very few European-origin immigrants until the rule of Perez Jimenez, from 1950 to 1958. About 332 000 persons, mainly of Italian origin, settled in Venezuela under his regime. However, the so-called open door policy stopped

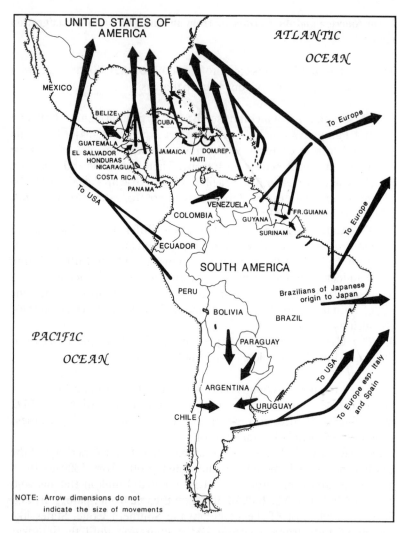

MAP 5.4   Migrations within and from Latin America

with the overthrow of the military government in 1958 (Picquet, Pelligrino and Papail 1986: 25–9).

As intercontinental inflows from Europe waned, intra-continental (or intra-regional) migrations developed. As in the Caribbean Basin back in the nineteenth century, labour migration predominated. The end of the Chaco War between Paraguay and Bolivia in 1935, for example, brought significant numbers of Bolivian army deserters into north-western Argentina. Some of them took jobs in agriculture. This marked the beginning of a seasonal labour migration from Bolivia to Argentina that lasted for over three decades, until mechanisation reduced the need for labour. This labour flow was largely unregulated until 1958 when a bilateral agreement was signed to help protect the Bolivian migrants (Barlán, 1988: 8–9).

Similarly Paraguayan and Chilean labour migrants began to find employment in north-eastern Argentina and in Patagonia respectively in the 1950s and 1960s. Foreign workers spread from agricultural areas to major urban centres. Single, mainly male, immigrants were soon joined by families, creating neighbourhoods of illegal immigrants in some cities. Their entry and employment appear to have been tolerated, as long as they were seen as contributing to economic growth and prosperity, a view challenged only in the 1970s (Sanz, 1989: 233–48). Beginning in 1948, the Argentine government adjusted laws and policies to enable illegal foreign workers to rectify their status. Irregular or illegal migration is the predominant form of migration in Latin America, but this was not viewed as a problem until the late 1960s (Lohrmann, 1987: 258).

Venezuela is another country where legalisation was deemed necessary. With the slowing of immigration from Europe and with oil-related economic growth, millions of Colombians flocked to Venezuela. Many arrived via the *caminos verdes* – the green highways – over which a guide would steer them across the frontiers (Mann, 1979). Other Colombians arrived as tourists and overstayed. By 1995, 2 million persons were thought to be residing illegally in Venezuela, most of them Colombian (Kratochwil, 1995: 33). Not only the oil industry but also agriculture, construction and a host of other industries attracted migrants. Declining incomes in Colombia and the attraction of the stronger Venezuelan currency were significant factors making work in Venezuela attractive in the 1980s (Martinez, 1989: 203–5). Many Colombians migrated to areas close to the Venezuelan–Colombian frontier and many were short-term migrants (Pelligrino, 1984: 748–66). However, most of the illegally resident alien population of about 10 per cent of Venezuela's total population lived in major cities (Kratochwil, 1995: 33).

Colombian seasonal workers traditionally helped harvest the coffee crop in Venezuela, and bilateral labour accords between the two countries were signed in 1951 and 1952. The Treaty of Tonchala in 1959 obliged the two governments to legalise illegally employed nationals from the other country if legal employment could be found. In 1979, the Andean Pact was signed, obliging member states to legalise illegally resident nationals from other member states (Picquet, Pelligrino and Papail, 1986: 30). This led to the Venezuelan legalisation of 1980. Despite estimates ranging from 1.2 to 3.5 million illegal residents out of a total Venezuelan population of some 13.5 million, only some 280 to 350 000 aliens were legalised (Meissner, Papademetition and North 1987: 11). Either the estimates were much too high, which seems likely, or the legalisation programme did not succeed in transforming the status of many illegal residents.

In the 1990s, drug-related violence and political turmoil in Colombia, where the government faced leftist insurgencies, drove tens of thousands of Colombians into Venezuela (Kratochwil, 1995: 15). An economic downturn and austerity measures in Venezuela sparked an attempted *coup d'état* and growing political unrest, contributing to significant outflows of Venezuelan citizens. Hundreds of Venezuelans, for instance, applied for asylum in Canada in 1995, prompting Canadian authorities to reinstate visa requirements for Venezuelan tourists (Kratochwil, 1995: 33). The Venezuelan government threatened to deport the illegally resident alien population *en masse*, but it was uncertain whether it had the intent and means to carry out the threat.

The legalisation policies implemented in Argentina and Venezuela testified to the changing character of migration within Latin America. Intra-regional labour migrations had supplanted immigration from Europe. According to a 1993 report, based on analysis of 1980s census information, some 2 million Latin Americans and Caribbeans lived within the region outside their country of birth. Although foreign Latin Americans and Caribbeans did not exceed 10 per cent of the total population of any country in the region 'there has been an increase in the last decade, both of the overall magnitude of mobility within Latin America, and of the relative importance of Latin Americans and Caribbeans in migration between regions' (Maguid, 1993: 41). The 1990 census counted 8 million Latin American and Caribbean-origin persons living in the USA, comprising almost half of the total resident alien population (Maguid, 1993: 41).

The post-Cold War period in Latin America and the Caribbean was marked by efforts to reinvigorate and expand the many regional integration instruments like MERCOSUR and the Andean Group (GRAN). The former includes Argentina, Brazil, Paraguay and Uruguay with a total population of 200 million. The latter consists of Bolivia, Colombia, Ecuador, Peru and Venezuela with a total population of 113 million. Movements of persons across national borders within these regional blocs were an important concern. However, coordination and cooperation was stymied by inadequate information (Maguid, 1993). Analysing earlier efforts within the Andean Group with regard to labour migration, Kratochwil concluded that 'the significant amount of work has been ultimately ineffective and the administrative agencies have collapsed erratically' (Kratochwil, 1995: 17). As in the Arab region and sub-Saharan Africa, Latin American and Caribbean regional integration projects had slender records of accomplishment in management of international migration.

A second significant feature of the post-Cold War period in Latin America and the Caribbean also echoed 1990 developments elsewhere. There were significant repatriations of refugees subsequent to peace accords in some countries but the eruption of new conflicts in the region produced new refugee flows. The most significant peace accords were reached in Central America where fighting in El Salvador, Nicaragua and Guatemala abated. In the 1980s, about 2 million Central Americans were uprooted, but only some 150 000 of these were recognised by the UNHCR as refugees (Gallagher and Diller, 1990: 3). There were significant repatriations of Guatemalans from Mexico, Nicaraguans from the USA and Costa Rica and of Salvadorans.

However, the political situation in all three countries continued to be tenuous. There were several reports of killings of returning Guatemalans, many of whom are Indians. Guatemalan migrants continued to come to the USA. Their presence was increasingly evident in labour-intensive agriculture and the poultry-processing industry. Most Guatemalans, Salvadorans and Nicaraguans in the USA did not repatriate despite the peace accords. When the USA adopted a new law in 1986 to curb illegal immigration, the then President of El Salvador, Napoleon Duarte, wrote to the US president complaining that this threatened El Salvador because remittances from Salvadorans in the USA were vital to the economy. In a similar vein, while there was some repatriation of

Nicaraguans from Costa Rica, many others stayed on. In 1993, Nicaragua and Costa Rica signed a bilateral labour agreement concerning employment of Nicaraguans in Costa Rican agriculture (Maguid, 1993: 88). Illegal employment of Nicaraguans was widespread and an increasingly salient question in bilateral relations between the two countries.

The Haitian outflow to the USA was part of a broader shift in the Latin American and Caribbean countries. By the 1970s, the region was a net exporter of people. The underlying reasons for this historic change are many, and the transition did not occur overnight. Since the colonial period, Caribbean migrants had been arriving on the eastern and southern shores of what is now the USA. These northward flows were accentuated during the Second World War, when Caribbean workers were recruited for defence-related employment in US Caribbean possessions, specifically the Virgin Islands, and for agricultural work on the US mainland. The origins of the British West Indies' Temporary Foreign Worker Programme, which recruited thousands of workers annually for employment in US agriculture, and which continued in to the 1990s as the so-called H-2A programme, were not unlike the far larger temporary foreign worker programme established between Mexico and the USA.

Temporary labour recruitment helped set in motion the massive northward flows of legal and illegal immigrants from Latin America and the Caribbean to the USA and Canada after 1970. But the causes of the shift are to be found in other factors as well: the declining economic fortunes of the region, its demographic explosion, rural–urban migration, political instability and warfare. Many of these additional factors cannot be viewed as strictly internal. Policies pursued by the USA, such as its intervention in Central America, clearly played a role in the sea-change that saw the area become a net area of emigration.

Up to 1990, the single most important factor behind the rise in emigration from the Latin American and Caribbean countries was the declining level of economic performance. GPD per capita fell in the 1980s. Between 1940 and 1980, the annual average rate of growth in Mexico was 6 per cent, which enabled the economy to absorb most of a rapidly growing workforce. Much the same was true of the Caribbean and Central American countries, but the declines of the 1980s undid those gains (CSIMCED, 1990: 13–14). A major problem affecting overall economic performance was the burden of repaying and financing debts contracted in the 1970s and 1980s.

EXHIBIT 5.3

Haitian *braceros* in the Dominican Republic

One of most notorious migrations in the Caribbean sub-region was the employment of Haitian *braceros* (strong armed ones) in the Dominican Republic's sugar cane harvest. Every year between November and May, Haitians entered for harvest-related employment, both legally and illegally. These workers were predominantly men, but some families followed, and settlement took place. In the early 1980s, the sugar crop represented only 12 per cent of cultivated land in the Dominican Republic but half of all exports and one-fifth of the revenue received by the government. Despite high unemployment and underemployment in the Dominican Republic, practically all the sugar crop was harvested by Haitians. One reason for the rejection of such work by Dominicans was the horrific working conditions and pay of Haitian *braceros*. In 1979, the London-based Anti-Slavery Society described the Haitian sugar cane workers' plight as slavery (Péan, 1982: 10).Every year, the government of the Dominican Republic would make a payment to the Haitian government for the provision of *braceros*. In 1980–1, US$2.9 million were paid for 16 000 *braceros* (French, 1990). This arrangement lapsed only in 1986 when the Haitian dictator 'Baby Doc' Duvalier was forced into his sumptuous exile in France. Since then, sugar interests in the Dominican Republic have relied increasingly on recruiters to find the estimated 40 000 workers needed for the harvest. In 1991, following democratic elections in Haiti and growing international criticism of the plight of Haitian workers, the Dominican government ordered a mass expulsion of Haitians. Of the more than 10 000 individuals expelled, many were persons of Haitian extraction who had long resided in the Dominican Republic or who had been born there (French, 1991: 15). The mass expulsion of Haitians contributed to the destabilisation of the fragile Haitian democracy. The overthrow of the democratically elected President Aristide in September 1991 led to a renewed outflow of Haitian emigrants to the USA. Most of them were intercepted by the US Coastguard and detained at the US naval installation at Guantanamo Bay in Cuba before being repatriated.

The downturn in economic performance exacerbated employment problems. Many Latin American and Caribbean countries experienced exponential population growth following the Second World War, in part as the result of improvements in public health which lowered mortality. Mexico's population tripled from 20 million in 1940 to more than 67 million in 1980, and its population grew by an estimated 21 million during the 1980s. In Central America, the population grew from 9 million in 1950 to 28 million in 1990 (CSIMCED, 1990: 11). Mexican fertility is now dropping. It declined 40 per cent from 1970 to

1989, but Mexico's population increased as much in 1990 as it did in 1970 (CSIMCED, 1990: 12). This suggests that rapid growth of the labour force will continue long into the future, virtually ensuring that international migration will remain a key issue in coming decades.

NAFTA the accord, reached by Mexico, the USA and Canada in 1993, was a North American response to the EU. But it was also viewed as a way to close the growing gap in economic performance between Mexico and its neighbours to the north which helped generate massive Mexican emigration. Differences between US and Mexican living standards grew sharply in the early 1980s after having narrowed between 1960 and 1980 (Tapinos, 1993: 10). In the early 1990s, the USA received 82 per cent of total Mexican exports and imports from the USA comprised 80 per cent of total Mexican imports. Meanwhile, US exports to Mexico were 8 per cent of total US exports and imports from Mexico comprised 6 per cent of total US imports (Tapinos, 1993: 12). Total Mexican GNP was approximately the size of Los Angeles county's.

NAFTA was originally proposed by Mexico's President Salinas. Concurrently, the CSIMCED in the USA was recommending liberal-isation of trade as an alternative way of curbing regional international migration. President Bush's National Security Council apparently endorsed the Salinas proposal on security grounds. By the 1990s, international migration had so interwoven Mexican and US societies that adverse political and socioeconomic developments in Mexico would affect the USA adversely. NAFTA was seen as a way to ensure modernisation of the Mexican economy with mutually beneficial results to the signatory states. Unauthorised Mexican immigration to the USA would recede if the Mexican economy grew and created adequate employment opportunities for the large cohorts entering the labour market each year.

NAFTA clearly has affected Mexico much more than the USA but its long-term implications for international migration between the USA and Mexico were still unclear several years after signature of the pact. The year 1994 witnessed another devaluation of the Peso and a debt crisis which was averted by a US-organised bail-out (Weintraub, 1996). Within Mexico, NAFTA-related economic liberalisation sparked sev-eral insurrections and the Salinas presidency ended in scandal and disgrace. There were mounting indications of political turmoil and instability linked to corruption, drug dealing and the decreasing ability of the long-dominant political party to rule. By 1997, the left-leaning

Party of the Democratic Revolution (PRD) was gaining strength with a withering critique of liberalisation.

Unauthorised Mexican migration to the USA probably increased after 1993 as had been expected even by most proponents of NAFTA. Development increases international migration over the short to medium term, before reducing it over the long run. There was a disjuncture between the politically destabilising, economically painful effects upon Mexico's poor and its emerging middle class, and the potential rewards of liberalisation and its promise of stemming Mexican emigration over the long run. This was suggestive of the contradictory temper of the post-Cold War period in general.

Conclusions

It is customary to differentiate between different categories of migrants, and regions of migration. But it is important to realise that all the movements have common roots, and that they are closely interrelated. Western penetration triggered off profound changes in other societies, first through colonisation, then through military involvement, political links, the Cold War, trade and investment. The upsurge in migration is due to rapid processes of economic, demographic, social, political, cultural and environmental change, which arise from decolonisation, modernisation and uneven development. These processes seem set to accelerate in the future, leading to even greater dislocations and changes in societies, and hence to even larger migrations.

Thus the entry of the countries of Eastern Europe and of the South into the international migration arena may be seen as an inevitable consequence of the increasing integration of these areas into the world economy and into global systems of international relations and cultural interchange. These new migratory movements are a continuation of historical processes that began in the fifteenth century with the European colonial expansion, and the ensuing diffusion of new philosophical values and economic and cultural practices around the globe.

The first effect of foreign investment and development is rural–urban migration, and the growth of cities. Leaving traditional forms of production and social relationships to move into burgeoning cities is the first stage of fundamental social, psychological and cultural changes which create the predispositions for further migrations. To move from peasant agriculture into a city like Cairo, Sao Paulo or

Lagos may be a bigger step for many than the subsequent move to a 'global city' like Paris or Los Angeles.

It is therefore inappropriate to analyse migration as an isolated phenomenon; it is one facet of societal change and global development. The different forms of migration – permanent emigration, contract labour, professional transients, students and refugees – all arise from these broader changes. The categories are interdependent: for instance, a refugee movement can start a permanent migration, or suspension of legal worker recruitment can lead to illegal movements. Migrations arise from complex links between different societies, and help to create new links. The mobility of people will remain a key issue in development strategies in the less-developed world, as well as a major element in North–South relations.

6 New Migrations in the Asia-Pacific Region

Over half the world's population and nearly two-thirds of the world's workforce lives in the Asia-Pacific region (Hugo, 1990). In the 1970s and 1980s international migration from Asia grew dramatically.[1] The main destinations were the Middle East, North America and Australia. In the 1990s, the major growth has been in migration within Asia, particularly from less-developed countries with massive labour surpluses to fast growing NICs. The international movements are often linked to large-scale internal migrations. For example, investment by Hong Kong in the Special Economic Zone of Shenzhen in southern China has created millions of manufacturing jobs, leading to mass rural–urban migration, especially of women (Skeldon, 1992: 44). Indonesia's *transmigrasi* programme is estimated to have shifted 6.5 million people from densely populated Java to more sparsely populated islands like Sumatra, Sulawesi and Irian Jaya since 1968 (*Time,* 11 November 1991). There are also large internal displacements of people fleeing volcanic eruptions, flood, earthquakes and political or ethnic persecution. Internal migration will not be dealt with here, but it is important to realise that it is often the first step in a process that leads to international movement.

The development of Asian migration

Asian migration is not new: westward movements from Central Asia helped shape European history in the Middle Ages, while movement of Chinese people to South-east Asia goes back centuries. Koreans trace their origins to migrants from Northern Siberia millennia ago. In the colonial period millions of indentured workers were recruited, often by force (see Chapter 3). The British took workers from India to the Caribbean and to Africa, as well as to Fiji. The Dutch recruited Chinese workers for construction work in Java. The British colonial administration in Malaya brought in Chinese, Indians and Indonesians to work in the tin mines and plantations. Chinese settlers in South-east

Asian countries and South Asians in Africa became trading minorities with an important intermediary role for colonialism. This often led to hostility – and even mass expulsions – after independence. In the nineteenth century there was considerable migration from China and Japan to the USA, Canada and Australia. In all three countries, discriminatory legislation was enacted to prevent these movements.

Migration from Asia was low in the early part of the twentieth century owing to restrictive policies by immigration countries and colonial powers.[2] However, movements within Asia continued, often connected with political struggles. For instance, Manchuria experienced mass migration from the late nineteenth century, while the Indian sub-continent had huge movements, especially at independence in 1947.

External movements started to grow from the 1960s. The reasons were complex (compare Fawcett and Cariño, 1987; Hugo, 1990; Skeldon, 1992: 20–2). Discriminatory rules against Asian entries were repealed in Canada (1962 and 1976), the USA (1965) and Australia (1966 and 1973). Increased foreign investment and trade helped create the communicative networks needed for migration. The US military presence in Korea, Vietnam and other countries in the region forged transnational links, as well as directly stimulating movement in the shape of brides of US personnel. The Vietnam War caused large-scale refugee movements. The openness of the USA, Canada and Australia to family migration meant that primary movements, whatever their cause, gave rise to entries of permanent settlers. The huge construction projects in the Middle East oil countries caused mass recruitment of temporary contract workers from Asia. Rapid economic growth in several Asian countries led to movements of both highly skilled and unskilled workers.

Asia's sudden and massive entry on to the world migration stage can be seen as the result of the opening-up of the continent to economic and political relationships with the industrialised countries in the post-colonial period. Western penetration through trade, aid and investment created the material means and the cultural capital necessary for migration. At the same time, the dislocation of existing forms of production and social structures through industrialisation, the 'Green Revolution' and wars (often encouraged by major powers as part of the Cold War) forced people to leave the countryside in search of better conditions in the growing cities or overseas. Later on, the rapid industrial take-off of some areas and the continuing stagnation or decline of others created new pressures for migration.

143

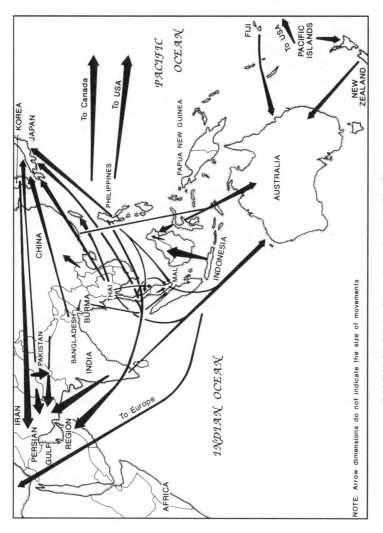

NOTE: Arrow dimensions do not indicate the size of movements

MAP 6.1 Migrations within the Asia-Pacific region

In recent years, social scientists have developed the notion of a 'migration transition'. Societies go through a number of fundamental changes in connection with economic development. The 'industrial transition' refers to the shift of economic activity and employment from agriculture to manufacturing, and then to the services. The 'demographic transition' involves falls in both mortality and fertility, leading to slower population growth and ageing populations. The 'migration transition' is seen as a result of all the preceding changes. At the beginning of the industrialisation process, there is frequently an increase in emigration, due to population growth, a decline in rural employment and low wage levels. This was the case in early nineteenth-century Britain, just as it was in late nineteenth-century Japan, or Korea in the 1970s. As industrialisation proceeds, labour supply declines and domestic wage levels rise; as a result emigration falls and labour immigration begins to take its place. Thus industrialising countries tend to move through an initial stage of emigration, followed by a stage of both in-and outflows, until finally there is a transition to being predominantly a country of immigration (Martin, Mason and Nagayama, 1996: 171–2). This model can be applied to recent changes in several Asian countries, although events do not always fully follow the pattern suggested.

By the mid-1990s, there were estimated to be about 3 million Asians employed outside their own countries within the Asian region, and another 3 million employed in other continents (Martin, Mason and Nagayama, 1996: 163). In addition there are millions of refugees and family members. It is possible to differentiate between labour-importing countries (Japan, Singapore, Taiwan and Brunei), countries which import some types of labour but export others (Hong Kong, Thailand, Malaysia, Korea), and countries which are predominantly labour exporters (China, Philippines, India, Bangladesh, Pakistan, Sri Lanka, Indonesia: compare Martin, 1991a: 187).

In this chapter, we will examine the main Asian migration systems: movement to Western countries, contract labour to the Middle East, intra-Asian labour migration, movement of highly skilled workers, student mobility and refugee movements. It is important to realise that these categories, although useful for analytical and administrative purposes, are often hard to keep separate in practice. All but the first and the last are supposed to be temporary, but in fact many people in other categories stay on permanently. In addition, there is substantial illegal migration. This often takes the form of tourist visa-holders who overstay their permits, but there is also a great deal of smuggling of undocumented workers over borders. The number of illegal migrants can only be guessed at, but may well exceed the number of legal migrants (Lim and Oishi, 1996).

Migration to Western Europe, the USA, Canada and Australia

Three European countries experienced Asian migrations connected with decolonisation: from the former Netherlands East Indies (Indonesia) to the Netherlands, from Vietnam to France, and from the Indian sub-continent and Hong Kong to Britain.[3] These movements had virtually ceased by the late 1970s. More recently there has been some migration of highly skilled workers from Asia to European countries, as well as recruitment of low-skilled workers, such as Filipino domestic servants in Italy.[4]

The largest movement was that to the USA after the 1965 Immigration Act. The number of migrants from Asia increased from 17 000 in 1965 to an average of more than 250 000 annually in the 1980s (Arnold, Minucha and Fawcett, 1987), and over 350 000 per year in the early 1990s (OECD, 1995: 236). Most Asians came to the USA through family reunion provisions of the 1965 Act, though refugee or skilled worker movements were often the first link in the migratory chain. Since 1978, Asia has been the main source of migrants to the USA, making up 40–50 per cent of total immigration. The main countries of origin were the Philippines, Vietnam, China, India and the Republic of Korea (OECD, 1997: 264). By 1990, there were 6.9 million Asian-Americans, and the number was expected to increase to over 10 million by the end of the century (Gardner, 1992: 93).

The picture for Canada and Australia is very similar. Asian immigration developed after the removal of restrictions in the 1960s and 1970s, with additional stimulus from Indo-Chinese refugee movement at the end of the 1970s. By the beginning of the 1990s, about half of new immigrants to Australia came from Asia. The five main Asian source countries in 1994–5 were Vietnam, Hong Kong, the Philippines, China and India. The 1996 Census counted 856 000 Asian-born people as permanent residents of Australia, making up 4.8 per cent of total population and 22 per cent of the overseas-born population.

In Canada it was the 1976 Immigration Act, with its non-discriminatory selection criteria and its emphasis on family and refugee entry, which opened the door to Asian migration. By 1981, 424 000 Asians had entered Canada, and the 1981 Census showed the presence of 674 000 people of Asian ethnic origin (Kubat, 1987: 237). Asian immigration – particularly from Hong Kong, India, the Philippines, China, Taiwan, Sri Lanka and Vietnam – grew in the 1980s and 1990s. In 1995, 113 000 out of Canada's total 212 000 immigrants were from Asia (OECD, 1997: 263). The 1991 Census counted over 1 million Asian-born residents, out of a total overseas-born population of 4.3 million.

New Zealand is a traditional immigrant country which built up its population through immigration from Britain, with racially-selective entry policies to keep out non-Europeans. However, since the 1950s, economic and political links with nearby Pacific islands have given rise to new inflows. There was considerable immigration from Tonga, the Cook Islands and other Pacific islands in the 1960s and 1970s (Trlin, 1987). Inflows from Asia are very recent. From 1991, official policy was for higher immigration, especially of people with professional skills and capital for investment. Most of these came from East Asia, especially Hong Kong, Taiwan, Korea and Japan. Total net migration to New Zealand from East Asia between 1986 and 1994 was 40 206 persons (Lidgard, 1996: 6). New Zealand's ethnic composition has become more complex: the Maori population has grown to over 10 per cent of the total population, Pacific Islanders make up about 5 per cent and Asians about 3 per cent (Pool and Bedford, 1996). This has led to heated public debates: anti-immigration calls by the mainly Maori New Zealand First Party played an important part in the October 1996 Election, and more restrictive immigration rules have since been introduced.

The movements from Asia to the classical immigration countries of North America and Oceania have certain common features. In all three countries, unexpectedly large movements have developed mainly through use of family reunion provisions. The countries of origin have been largely the same, with increasing participation of China and Hong Kong in recent years. Hugo notes a trend to feminisation of Asian migration to the USA and other developed countries, partly through family reunion, but also owing to the increasing number of women as primary migrants. A further trend is the growing involvement of brokers and agents of various types, who provide contacts and knowledge of immigration regulations (Hugo, 1990). In the last few years all these immigration countries have changed their immigration rules to encourage entry of skilled and business migrants. A global labour market for highly skilled personnel has emerged, with Asia as the main source, and immigration countries are competing to attract this group (compare Borjas, 1990: 199–228).

Contract labour migration to the Middle East

Large-scale migrations from Asia to the Middle East developed rapidly after the oil price rise of 1973. Labour was imported at first mainly from India and Pakistan, in the 1980s also from the Philippines, Indonesia, Thailand and the Republic of Korea, and later increasingly from Bangladesh and Sri Lanka. Movements grew rapidly with flows of between 0.7 and 1 million workers per year from 1981 to 1984. By 1985, there were 3.2 million Asian workers in the Gulf states, of whom over 2 million were in Saudi Arabia. Then recruitment declined as oil prices fell sharply. However, by the beginning of the 1990s, movements had reached their former levels, with 933 000 Asian migrants to the Gulf in 1991.

The Iraqi invasion of Kuwait and the Gulf War in 1990–1 led to the forced return of some 450 000 Asians to their countries of origin. After the War, recruitment of Asian workers increased again, partly due to reconstruction needs in Kuwait, but also due to the replacement of 'politically unreliable' Palestinians in Kuwait and Yemenis in Saudi Arabia (Abella, 1995; see also Chapter 5 above). Israel also began to recruit large numbers of Thais and Filipinos for agriculture, construction and domestic work, after security measures blocked entry of Palestinians from the West Bank and Gaza.

In the 1970s, most of the migrants were male workers employed in the many construction projects on which the oil dollars were being spent. Governments of sending countries like the Philippines, the Republic of Korea and even China actively marketed their labour abroad, and made labour-supply agreements with Gulf countries. Construction companies were encouraged to take on contracts in the Middle East, which included provision of labour. The Asian labour-sending countries also allowed private agencies to organise recruitment (Abella, 1995).

The temporary decline of the construction sector after 1985 encouraged more diverse employment of contract workers, particularly a shift into the services sector, such as hotels and personal services. There was an upsurge in demand for domestic servants, leading to a feminisation of contract labour flows. Most women workers came from the Philippines, Indonesia, Thailand, Korea or Sri Lanka, while neither Pakistan nor Bangladesh sent females abroad (Martin, 1991a: 189; Skeldon, 1992: 40–1). Many Filipino and Korean workers were well educated; they took skilled jobs as drivers, carpenters, mechanics or building tradesmen. Some were professionals or para-professionals, especially engineers, nurses and medical practitioners. It is clear that labour migrants were often not part of a surplus population of the unemployed rural and urban poor, but rather skilled workers, whose departure could have a negative effect on the economy (Skeldon, 1992: 38).

Asians in Arab countries encounter difficult conditions, due both to the lack of worker rights and the very different cultural values, especially with regard to the position of women. Migration takes place within rigid contract labour frameworks: workers are not allowed to settle or bring in dependants, and are often segregated in barracks. They can be deported for misconduct and often have to work very long hours. Women domestic workers are often subjected to exploitation and sexual abuse. The big attraction for workers is the wages: during the boom of the 1970s often ten times as much as could be earned at home. However, wage levels declined during the 1980s as labour demand fell, and competition between labour-sending nations increased. Many migrant workers are exploited by agents and other intermediaries, who take large fees (up to 25 per cent of their pay). Agents sometimes fail to keep their promises of providing work and transport, and wages and working conditions are often considerably inferior to those originally offered.

The governments of labour-sending countries see the migrations as economically vital, partly because they hope they will reduce unemployment and provide training and industrial experience, but mainly because of the worker remittances. These make a major contribution to the balance of payments of countries with severe trade deficits. For instance, Pakistani workers remitted over US$2 billion in 1988, which covered 30 per cent of the cost of imports. Indian workers remitted US$2.6 billion, the equivalent of 15 per cent of imports (ILO, 1991).[5] Between 1978 and 1987, Pakistan received a total of US$22 billion through official banking channels, which does not include unofficial transfers or transfers in the form of consumer goods (Abella, 1995: 421).

Millions of families have become dependent on remittances, and have improved living standards because of them. However, it is not clear what contribution migration actually makes to development, since money is often spent on luxury goods, dowries and housing, rather than on productive investments. In some cases the increased inflow of money has led to inflation, disadvantaging non-migrant families. Since the migrants generally come from the middle strata rather than the poorest groups in the areas of origin, remittances often exacerbate social inequality, and lead to increased concentration of land ownership.

Asian governments have attempted to regulate migration to protect workers and to ensure transfer of remittances through official channels. Control appears to have been most effective in the Republic of Korea, where the majority of migrants were hired by Korean firms which had construction contracts in the Middle East. Korean workers were provided with transport and accommodation, and earned up to three times what they could expect at home. However, working hours were long (up to 60 hours a week) and conditions were highly regimented (Skeldon, 1992: 40).

The Philippine authorities have also made considerable efforts to develop systems of control and protection: the Philippine Overseas Employment Administration controls recruitment, while the Overseas Workers' Welfare Administration is meant to protect workers from abuse. Pre-departure orientation seminars are provided for entertainers, domestic workers and nurses. The Philippines has special officials at its consulates in labour-importing countries to help migrants who get into difficulties. Yet these are too few to be effective: in 1993 there were 31 labour attachés, 20 welfare officers and 20 coordinators to respond to the needs of 4.2 million migrant workers in 120 countries (Lim and Oishi, 1996: 120). Philippine officials often find themselves powerless against unscrupulous agents and abusive employers, who may have the backing of the police and other authorities in countries like Saudi Arabia.

Labour migration within Asia

Since the mid-1980s, rapid economic growth and declining fertility have led to considerable demand for migrant labour in such countries as Japan, the Republic of Korea, Hong Kong, Taiwan, Singapore and oil-rich Brunei. Malaysia and Thailand have both emigration and immigration. Labour migration within Asia grew exponentially in the first half of the 1990s. Throughout the fast-growing 'tiger economies', migrant workers are doing the '3D jobs' – dirty, dangerous and difficult – that nationals can increasingly afford to reject. Asian governments treat migrants as temporary workers, with very limited rights and no entitlement to settlement and family reunion. Some significant examples of intra-Asian labour migration will be discussed here, but it is impossible to give a comprehensive account of the complex patterns.

A key development in recent years has been the increasing feminisation of migration: about 1.5 million Asian women were working abroad by the mid-1990s, and in many migratory movements they outnumbered men. For instance, two-thirds of Indonesian migrants from 1984 to 1994 were women. About half of Philippine overseas contract workers (OCWs) in 1994 were female (Amjad, 1996: 346–9). Most migrant women are concentrated in jobs regarded as 'typically female': domestic workers, entertainers (often a euphemism for prostitution), restaurant and hotel staff, assembly-line workers in clothing and electronics. These jobs are low in pay, conditions and status, and are associated with patriarchal stereotypes of female characteristics, such as docility, obedience and willingness to give personal service. Domestic service leads to isolation and vulnerability for young women migrants, who often have little protection against the demands of their employers (Lim and Oishi, 1996). One form of Asian female migration, particularly from the Philippines, Thailand and Sri Lanka, is as 'mail order' brides to Europe, Australia and Japan (Cahill, 1990).

Japan has been experiencing severe labour shortages since the mid-1980s. Japanese school-leavers are unwilling to take factory jobs, and there is little further potential for rural–urban movements or for increasing female labour force participation. Government industry policy encourages investment in new technology to raise labour productivity, while many companies invest overseas, in order to shift labour-intensive workplaces to low-wage countries. But there are limits to these approaches: it is hard to increase productivity in certain service branches, while construction and services jobs cannot be relocated, and many factory jobs, such as making car components, are part of complex supply chains which cannot easily be spatially divided. In the 1980s, increasing numbers of women were admitted, mainly from the Philippines and Thailand, to work as dancers, waitresses and hostesses. They were followed by men from these countries as well as Pakistan and Bangladesh, who worked – generally illegally – as factory or construction workers.

According to official figures, the foreign population of Japan increased from 817000 in 1983 to 1.4 million in 1995 (1.1 per cent of the total population). About three-quarters are permanent or long-term residents (OECD, 1997: 122–5): mainly Koreans, who were recruited as workers before and during the Second World War. Many current Korean residents are in the third or fourth generation, but still find it hard to obtain Japanese citizenship. They remain a segregated and discriminated-against minority (Esman, 1992). The overall naturalisation rate is about 1 per cent of foreign residents per year. Other foreign groups have grown rapidly in recent years: the number of Chinese went up from 75000 in 1985 to 223000 in 1995; Brazilians increased from 2000 to 176000, and Filipinos from 12000 to 74000. Official estimates put the number of illegal immigrants in Japan in 1995 at 285000 (OECD, 1997: 122–5 and 229). These illegals are extremely vulnerable to exploitation through substandard wages and working conditions, and are prone to high rates of industrial accidents (Mori, 1995: 417).

The Japanese government encouraged emigration after the Second World War, and is strongly opposed to immigration, owing to fears of overpopulation and concern to preserve ethnic homogeneity. There was considerable debate on the need for foreign labour in the late 1980s, with business associations favouring recruitment, while trade unions and the government were opposed (Suzuki, 1988; Sekine, 1990; Martin, 1991a). In 1989, revisions to the Immigration Control Act introduced severe penalties for illegal foreign workers, brokers and employers. However recruitment of unskilled foreigners of Japanese origin was permitted, leading to a scramble to recruit 'Japanese Brazilians'. Other ways of getting round the law are to employ 'trainees' from developing countries, or to give work to foreigners who register as students of Japanese language schools and are permitted to work 20 hours per week. Research has shown that there are many abusive cases where proper training is not provided, and the trainees are used as cheap labour (Oishi, 1995: 369).

Singapore is heavily dependent on unskilled workers from Malaysia, Thailand, Indonesia, the Philippines and Sri Lanka. About 300000 foreign workers make up 19 per cent of the labour force (Huguet, 1995: 525–6). Foreign men work in construction, ship-building, transport and services; women are mainly in domestic service and other services. The government imposes a foreign worker levy to equalise the costs of foreign and domestic workers. Unskilled workers have to rotate every few years and are not permitted to settle or to bring in their families. Migrants are forbidden to marry Singaporeans, and women have to undergo regular pregnancy tests. In 1989, there was an amnesty for illegal workers, after which a mandatory punishment of three months' jail and three strokes of the cane were introduced. This led to strong protests from the Thai government. The Singapore government is worried about dependence on foreign labour, and has imposed quotas for various industries, yet lack of local labour has forced the government to raise the quotas continually. On the other hand, Singapore is eager to attract skilled and professional workers, particularly those of Chinese ethnicity from Hong Kong. They are encouraged to settle permanently (Martin, 1991a: 182–4; Skeldon, 1992: 44–6).

Due to attractive job opportunities for Singaporean women, employment of foreign domestic servants is very high: 15 per cent of households have a live-in servant. In 1993, there were estimated to be 81 000 foreign domestic servants, of whom 50 000 were from the Philippines, 17 000 from Sri Lanka and 10 000 from Indonesia. Fees for recruitment (mainly through specialised agencies) are up to S$2000, which is deducted from the maid's wages. Frequent cases of abuse have been reported to Philippine authorities, leading to a ban on recruitment in 1987. This, however, was circumvented by the Singaporean authorities, who admitted Filipinas as tourists and then gave them work permits (Wong, 1996).

Public concern in the Philippines came to a head in 1995 when a Filipino maid, Flor Contemplacion, was hanged in Singapore, after being found guilty or murder. The case strained relations between the two countries and led to a heated debate in the Philippines about the situation of the estimated 700 000 Filipinos who go to work overseas each year (*Asian Migrant,* January–March 1995). The Philippine government banned migration of domestic workers to Singapore (a ban which was again largely circumvented). In June 1995, the Philippines passed the Migrant Workers and Overseas Filipinos Act to improve monitoring of the conditions of OCWs (Lim and Oishi, 1996: 106). The Flor Contemplacion case highlighted the human cost of emigration and gave impetus to economic development programmes designed to reduce the need to work abroad.

Malaysia, with its complex ethnic mix (56 per cent Malay, 33 per cent Chinese, 10 per cent Indian and other) has both emigration and immigration. Many low-skilled Malays still work in Singapore, while many ethnic Chinese and Indians migrate to Australia and North America, since they feel disadvantaged by policies which encourage education and business activity for Malays. But inflows now exceed departures: by 1995, there were 533 000 registered foreign workers in Malaysia, of whom 253 000 were from Indonesia and the rest mainly from Bangladesh, the Philippines and Thailand (Huguet, 1995: 525). Estimates of illegals were as high as 1.2 million in 1993, making up 15 per cent of the total 7.4 million employed workers (Lim, 1996: 321). As Lim (1996) points out, Malaysia made the migration transition relatively early in its development process, at a time when increase in the domestic labour force was still high and GDP per capita was still fairly low (US$1800 in 1987). She attributes this to two special features of Malaysia: the multi-ethnic population; and the open export-orientated economy, with high rates of foreign investment.

The East Malaysian island states of Sabah and Sarawak are even more dependent than peninsular Malaysia on foreign workers, with over half a million Filipinos and Indonesians working on plantations and in construction. They account for up to half the population of Sabah (Stahl, 1990; Martin, 1991a: 186–7). In 1996, following a legalisation campaign which enabled hundreds of thousands of workers to gain legal status, Malaysia started building a 500 kilometre long wall along its northern border with Thailand, to stop illegal entries (*Guardian Weekly*, 23 June 1996). In early 1997, the government announced plans for mass deportations of illegals, now claimed to be as numerous as 2 million. They were blamed for crime, disease and immorality. Scapegoating of migrant workers for social evils is a new trend throughout Asia.

Fast-growing countries like the Republic of Korea and Thailand are sending fewer workers abroad, as job opportunities open up locally. The number of Korean workers abroad declined from 225 000 in 1983 to 76 000 in 1989 (Martin, 1991a: 188). Korea has now passed through the migration transition: by 1995, the GDP per capita was US$10 000, labour departures had fallen sharply and there were estimated to be 150 000 foreign workers in Korea. As in Japan, the official reaction was denial: there is no coherent long-term policy on foreign workers, and unskilled migrants are barred. Some foreign workers are brought in as 'trainees', but in fact carry out labouring jobs. The majority (about 60 per cent) are illegals, who are paid low wages and lack basic rights. Many are Chinese citizens of Korean ethnic origin (Kang, 1996). South Koreans became increasingly apprehensive about the possibility of mass migration from North Korea. As indications of political instability and famine grew, the Government of the Republic of Korea began to build camps to house potential refugees. The parallels between the Koreas and the former Germanies were striking.

Many Thai workers still go to the Gulf, while Thai women travel as domestic workers and entertainers to Hong Kong, Taiwan and Japan. However, more workers now enter than leave, though it is sometimes hard to distinguish clearly between migrant workers and the refugees who came from Vietnam and Cambodia in the 1970s and 1980s, and from Burma in the 1990s. Burmese and Cambodians work on the farms of the north-east, many of which belong to migrants who are in the Middle East (Martin, 1991a: 187). In recent years up to a million illegal

Burmese workers have entered, and many now carry out '3D jobs' in Bangkok and other cities.

Hong Kong has been transformed from a labour-intensive industrial economy to a post-industrial economy based on trade, services and investment, leading to shortages of both skilled and unskilled workers. Highly-qualified expatriate workers from North America, Western Europe and India are recruited for well-paid jobs in finance, management and education. Unskilled workers from China have entered illegally in large numbers. Maids are recruited in the Philippines and elsewhere, under arrangements rather like Singapore's, to facilitate the labour market participation of Hong Kong women. The situation in Hong Kong has been complicated by political concerns about reunification with China. Many highly skilled Hong Kong workers emigrated, especially to the USA, Canada and Australia, to seek a safe domicile after reunification (Skeldon, 1994). Many stay in the receiving country only long enough to gain permanent resident status or citizenship, and then return to Hong Kong to work. Often they commute back and forwards regularly; this group is known as 'astronauts', while the children they leave in Canada or Australia are known as 'parachute children' (Pe-Pua et al., 1996). It is too early to say what effects reunification with China in July 1997 will have on migration patterns.

Taiwan is one of the world's most densely populated countries, yet economic growth has led to labour shortfalls and illegal immigration. In 1992, a foreign labour policy was laid down permitting recruitment of migrant workers for occupations with severe labour shortages. Duration of employment was limited to two years. In January 1996, there were 200 000 legal foreign workers and up to 250 000 illegals. Workers came mainly from Thailand (68 per cent of foreign workers), the Philippines (25 per cent), Malaysia (3.5 per cent) and Indonesia (3.2 per cent). Most recruitment is carried out by labour brokers, who charge workers from US$730 to US$3000 (the latter figure being the equivalent of 4–6 months' wages). Despite rigid regulations, including prohibition of job-changing, the authorities have lost control of movements. Many workers stay on illegally after two years, or change jobs to get higher wages, and to escape repayments to brokers (Lee and Wang, 1996).

Just as the Mediterranean periphery fuelled Western European industrial expansion up to the 1970s, industrialising Asia now has its own labour reserve areas: China, the South Asian countries, the Philippines and Indonesia have all become major labour providers for the region and indeed for the rest of the world. The Philippines is the labour-exporter *par excellence* of the modern age (rather like Italy a generation ago), with over 4 million of its people scattered across the world (Battistella and Paganoni, 1992). About half of these are permanent settlers in the USA, while the rest are temporary OCWs (both legal and illegal) in the Gulf states and Asia. Filipino emigration is still growing: the highest outflows of OCWs ever were in the years 1991–4. In 1994 a total of 565 000 workers were recruited to work in other countries, and a further 154 000 took jobs as sailors on foreign-owned ships as 'guestworkers of the sea'. Export of labour is crucial to the Philippine economy. It has been estimated that unemployment levels would be 40 per cent higher without labour emigration. Official remittances from migrants in 1994 were US$2.94 billion, which financed 50 per cent of the external trade deficit (Amjad, 1996).

A significant feature of Asian labour migration is the major role played by the 'migration industry'. Most recruitment of migrant workers both to the Gulf and within Asia is organised by migration agents and labour brokers. Governments and employers in receiving countries find it easier to rely on such intermediaries than to organise movements themselves. Authorities of labour-sending countries have found themselves powerless to stop or control the frequently exploitative activities of the industry. Martin (1996: 201) estimates that migrants typically pay fees equal to 20–30 per cent of their first year's earnings. For the whole of Asia, the labour broker industry could be worth US$2.2 billion per year.

While some agents carry out legitimate activities, others indulge in illegal practices, such as tricking women into prostitution, or smuggling human cargoes over borders. For instance certain Thai agents dupe young rural women into coming to Japan, ostensibly to work in restaurants or factories, then hand them over to *Yakuza* gangsters, who keep them in conditions of near-slavery as prostitutes (Okunishi, 1996: 229-30). The Indians, Pakistanis and Sri Lankans who drowned between Malta and Sicily on Christmas Day 1996 – as many of 280 of them – were the victims of an international network of migrant smugglers, with tentacles in South Asia, the Middle East and Southern Europe. The migrants had paid up to US$9000 for the fatal voyage to a dream of prosperity in Europe (Ferguson, 1997: 29). Similar disasters have befallen Asians being smuggled into the USA and Canada. Even when they arrive safely in North America, many illegal entrants have to work for years to pay off their debts to the smugglers, who frequently use coercion to ensure that migrants pay up. Many Chinese and Thais who are smuggled into North America end up working in slave-like conditions.

Highly qualified migrants

Another growing movement is that of professionals, executives, technicians and other highly skilled personnel (see Chapter 4 above). One form is the 'brain drain': university-trained people moving from less-developed to highly developed countries. Europe, North America and Australia have obtained thousands of doctors and engineers from India, Malaysia, Hong Kong and similar countries. This is a drain on the resources of the poorer countries, and may lead to bottlenecks in supply of skilled personnel. On the other hand, the remittances of the skilled migrants may be beneficial, and many do return when opportunities become available, bringing with them new experience and sometimes additional training. Unfortunately many highly skilled migrants find their entry to appropriate employment in highly developed countries restricted by difficulty in securing recognition of their qualifications, or by discrimination in hiring and promotion practices. If they fail to get skilled jobs, their migration is both a loss to their countries of origin and a personal disaster.

Another form of highly-qualified migration is of executives, professionals and experts sent overseas by their companies to work overseas or by international organisations. Capital investment in less-developed countries may be seen as an alternative to low-skilled migration to developed countries, but it leads to movements of skilled personnel in the opposite direction. These migrations may be of considerable economic and cultural importance. For example, 83 000 Japanese were assigned to work in overseas branches of Japanese companies in 1988, while a further 29 000 (not including students) went overseas to engage in scientific study. Over 1 million Japanese went abroad in the same year for a 'short stay for business' (Skeldon, 1992: 42–3). There is little information on such movements from other countries, but there is no doubt that professional transients from the industrialising Asian economies are playing an increasing role throughout Asia, alongside their counterparts from North America, Europe and Australia.

Capital investment from overseas is a catalyst for socioeconomic change and urbanisation, while professional transients are not only agents of economic change, but also bearers of new cultural values. The links they create may encourage people from the developing country to move to the investing country in search of training or work. For instance Lim (1996: 329) has shown that 'the three largest foreign investors in Malaysia – Taiwan, Japan and Singapore – are also the three main destinations of Malaysian emigrant workers'. The returning professional transients bring new experiences and values with them. Some Japanese observers see the stationing of highly trained personnel overseas as part of the 'internationalisation' of Japan, and a powerful factor for cultural change (Suzuki, 1988: 41).

Students

Considerable numbers of Asians have gone to developed countries to study in recent years. By the late 1980s, there were 366 000 foreign students in the USA, of whom nearly half came from Asia. In the case of Canada, seven East and South-east Asian countries made up 45 per cent of the 71 000 foreign students present in 1989 (Skeldon, 1992: 35). Australia had 104 000 foreign student arrivals in 1994–5, with the largest groups coming from Indonesia (14 500), Malaysia (12 000), Singapore (10 700), Hong Kong (10 400), Korea (8600) and Japan (8500: see Bureau of Immigration, Multicultural and Population Research, or BIMPR, 1996: 39). There is considerable competition among developed countries to attract fee-paying students from Asia. Many Australian universities now have Asian campuses. In 1996, when racist speeches and attacks on Asian students took place in Australia, university vice-chancellors demanded action from the government to counter a feared decline in student enrolments.

Student movements to developed countries may be part of the brain drain, since many do not return. A study of Taiwanese students showed that only about 5 per cent returned home after studying overseas between 1960 and 1968. By the 1980s, the proportion of returnees had risen to a quarter (Skeldon, 1992: 35–7). However schemes to provide student scholarships as part of development aid often impose legal requirements to return home upon completing studies. Research in the Republic of Korea found that three-quarters of those who studied abroad did return home; 20–30 per cent of that country's professionals were estimated to have been trained abroad, mainly in the USA and Japan. Movements of students need to be examined as part of the more general linkages which include professional migrations and capital flows. In the long term, it is likely that many do return, and that they play a role in both technology transfer and cultural change.

Refugees

About one-third of the world's 27 million 'refugees and other persons of concern' to the UNHCR have their origins in Asia (UNHCR, 1995: 247). The two largest forced exoduses since 1945 have been from Indo-China and from Afghanistan.[6]

Over 2 million people fled from Vietnam, Laos and Cambodia following the end of the Vietnam War in 1975. Many left as 'boat-people', sailing long distances in overcrowded small boats, at risk of shipwreck and pirate attacks. Over a million were resettled in the USA, with smaller numbers in Australia, Canada and Western European countries. China accepted about 300 000 refugees, mainly of ethnic Chinese origin. Other Asian countries were unwilling to accept perma-nent settlers (Hugo, 1990; UNHCR, 1991; Skeldon, 1992: 49–52). Vietnamese continued to leave in the late 1980s, even though political conditions in Vietnam had stabilised. The UNHCR considered that many of these departures were induced by hopes of economic prosper-ity in the West, rather than by persecution at home.

In 1989, a 'Comprehensive Plan of Action' was adopted by all the countries concerned. People already in the camps were to be resettled, while any new asylum seekers were to be screened to see if they were really victims of persecution. Those found to be economic migrants were to be repatriated. Vietnam introduced an 'Orderly Departure Programme' to permit legal emigration, particularly of people with relatives in overseas countries. In 1991, there were 113 000 Vietnamese in camps in Thailand, Malaysia, Hong Kong, Indonesia and the Philippines. By 1995, the camp population had declined to 50 000. This had been achieved through voluntary or even forced repatriation, particularly from the overcrowded camps of Hong Kong (UNHCR, 1995: 208–9).

Up to a third of Afghanistan's 18 million people fled the country following the Soviet military intervention in 1979. The overwhelming majority remained in the neighbouring countries of Pakistan (3.6 million in 1989) and Iran (over 2 million). There was hardly any resettlement overseas. The Afghan exodus came just after the Indo-Chinese exodus, and there was little willingness in Western countries to provide homes for new waves of refugees. Moreover the guerilla leaders wanted to use the refugee camps as bases for recruitment and training. For political, humanitarian, religious and cultural reasons, Pakistan and Iran were willing to provide refuge for extended periods. Pakistan received substantial compensation from the USA in the form of military, economic and diplomatic support. Iran, on the other hand, received very little external assistance, despite being one of the world's principal havens for refugees.

The different handling of the Vietnamese and Afghan cases is an example of the way refugee movements can become part of wider foreign policy considerations for major powers (Suhrke and Klink, 1987). With the end of the Soviet intervention in 1992, about 1.5 million Afghan refugees returned home. However, the outbreak of new conflicts and the devastated condition of the country delayed the return of the rest. In 1995, 2.8 million Afghans (20 per cent of total population) remained outside the county, while over a million were internally displaced. Some Afghan men went to work in the Gulf states, to help fund the costs of rebuilding their villages (UNHCR, 1995: 182–3).

Apart from these two huge refugee movements, there have been many exoduses smaller in number, but no less traumatic for those concerned. They include Tibetans in India and Nepal, East Timorese in Australia and Portugal, and Fijian Indians in Australia. Large numbers of Sri Lankans have been forced to seek refuge from the long-running civil war. After the failure of the democracy movement in 1989, thousands of Chinese sought asylum in a wide range of countries. In 1991–2, there were large movements of refugees from Burma into Thailand and Bangladesh. The latter case was especially poignant: one of the world's poorest countries, recently subject to catastrophic flooding, was struggling to help political and ethnic refugees, with little initial support from the international community. In the meantime, the UNHCR has organised a voluntary repatriation scheme, and the majority of the refugees have returned. Conflicts linked to the breakup of the former Soviet Union led to mass displacements in the 1990s affecting many new states, including Georgia, Chechnya, Armenia, Azerbaijan and Tajikistan. Around two million people were internally displaced or forced to flee across borders (UNHCR, 1995: 24–5).

The Asian experience shows the complexity of refugee situations in less-developed countries: they are hardly ever a simple matter of individual political persecution. Almost invariably, economic and environmental pressures play a major part. Long-standing ethnic and religious differences exacerbate conflicts and often motivate high levels of violence. Resolution of refugee-producing situations and return home of refugees is hampered by scarcity of economic resources and lack of guarantees for human rights in weak and despotic states. Where refugees do find a haven and a certain level of support – such as adequate food and shelter, basic education and health care – there may be little motivation for returning to devastated and impoverished homelands, even if the hostilities which led to flight have ended. Refugee movements, like mass labour migration, are the result of the massive social transformations currently taking place in Asia.

Perspectives for Asian migration

Asian migration has grown rapidly since the 1970s. By the mid-1990s there were at least 3 million Asians outside the region and another 3 million foreign workers in the major Asian labour-importing countries: Japan, Korea, Hong Kong, Taiwan, Singapore, Malaysia and Thailand. Most of them came from just a few source areas, especially the Philippines, Indonesia, China, Thailand and South Asia. The majority of the Asian migrants are low-skilled workers, but flows of highly skilled personnel are on the increase. Although most movements are temporary in intention, trends towards permanent settlement are beginning to emerge in some places.

Every migratory movement in Asia has its own special features, yet there are significant general trends. One is the lack of long-term planning: movements have been shaped not only by government labour policies, but also by the actions of employers, migrants and the migration industry. Illegal migration is very high, and agents and brokers play a major role. Official policies range from 'near-denial' of the presence of foreign labour (Japan and Korea) to 'active management' (Singapore), with most countries somewhere in-between (Miller and Martin, 1996: 195).

Fairly general features of labour migration systems in the Middle East and Asia include the attempt at rigid control of foreign workers, the prohibition of settlement and family reunion, and the denial of basic rights. Many of the governments concerned refer explicitly to the European experience, in which temporary guestworkers turned into settlers and new ethnic minorities. The strict regulatory systems are designed to prevent this. Will they succeed? Countries like Germany and Switzerland found it hard to maintain rigid controls, because they contradicted both employers' interests in a stable labour force and democratic principles. It is easier for authoritarian governments to disregard human rights than it is for Western democracies, but certain pressures for longer stay are common to both situations.

There are clear signs of increasing dependence on foreign workers for the '3D jobs', as labour force growth slows in industrialising countries and local workers reject menial tasks. Some employers seek to retain 'good workers', many migrants prolong their stays (Martin, Mason and Nagayama, 1996: 173), and family reunion or formation of new families in the receiving country cannot be completely prevented. Trends towards democratisation in some Asian countries also make it hard to ignore human rights considerations. It therefore seems reasonable to predict that settlement and increased cultural diversity will affect many Asian labour-importing countries; yet no Asian government has plans to deal with long-term effects of migration – even to discuss the matter is still almost taboo.

Despite the rapid growth, movements are still quite small in comparison with Asia's vast population. Migrant workers make up a far smaller proportion of the labour force in countries like Japan and Korea than they do in European countries (although the proportion is large in Singapore and Malaysia). However, the potential for growth is obvious. The Indian sub-continent provides a vast labour reservoir. Economic and political reform in China could open the door for mass labour migration, while setbacks to reform could lead to refugee movements. Indonesia and the Philippines have considerable population growth, and regard labour export as a vital part of their economic strategies. The fast-growing economies of East and South-east Asia seem certain to pull in large numbers of migrant workers in the future. It is hard to believe that this will not lead to some degree of settlement, with far-reaching social and political consequences. The twenty-first century has been dubbed the 'Pacific century' in terms of economic and political development, but it will also be an epoch of rapidly growing population mobility.

7 Migrants and Minorities in the Labour Force

Of the world's estimated 120 million recent migrants, perhaps a quarter are legally admitted workers, another quarter illegally resident aliens, one-quarter spouses and children and the remainder refugees and asylum-seekers (Falchi, 1995: 5; Widgren, 1987: 4). In Western Europe, foreign labour employment generally stagnated or declined between 1975 and 1985, but then the overall pattern became one of increase until 1992. In Germany, 400 000 new foreign workers entered in 1992, including many seasonal and contract workers recruited for temporary employment from Poland and other former Warsaw Bloc countries. This was double the number of new foreign workers recorded in 1991 and triple the number who entered in 1990 (OECD, 1994: 21).

However, about 1993, a downward trend in overall migration and immigrant employment became discernible within the OECD area, although there were exceptions to the general pattern such as the USA. The downturn was connected to slower economic growth and mounting unemployment but also to changes in regulations which made it more difficult for aliens to take up employment (OECD, 1994: 13–14). French statistics on the economically active foreign population were not untypical of the period: 1.59 million in 1994, 1.57 million in 1995 and 1.6 million in 1996 (Lebon, 1996: 41). Behind the modest ups and downs were important trends that were typical for the OECD countries.

There was a steady increase in new employment authorisations for highly skilled workers in France: indeed, US citizens were the single largest nationality in 1996 (Lebon, 1996: 3). Unemployment of foreigners also increased: in 1996, one out of every ten French citizens was unemployed, compared with one out of every four foreigners and one out of every three non-EU immigrants (Lebon, 1996: 44). Admissions of seasonal foreign workers, mainly for agricultural employment, continued to decline. Foreign women's labour force participation continued to increase, but about 40 per cent of economically active foreign women were unemployed in 1996 (Lebon, 1996: 42).

The OECD's 1986 Conference on the Future of Migration identified the underlying reasons for the long-term prospects for increasing

162

employment of immigrants: the ageing of Western societies, demographic imbalances between developed and developing regions in close proximity to each other, the North–South gap, continuing employer demand for foreign labour and the growth of illegal migration (OECD, 1987). Furthermore the conference stressed the necessity of understanding immigration in its global context as something inextricably bound up with economic and foreign policies, developments in international trade and growing interdependence.

This book has shown how most post-1945 movements started as labour migration, often organised by employers and governments. The movements have changed in character over time, with increasing participation of non-economic migrants, including dependants and refugees. The economic migrants too have become differentiated, with increasing participation of highly skilled personnel and entrepreneurs. The political economy-based theories of labour migration which developed in the 1960s and 1970s emphasised the crucial role of migrant workers in providing low-skilled labour for manufacturing industry and construction, and in restraining wage growth in these sectors. In the 1990s, there is a need to re-examine this political economy in the light of the shift from temporary labour to permanent settlement and the increasing economic differentiation of migrant workers. Key questions to be asked include the following.

1. What has been the impact of economic restructuring since the 1970s on migrant workers?
2. Have the patterns of labour market segmentation by ethnic origin and gender which had emerged by the 1970s persisted, or have there been significant changes?
3. What variations are there in employment patterns according to such criteria as ethnic background, gender, recentness of arrival, type of migration, legal status, education and training?
4. What variations are to be found between immigration countries, and how are they to be explained?
5. What is the situation of second and subsequent generation immigrants in the labour market (is disadvantage passed on from generation to generation)?
6. Is institutional or informal discrimination a major determinant of employment and socioeconomic status?
7. What strategies have migrants adopted to deal with the labour market disadvantage (for example, self-employment, small business, mutual aid, finding 'ethnic niches')?

This chapter addresses the above questions by reviewing some of the major theoretical and empirical findings concerning immigrants and labour markets since the 1970s. The growing complexity of immigrant labour market effects is examined, along with illustrative material concerning cross-national trends in labour market segmentation and the growing polarisation of immigrant labour market characteristics. A case-study of the evolution of foreign employment in the French motor and building industries is included to demonstrate the adverse effects of economic restructuring since the early 1970s on foreign labour in certain industries and to illustrate processes of labour market segmentation.

Perhaps what is most distinctive about immigrant employment is clustering or concentration in particular jobs, industries and economic sectors. The sectoral nature of immigrant employment concentration varies from country to country due to historical factors and other variables, such as entrepreneurial strategies and those of foreign workers (OECD, 1994: 37). The pattern of immigrant employment concentration within a particular state and society often evolves through time. In France, declines in alien employment in the motor and building industries since 1973 have been paralleled by new concentrations of aliens in the rapidly growing services sector. A nine-country OECD study revealed:

> contrasting situations in the structure of foreign labor compared with national employment in each type of economic activity. The role of foreign labor differs in the countries covered by the study . . . Despite these differences, concentrations of foreign workers persist in sectors often neglected by nationals, though at the same time there has been a spread of foreign labor throughout all areas of economic activity, especially services. (OECD, 1994: 37)

Globalisation and international migration

The international migration and employment nexus has been the object of extensive but inconclusive scholarship and acrimonious political debate. Comparison of immigrant employment characteristics is particularly difficult. The statistics recorded by national governments vary enormously in scope and quality. A passage from a 1989 government report, *The Effects of Immigration in the US Economy and Labor Market,* summarised the state of knowledge in the USA as follows:

The assessment of the effects of immigration on the US economy and labor market is a complex undertaking and a definite response remains essentially elusive. In addition to difficulties in isolating the labor market behaviour of such groups as illegal immigrants and non-immigrants, larger questions of data adequacy also conspire to make what is a particularly contentious analytical exercise even more so . . . few unequivocal answers can be offered regarding the role of the foreign born in the various US labor markets.

The shortage of appropriate data allows the analysts' predispositions to influence the outcome of the research to a significant degree. Differences in academic disciplines, for instance, influence the research questions asked and often dictate the choice both of the unit of analysis and the analytical tools used. Furthermore, the level of data aggregation, and the focus and location of the investigation, often lead to different findings and influence their interpretation. Finally, theoretical and philosophical differences often intrude to the point of creating an analytical and interpretative morass. (US Department of Labor, 1989: 179)

In spite of these caveats, the report went on to conclude that immigration was increasingly important to understanding the US economy and, on balance, had a slight but beneficial overall effect. It noted, for instance, that the foreign-born constituted nearly 7 per cent of all US workers and accounted for some 22 per cent of annual growth of the workforce in the 1980s (US Department of Labor, 1989: xi). Its upbeat conclusion influenced adoption of the Immigration Act of 1990 which increased annual legal migration to the USA by 35 per cent.

One of the principal themes emerging from the analysis of international labour migration in the 1980s was its interconnections with economic globalisation. The US Department of Labor report was emblematic:

The underlying economic and social conditions that create, organise and sustain international migration result from the degree and manner in which regional economies become integrated, and not simply from stagnation or economic crisis found in individual countries . . . To the extent that US policies and practices contribute to the pace and pattern of regional integration, they help organise the expansion of regional labor flows. International trade, investment, communication and transportation facilitate the narrowing of differences between regions and countries and contribute to the expansion of opportunities and possibilities for international migration . . . Just as a firm expands from production for a local market to sell overseas in an international market, local labor markets are transformed through economic development into regional and international labor exchanges . . . The timing, direction, volume, and composition of international migration, therefore, are fundamentally rooted in the structure and growth of the regional economy in which the United States is most actively involved. Flows of labor occur within an international division of labor with increasingly integrated production, exchange and consumption processes that extend beyond national boundaries. (US Department of Labor, 1989: 5)

Other major factors affecting global patterns of immigrant employment include the decline in manufacturing employment in 'old' industrial areas, the rise of the NICs, the reorganisation of production and distribution within transnational corporations, more emphasis on control and communications using new technologies, the increased role of globally mobile financial capital and the emergence of 'global cities' as centres of corporate finance, marketing and design.

The growth of manufacturing in the NICs does not generally reduce labour emigration. The capitalist revolution in traditional agricultural societies has spurred massive rural–urban migration, bringing more peasants to urban areas than can be employed by new world market factories. Thus many of the exploding cities of Asia and Latin America become way stations on the road to urban centres in industrial democracies. Many of these new labour migrants confront an erosion of the relatively favourable and protected wages and employment conditions achieved by generations of blue-collar unionism. They take low-skilled non-unionised jobs where they have little bargaining power or security of employment. Hence new migrations and new patterns of ethnic segmentation have been hallmarks of the transformation of the global economy since the 1970s.

Growing fragmentation and polarisation of immigrant employment

The persistence of labour market segmentation is a theme common to many studies on immigrants and labour markets. Castles and Kosack demonstrated a general pattern of labour market segmentation between native and immigrant workers in Western Europe in the 1970s (Castles and Kosack, 1973). Collins regards the 'impact of post-war immigration on the growth and fragmentation of the Australian working class' as 'one of the most salient aspects of the Australian immigration experience' (Collins, 1991: 87). The US Department of Labor report concluded:

the most important current consequence of internationalisation, industrial restructuring, and the increase in the national origins and legal status of new immigrants is the dramatic diversification of conditions under which newcomers participate in the US labor market. Newcomers arrive in the United States with increasingly diverse skills, resources and motivations. In addition, on an increasing scale, they are arriving with distinct legal statuses. In turn, this proliferation of legal statuses may become a new source of social and economic stratification. (US Department of Labor, 1989: 18)

The range and significance of immigrant labour market diversity is obscured by policy and analytical perspectives that stress the homogeneity of competitive labour markets or sharp contrasts between primary and secondary labour markets (US Department of Labor, 1989: 18). It is often meaningless to generalise about average earnings and other labour market effects of immigration, just as it is meaningless to assume a general interest in discussions of immigration policy. Immigration has extremely unequal effects upon different social strata. Some groups gain from policies facilitating large-scale expansion of foreign labour migration, while other groups lose. The winners are large investors and employers who favour expanded immigration as part of a strategy for deregulation of the labour market. The losers are many of the migrants themselves, who find themselves forced into insecure and exploitative jobs, with little chance of promotion. Among the losers are also some existing members of the workforce, whose employment and social condition might be worsened by such policies.

In the 1980s, awareness grew that immigrant workforces were becoming increasingly bipolar with clustering at the upper and lower levels of the labour market. The head of ILO's migrant workers section termed Western Europe's growing number of professionals, technicians and kindred foreign workers the 'highly invisible' migrants (Böhning, 1991a: 10). He estimated that they comprised one-quarter of legally resident aliens living in the EC and included 2 million citizens of European Free Trade Association (EFTA) countries, which have since joined with the EC to create the world's most populous free trade zone, the European Economic Area. Americans, Canadians and Japanese comprised most of the remainder of the EC's highly invisible migrants. However resident alien populations, such as Turks in Germany, who are stereotypically seen as blue-collar workers, also include surprising numbers of professionals and entrepreneurs.

The growing number of professional level foreign workers reflects the globalisation of the economy (see Chapter 4; and Salt, 1989). In Germany, for instance, the unqualified share of the workforce was expected to decline from 27 per cent in 1985 to 18 per cent in 2010, whereas the highly qualified component would expand from 28 to 39 per cent (Böhning, 1991b: 11; the figures are for the area of the former West Germany only). In a little over a generation, 2 million jobs for unskilled workers were expected to be eliminated while 3.4 million additional highly skilled jobs will be created. While labour force need projections must be contemplated with caution, the unavoidable implication of the German projections is that there will be no resumption of large-scale recruitment of unskilled foreign workers as in the 1960s (Werner, 1992: 89). Some Germans, however, disagree and foresee a need for large-scale immigration on demographic grounds (Tichy, 1990). The introduction of new 'guestworker' schemes for migrants from Poland and other former Warsaw Bloc countries in the early 1990s reflects both a need for low-skilled labour, and the political objective of improving Germany's relations with these countries.

The trend towards higher skill levels for foreign employees is illustrated by Seifert's (1996) study of the German labour market. Using data from a large longitudinal survey, he finds that the proportion of foreign workers in unskilled or semi-skilled occupations declined from 70 per cent in 1984 to 60 per cent in 1994. However, at the same time the proportion of Germans in such jobs declined from 16 per cent to 12 per cent. As for the second generation (German-born children of immigrants), the proportion in unskilled and semi-skilled work declined from 47 per cent in 1984 to 34 per cent in 1994, which is an improvement but still unfavourable when compared with just 6 per cent of the same age cohort of Germans. The picture is similar with regard to sectoral distribution: immigrants are not as concentrated in manufacturing as they used to be, but are still considerably over-represented compared with Germans (Seifert, 1996: 423–7).

A bifurcation in the labour market characteristics of immigrants was apparent in the USA as well. Borjas found an overall pattern of declining skills in post-1965 immigrant cohorts as compared to earlier immigrants. This is a result of the 1965 changes in immigration law which opened up the USA to immigration from around the world (see

Chapter 4). As entries from Western Europe declined in favour of those from Asia and Latin America, the differences in the prevailing socioeconomic and educational standards between the regions were reflected in the declining skills and rising poverty of post-1965 immigrants (Borjas, 1990). The USA is far more attractive to poorer and less privileged Mexicans than it is to the Mexican middle and upper classes, who are little inclined to emigrate from a society marked by extreme inequality in income distribution and life chances (Borjas, 1990: 126). Hence it was scarcely surprising that the Mexican immigrants who were legalised after 1986 on average possessed only four years of schooling.

The growing bifurcation of immigrants to the USA was apparent in the sharply contrasting poverty rates of various national origin groups. The fraction of immigrants from Germany and Italy living in poverty was 8.2 per cent, whereas Chinese and Koreans had poverty rates of 12.5 and 13.5 per cent respectively, and immigrants from the Dominican Republic and Mexico suffered poverty rates of 33.7 and 26 per cent (Borjas, 1990: 148). Similarly Borjas found a strong link between rising welfare utilisation by immigrants and the changing character of immigration to the USA (Borjas, 1990: 150–62). These trends prompted Borjas to advocate changes in US immigration law to increase the skill levels of immigrants. The Immigration Act of 1990 aimed to nearly triple the number of visas reserved for qualified workers from 54 000 to 140 000 yearly. Moreover, 10 000 visas were set aside for investors annually. However, by 1995, employment-based immigration had declined to 85 000 (OECD, 1997: 173).

As in Western Europe, labour market projections for the USA forecast growing shortages of highly-qualified personnel. The Immigration Act of 1990 was designed to enhance US competitiveness in what was perceived as a global competition to attract highly skilled labour. One of the major challenges facing the USA in the future is finding gainful employment for existing and projected stocks of low and unskilled workers, many of whom are minorities. None the less advocacy of temporary foreign worker recruitment for industries such as agriculture, restaurants and hotels, and construction continues on both sides of the Atlantic, and many employers complain about labour shortages despite relatively high unemployment rates. Congressional hearings on numerous bills seeking to authorise expanded temporary foreign worker recruitment to the USA were held in 1996, but the 1996 immigration law did not alter policy towards recruitment of temporary foreign labour. President Clinton threatened to veto any legislation that significantly expanded guestworker recruitment.

A sharp pattern of labour market segmentation is also apparent in Australia (see Chapter 8). In 1978, Collins identified four major groups: (1) men born in Australia, in English-speaking countries and Northern Europe, who were disproportionately found in white-collar, highly skilled or supervisory jobs; (2) men from non-English speaking countries who were highly concentrated in manual manufacturing jobs; (3) women with an Australian or English-speaking background, found disproportionately in sales and services; and (4) women with a non-English-speaking background who tended to get the worst jobs with the poorest conditions (Collins, 1978). For Collins: '[p]erhaps the crucial point in understanding post-war Australian immigration is that [English-speaking and non-English-speaking] migrants have very different work experiences' (Collins, 1991: 87).[1]

Significant labour market segmentation is thus evident in industrial democracies. Traditional gender divisions, which concentrated women in low-paid and low-status work, have been overlaid and reinforced by new divisions affecting immigrant workers of both sexes. As migration is globalised there are widening gaps both between immigrants and non-immigrants, and among different immigrant categories. Future trends in the labour market will favour highly skilled immigration, but the pool of aspiring low-skilled immigrants is enormous and will expand exponentially in coming years.

Labour market segmentation leads to long-term marginalisation of certain groups, including many of the new immigrants from non-traditional sources. Generally there are not rigid divisions based on race, ethnicity or citizenship status. Instead, certain groups have become over-represented in certain disadvantaged positions. Some individual members of disadvantaged groups do well in the labour market, but most do not. The causes for this are not only found in specific factors like education, length of residence, prior labour market experience or discrimination. Much more complex explanations are usually required, which provide historical understanding of the processes of labour migration and settlement, along with its role in a changing world economy.

Global cities, ethnic entrepreneurs and immigrant women workers

Patterns of international migration are tightly bound up with capital flows, investment, international trade, direct and indirect foreign military intervention, diplomacy and cultural interaction. Pioneering work by Sassen (1988) stressed how patterns of foreign investment and displacement of certain US manufacturing jobs abroad have fostered new migratory streams to the USA (or have tended to expand preexisting flows). Sassen underscores the significance of the emergence of global cities, like New York or Los Angeles, for understanding future patterns of migration. Linkages between global cities and distant hinterlands create paradoxes wherein enormous wealth and highly remunerated professional employment uneasily coexist with growing unskilled service industry employment and Third-World-like employment conditions in underground industries. The casualisation of labour and growing illegal alien employment are characteristic of global cities. Considerable illegal employment of aliens often coincides with high unemployment of citizens and resident aliens. The latter are likely to belong to minorities and have often been victims of job losses in industries that have shifted manufacturing operations abroad.

As noted in previous chapters, some immigrant groups have traditionally played key economic roles as traders and entrepreneurs. Since the 1970s recession, a growing body of research has examined immigrant entrepreneurship and its effects. Across industrial democracies, growing numbers of immigrants are self-employed and owners of small businesses (Waldinger *et al.,* 1990). Most typical are ethnic restaurants, 'mom and pop' food stores and convenience stores. Immigrant-owned businesses frequently employ family members from the country of origin. Light and Bonacich, in their influential study, *Immigrant Entrepreneurs* (1988) traced the origins of the Korean business community in Los Angeles to the Korean War, which led to the establishment of extensive transnational ties and eventually migration between the Republic of Korea and the USA.

Studies in France similarly stressed the complex historical genesis of immigrant entrepreneurship. Sayad noted that 'sleep merchants' who supplied lodging for illegal aliens, usually compatriots, figured among the first North African businessmen in France (Vuddamalay, 1990: 13). In Germany, there were 150 000 foreigner-owned businesses by 1992, including 33 000 owned by Turks. The Turkish-owned businesses generated 700 000 jobs in 1991 and recorded sales of DM25 billion (about US$17 billion) and invested DM6 million in Germany (*This Week in Germany,* 18 September 1992: 4).

Firms owned by Asian Americans, Pacific Islanders, American Indians and Alaska natives increased 87 per cent from 1982 to 1987, from 201 264 to 376 711. This compared with a 14 per cent increase over the same period for all US firms (Census Bureau press release of

2 August 1991). Similarly, Hispanic firms in the USA increased from 233 975 in 1982 to 422 373 in 1987, an 81 per cent increase (Census Bureau press release of 16 May 1991). Hispanic-owned firms accounted for 3 per cent of all US firms and generated 1 per cent of gross receipts. Immigrant entrepreneurship has been assessed divergently. Some scholars, such as Fix and Passel, stress the economic dynamism of immigrant entrepreneurs with their positive effects upon economic growth and quality of life for consumers:

> Another source of job creation is the entrepreneurial activities of immigrants themselves. In 1990 almost 1.3 million immigrants (7.2 percent) were self-employed, a rate marginally higher than natives (7.0 percent) . . . During the 1980's, immigrant entrepreneurship increased dramatically. In 1980, 5.6 percent of immigrants living in the United States were self-employed but by 1990 the same group of pre-1980 immigrants (who had now been in this country for an additional decade) had a self-employment rate of 8.4 percent. (Fix and Passel, 1994: 53)

A more critical viewpoint stresses the human suffering entailed by intense competition, the long hours of work, exploitation of family labour and of illegally employed aliens, resultant social problems and so on (Light and Bonacich, 1988: 425–36; Collins *et al.*, 1995). The Los Angeles riots of 1992 revealed an undercurrent of tension between blacks and Korean businesspeople in Los Angeles. Tensions between urban black Americans and Korean entrepreneurs were manifested in other major US cities, frictions that were similar to anti-Jewish business sentiments when US ghettoes boiled over in the 1960s. Such tensions again point to the need for a broad-gauged approach to apprehension of immigration. The downside of immigrant entrepreneurship was summarised in a 1997 report:

> The ethnic solidarity hypothesised to be conducive to immigrant business can be seen in another light, as exclusionary and clannish, impeding access to business and employment opportunities for the native-born . . . The informal business transactions in immigrant communities that are normally regulated by gossip and ostracism can sometimes be enforced in ways that are distinctly illegal. To some of the relatives involved, the much-vaunted 'strong family ties' that keep a corner store open 24 hours a day may seem exploitative and unfair. There is even reason to suspect that migrant self-employ-

ment is more of a survival strategy than an indication of socio-economic success – more, that is, of a lifeboat than a ladder. (*Research Perspectives on Migration*, 1997: 11)

Research in the 1980s shed a great deal of additional light on the labour market role of immigrant women. Houstoun, Kramer and Barrett (1984) documented a female predominance in legal immigration to the US since 1930. They concluded that deployment of USA military forces abroad played a significant role in this. They noted that an estimated 200 000 Asian-born wives of US servicemen resided in the USA in the early 1980s. While working-age immigrant men reported a labour force participation rate (77.4 per cent) similar to US men, female immigrants were less likely to report an occupation than US women. The bifurcation pattern considered above was more pronounced with immigrant women. They were more concentrated in highly skilled occupations (28.1 per cent) than US women but also more concentrated in low-status, white-collar clerical employment (18.0 per cent), semi-skilled blue-collar operation jobs (17.9 per cent) and in private household work (13.9 per cent: see Houstoun, Kramer and Barrett, 1984).

Data on female immigrant employment in Australia revealed sharp segmentation. Collins and Castles used 1986 Census data to examine the representation of women in manufacturing industry. The index figure 100 indicates average representation. They found high degrees of overrepresentation for women born in Vietnam (494), Turkey (437), Yugoslavia (358) and Greece (315). Women born in the USA (63), Canada (68) and Australia (79) were underrepresented (Collins and Castles, 1991: 15). Female clustering in manufacturing industries undergoing restructuring rendered them disproportionately vulnerable to unemployment. Immigrant women of a non-English speaking background were thought to be overrepresented in outwork for industries such as textiles, footwear, electronics, packing and food and groceries. Collins and Castles considered these workers as perhaps the most exploited section of the Australian workforce (Collins and Castles, 1991: 19).

Morokvasic has argued that, in general, immigrant women from peripheral zones living in Western industrial democracies:

represent a ready made labour supply which is, at once, the most vulnerable, the most flexible and, at least in the beginning, the least demanding work force. They have been incorporated into sexually segregated labour markets at the lowest stratum in high technology industries or at the 'cheapest' sectors in those industries which are labour intensive and employ the cheapest labour to remain competitive. (Morokvasic, 1984: 886)

Patterns of labour migration in the 1990s are continuing this type of incorporation of women's labour, and extending it to new areas of immigration, such as Southern Europe and South-east Asia.

Foreign labour in France's car and building industries

In many highly-developed countries, migrant workers have become highly concentrated in the car and building industries. Employer recourse to foreign labour in these sectors has been particularly significant – both in quantitative and in political terms – in France. At the height of labour immigration in the early 1970s, some 500 000 foreigners were employed in the building industry. About a quarter of all foreigners employed in France were in the building industry. In motor car construction, some 125 000 foreigners were employed, representing one out of every four car workers. Only the sanitation services industry had a higher ratio of foreign to French employees by 1980 (M. J. Miller, 1984).

The disproportionate effects of the 1970s recession upon foreign workers in the car and building industries were incontrovertible. Although foreigners comprised one-third of building sector employees, they suffered nearly half of the total employment loss from 1973 to 1979, and declined to 17 per cent of the building industry workforce by 1989 (OECD, 1992: 24). In the car industry, total employment actually increased by 13 000 in the same period, yet foreign workers were hard hit by layoffs, their number falling by 29 000. During the 1980s, tens of thousands of additional jobs were lost, with aliens again being disproportionately affected.

A report compiled by the *Féderation Nationale du Bâtiment,* the main French building sector association, revealed that total employment in the building sector declined by 11.7 per cent from 1974 to 1981. But the reduction of the foreign employee component, some 150 000 jobs, represented a loss of 30 per cent of the 1974 foreign workforce, whereas the 45 000 decrease in the number of French workers employed represented only a 3.9 per cent decline from 1974 employment levels.

In other words, three out of every four jobs lost in the building industry from 1974 to 1981 had been held by foreigners. Foreign worker employment in the building and car industries reached its height in 1974 and then contracted sharply. None the less, according to a Ministry of Labour survey, foreign workers still comprised 28 and 18.6 per cent of the building and car construction industries workforces respectively in 1979. This was all the more remarkable because, in addition to the halt in recruitment, the French government sought to reduce foreign worker employment through a programme offering a cash incentive for repatriation. There was also a *revalorisation du travail manuel* programme, which sought to substitute French for foreign workers through improving the conditions of manual jobs. Both the repatriation and *revalorisation* programmes fared poorly.

Foreign workers were routinely given jobs with unskilled or semi-skilled manual labour classifications which belied their actual level of training or the skill required to perform the job. In both industries it was often charged that there was not equal pay for equal work. This perception, coupled with a lack of foreign worker integration into unions, which in the 1960s motor plants were mainly representative of French workers, made foreign workers a primary target of extreme Leftist organisational efforts in the wake of the May/June 1968 events. A *grève bouchon* or bottleneck strike at the sprawling Renault-Billancourt factory in 1973 caused consternation (Mehideb, 1973). A shop of some 400 workers succeeded in paralysing production. Similar strikes disrupted the German car industry at roughly the same time and, in Switzerland, Spanish seasonal workers in construction stunned the country with strikes and demonstrations over their housing conditions (Castles and Kosack, 1973; M. J. Miller, 1981; Castles, 1989: 28–42).

Prior to 1974, the car assembly industry was characterised by a high rate of foreign employee turnover. This pattern was profoundly altered by the 1974 recruitment ban. Major consequences of the stabilisation of the foreign workforce in motor manufacturing were the ageing of the foreign workforce, its mounting unionisation and sociopolitical cohesiveness as well as resentment of perceived discrimination against foreigners in terms of career opportunities. By the 1980s, most foreign car workers had been employed for at least five years by their company. At the Talbot-Poissy plant by 1982, for example, only one out of the 4400 Moroccan manual workers had worked there less than five years. Some 3200 of the Moroccans had worked there for ten years or more (Croissandeau, 1984: 8–9).

Foreign workers often chose to join or to vote for various unions by groups, whether from a specific nationality or from a specific shop.[2] Hence support could swing sharply from one union to another, depending on foreign workers' views of a union's specific programme on issues of concern to them. The volatility of ties to French unions stemmed in part from the parallel development of largely autonomous shop-floor organisation among foreign workers. In many cases, shop-floor cohesion was based upon national or religious solidarity. By the 1980s, Islamic solidarity groups, whose loci of contact were Muslim prayer-rooms provided by management within the factories, had become an important force. In other instances, underground revolutionary groups affected the form of foreign worker integration into union structures.

In some factories, such as Citroën's Aulnay-sous-Bois plant and Talbot's-Poissy plant in the Parisian suburbs, alleged violations of French labour law and other means of management pressure resulted in foreign worker enrolment in so-called house-unions affiliated with the right-wing *Confédération des Syndicats Libres* (CSL). Foreign workers risked losing work and residence permits if they did not support the house union, or they stood to lose company housing and the opportunity to participate in CSL-controlled holiday programmes. It was alleged that factory elections were fraudulent. This led to an accumulation of foreign worker grievances and bitter antagonism between pro-CSL and anti-CSL employee factions which would explode into violence after the left-wing election victory of 1981.

The extraordinary sense of collective identity evidenced by foreign car workers by the 1980s stemmed from the stratification which bound workers of similar ethnic and religious backgrounds together in assembly line and other manual jobs. The striking concentration of foreign workers in unskilled or lowly qualified jobs at Renault-Billancourt was typical of car plants which employed large numbers of foreign workers. Any explanation for the low certified skill levels of most foreign car workers must return to the recruitment process. Citroën, and to a lesser extent other French motor manufacturers, deliberately sought out physically able but poorly educated foreigners to fill manual labour positions. It was felt that their low levels of education and general backwardness made them better suited for monotonous and often physically taxing jobs than Frenchmen. Hence many foreign car workers were illiterate.

Illiterate foreign workers and those lacking in primary education could not compete in written exams required for professional advancement. Foreign workers frequently possessed skills which were not reflected in their professional rankings because they could not obtain certificates based on examinations and successful completion of courses. Foreign workers frequently charged that the industry's system of remuneration based on a worker's formal qualifications and job descriptions discriminated against them. The issue remained a bone of contention between French and non-French workers in the industry and strained foreign worker ties to French unions as well.

With few hopes for professional advancement, many foreign car industry workers grew frustrated with their jobs. Their frustration and the difficulty of their work was reflected in rising absenteeism and generally less disciplined work habits (Willard, 1984). Whereas employers once prized foreign workers for their industry and discipline, they began to complain of production and quality control problems. Employer misgivings over hiring of foreign labour were crystallised by a primarily foreign worker strike wave which plagued the industry in the 1970s before rocking its very foundations in the 1980s. The 1973 Renault-Billancourt strike was portentous.

Foreign worker unrest was evident by 1978 throughout the industry. However, it took the dramatic left-wing coalition electoral victories of 1981 to embolden foreign workers at Talbot and Citroën to strike. The change of government meant that labour laws would be applied at the Talbot and Citroën factories, and that foreign workers would no longer have to fear sanctions if they expressed themselves freely. The announced intention of the new government to strengthen the rights of labour through the Auroux laws buoyed support for anti-CSL forces in works council elections at the two companies. The pro-communist *Confédération Générale du Travail* (CGT) in particular scored impressive gains. The elections were marred by violent confrontations between CGT supporters, most of whom were foreign assembly line workers, and CSL supporters, many if not most of whom were skilled French workers (Ewald, 1983). During and after these employee elections, violence periodically erupted at the two plants.

The strike movements at Talbot-Poissy and Citroën-Aulnay sparked foreign worker dominated strikes at other car companies. They generally demanded upgrading of their pay and professional status along with the creation of career opportunities. Many of the strikes were *grèves bouchons* where one or several shops of foreign workers would shut down production and thereby force layoffs of non-striking workers. This situation led to confrontations between strikers and non-strikers, but the violence witnessed at Talbot and Citroën plants was generally avoided elsewhere.

The car workers' strikes hastened plans to restructure and modernise the French motor manufacturing industry. Both Peugeot and Renault, the two major automobile firms (Peugeot having acquired Citroën and Chrysler Europe in the late 1970s), announced plans to automate production through the use of industrial robots. Unrest in French car factories continued sporadically into the early 1990s, but would never again reach dimensions comparable to those of the 1973 to 1983 period. The building industry, with its weaker unionisation rate, rampant illegal alien employment, widespread sub-contracting and predominance of small and medium-sized employers, did not experience parallel unrest. However, economic restructuring, as seen through the window of these two French industries, had disproportionately affected immigrant employment, with far-reaching political consequences.

In other French industries, however, immigrant employment grew over the 1973 to 1993 period. This was particularly true of services and the apparel industry. In other countries, similar seemingly contradictory developments have been documented. Migrants are disproportionately vulnerable to job loss during recessions and periods of economic restructuring in declining industries but not in others. Tapinos and de Rugy suggest that 'immigrant workers, more sensitive to fluctuating demand, would appear to be more popular than nationals in sectors subject to strong cyclical swings, but also more at risk during a recession' (OECD, 1994: 168).

The process of labour market segmentation

The French car and building industries were typical of the situation in all highly-developed countries, in that they exhibited a pattern of foreign worker concentration in less desirable jobs. These jobs were frequently unhealthy, physically taxing, dangerous, monotonous or socially unattractive. This state of affairs was shaped by many factors. In both industries, employment of foreign and colonial workers had already become traditional before the Second World War. In the post-1945 period, both industries faced a serious shortfall of labour, a problem solved by recourse to aliens. The legal foreign worker recruitment system aided employers by making employment and residence contingent on employment in a certain firm or industry – usually within one city or region – for a period of several years. Many foreign workers only gradually earned freedom of employment and residential mobility. The recruitment system funnelled foreign workers into less attractive jobs. Employers might have had to improve working conditions and wages if it had not been for the availability of foreign labour, or they might have been unable to stay in business. Illegal alien employment was rare in the car industry: the size of firms and the presence of strong unions made it difficult. Illegal employment was common in the building industry, where it adversely affected wages and working conditions. This had the paradoxical effect of making the industry all the more dependent on foreign labour. As employment in the industry became socially devalued, employers often could find only foreigners to work for them. Similar processes affected female foreign workers, who became highly concentrated in certain sectors of manufacturing, such as clothing and food processing, and in service occupations such as cleaning, catering and unskilled health service work. Undocumented employment of women was even more common than for men, since ideologies about foreign women as mothers and housewives made it easy to conceal their role in the labour force.

There was little direct displacement of French workers by foreigners. Certain types of jobs became socially defined as jobs for foreign labour, and were increasingly shunned by French workers who, during the long period of post-war expansion, could generally find more attractive employment elsewhere. Indeed, massive foreign worker employment enabled the upward mobility of many French workers. This general process prevailed until the late 1970s or early 1980s, when France went into a prolonged recession and unemployment grew.

Employer recruitment strategies also contributed to labour market segmentation between French and alien workers. Some building in-dustry employers preferred to hire illegal aliens because they could increase profits, through non-payment of bonuses and payroll taxes for instance, and they ran little risk of legal sanctions until the 1980s. Some motor industry employers deliberately sought to hire poorly educated peasants without industrial experience in order to frustrate left-wing unionisation efforts. This strategy had the effect of making assembly line work even less attractive to French workers. In the same way, clothing industry employers found it particularly easy to pressure foreign women into undocumented and poorly-paid outwork; again a situation to be found in virtually all industrial countries (Phizacklea,

1990). In France, between 1983 and 1991, overall employment in the clothing industry fell by 45 per cent, but foreign worker employment rose by 53 per cent (OECD, 1994: 40). Eventually the pattern of ethnic stratification within French car plants became a major factor in labour unrest. The strategy of divide and rule practised by some employers ultimately boomeranged when foreign car workers struck for dignity in the late 1970s and the early 1980s. The ethnic solidarity produced by the process of labour market segmentation in many French car factories was a key factor in the prolonged unrest. Again parallels can be found in migrant worker movements in other countries (for Australia, for instance, see Lever-Tracy and Quinlan, 1988).

The process of labour market segmentation usually results from a combination of institutional racism and more diffuse attitudinal racism. This applies particularly in countries which recruit 'guestworkers' under legal and administrative rules which restrict their rights in a discriminatory way. The legally vulnerable status of many foreign workers in turn fosters resentment against them on the part of citizen workers, who fear that their wages and conditions will be undermined. This may be combined with resentment of foreign workers for social and cultural reasons, leading to a dangerous spiral of racism. Such factors have profoundly affected trade unions and labour relations in most countries which have experienced labour immigration since 1945.

Immigration, minorities and the labour market needs of the future

The plight of laid-off Moroccan car workers in France was emblematic of a host of critical problems facing many industrial democracies. Even in the early 1980s, a Paris-area car plant typically finished painting cars by hand. Teams of immigrant workers generally did the work and, in many cases, it was done by Moroccans. One-quarter of all Moroccans employed in France in 1979 were employed by the car industry alone. The Moroccans were recruited because they were eager to work, recruitment networks were in place and because they were reputed to be physically apt and hardworking people. By 1990, most of the painting teams had been replaced by robots. Many of the workers were unemployed and, owing to their lack of educational background, there was little hope of retraining them to take jobs requiring more advanced educational backgrounds. Their only hope for re-employment lay in finding another relatively low-skilled manual labour job, but such jobs were disappearing.

Throughout Western Europe, economic restructuring led to alarmingly high unemployment rates for foreign residents by the mid-1980s. In the mid-1990s, their unemployment rates remain well above those for the population as a whole. All indications are that there will continue to be an aggregate surplus of manual workers over employment opportunities for the foreseeable future. Job opportunities will be found primarily in the highly skilled sector where shortages are already apparent and will continue into the future.

The labour market difficulties of laid-off foreign workers were compounded by several other worrisome trends. Immigrant children comprised a growing share of the school age population but were disproportionately likely to do poorly in school, to be early school leavers or to enter the labour force without the kind of educational and vocational credentials increasingly required for gainful employment (Castles, Booth and Wallace, 1984: Chapter 6). The worst scenario for the French socialists involved the sons and daughters of the recently laid-off Moroccan car workers leaving school early and facing bleak employment prospects. The fear was of a US-style ghetto syndrome in which successive generations of an ethnically distinctive population would become entrapped in a vicious cycle of unemployment leading to educational failure and then socioeconomic discrimination, and finally housing problems.

France faced an uphill struggle to ensure that the most vulnerable members of its society enjoyed a reasonable measure of equality of opportunity. Immigrants and their descendants comprised a large share of the at-risk population. This was the major motivation behind Western European efforts to curb illegal immigration. It was generally felt that the population that was the most adversely affected by competition from illegal aliens on labour markets was existing minority populations. The overall economic effects of immigration may well be marginally positive. But labour market effects of immigration, and particularly of illegal immigration, are uneven and spatially concentrated. In the USA, it was thought by some specialists that Afro-Americans and Hispanic citizens were the two groups most affected by illegal migration. These conclusions were disputed, however, and many Hispanic advocacy groups in the USA viewed illegal immigration as a benign, if not positive, inflow, since it provided much-needed workers and helped in family reunion and community formation processes.

Conclusions

This chapter has argued that the economic restructuring since the 1970s has given rise to new immigration flows and new patterns of immigrant employment. One major result has been increasing diversification of immigrants' work situations and of their effects on labour markets. A major review of the literature on macro-economic impacts of immigration since the mid-1970s found that studies converge 'in concluding that immigration causes no crowding-out on the labor market and does not depress the income of nationals . . . [T]his is probably the most important contribution economists have made toward clarifying the issues involved' (OECD, 1994: 164).

Patterns of labour market segmentation by ethnic origin and gender which had emerged by the 1970s have generally persisted and, in many ways, become even more pronounced in the 1990s. However, the growth of illegal migration, continuing deficiencies in statistics, and the growing transnational interdependence of which international migration is an integral part make it difficult to generalise about the labour market effects of immigrants. Writing of immigrant women, Morokvasic observed that 'it is probably illusory to make any generalisations based on these findings in different parts of the world . . . They can only be interpreted within the specific socioeconomic and cultural context in which these changes are observed' (Morokvasic, 1984: 895). There are tremendous variations in immigrant employment patterns according to ethnic and national background, gender, recentness of arrival, legal status, education and training. Varying economic structures, governmental policies, patterns of discrimination and legal traditions further complicate matters.

In Western Europe, an authoritative EC study (Commission of the European Communities, 1990) has documented the continuing pattern of employment, educational and housing disadvantages encountered by immigrants. Discrimination endures despite the integration policies of many governments. Disadvantage is often intergenerational and poses a grave challenge to Western European social democratic traditions. In the USA, the passage of time has generally witnessed inter-generational upward mobility for European-origin immigrants. The quintessential question asked about immigrants to the USA is: will the Mexican or Dominican immigrants be like the Irish and Italian immigrants of the nineteenth and early twentieth centuries? It seems too early to answer this question, but the intergenerational mobility evinced by earlier immigrant waves to the USA has created a more optimistic context and expectation than prevails in Western Europe. Much the same could be said for Australia and Canada.

Institutional and informal discrimination has clearly contributed to immigrant disadvantage. In Western Europe, the discrimination inherent in the employment and residential restrictions characteristic of guestworker policies funnelled immigrants into specific economic sectors and types of jobs. The analysis of foreign worker employment in the French motor manufacture and building industries demonstrated the disproportionate effects of job losses through economic restructuring since the 1970s upon foreign workers. However, in the 1980s, immigrant employment in France grew sharply in the expanding services sector. Legally-resident aliens enjoyed more secure legal status and more extensive rights than in the past. This enabled many foreigners to adjust to restructuring. Some migrants have developed their own strategies to cope with labour market disadvantage. The growing unionisation of foreign employees in Western Europe and strike movements like those witnessed in the French car industry were forms of adaptation. The proliferation of immigrant entrepreneurs was another.

Labour market segmentation is a central element in the process which leads to formation of ethnic minorities. Labour market segmentation has complex links with other factors that lead to marginalisation of immigrant groups (see Chapters 2, 8 and 9). Low-status work, high unemployment, bad working conditions and lack of opportunities for promotion are both causes and results of the other determinants of minority status: legal disabilities, insecure residency status, residential concentration in disadvantaged areas, poor educational prospects and racism.

Some sociologists argue that, in the 1990s, the conflict between labour and capital is no longer the major social issue in advanced societies. It has been replaced by the problem of the *exclusion* of certain groups from the mainstream of society. These groups are economically marginalised through insecure work, low pay and frequent unemployment; socially marginalised through poor education and exposure to crime, addiction and family breakdown; and politically marginalised through lack of power to influence decision making at any level of government. All these factors join to produce spatial marginalisation: concentration in certain urban and suburban areas, where minorities of various kinds are thrown together, virtually cut off from and forgotten by the rest of society (Dubet and Lapeyronnie, 1992). Certain immigrant groups have a very high propensity to suffer social exclusion. These immigrants are doubly disadvantaged: they are not only amongst the most disadvantaged groups in contemporary society, but they are also frequently labelled as the cause of the problems. Thus immigrants experience a rising tide of racism, which isolates them even more. This process of ethnic minority formation will be discussed in the next three chapters.

8 The Migratory Process: A Comparison of Australia and Germany

This chapter presents comparative case studies of the migratory process in two countries with very different traditions and institutional frameworks. As will become apparent, there are significant parallels in the development of migration and ethnic diversity. This leads to the conjecture that the dynamics of the migratory process (as discussed theoretically in Chapter 2) can be powerful enough to override political structures, government policies and subjective intentions of the migrants. This does not mean, however, that these factors are unimportant: settlement and ethnic group formation have taken place in both cases, but under very different conditions. This has led to differing outcomes, which can be characterised as the formation of ethnic *communities* in the Australian case, as against ethnic *minorities* in Germany.

Australia and Germany: two opposing cases?

Australia and the Federal Republic of Germany (FRG)[1] have both experienced mass population movements since 1945. In both cases, foreign immigration started through the official recruitment of migrant workers. In some periods, the areas of origin of migrants have been the same. However, there the similarities seem to end, and the two countries are often seen as opposite poles on the migration spectrum.

Australia is considered one of the classical countries of immigration: a new nation which has been built through colonisation and immigration over the last two centuries. Like the USA and Canada, it is part of the 'new world', a sparsely populated country open to settlement from Europe and, more recently, from other continents too. Since 1947, there has been a continuous policy of planned immigration, designed both to build population and to bring about economic growth.

Immigration has been mainly a permanent family movement of future citizens and has made Australia into a country of great ethnic diversity, with official policies of multiculturalism.

Germany, by contrast, is generally seen as a 'historical nation', with roots that go back many centuries, even though unification as a state was not achieved until 1871. Post-1945 policies emphasised the recruitment of temporary 'guestworkers', although there have also been large influxes of refugees and 'ethnic Germans' from Eastern Europe. Today leaders still claim that Germany is 'not a country of immigration'. The end of the Cold War and German reunification have led to massive new population movements since 1989, making immigration and ethnic diversity into central political issues.

In comparing the two countries, we shall look at the way the overall migratory process is shaped by a number of factors: the origins and developments of migratory flows; labour market incorporation; the development of immigrant communities; the evolution of legal frameworks and government policies; and the immigrants' various forms of interaction with the society of the receiving country.

Tables 8.1 and 8.2 give the most recent available figures on the immigrant populations in the two countries. The figures for Australia

TABLE 8.1 Australia: immigrant population by birthplace (thousands)

Country of birth	1971	1981	1991	1996
Europe	2 197	2 234	2 299	2 217
UK and Ireland	1 088	1 133	1 175	1 124
Italy	290	276	255	238
Former Yugoslavia	130	149	161	n.a.
Greece	160	147	136	127
Germany	111	111	115	110
Other Europe	418	418	457	618
Asia (incl. Middle East)	167	372	822	1 007
New Zealand	81	177	276	291
Africa	62	90	132	147
America	56	96	147	151
Other and not stated	18	36	75	95
Total	2 581	3 005	3 751	3 908

n.a. = not available.
Sources: All data is from Australian Censuses. OECD (1997): Table C1; 1996 Census, preliminary data.

are birthplace figures, for many overseas-born people have become citizens. About 22 per cent of the total population were overseas-born in 1996. In addition about 20 per cent of those born in Australia had at least one immigrant parent. Thus about 7.5 million of the 17.9 million people living in Australia in 1996 were either born overseas or had one or both parents born overseas, which indicates the great significance of the migration experience for Australia. There were also 353 000 Aboriginal people and Torres Strait Islanders (2.1 per cent of the total population) who are the only true 'non-immigrants' in Australia.

The figures for Germany show the foreign resident population for 1995: 7.2 million people who make up 8.8 per cent of the total population. These figures are for the whole of Germany. In 1990, prior to reunification, there were 5.3 million foreign residents in the old *Länder* (states) of the Federal Republic. In addition, Germany has

TABLE 8.2   Foreign residents in Germany (thousands)

Country	1980	1985	1990	1995
Turkey	1 462	1 402	1 695	2 014
Former Yugoslavia	632	591	662	1 299
Italy	618	531	552	586
Greece	298	281	320	360
Poland	..	105	242	277
Austria	173	173	183	185
Spain	180	153	135	132
Netherlands	..	108	111	113
United Kingdom	..	88	96	113
Iran	..	51	92	107
France	..	75	85	99
Portugal	112	77	85	125
Morocco	36	48	70	82
Romania	..	14	60	109
Hungary	..	21	37	67
Tunisia	23	23	26	26
Other countries	921	638	891	1 480
Total	4 453	4 379	5 342	7 174
of which EC/EU	–	1 357	1 439	1 812

Notes: Figures refer to the old *Länder* of the pre-reunification Federal Republic of Germany up to 1990, to the whole of Germany for 1995. 'Former Yugoslavia' includes Bosnia-Herzegovina, Croatia, Macedonia, etc.
Sources: OECD (1992): Table 10; OECD (1997): Table B1.

large numbers of 'ethnic German' immigrants (or *Aussiedler*) with a claim to German citizenship. The figures also omit foreign settlers who have become citizens. However, this is a fairly small group, since naturalisation rates are low.

Origins and development of the migratory movements

Migratory movements to Australia and Germany were described in Chapters 3 and 4. Here, we will discuss differences and similarities in the post-1945 immigration experiences.

In 1947, the Australian government started a large-scale immigration programme, designed to increase the population for strategic reasons and to provide labour for new manufacturing industries. The original aim was to attract British settlers, but areas of origin quickly became more diverse. In the late 1940s, many immigrants came from Eastern and Central Europe, while in the 1950s and 1960s Southern Europeans predominated. The main motive force was Australian government policy. British migrants were encouraged to come by advertising campaigns and subsidised fares (the famous £10 family passages). Many Eastern Europeans were selected in Displaced Persons camps, while Southern Europeans were recruited through bilateral agreements with the Italian, Greek and Maltese governments. Since the Australian government wanted both workers and settlers, initial recruitment led to processes of chain migration, through which early migrants helped relatives, friends and fellow villagers to come and join them. The assimilationist policies of the 1950s and 1960s were designed to turn these 'New Australians' into citizens.

Germany has had several major migratory movements since 1945. The first and largest was that of over 8 million expellees (*Heimatver-triebene*) from the lost eastern parts of the *Reich* and 3 million refugees (*Flüchtlinge*) who came to the FRG from the GDR up to 1961. These people were of German ethnicity, and immediately became citizens of the FRG. Despite initial strains, they were absorbed into the population, providing a willing source of labour for Germany's 'economic miracle' (Kindleberger, 1967).

The next major movement – that of 'guestworkers' from the Mediterranean area – was to be the one that did most to turn Germany into a multi-ethnic society. As in Australia, government labour recruitment was the driving force, but there was a major difference: 'guestworkers' were not meant to settle permanently. The 'guestworker system' was described in Chapter 4 (see also Castles and Kosack, 1973; Castles, Booth and Walace, 1984). Foreign labour was recruited to meet German labour needs from 1955 to 1973 through agreements signed with Southern European countries, Turkey, Morocco and Tunisia. Recruitment was carried out by the German Federal Labour Office working closely with the authorities of the countries of origin. The 'guestworker' system was designed to recruit manual workers (both male and female) to work in factories and other low-skilled jobs in Germany. The foreign workers' special legal status restricted family reunion, limited labour market and social rights, and gave little chance of becoming citizens.

The ending of labour recruitment in 1973 led to unplanned trends towards family reunion and permanent settlement, which radically changed the position of immigrants in Germany. Many Southern Europeans did leave, partly because of lack of opportunities in Germany and partly because conditions were improving in their home countries. Those who stayed were mainly those from the most distant and culturally-different sending countries, especially Turkey and Yugoslavia. The Turkish case illustrates how temporary migration became transformed into settlement and community formation. Turkey had no tradition of international labour migration: the initial movement was a result of German recruitment policies. The Turkish government hoped to relieve domestic unemployment and to obtain foreign exchange through worker remittances. The migrants themselves sought an escape from poverty, unemployment and dependence on semi-feudal landowners. There was an expectation that money earned and skills gained abroad would encourage economic development. Thus the Turkish participants initially shared the German expectation of temporary migration.

When the German authorities stopped labour recruitment in 1973, however, many Turkish workers stayed on, and family reunion continued. Migrants realised that economic conditions at home were bad, and that there would be no opportunity to re-migrate to Germany later. In 1974, there were just over 1 million Turkish residents (including family members) out of a total foreign population of 4.1 million. Their number grew to 1.6 million by 1982, and to 2 million in 1995. Family reunion was not the only form of continued migration: political unrest and ethnic conflict in Turkey generated waves of asylum seekers, who found shelter in Turkish and Kurdish communities abroad. German government policies, which were not based on any understanding of the migratory process, were ineffective in preventing further immigration and settlement. Mass deportation, though debated, was never a real option for a democratic state, committed to a wide range of international agreements.

By the mid-1970s, both Australia and Germany had large permanent settler populations and emerging ethnic communities. Australian authorities accepted settlement and were beginning to seek ways of managing cultural diversity. Germany, by contrast, officially denied the reality of settlement. In the late 1970s and early 1980s, both countries experienced new forms of immigration, leading to even greater diversity.

Australia's immigration intakes became global in scope. The White Australia policy was formally abandoned in 1973, and large-scale Asian immigration began in the late 1970s with the arrival of Indo-Chinese refugees. By the mid-1980s, Asia was the main source of immigrants, making up 40–50 per cent of entries. But Australia also attracted Latin Americans (both workers and refugees) and Africans (in fairly small numbers). Immigration of New Zealanders (who can enter freely) also grew. In the mid-1990s, economic and political crises brought about new inflows from the former Soviet Union, former Yugoslavia, the Middle East and South Africa. The immigrants of the 1980s and 1990s were more economically and socially diverse than their predecessors. Most economic migrants were highly-skilled, but refugees often lacked skills and were hampered in their settlement by severe dislocation and trauma. Both skilled migration and refugee entry led to entry of dependents, whose educational and cultural backgrounds were very diverse. Table 8.3 illustrates how the areas of origin have changed. The most telling figure is the decline of the UK and Ireland from 54 per cent of all entrants in 1967 to just 12 per cent in 1995.

Germany has had three very diverse types of migration in recent years.

1. Largely spontaneous entries both of asylum seekers and of economic migrants from Eastern Europe and from non-European countries.
2. Mass migration from the GDR to the FRG, especially in 1989–90. This movement continued as internal migration after reunification in 1990.
3. Immigration of *Aussiedler* or 'ethnic Germans' from the former Soviet Union, Poland, Romania and other Eastern European countries.

TABLE 8.3   **Australia, settler arrivals: top 10 countries of birth, 1966–7 and 1994–5**

1966-7 Country of birth	Number	Per cent	1994-7 Country of birth	Number	Per cent
UK and Ireland	75 510	54.4	UK and Ireland	10 689	12.2
Italy	12 890	9.3	New Zealand	10 498	12.0
Greece	9 830	7.1	Former Yugoslavia	6 665	7.6
Yugoslavia	7 550	5.4	Vietnam	5 097	5.8
Germany	3 410	2.5	Hong Kong	4 135	4.7
New Zealand	2 750	2.0	Philippines	4 116	4.7
USA	2 340	1.7	India	3 908	4.5
Netherlands	1 870	1.3	China	3 708	4.2
Lebanon	1 720	1.2	South Africa	2 792	3.2
India	1 650	1.2	Iraq	2 539	2.9
Sub-total	119 520	86.2	Sub-total	54 147	6.9
Other	19 160	13.8	Other	33 281	38.1
Total	138 680	100.0	Total	87 428	100.0

Sources: Bureau of Immigration Research, or BIR (1991); BIMPR (1996): Table 3.3.

Article 16 of Germany's Basic Law lays down a right for victims of persecution to seek asylum. Until 1993, anybody who claimed to be an asylum seeker was permitted to stay pending an official decision on refugee status, which often took several years. South–North asylum-seeker movement became significant in the late 1970s, with about a quarter of a million entrants from Turkey, Eritrea, Afghanistan, Vietnam, Chile and other countries. Measures were taken to deter asylum seekers and inflows declined temporarily, but then started to increase, reaching 100 000 in 1986, 193 000 in 1990, and 438 000 in 1992 (OECD, 1995: 195). Fears of mass East–West and South–North migrations of desperate and impoverished people were seized on by the extreme right, and there was an upsurge in racist incidents. After a lengthy and emotional debate, Paragraph 16 of the Basic Law was amended in 1993, allowing German frontier police to reject asylum seekers for a variety of reasons. Measures were also taken to speed up the processing of applications. As a result, asylum applications fell to 322 600 in 1993 and 127 200 in 1994 (OECD, 1995: 195).

Many Polish asylum seekers came to Germany in the early 1990s, but this flow declined as conditions improved in Poland and new international agreements came into force. At the same time, temporary labour migration from Poland increased. In 1992, there was an upsurge in asylum seekers from war zones of the former Yugoslavia. At first, many were gypsies, as were the majority of asylum seekers from Romania. This ethnic group became the main target of racist violence in mid-1992. By 1996, there were estimated to be 320 000 Bosnians in Germany, as well as 135 000 Kosovo-Albanians. With the ending of warfare in former Yugoslavia, Germany made agreements with the Bosnian and Serbian governments to begin returning refugees in 1997, although continuing tensions made this difficult (*Migration News*, 3:12, December 1996).

The *Aussiedler* are people of German origin whose ancestors have lived in Eastern Europe for centuries. Like the post-1945 expellees, they have the right to enter Germany and to claim citizenship. *Aussiedler* are generally of rural origin, and may have considerable problems of social adaptation and labour market entry. They are provided with a range of services and benefits to facilitate settlement, which act as a powerful attracting factor. *Aussiedler* arrivals rose from 86 000 in 1987 to a peak of 397 000 in 1990. In the latter year, 148 000 were from the Soviet Union, 134 000 from Poland and 111 150 from Romania. At a time of social stress and growing unemployment, the influx of *Aussiedler* became unpopular. Despite the principle of free admission, the German government introduced a *de facto* quota system, based on complex bureaucratic rules (Thränhardt, 1996: 237–8). Entries of *Aussiedler* declined to an average of around 220 000 per year from 1991 to 1995. In 1995, 96 per cent of new *Aussiedler* came from the former Soviet Union (OECD, 1997: 106).

Australia still maintains a regular immigration intake planned by the government on the basis of economic, social and humanitarian considerations. Permanent arrivals in the 1990s have ranged from 70 000 to 100 000 per year. Policy is designed to admit people with economically-useful skills, although the family category remains the largest one. Humanitarian entrants average 12 000–15 000 per year. Most immigrants in the permanent categories are expected to settle and to become citizens. However, temporary migration is growing in significance.

There were 124 400 'temporary residents' in 1994–5, many of whom were highly-skilled personnel who came to work for limited periods. Another important temporary group is students, of whom 104 000 entered Australia in 1994–5 (BIMPR, 1996: 38–9). The growing number of temporary residents reflects increasing internationalisation of the economy.

Australia has had over 5 million immigrants since 1947. The overall pattern has been a policy of permanent immigration, with control facilitated by Australia's isolated geographical position. Although settlement was always planned, it has had unforeseen consequences: the ethnic composition of the population has changed in a way that was never desired by the architects of the migration programme. This has been partly because the need for labour during expansionary phases has dictated changes in recruitment policies. It has also been due to the way chain migration has led to self-sustaining migratory processes. Current economic and demographic developments in Asia are likely to change migratory patterns further.

Altogether around 20 million people have migrated into Germany since 1945. Population inflows of the 1990s have ranged from 788 000 to 1.2 million per year, although these have been partly balanced by outflows. The net average annual inflow from 1990–5 was 340 000 (calculated from OECD, 1997: 219–20). The neat categories of the 'guestworker system' have completely broken down. Current movements are volatile and unpredictable. Their causes lie in a mixture of long-standing historical patterns, new political constellations, emerging economic interests, uncertain social developments and complicated ethnic conflicts. Today, German capital is seeking a major role in investment, industry and trade throughout Central and Eastern Europe. The financial and communicative links which this is creating are likely to encourage future migrations.

Labour market incorporation

Up to about 1973, both Australian and German immigration policies were concerned with the recruitment of a manual labour force. Non-British migrants who received assisted passages to Australia were directed into jobs on construction sites such as the Snowy Mountains Hydro-electric Scheme, in heavy industry, or in factories (Collins, 1991). Similarly, the German Federal Labour Office channelled foreign workers into unskilled and semi-skilled jobs on building sites and in factories, and used restrictionary labour permit rules to keep them there as long as possible. Foreign workers were attractive to employers. A manager of Australia's largest steel company, BHP, described Italians as a 'hardworking race, especially those in the unskilled category', while company records showed a preference for Southern Europeans who were seen as 'readily available, eager to migrate and less reluctant to undertake hazardous, dirty and enervating jobs' (Lever-Tracy and Quinlan, 1988: 47–8). In Germany, economists suggested that failure to recruit foreign workers would lead to increased upward wage pressure and a decline in the competitivity of German industry (Castles and Kosack, 1973: 378).

The pre-1973 movements were mainly rural–urban migration: Mediterranean farmers and rural workers emigrated because of poverty, population growth, breakdown of social structures through war, and decline of local industries. Many intended to work temporarily in industrial economies, in order to use their earnings to improve their farms or set up small businesses upon return. Even in Australia, many Southern European workers expected to return home, and indeed did so in the 1960s and 1970s, as conditions improved in their countries of origin. However, this apparent agreement of interests between migrant workers and employers was neither complete nor durable. Some migrants were skilled, but in both countries there was a widespread policy of refusing to recognise their qualifications, compelling them to start off in low-skilled jobs. In time, many migrant workers' intentions changed: it became clear that it would not be possible to achieve their objectives in the home country as quickly as originally expected. Sometimes a failed attempt to set up a business at home led to re-migration. The result was an increasing orientation towards long-term stay and occupational mobility in the immigration country (a trend which went hand-in-hand with family reunion: Piore, 1979: 50ff).

However, workers found that, having entered the labour market at the bottom, it was hard to gain promotion. Certain types of workplace turned into a 'Southern European occupational ghetto' (Lever-Tracy and Quinlan, 1988: 82) or into *Gastarbeiterbeschäftigungen* (guest-worker jobs). Typical of such jobs for men were car assembly lines, construction sites and foundry work; and, for women, clothing, textiles and food processing. Services occupations such as catering, refuse collection, office cleaning and unskilled jobs in public utilities also became known as 'migrant work' (see Castles, Booth and Wallace, 1984; Collins, 1991). The structural factors and discriminatory rules which led to initial low status caused enduring patterns of labour market segmentation. Two decades on, the migrant workers of the early waves remained highly concentrated in the original sectors (Collins, 1991; Funcke, 1991: 9). This applied particularly to migrant women, whose situation was affected both by patriarchal structures in the countries of origin and gender discrimination in the country of immigration. Their situation in terms of occupational status, wages and conditions was generally the worst of all groups in the labour market (Phizacklea, 1983, 1990; Morokvasic, 1984).

Economic restructuring since the 1970s has brought significant changes. In both countries the pre-1973 entrants bore the brunt of restructuring, as low-skilled jobs in manufacturing declined. Research in Australia has shown that unemployment during the recessions of 1974–5, 1982–3 and 1990–2 was significantly higher for non-English-speaking background immigrants than for other workers (Ackland and Williams, 1992). Certain groups were very hard hit: the May 1993 unemployment rate for Vietnamese aged 15–34 years was 52 per cent and for Lebanese 43 per cent; four to five times the average (Moss, 1993: 258). In Germany the unemployment rate for foreigners in 1995 was 16.6 per cent, compared with only 9.3 per cent for the workforce as a whole. The unemployment rate for Turks was 24.4 per cent (OECD, 1997: 108).

OECD research in Germany and other countries has found that once older unskilled foreign workers are laid off in recessions, they have little chance of being re-employed (OECD, 1995: 37). As unskilled manufacturing jobs disappear, many immigrants lack the language skills and basic education needed for retraining. In Australia, studies in the communications industry (Baker and Wooden, 1992) and the automobile industry (Levine, McLenna and Pearce, 1992) found that workers with poor English skills are far less likely than other workers to be able to gain retraining.

As for newer migrants, there has been a differentiation in qualification and occupational status. In Australia, many immigrants from countries such as Taiwan, Korea, China, Hong Kong and Malaysia find work in business and in skilled, professional and managerial occupations. Germany, like other EU countries, experiences increasing international interchange of managers and experts. But people who come through family reunion or as refugees often lack skills and education. Such job-seekers have high rates of unemployment or find themselves in insecure and poorly-paid casual or informal-sector employment.

At the same time, the segmentation of migrant workers into specific forms of work means that they cannot be replaced by local labour, even at times of high unemployment. In Germany prior to reunification, the low birth rates of the 1970s and 1980s were leading to new demands by employers for migrant workers (Tichy, 1990). After a period of concern about mass immigration, by the mid-1990s the old worries about demographic decline and the need for immigrants to compensate for an ageing population were being re-asserted (Thränhardt, 1996). In Australia, new migrants are needed to make up for skill deficits. The entry of Asian entrepreneurs and executives is also seen as vital for linking the Australian economy to the fast-growing 'tiger economies' of the region.

Children of migrants who have obtained education and vocational training in the immigration country often secure better jobs than their parents. There is strong statistical evidence of such intergenerational mobility in Australia (Hugo, 1986: 225). However, second-generation immigrants with poor educational qualifications have little chance of steady employment. They often share this fate with local school-leavers, but it is members of ethnic minorities who were most likely to have had poor educational opportunities. This uneven picture is reflected in some of the research findings cited in Chapter 7 above.

Up to the mid-1980s many foreign children were failing in German schools, while few employers were willing to give them training places (Castles, Booth and Wallace, 1984: Chapter 6). More recently school achievement rates have improved, while the declining availability of young Germans owing to demographic factors should make it easier to get apprenticeships. However, even now many young foreigners are refused training places because of prejudice (Funcke, 1991: 11). Thomas Faist (1993) found an increase in access to vocational training for young Turkish nationals in the 1980s. However, ethnic inequality persisted: while two-thirds of German youths aged 15–24 had completed or were enrolled in apprenticeships, less than one-third of Turkish youths had done so. Moreover, Turkish apprentices were heavily overrepresented in craft occupations (such as hairdressers, bakers or motor mechanics). They were underrepresented in industrial occupations and almost completely absent from advanced services (banking, insurance and public administration). Many Turkish youths were enrolled in special programmes for the unemployed or disadvantaged. Such programmes were meant to improve basic work skills, but in fact most companies refused to hire youths who had done them. The situation was particularly bad for young Turkish women: a third were not in the labour force and nearly a quarter were in programmes for the disadvantaged. When the original immigrants arrived in the 1950s and 1960s, it was easy to find entry-level jobs in industry. Such jobs are now few and far between, so that many young ethnic minority members face a future of casual work and frequent joblessness. Some groups and individuals break out of this situation, but many are caught in a vicious circle: initial incorporation in low-skilled work and residential areas with poor educational opportunities is reinforced by processes of racialisation. Young job-seekers may be rejected because the combination of poor educational credentials, ethnic appearance and living in certain neighbourhoods has become a stigma, denoting marginality and unreliability (Häussermann and Kazapov, 1996: 361).

One route out of factory work is self-employment: 'ethnic small business' has become significant in virtually all industrial countries (Waldinger *et al.*, 1990). In Australia, some migrant groups have higher rates of self-employment or business ownership than locally born people. However, many small businesses fail, and the rate of self-exploitation (long working hours, poor conditions, use of family labour power, insecurity) is high. In Germany, the move into small business was delayed for non-EC migrants by a refusal to grant official permission to become self-employed. Turkish or Yugoslav entrepreneurs often had to pay a German or EC citizen to be the front for a business. This obstacle is less significant today, as most immigrants now have long-term residence permits. Many ethnic entrepreneurs are concentrated in 'ethnic niches' such as retail trade, catering, construction and transport (Waldinger *et al.*, 1990; Collins *et al.*, 1995). By 1990, it was estimated that 150 000 foreigners (of whom 100 000 came from Mediterranean countries) had set up businesses in Germany. In catering they made up 26 per cent of all business owners (Funcke, 1991: 10).

Community development

In Germany, many foreign workers were at first housed by employers in hostels or camps near the work site. In Australia, the Department of Immigration provided hostels for new arrivals, and they often sought work and longer-term housing around these. As relatives and friends arrived through chain migration, they tended to go where the earlier arrivals could give them support and help.

As the need for family accommodation grew, migrants had to enter the general housing market. Several factors put them at a disadvantage. Most had low incomes and few savings. Early arrivals lacked the local knowledge and informal networks needed to find good housing. There was much discrimination against migrants: some landlords refused to rent to them, while others made a business out of it, taking high rents for sub-standard and overcrowded accommodation. In some cases there was discrimination in the allocation of public housing, with rules that effectively excluded migrants, or put them at the end of long waiting lists (see Castles and Kosack, 1973: Chapter 7). Migrants therefore tended to become concentrated in the inner city or industrial areas where relatively low-cost housing was available. The quality of the accommodation and of the local social amenities (such as schools, health care facilities and recreational facilities) was often poor.

In Germany, such concentration has persisted long after settlement. According to an official report, the housing situation of foreign residents was 'generally bad' in 1991. They tended to have rented accommodation in low-standard or derelict housing, and were often rejected by German landlords because of prejudice. Public housing authorities often denied housing even to 'well-integrated foreigners' (Funcke, 1991: 11). In Australia, where there is a strong tradition of owner-occupation, many migrants were able to improve their situation over time. By the 1986 Census, most Southern Europeans owned their own homes, and their rate of owner-occupation was higher than for the Australian-born population (Australian Bureau of Statistics, or ABS, 1989). Many still remained in the original areas of settlement, though some had moved to outer suburbs. Newer groups, such as Indo-Chinese immigrants, seem to be following the same trajectory, which requires considerable time and thrift.

There has been much debate in both countries about the formation of 'ethnic ghettoes'. In fact, unlike the USA, there are very few areas with predominantly minority populations. Rather we find class-based segregation, with migrants sharing certain areas with disadvantaged groups of the local population: low-income workers, the unemployed, social security recipients and pensioners (see Castles, Booth and Walace, 1984: 117–20). However there are neighbourhoods where a specific ethnic group is large enough to have a decisive effect on the appearance, culture and social structure. Areas with a visible Turkish, Greek, Yugoslav or Italian presence (or a mixture of all of these) can be found in most German cities. The Turkish community of Kreuzberg in West Berlin is a well-known example. In Australia, a strong Italian flavour can be found in the Carlton area of Melbourne, or in the Leichhardt and Fairfield areas of Sydney. There are Chinatowns in the centre of Melbourne and Sydney, and Indo-Chinese neighbourhoods have developed in Richmond (Melbourne) and Cabramatta (Sydney).

Residential segregation of migrants has a double character: on the one hand, it can mean poor housing and social amenities, as well as relative isolation from the majority population; on the other hand, it offers the opportunity for community formation and the development of ethnic infrastructure and institutions. The most visible sign of this is the establishment of shops, cafés, and agencies which cater for migrants' special needs. 'Ethnic professionals' – health practitioners, lawyers, accountants – also find opportunities in such areas. A further development was the establishment of newspapers in migrant languages, followed (at least in Australia) by the setting-up of ethnic radio stations.

Small business owners and professionals form the core of ethnic middle classes, and take on leadership roles in associations. Welfare organisations cater for special needs of immigrants, sometimes compensating for gaps in existing social services. Social associations establish meeting places, such as the sports and recreation clubs of Italian, Greek and other communities in Australia (Alcorso, Popoli and Rando, 1992). Cultural associations aim to preserve homeland languages, folklore and tradition, and often set up mother-tongue or religious classes. Political associations of all complexions struggle for influence within the community. Often their starting-point is political and class divisions in the country of origin, but with increasing length of stay their aims become more oriented to the situation in the country of immigration.

Religion plays a major part in community formation. Sometimes migrants can join existing structures: for instance, many Southern Europeans in Germany and Australia entered the Catholic Church. However, they often found that religion was practised in different ways, and that the existing ways were not always sensitive to their needs (Alcorso, Popoli and Rando, 1992: 110–12). Often priests or religious orders (such as the Scalabrinians from Italy) accompanied the migrants, giving churches in areas of migrant settlement a new character. Orthodox Christians from Greece, Yugoslavia and Eastern Europe had to establish their own churches and religious communities. In recent years, the most significant religious development has been connected with migrations of Muslims: Turks and North Africans to Germany; Lebanese, Turks and Malaysians to Australia. The establishment of mosques and religious associations has had a high priority. Bhuddist, Hindu and Bahai temples can also be found in what were formerly almost exclusively Christian countries.

Such developments can be found in all countries of immigration. They are at the nexus of the migratory process, where transitory migrant groups metamorphose into ethnic communities. Establishing community networks and institutions means an at least partially conscious decision to start 'placemaking' and building a new identity (Pascoe, 1992). Community formation is linked to awareness of long-term or permanent stay, to the birth and schooling of children in the country of immigration, to the role of women as 'cultural custodians' and above all to the coming of age of the second generation (Vasta, 1992). In Germany, growing awareness of the long-term nature of stay led to formation of Turkish associations. Though many had an Islamic character, they were increasingly aimed at obtaining social and political rights in Germany. Moreover they were linked to a new collective identity which found expression in the demand for dual citizenship: that is, the recognition of being both Turkish and German.

The concept of the ethnic community plays a central part in debates on assimilation and multiculturalism. Community formation is not a mechanistic or predetermined process, and the communities that emerge are neither static nor homogeneous. Not all migrants form communities: for instance, one cannot speak of an English community in Australia, or an Austrian community in Germany. Communities are based not just on culture, but also on socioeconomic differentiation (labour market segmentation and housing segregation) and on discrimination (legal disadvantage, racist attitudes and behaviour). Community formation is not just concerned with cultural maintenance, but is also a strategy to cope with social disadvantage and to provide protection from racism.

The relationships and institutions which make up the community are initially based simply on individual and group needs. However, as economic enterprises, cultural and social associations, and religious and political groups develop, a consciousness of the community emerges. This is in no way homogeneous; rather it is based on struggles for power, prestige and control. The ethnic community can best be conceived as a changing, complex and contradictory network. The network is most intense and easily identifiable at the local level (for example, 'the Italian community of Fairfield' or the 'Turkish community of Kreuzberg'), but is in turn linked in many ways to wider networks: co-ethnics in the same country, the social groups and the state of the immigration country, and finally the social groups and the state of the country of origin.

Ethnic community formation may take on a transnational character, and provide the basis for long-lasting communicative networks which unite people across borders and generations. A special form of this is the *diaspora*, which denotes a persistent sense of community between people who have left their homeland (usually involuntarily) and who may be scattered all over the world. Such diasporas as the Jewish, the Armenian, the Kurdish and the Palestinian may play a crucial role in maintaining the national identity of a conquered or divided homeland, and in bringing about political change. Even economically-motivated migrants – such as Greeks, Italians or Filipinos – may consider themselves part of a diaspora, with dreams of changing their country of origin to make return a possibility.

Legal frameworks and government policies

There are important parallels in the migratory process in Australia and Germany, but the laws and policies regulating migration have been very different. Australian governments aimed to attract permanent settlers from Britain and, as a second best, other Europeans. According to Immigration Minister Harold Holt, speaking in 1950, this was the only way to hold Australia against 'the hungry millions of people in the resurgent continent of Asia' (Vasta, 1991). However, changes in Australia's international position led to the abolition of the White Australia Policy, opening the door to Asian immigration. Family reunion was accepted from the outset, so primary migration led quickly to migratory chains and to community formation.

Newcomers were encouraged to become Australian citizens. The initial five-year waiting period for naturalisation was reduced to three and then two years. In 1991, over 60 per cent of overseas-born residents were Australian citizens. The highest rates of naturalisation of immigrants in Australia for at least ten years (over 95 per cent) are shown by people from Greece, Lebanon, Poland, Vietnam and the Philippines. The lowest rates (below 50 per cent) are found among people from the United Kingdom and New Zealand (ABS, 1993: 19).[3] Citizenship is based primarily on the *ius soli* (law of the soil) principle, so that children born to legal immigrants in Australia are automatically citizens.

For Germany there are two separate legal frameworks: the first applies to people who can claim German *Volkszugehörigkeit* (ethnicity) such as post-1945 expellees and refugees and current *Aussiedler*. They have a right to citizenship, and are not considered foreigners. The second framework applies to foreign immigrants, who find it very hard to become citizens. By the mid-1980s over 3 million foreigners fulfilled the 10-year residence qualification, but only about 14 000 per year actually obtained citizenship (Funcke, 1991). In the early 1990s, rules were changed to make naturalisation easier. There were 27 295 naturalisations in 1991, 44 950 in 1993 and 31 888 in 1995 (OECD, 1997: 252). The rate of naturalisation is still low in relation to Germany's large foreign population. Children born in Germany to foreign parents do not have an automatic right to citizenship, although the Foreigners Law of 1990 has made it easier to obtain. Second-generation immigrants can, under certain circumstances (such as conviction for criminal offences or long-term unemployment), be deported. Even the third generation (children born to parents who were themselves born in Germany of immigrant parents) are not automatically German. However, new rules introduced in 1993 do give the third generation a strong claim to naturalisation.

The difference between Australian and German policies is connected with different historical experiences of nation-state formation. The Australian model embodies an inclusionary territorial concept of the nation: if immigration policy allows someone to be resident in the country and to participate in society, then citizenship policy allows him or her to become a member of the political community (or state) and of the nation (or people).

By contrast, when the German *Reich* emerged as the first modern German state in 1871, nationality was defined not through territoriality, but through ethnicity as shown by language and culture. A person could only obtain German nationality by being born into the German community, so that 'blood' became a label for ethnicity. When Hitler annexed Austria in 1938, he could claim that its people were coming 'home to the *Reich*', though they had never actually belonged to it. The same principle was used to take citizenship away from Jews and gypsies whose ancestors had lived on German soil for centuries. Today German citizenship is still mainly based on *ius sanguinis* (law of the blood). The German model is an exclusionary one. Millions of foreigners have become part of society, but they are excluded from the state and nation. This is the rationale behind the seemingly absurd slogan 'the FRG is not a country of immigration' (see Hoffmann, 1990).

This fundamental difference affects all aspects of public policy towards immigrants and minorities. The Australian model for managing diversity has had two main stages. In the 1950s, the government introduced a policy of *assimilationism,* based on the doctrine that non-British immigrants could be culturally and socially absorbed, and become indistinguishable from the existing population (Wilton and Bosworth, 1984). The central principle of assimilationism was the treatment of migrants as 'New Australians', who were to live and work with Anglo-Australians and rapidly become citizens. There was no special educational provision for migrant children, who were to be brought up as Australians. Cultural pluralism and the formation of 'ethnic ghettoes' were to be avoided at all costs.

By the 1960s, it became clear that assimilationism was not working, due to labour market segmentation, residential segregation and community formation. By the 1970s, political parties were also beginning to discover the political potential of the 'ethnic vote'. Assimilationism was replaced by *multiculturalism:* the idea that ethnic communities, which maintain the languages and cultures of the areas of origin, are legitimate and consistent with Australian citizenship, as long as certain principles (such as respect for basic institutions and democratic values) are adhered to. In addition, multiculturalism means recognition of the need for special laws, institutions and social policies to overcome barriers to full participation of various ethnic groups in society (Castles *et al.,* 1992b). In the early 1990s, the Australian Labor Party (ALP) Government emphasised 'Access and Equity' policies, designed to ensure that government services met the varying needs of all the different groups of the population. The Liberal-National Party Coalition Government elected in 1996 made cuts in special services for minorities, but claimed that it would maintain the principles of multiculturalism.

In Germany there was no question of assimilation in the early years. 'Guestworkers' were controlled by a network of bureaucracies. The Federal Labour Office organised recruitment and granted work permits. The *Ausländerpolizei* (foreigners' police) issued residence permits, kept foreign workers under surveillance and deported those who offended against the rules (for instance, by changing to a better-paid job without permission). The personnel departments of the employers provided some basic social services and managed company hostels. To deal with personal or family problems of foreign workers, the government provided funding to church and private welfare bodies (see Castles and Kosack, 1973).

By the 1970s, foreign children were entering German schools in large numbers. The educational authorities worked out a 'dual strategy' designed both to integrate foreign children temporarily during their stay in Germany, and to prepare them for return to their country of origin. The result was a system of 'national classes', 'preparatory classes' and 'mother-tongue classes' which separated foreign from German students, and prevented many foreign children from achieving educational success (see Castles, Booth and Wallace, 1984: Chapter 6). Family reunion also meant that workers were leaving company accommodation and seeking housing in the inner cities. The result was a debate on 'foreigners policy' which was to continue up to the present.

Up to the early 1990s, there were three main positions: the first was the call for a continuation of exclusionary policies, including restriction of family entry, limitation of rights for immigrants and widespread use of deportation powers. This was the position of the extreme right, but also of much of the ruling Christian Democratic Union (CDU). The second position recognised that settlement was irreversible, and called for policies of assimilation or integration. This was sometimes coupled with the idea that some people (Europeans) could be integrated, while others (Turks and other non-Europeans) could not. Such positions were associated with the right of the Social Democratic Party (SPD), but also with some sections of the CDU. The third and most recent position was that assimilation was no longer possible in view of the emergence of ethnic communities, and that multicultural models were needed. This view was held in the Green Party, some parts of the SPD, the churches and the trade unions (Castles, 1985; Leggewie, 1990; Tichy, 1990).

After reunification in 1990, immigration control became a major policy aim of the ruling centre-right parties. But, at the same time, the myth of not being 'a country of immigration' became unsustainable (see Bade, 1994). After the murder of several Turkish immigrants in arson attacks in Mölln in 1992 and Solingen in 1993, there were large anti-racist demonstrations all over Germany. One of the main slogans was the demand for dual citizenship. This is an important issue for Turks, who cannot easily give up their previous citizenship. In fact, there are growing numbers of people in Germany with dual or multiple citizenship, as a result of bicultural marriages. The official estimate is 1.2 million people (Beauftragte der Bundesregierung, 1993: 9). The German left now campaigns for dual citizenship, but has ambivalent attitudes towards multiculturalism. Some see it as a model for cementing the identity of ethnic groups, and for maintaining cultures perceived as anti-modern and repressive, especially towards women. Other people on the left, however, support multiculturalism as a way of enriching German cultural life (see Cohn-Bendit and Schmid, 1993; and also Leggewie, 1990).

The centre-right is also rethinking its position. From the mid-1980s, a group around then CDU General Secretary Geißler called for recognition of permanent settlement, and significant improvements in immigrant rights. The initiative was unpopular, and contributed to Geißler's dismissal from his post. More recently, some theorists of the right have called for radical changes. A book by Dieter Oberndörfer, a prominent adviser to the CDU, has called for the replacement of the nation-state by an 'open European republic', based not on ethnic belonging but on liberal-democratic principles. The key principle would be '*Verfassungspatriotismus* [constitutional patriotism], the active identification of the citizens with the political order and values of the republic' (Oberndörfer, 1993: 14).[4] This would involve a move away from the traditional German model of ethnic nationalism, in favour of civic nationalism, closer to the French approach (see Chapter 9).

German government policies remain contradictory. The myth of temporary residence still shapes the legal status of foreigners, except those from EU countries, who largely enjoy social and economic parity with German citizens. Other immigrant groups still have a marginal position. They are excluded from certain rights, and denied political participation and representation. A proposal for allowing long-standing foreign residents voting rights for local government was rejected by the Federal Constitutional Court in 1990. Yet the state cannot escape the realities of settlement. A market economy requires mobility and flexibility, and democratic societies cannot function well if large sections of the population are excluded from full participation. The current German model is not stable, and a move towards recognition of settlement and the introduction of some elements of multicultural policy seems probable in the long run (Bade, 1994).

Interaction with the society of the receiving country

The attitudes and actions of the population and state of the country of immigration have crucial effects on the migratory process. In turn, migrant community formation may modify or reinforce these effects.

In both countries the control of migrant labour by the state, and its incorporation by employers, set the conditions for settlement processes. Discrimination in hiring and promotion, non-recognition of skills and regulations explicitly designed to limit migrant workers' right to equal treatment in the labour market can be seen as forms of institutional racism.[5]

Local workers and their unions generally supported such discrimination, at least initially. In both countries there were strong traditions of opposition to foreign labour. In Australia, the labour movement supported the White Australia Policy and was hostile to all non-British immigration. German workers had been exposed to Nazi ideologies, and many had participated in racism towards Jews and Polish, Russian and other forced labourers in the Second World War. Australian unions only agreed to recruitment of Eastern and Southern Europeans in the 1940s after getting official guarantees that they would not compete with local workers for jobs and housing (Collins, 1991: 22–3). German unions demanded that foreign workers should get the same work and conditions as Germans doing the same jobs, but otherwise supported discriminatory 'guestworker' regulations, which ensured that most foreigners got inferior positions (Castles and Kosack, 1973: 129). Later on the unions in both countries realised that a split in the working class harmed local workers too, and made efforts to organise migrants and to fight the more blatant forms of exploitation, but by then discriminatory attitudes and structures were well established.

The attitude of local workers towards migrants was part of a wider picture. Many Australians were highly suspicious of foreigners. In everyday terms this meant reluctance to rent housing to migrants or to have them as neighbours, hostility towards anyone speaking a foreign language in public, mistrust of visible foreign groups and resentment towards foreign children at school. The 1960s and the 1970s were years of growing acceptance of difference and a decline in open racism, no doubt due to the recognised contribution of immigration to economic growth and prosperity. This permitted such dramatic changes as the abolition of the White Australia Policy, the first large-scale Asian entries and the introduction of multicultural polices.

In the 1980s (most notably in 1984 and again in 1988), there were attacks by various public figures and sections of the media against immigration (particularly from Asia) and multiculturalism. These corresponded with increases in racist violence mainly against Aboriginal people and Asian immigrants (HREOC, 1991). However, the

ALP Government took a strong anti-racist line, and there was considerable public support for multiculturalism. In the 1996 Federal Election, a number of right-wing candidates attacked the provision of services for Aborigines and immigrants. Pauline Hanson, an Independent Member of Parliament, became the figure-head for a populist backlash which mobilised considerable support among working-class and middle-class Australians threatened by change. This time, the newly elected Liberal-National Government did little to combat racism or to support multiculturalism. Indeed, cuts in services for Aborigines and immigrants was a part of its policy, and the onslaught on multiculturalism seemed to reflect a desire to return to a more traditional monocultural identity.

In Germany, most social groups supported the 'guestworker' system and there was little public hostility in the early stages, although there was informal discrimination, such as refusal to rent to foreigners, or exclusion from bars and dance halls. An escalation of racism came in the 1970s: unemployment of Germans was a problem for the first time since the 'economic miracle', because the foreign workers were not going home as expected but instead were bringing in their families. The Turks had become the largest and most visible group, and fear of Islam remains a powerful historical image in central European cultures. The upsurge of Third World refugee entries was exploited by the extreme right, and anti-immigrant themes were taken up by the leadership of the Christian Democratic Party (Castles, Booth and Wallace, 1984: Chapter 7; Castles, 1985). Reunification in 1990 was accompanied by vast population movements and by growing economic and social uncertainty, particularly in the area of the former GDR. The result was widespread hostility towards immigrants and an upsurge of organised racist violence.

These tendencies influenced the processes of community formation described above. The development of ethnic communities has reciprocal effects on the attitude and behaviour of the population, as well as on state policies. For people who fear the competition of migrants or who feel threatened by difference, the visible existence of such communities may confirm the idea that 'they are taking over'. Ethnic areas can become the target for organised racist attacks, and ethnic minorities can become the focus for extreme right mobilisation. On the other hand, contact with new cultures and some of their more accessible symbols, such as food and entertainment, may break down prejudices. Where ethnic small business and community efforts rehabilitate inner-city neighbourhoods, good intergroup relationships may develop.

Complex links emerge between ethnic communities and the wider society. Political parties seek cooperation with ethnic political groups of similar complexion. Local party branches in ethnic community areas need foreign members, and must take account of their needs in order to attract them. For instance, the ALP set up Greek branches in Melbourne in the 1970s. Unions need to attract immigrant members. Churches find that they must overcome barriers on both sides, and work with mosques and Islamic associations if they are to maintain their traditional social role. Artists and cultural workers of minorities and the majority find they can enrich their creativity by learning from each other. Multifaceted new social networks develop in the ethnic community areas of the cities. These give members of the majority population greater understanding of the social situation and culture of the minorities, and form the basis for movements opposed to exploitation and racism (Castles, Booth and Wallace, 1984: Chapter 8).

Similar tendencies prevail in the public sector. Both the German and the Australian state have experimented with using ethnic associations as instruments for delivery of social services, such as counselling, family welfare and youth work. Education authorities work with ethnic parents' organisations. The relationship is often an uneasy one, for aims and methods can differ widely. Government agencies may see traditionalist ethnic organisations with petit-bourgeois leaderships as effective instruments of social control of workers, young people or women. On the other hand, ethnic leaders may use their new role to preserve traditional authority, and slow down cultural and political change. The state can choose which ethnic leaders it wants to work with, and reward desired behaviour by providing patronage and funding (Jakubowicz, 1989; Castles *et al.,* 1992b: 65–71). But cooption is a two-way process: state agencies try to use ethnic community structures and associations, but have to make concessions in return.

Cooption has gone much further in Australia than in Germany, because of the acceptance of permanent settlement and the granting of citizenship. Here ethnic leaderships have a power base which is important to the state and the 'ethnic vote' is thought to affect the outcome of elections (Castles, Rando and Vasta, 1992c: 131–3). Members of ethnic communities are accepted as members of the wider society who may have special needs or interests. In Germany, members of ethnic communities lack political clout and are perceived as not really belonging to society. Indeed, recognition of ethnic community leaderships has often been seen as a way of maintaining migrants' capability of return to the country of origin, however illusory that might be.

The main expression of the Australian approach is to be found in the policy of multiculturalism, with its network of consultative bodies, special agencies and equal opportunities legislation. Even though the conservative government elected in 1996 questions multiculturalism as a principle for national identity, it is hard to see how this social policy framework could be dispensed with. In Germany, links between state and ethnic communities are far less developed. The office of the 'Plenipotentiary of the Federal Government for the Integration of Foreign Workers and their Families' has few resources and little power. Its long-time head, Liselotte Funcke, resigned in despair in mid-1991 (Nirumand, 1992: 214–18). But in the big cities with large ethnic community populations, the need for cooperation cannot be denied. In Berlin, Frankfurt and elsewhere 'commissions for foreigners' or 'offices for multicultural affairs' have been set up. These are actively seeking to build structures to work with ethnic community groups and to propagate legal and administrative reforms.

Conclusions

Many people reject the validity of a comparison between Australia and Germany, arguing that Australia is a 'classical country of immigration', which set out to build its economy and nation through settlement from overseas, while Germany is a 'historical nation' which has recruited temporary workers and is not a 'country of immigration'. This argument does not stand up to analysis. Both countries have had mass immigration. Germany has had around 20 million immigrants since 1945, one of the biggest population movements to any country ever. Australia – with immigration of over 5 million people since 1945 – has had a very high inflow relative to its fairly small population. Both countries initially recruited migrant workers in roughly the same areas at the same time. Whatever the intentions of policy-makers, both movements led to similar patterns of labour market segmentation, residential segregation and ethnic group formation. In both cases, racist attitudes and behaviour on the part of some sections of the receiving population have been problems for settlers.

Thus there are great similarities in the migratory process, despite the differences in migration policies and attitudes towards permanent settlement. In both countries we can observe the four stages of the migratory process outlined in Chapter 2. The initial stage was one of labour recruitment, although with differing expectations: temporary sojourn in the German case, settlement in the Australian one. The second stage was one of prolonging of stay and the emergence of social networks for mutual assistance among migrants. The third stage was that of family reunion, increasing orientation towards the receiving country and emergence of ethnic community institutions. In fact it is hard to clearly separate these two stages: in Australia especially, family reunion often came fairly early in the process. The fourth stage, that of permanent settlement, was reached in the 1970s in both countries.

The parallels in the migratory process in Australia and Germany are important because, if these apparently opposing examples show corresponding patterns, it should be possible also to find them for other countries, which are somewhere between these cases on the migration spectrum. But the differences are also significant and require analysis. They go back to the different historical concepts of the nation and to the intentions of the post-war migration programmes. The Australian authorities wanted permanent settlement, and went to considerable lengths to persuade the public of the need for this. Chain migration and family reunion were therefore seen as legitimate, and the model for settlement was based on citizenship, full rights and assimilation. Assimilationism eventually failed in its declared goal of cultural homogenisation, but it did provide the conditions for successful settlement and the later shift to multiculturalism.

The German government planned temporary labour recruitment without settlement, and passed this expectation on to the public. Official policies were unable to prevent settlement and community formation. But these policies (and the persistent failure to adapt them to changing conditions) did lead to marginalisation and exclusion of immigrants. The results can be summed up by saying that the Australian model led to the formation of ethnic communities which are seen as an integral part of a changing nation, while the German model led to ethnic minorities, which are not seen as a legitimate part of a nation unwilling to accept a change in its identity. This is an over-simplification, for there are ethnic minorities in Australia too: Aboriginal people and some non-European immigrant groups. All the same, the distinction between ethnic communities and minorities does apply in most cases, and captures the essential difference in the outcomes of the two models.

Herein lies the usefulness of the concept of the migratory process. It means looking at all the dimensions of migration and settlement, in relation to political, economic, social and cultural practices and structures in the societies concerned. The grasp of these complex dynamics can help us understand specific problems and events, in a way which transcends short-term and local considerations. If the architects of the post-war European 'guestworker systems' had studied the migratory process in their own histories or elsewhere, they would never have held the naive belief that they could turn flows of migrant labour on and off as if with a tap. They would have understood that movement of workers almost always leads to family reunion and permanent settlement. The very fears of permanent ethnic minorities held by some governments turned into self-fulfilling prophecies: by denying legitimacy to family reunion and settlement, governments ensured that these processes would take place under unfavourable circumstances, leading to the creation of minorities and to deep divisions in society.

9   New Ethnic Minorities and Society

The migrations of the last half century have led to growing cultural diversity and the formation of new ethnic groups in many countries. Such groups are visible through the presence of different-looking people speaking their own languages, the development of ethnic neighbourhoods, the distinctive use of urban space, and the establishment of ethnic associations and institutions. In Chapter 8 we discussed the migratory process and its outcomes in two very different immigration countries. In this chapter we will compare the position of the new ethnic communities or minorities in a wider range of Western societies.

The topic is a broad one, and should entail detailed description of the situation in each immigration country. That is not possible here for reasons of space. Instead brief summaries of the situation in selected countries – USA, Canada, United Kingdom, France, the Netherlands, Switzerland and Sweden – will be presented as 'Exhibits' within the text. The comparative analysis will draw on these, as well as on the case-studies of Australia and Germany in Chapter 8. Many of the immigration countries of Europe and of the new immigrant-receiving areas of the rest of the world are not discussed here, although there may well be parallels.

The aim of the chapter is to show similarities and differences in the migratory process, and to discuss why ethnic group formation and growing diversity have been relatively easily accepted in some countries, while in others the result has been marginalisation and exclusion. We will then go on to examine the consequences for the ethnic groups concerned and for society in general. The argument is that the migratory process works in a similar way in all countries with respect to chain migration and settlement, labour market segmentation, residential segregation and ethnic group formation. Racism and discrimination are also to be found in all countries, although their intensity varies. The main differences are to be found in state policies on immigration, settlement, citizenship and cultural pluralism. These differences, in turn, are linked to different historical experiences of nation-state formation.

212

Immigration policies and minority formation

Three groups of countries may be distinguished. The so-called 'classical immigration' countries – the USA, Canada and Australia – have encouraged family reunion and permanent settlement and treated most legal immigrants as future citizens. Sweden, despite its very different historical background, has followed similar policies. The second group includes France, the Netherlands and Britain, where immigrants from former colonies have received preferential treatment and have often been citizens at the time of entry. Permanent immigration has generally been accepted (though with some exceptions) and family reunion has been permitted. Immigrants from other European countries have had a less privileged situation, although settlement and naturalisation have often been permitted. The third group consists of those countries which have tried to cling to rigid 'guestworker' models, above all Germany and Switzerland. Belgium and Austria are similar in many ways. Such countries have tried to prevent family reunion, have been reluctant to grant secure residence status and have highly restrictive naturalisation rules.

The distinctions between these three categories are neither absolute nor static. The openness of the USA, Canada and Australia only applied to certain groups: all three countries had exclusionary policies towards Asians until the 1960s. The USA tacitly permitted illegal farmworker migration from Mexico, and denied rights to such workers. France had very restrictive rules on family reunion in the 1970s. In response to growing international competition for migrant labour in the late 1960s, Germany and Switzerland improved family reunion rules and residence status. These countries could not completely deny the reality of settlement. By the early 1980s, three-quarters of foreign residents in Switzerland had Establishment Permits (*Niederlassungsbewilligungen*), obtainable only after ten years' residence (five for some nationalities), and conferring much greater protection from deportation. Germany has a complicated system of residence 'authorisations', 'permits' and 'consents', granted to different categories of foreigners and offering differing entitlements (Frey and Mammey, 1996). There is a gradual trend towards greater rights and security.

One important change has been the erosion of the privileged status of migrants from former colonies in France, the Netherlands and Britain. Making colonised people into subjects of the Dutch or British crown, or citizens of France, was a way of legitimating colonialism. In the period of European labour shortage it also seemed a convenient

---

EXHIBIT 9.1

Minorities in the USA

US society is a complex ethnic mosaic deriving from five centuries of immigration. The white population is a mixture of the white Anglo-Saxon Protestant (WASP) group, which achieved supremacy in the colonial period, and later immigrants, who came from all parts of Europe in one of the greatest migrations in history between 1850 and 1914. Assimilation of newcomers is part of the 'American creed', but in reality this process has always been racially selective.

Native American societies were devastated by white expansion westwards. The survivors, forced into reservations, still have a marginal social situation. Millions of African slaves were brought to America from the seventeenth to the nineteenth century to labour in the plantations of the South. Their African-American descendants were kept in a situation of segregation and powerlessness, even after the abolition of slavery in 1865. After 1914, many migrated to the growing industrial cities of the north and west. Since the changes to immigration law in 1965 (see Chapter 4), new settlers have come mainly from Latin America and Asia. Hispanics are the descendants of Mexicans absorbed into the USA through its south-western expansion, as well as recent immigrants from Latin American countries. The main Asian countries of origin are the Philippines, China, South Korea, Vietnam and India.

Today the population is officially classified according to place of birth, but also according to race. In 1996, 24.6 million people (9.3 per cent of the population) were foreign-born. This compares with only 4.8 per cent in 1970, but is much lower than the 14.7 per cent foreign-born quota in 1910. A third of all the foreign-born – 7.7 million persons – lived in California in 1994. New York came second with 2.9 million and Florida third with 2.1 million foreign-born. Texas, Illinois and New Jersey all had over 1 million foreign-born residents. The table below shows the classification by race according to the 1990 Census. Ethnic minorities now make up one-fifth of the USA's population. The greatest divide in US society remains that between blacks (African-Americans) and whites. However, the number of Hispanics is rapidly approaching that of blacks. Hispanics can be of any race, but are seen as a distinct group based on language and culture and are listed separately. The Asian population is also growing fast.

The movement of Europeans and African-Americans into low-skilled industrial jobs in the first half of the twentieth century led to labour market segmentation and residential segregation. In the long run, many 'white ethnics' achieved upward mobility, while African-Americans became increasingly ghettoised. Distinctions between blacks and whites in income, unemployment rates, social conditions and education are still extreme. Like African-Americans, Hispanics and Asians are subject to complex processes of racialisation, in which racial stereotyping interacts with socio-economic position and spatial location to produce social

$\longrightarrow$

→

exclusion. Members of some recent immigrant groups, especially from Asia, have high educational and occupational levels, while most Latin Americans lack education and are concentrated in unskilled categories.

Population by race and Hispanic origin, 1990

	Millions	Per cent
White	199.7	80.3
Black	30.3	12.1
American Indian, Eskimo or Aleut	2.0	0.8
Asian or Pacific Islander	7.3	2.9
Other race	9.8	3.9
Total population	248.7	100.0
Hispanic origin (of any race)	22.4	9.0

Source: US Census Bureau, US Census Data, Database C90STF1C.

Incorporation of immigrants into economy and society has been largely left to market forces. The egalitarian character of US society has been seen as providing the best possible chances for immigrant groups to become assimilated into the 'American dream'. None the less government has played a role by making it easy to obtain US citizenship, and through education policies in which the compulsory public school has been used as a way of transmitting the English language and American values. Legislation and political action following the Civil Rights Movement of the 1950s and 1960s led to an enhanced role for a black middle class, and changes in stereotypes of blacks in the mass media. However, commitment to equal opportunities and anti-poverty measures declined during the Reagan–Bush era, leading to increased community tension. Racist violence by whites remains a serious problem for African-Americans, Hispanics, Asians and other minorities.

The increase in migrant entries in the 1980s caused anxieties about 'alien control' or loss of national identity. One reaction was the 'US English movement', which campaigned for a constitutional amendment to declare English the official language of the country. Such amendments were passed in some states, including California, where a high proportion of the population speaks Spanish as the mother tongue. In the 1990s, illegal migration and the costs of welfare for immigrants became major political issues. In 1994, Californian voters passed Proposition 187 which denied social services and education to illegal immigrants, although implementation of many of its restrictions was suspended by the courts. In September 1996 the US Congress approved a law designed to cut illegal entries, and to deny welfare benefits to both legal and illegal immigrants.

Sources: Anti-Defamation League (1988); Coffey (1987); Feagin (1989); Portes and Rumbaut (1990); *Migration News* 3:10 (October 1996); US Census Bureau (1996).

way of bringing in low-skilled labour. But citizenship for colonised peoples became a liability when permanent settlement took place and labour demand declined. All three countries have removed citizenship from their former colonial subjects (with a few exceptions) and put these people on a par with foreigners.

There has been some convergence of policies: the former colonial countries have become more restrictive, while the former guestworker countries have become less so. But this has gone hand-in-hand with a new differentiation: the EC countries granted a privileged status to intra-Community migrants in 1968. The establishment of the EU in 1993 was designed to create a unified labour market, with all EU citizens having full rights to take up employment and to obtain work-related social benefits in any member country. At the same time, entry and residence have become more difficult for non-EU nationals, especially those from outside Europe. Political discourses which portray immigration as threatening to the nation, and which conflate illegal and legal immigration, create problems for long-standing immigrants and even for their descendants born in Western Europe. Anyone who looks different becomes suspect and may forced to prove their identity as legal residents.

Immigration policies have consequences for most other areas of policy towards immigrants, such as labour market rights, political participation and naturalisation. If the original immigration policies were designed to keep migrants in the status of temporary mobile workers, then they make it likely that settlement will take place under unsatisfactory and discriminatory conditions. Moreover, official ideologies of temporary migration create expectations within the receiving population. If a temporary sojourn turns into settlement, and the governments concerned refuse to admit this, then it is the immigrants who are blamed for the resulting problems.

One of the most important effects of immigration policies is on the consciousness of migrants themselves. In countries where permanent immigration is accepted and the settlers are granted secure residence status and most civil rights, a long-term perspective is possible. Where the myth of short-term sojourn is maintained, immigrants' perspectives are inevitably contradictory. Return to the country of origin may be difficult or impossible, but permanence in the immigration country is doubtful. Such immigrants settle and form ethnic groups, but they cannot plan a future as part of the wider society. The result is isolation, separatism and emphasis on difference. Thus discriminatory immigration policies cannot stop the completion of the migratory process, but they can be the first step towards the marginalisation of the future settlers.

Labour market position

As Chapter 7 showed, labour market segmentation based on ethnicity and gender has developed in all immigration countries. This was intrinsic in the type of labour migration practised until the mid-1970s: obtaining cheaper labour or using increased labour supply to restrain wage growth was a major reason for recruiting immigrant workers. The situation has changed; new migrants are much more diverse in educational and occupational status. There is a trend towards polarisation: highly-skilled personnel are encouraged to enter, either temporarily or permanently, and are seen as an important factor in skill upgrading and technology transfer. Low-skilled migrants are unwelcome as workers, but enter through family reunion, as refugees or illegally. Their contribution to low-skilled occupations, casual work, the informal sector and small business is of great economic importance, but is officially unrecognised.

In any case, labour market segmentation is part of the migratory process. When people come from poor to rich countries, without local knowledge or networks, lacking proficiency in the language and unfamiliar with local ways of working, then their entry point into the labour market is likely to be at a low level. The question is whether there is a fair chance of later upward mobility. The answer often depends on whether the state encourages the continuation of segmentation through its own discriminatory practices, or whether it takes measures to give immigrants equal opportunities.

Again it is possible to discern three groups. Some countries have active policies to improve the labour market position of immigrants and minorities through language courses, basic education, vocational training and anti-discrimination legislation. These countries include Australia, Canada, Sweden, Britain, France and the Netherlands. The USA has a special position: there are equal opportunities, affirmative action and anti-discrimination legislation, but little in the way of language, education and training measures. This fits in with the *laissez-faire* model of social policy and with cuts in government intervention in recent times.

The former 'guestworker' countries form a third category. Although there are education and training measures for foreign workers and

EXHIBIT 9.2

Minorities in Canada

In 1991 the 4.3 million foreign-born residents made up 16 per cent of Canada's population of 27 million. The most notable feature is the increase in the Asian and American groups since 1981 (see the table below). The 1991 Census also asked respondents to state their 'ethnic origins': the largest single category was 'multiple origins' (mainly British plus some other origin) with 7.8 million people (29 per cent of the population). Of the 'single origins' French came first with 23 per cent, followed by English (15 per cent). Descent-groups between 1.5 and 3.5 per cent of the population included Scots, Irish, Germans, Italians, Chinese and Ukrainians. Aboriginal (or First Nations) peoples made up 1.7 per cent of the population.

Canadian history has been shaped by the struggle between the British and French. After 1945, separatist movements in French-speaking Quebec made language and culture into crucial areas of struggle. This led to devolution of power to the provinces and to a policy of bilingualism and two official languages. The most recent referendum on independence for Quebec was lost in 1995, mainly because of fears by First Nation people and immigrants that they would be marginalised in a Francophone state.

Legal and political conflicts on land rights and the social position of First Nation peoples play an important role in Canadian public life. The land claims of the Inuit people have been settled through the establishment of Nunavut, which will give the Inuit control of one-fifth of Canada's land mass in the Arctic region by 1999. Other groups remain socially marginalised and are struggling for recognition of their claims.

In 1971, multiculturalism was proclaimed an official policy and a Minister of State for Multiculturalism was appointed. There were two main objectives: maintaining ethnic languages and cultures and combating racism. The Canadian Human Rights Act of 1977 prohibited discrimination based on race, origin or religion. In 1982, equality rights and multiculturalism were enshrined in the Canadian Charter of Rights and Freedoms. The Employment Equity Act of 1986 required all federally regulated employers to assess the composition of their workforces, in order to correct disadvantages faced by women, visible minorities, native people and the disabled. The Multiculturalism Act of 1987 proclaimed multiculturalism as a central feature of Canadian citizenship and laid down principles for cultural pluralism.

$\longrightarrow$

→

Since the 1980s, public opinion on multiculturalism has become more negative. Community relations have deteriorated through increased discrimination against Aboriginal people and racial assaults against blacks and Asians. The unwillingness of the authorities to respond to racist attacks has been a major cause of politicisation and resistance among 'visible minorities'. In 1993 the Federal Government took steps to reduce the emphasis on multiculturalism, most notably by merging the multicultural bureaucracy into an amorphous new department called Heritage Canada.

Immigrant population by birthplace, census figures (thousands)

Country of origin	1981 total	1991 total
Europe	2 568	2 365
of which:		
United Kingdom	879	718
Italy	385	352
Germany	155	181
Poland	149	185
Portugal	139	161
America	582	701
of which:		
United States	302	249
Caribbean	173	233
South and Central America	107	151
Asia	541	1 065
of which:		
India	109	174
China	52	157
Africa	102	114
Oceania	33	38
Other and not stated	23	52
Total	3 848	4 343

Sources: Stasiulis (1988); Naidoo (1989); Breton *et al.* (1990); Immigration Canada (1991); OECD (1992; 1995: Table C1); Stasiulis and Jhappan (1995); Statistics Canada (1996).

foreign youth, there are also restrictions on labour market rights. During the period of mass labour recruitment, work permits often bound foreign workers to specific occupations, jobs or locations. Swiss rules on frontier and seasonal workers still maintain such restrictions, as do the German rules for the temporary workers from Eastern Europe recruited in the 1990s. However, the overwhelming majority of workers in the two countries have now gained long-term residence permits, which give them virtual equality of labour market rights with nationals. Long-term unemployment can under certain circumstances still lead to loss of secure residence status and eventually to deportation. This is, however, very rare.

Residential segregation, community formation and the post-modern city

Some degree of residential segregation is to be found in all the immigration countries, though nowhere is it as extreme as in the USA, where in certain areas there is almost complete separation between blacks and whites, and sometimes Asians and Hispanics too. In the other countries there are city neighbourhoods where immigrant groups are highly concentrated, though they rarely form the majority of the population. Their influence is often sufficient to bring about visible changes and to give areas a special character. Residential segregation has several causes.

Migrant workers generally start work in low-income jobs and have few savings. Often they have to remit money home. Therefore they tend to seek cheap housing in working-class areas. Proximity to work reinforces this choice of location. Many local people find housing through friends and relations, but such networks are at first not available to migrants. As a group becomes established, the earlier arrivals can assist the newcomers, which strengthens the tendency to ethnic clustering. Another factor is discrimination by landlords. Some refuse to rent to immigrants, while others make a business of charging high rents for poor accommodation. In Germany in the 1980s, some landlords crowded migrants into poorly-equipped apartments, in order to make conditions unbearable for long-standing German tenants who could not be legally evicted. When the Germans gave up and left, the foreigners were evicted too, and the block could be demolished to make way for offices or luxury housing. Such practices increased racism towards the immigrants, who became the scapegoats for ruthless urban development speculation.[1]

Institutional practices may also encourage residential segregation. Many migrant workers were initially housed by employers or public authorities. There were migrant hostels and camps in Australia, barracks provided by employers in Germany and Switzerland, and hostels managed by the government *Fonds d'Action Sociale* (FAS, or Social Action Fund) in France. These generally provided better conditions than private rented accommodation, but led to control and isolation for migrant workers. Hostels also encouraged clustering: when workers left their initial accommodation they tended to seek housing in the vicinity.

In countries where racism is relatively weak, immigrants often move out of the inner-city areas to better suburbs as their economic position improves. Sometimes a process of 'ecological succession' takes place,[2] whereby a large proportion of one immigrant group moves out over time, only to be replaced by a newer group. The replacement of Greeks by Vietnamese in Richmond (Melbourne) and Marrickville (Sydney) is a good example. However, where racism is strong, concentration persists or may even increase. In 1991, Greater London contained 58 per cent of Britain's black population and 35 per cent of those of South Asian origin. Some groups are highly concentrated in disadvantaged areas, such as housing estates inhabited mainly by Bengalis in Tower Hamlets (London). In Amsterdam, a quarter of the population belongs to ethnic minorities, such as Surinamese, Antilleans, Turks and Moroccans, and these are mainly concentrated in certain inner-city and peripheral locations. Such groups tend to have extremely high rates of unemployment: for instance, over half of all Turks in Amsterdam were jobless in 1991 (Cross, 1995).

Residential segregation is a contradictory phenomenon. In terms of the theory of ethnic minority formation set out in Chapter 2, it contains elements of both other-definition and self-definition. The relative weight of the two sets of factors varies from country to country and group to group. Immigrants cluster together for economic and social reasons arising from the migratory process, and are often forced out of certain areas by racism. But they also frequently want to be together, in order to provide mutual support, to develop family and neighbourhood networks and to maintain their languages and cultures. Ethnic neighbourhoods allow the establishment of small businesses and agencies which cater for immigrants' needs, as well as the formation of associations of all kinds (see Chapter 8). Residential segregation is thus both a precondition for and a result of community formation.

EXHIBIT 9.3

Minorities in the UK

No table is given for the UK, due to the difficulty in aggregating the foreign population and the ethnic minority population. In 1995, there were 2.1 million foreign citizens in the UK (3.5 per cent of the total population). EU citizens made up 44 per cent of the foreigners. The largest groups were the Irish (443 000), Indians (114 000), US citizens (110 000), West Africans (87 000) Caribbean and Guyana (82 000), and Pakistanis (81 000). The ethnic minority population, most of whom are British-born people of non-European ancestry, totalled about 3 million (5.5 per cent of the total population). Half of them have their origins in the Indian sub-continent (India, Pakistan and Bangladesh) and about one-fifth in the Caribbean. The overall population of immigrant origin may be estimated at about 5 million or 9 per cent of the total population.

Labour market segmentation developed in the 1950s and 1960s, with Asians and Afro-Caribbeans concentrated in the least desirable jobs. Today black workers still have mainly unskilled jobs and low average socioeconomic status. In 1995, the ethnic minority unemployment rate was 19 per cent, compared with 8 per cent for the workforce as a whole. Ethnic minorities are heavily concentrated in the most run-down inner-city areas.

Commonwealth immigrants who came before 1971 were British subjects, who enjoyed all rights once admitted. This situation was ended by the 1971 Immigration Act and the 1981 British Nationality Act, which put Commonwealth immigrants on a par with foreigners. Irish settlers

⟶

Interestingly, the countries where community formation has been able to take place most easily have been those with open and flexible housing markets, based mainly on owner occupation, such as Australia, Britain and the USA. The continental European pattern of apartment blocks owned by private landlords has not been conducive to community formation, while large publicly owned housing developments have frequently led to isolation and social problems, which are the breeding-ground for racism.

Some members of the majority population perceive residential segregation as a deliberate and threatening attempt to form 'ethnic enclaves' or 'ghettoes'. The result may be citizens' movements which campaign to keep out immigrants. For instance, the Residents' Association of Monterey Park was set up in the mid-1980s to combat the 'Chinese take-over' of a predominantly white suburb of Los Angeles. The group did well in city council elections and was able to get the

$\longrightarrow$

enjoy virtually all rights, including the right to vote. It is relatively easy for foreigners to obtain citizenship after five years of legal residence in Britain.

Since 1965, a series of Race Relations Acts has been passed, outlawing discrimination in public places, in employment and housing. A Commission for Racial Equality (CRE) was set up, to enforcement anti-discrimination laws and promote good community relations. Despite all this, black people experience institutional discrimination, and black youth allege that they are frequently subjected to police harassment.

Organised racist groups such as the National Front, grew rapidly in the 1970s. Their electoral success was limited, but they recruited members of violent youth sub-cultures, such as skinheads. Racist violence became a major problem for Asians and Afro-Caribbeans. Black youth discontent exploded into riots in inner-city areas in 1980–1 and again in 1985–6 and 1991. Such problems led to government measures in the 1980s to combat youth unemployment, to make education more accessible to minorities, to improve the conditions in urban areas and to change police practices. In the 1990s, however, there was a shift away from interventionist anti-racist policies. Instead there was a move to market-orientated approaches which emphasised service to local authority 'customers'. The role of the local state in bringing about change was severely restricted.

Sources: Home Office (1981, 1989); Banton (1985); Beynon (1986); Layton-Henry (1986); OECD (1992, 1997); Solomos (1993); Solomos and Back (1995).

council to pass a resolution declaring English to be the 'official language' of Monterey Park (Davis, 1990: 207). Such movements may be found in all immigration countries. Sometimes they constitute themselves as formal organisations, working within local political structures; in others they are more diffuse, and their members resort to racial harassment and violence.

Racism is thus a self-fulfilling prophecy: by forcing immigrants to live together for protection, it creates the very 'ghettoes' it fears. In any case many immigrants are forced by powerful social and economic factors into isolated and disadvantaged urban areas, which they share with other marginalised social groups (Dubet and Lapeyronnie, 1992). One official reaction has been dispersal policies, designed to reduce ethnic concentrations (see below).

Immigration and ethnic minority formation are transforming post-industrial cities in contradictory ways. The work of Sassen (1988) and others has shown how new forms of global organisation of finance, production and distribution lead to 'global cities'. These attract influxes of immigrants, both for highly-specialised activities and for low-skilled service jobs which service the high-income life styles of the professional workforce. In turn, this leads to a spatial restructuring of the city, in which interacting factors of socioeconomic status and ethnic background lead to rapidly changing forms of differentiation between neighbourhoods. Areas of concentration of specific immigrant groups are often the focus of conflicts with other disadvantaged sections of the population. The mobilisation by the extreme right in Belgium, France and elsewhere since the 1970s illustrates this. Areas of immigrant and ethnic minority concentration can also be the site of confrontations with the state and its agencies of social control, particularly the police (as will be discussed in Chapter 10).

Ethnic clustering and community formation may be seen as necessary products of contemporary forms of migration to the global cities. They may lead to conflicts, but they can also lead to renewal and enrichment of urban life and culture. Gilroy (1987) has taken up Castells' (1983) theory of the emergence of urban social movements, and linked it to the experience of black communities in Britain. Castells argued that such movements were locally based, and that they tended to mobilise around three central goals: (1) collective consumption (that is, of goods and services provided by the state), (2) cultural identity and (3) political self-management. Gilroy shows how each of these features can be found in the recent history of Britain's black communities. He emphasises the significance of cultural symbols (such as music) and style in drawing the boundaries of the community.

However, specific ethnic groups can never be completely isolated or self-sufficient in modern cities. Cultural and political interaction is negotiated around complex processes of inclusion and exclusion, and of cultural transference. Much of the energy and innovative capacity within the cities lies in the cultural syncretism of the multi-ethnic populations, as Davis (1990) has shown so convincingly in the case of Los Angeles. This syncretism can be seen as a creative linking and development of aspects of different cultures, in a process of community formation, which always has political dimensions. This process raises questions of burning interest about the way our cities and cultures are likely to develop in the future. Just as there can be no return to mono-ethnic populations (always a myth in any case), so there is no way back to static or homogeneous cultures. The global city with its multicultural population can be seen as a powerful laboratory for change.

Social policy

As migrants moved into the inner cities and industrial towns, social conflicts with lower-income groups of the majority population developed. Immigrants were blamed for rising housing costs, declining housing quality and deteriorating social amenities. In response, a whole set of social policies developed in most immigration countries. Sometimes policies designed to reduce ethnic concentrations and ease social tensions achieved the opposite.

Nowhere were the problems more severe than in France. After 1968, measures were taken to eliminate *bidonvilles* and make public housing more accessible to immigrants. The concept of the *seuil de tolérance* (threshold of tolerance) was introduced, according to which the immigrant presence should be limited to a maximum of 10 or 15 per cent of residents in a housing estate or 25 per cent of students in a class (Verbunt, 1985: 147–55; MacMaster, 1991: 14–28). The implication was that immigrant concentrations presented a problem, and that dispersal was the precondition for assimilation. Subsidies to public housing societies (*habitations à loyers modestes,* or HLMs) were coupled to quotas for immigrants based on the *seuil de tolérance.* The HLMs used the subsidies to build new estates, where mainly French families were housed. In order to minimise conflicts with the French, immigrant families were concentrated in run-down older estates. The HLMs could claim that they had adhered to the quotas – on an average of all their dwellings – while in fact creating new ghettoes (Weil, 1991b: 249–58).

By the 1980s, the central social policy issue was therefore the situation of ethnic minorities in the inner-city areas and in the great public housing estates constructed around the cities in the 1960s and 1970s. These were rapidly turning into areas of persistent unemployment, social problems and ethnic conflicts. Social policies focused on urban youth, and the Socialist Government developed a range of programmes. The three most important were the *zones d'Education prioritaire* (ZEP, or educational priority zones) designed to combat social inequality through educational action in areas of disadvantage; programmes to combat youth unemployment which paid special attention to youth of North African background; and the *Développement social des quartiers* (neighbourhood social development) programme aimed at improving housing and social conditions in the most run-down areas. Special measures for immigrants, especially with regard to housing, were coordinated by the FAS, with considerable

---

EXHIBIT 9.4

Minorities in France

Foreign residents made up 6.4 per cent of France's total population in 1990 (see Table 9.1). In addition there were over 1 million immigrants who had become French citizens, and up to half a million French citizens of African, Caribbean and Pacific Island origin from overseas Departments and territories.

Official policies are based on individual assimilation of immigrants, through easy naturalisation and equal social rights. In reality, however, there is considerable differentiation. EU citizens enjoy all basic rights, except the right to vote. Immigrants from non-EU European countries (such as Poland and former Yugoslavia) lack many rights, and many have an irregular legal situation. People of non-European birth or parentage (whether citizens or not) constitute the ethnic minorities. These include Algerians, Tunisians and Moroccans, young Franco-Algerians, black Africans, Turks and settlers from the overseas departments and territories. They may have formal rights as French citizens, but they still suffer socioeconomic exclusion and racism.

The *bidonvilles* (shanty-towns) which developed around French cities in the 1960s have disappeared, but there is still residential concentration in inner-city areas and in the public housing estates on the periphery of the cities. The work situation of ethnic minorities is marked by low status, insecure jobs and high unemployment rates, especially for youth. Racist discrimination and violence, especially against North Africans, have been a problem for many years.

In the 1970s, policies towards immigration (especially family reunion) became increasingly restrictive. Police raids, identity checks and deportations of immigrants convicted of even minor offences were common. In the early 1980s, the Socialist Government improved residence rights, granted an amnesty to illegals and allowed greater political participation.

$\longrightarrow$

---

financial resources (FF 1222 million in 1988: Lapeyronnie *et al.*, 1990: 65–76).

Weil concludes that the social policy measures of the 1980s failed: they were designed to achieve integration into French society, but in fact they 'linked all the problems of these towns and neighbourhoods to immigration'. Thus social policy has encouraged concentration of minorities, which slows integration, encourages the formation of ethnic communities, and strengthens group religious and cultural affiliations (Weil, 1991b: 176–9).

⟶

In the late 1980s, growing racism and serious social problems in areas of immigrant concentration led to a series of special programmes to improve housing and education and combat youth unemployment.

In the 1990s, however, the centre-right government became increasingly restrictive towards minorities. This was partly due to the increasing influence of the extreme-right FN, which regularly gets around 15 per cent of the votes in national elections, and which now controls the local authorities of several major cities. The 1993 *Loi Pasqua* tightened up immigration and nationality rules. Conditions for entry and family reunion became stricter, while deportation was facilitated. Rules on citizenship for children of immigrants tightened up. Fears about Islamic fundamentalism turned into near-panic when violence in Algeria spilled over into bomb attacks on the Paris Métro in 1995. Immigration rules were further tightened, and there were mass deportations of people in irregular situations. However, the Socialist Government elected in mid-1997 promised to restore rights to immigrants.

The position of ethnic minorities in French society has become highly politicised. Immigrants have taken an active role in major strikes, and demanded civil, political and cultural rights. Second-generation North African immigrants (known as *beurs*) and Muslim organisations are emerging political forces. Youth discontent with unemployment and police practices led to riots in Lyons, Paris and other cities in the 1980s. More recently, campaigns by the *beurs* have asserted the need for a new type of 'citizenship by participation', based on residence rather than nationality or descent. This means demanding a form of pluralism quite alien to the French assimilationist model.

Sources: Verbunt (1985); Wihtol de Wenden (1987, 1995); Noiriel (1988); Costa-Lascoux (1989); Lapeyronnie *et al.* (1990); Weil (1991b); OECD (1992): Table 9.

This is clearly a complex issue which requires careful analysis in each country. Special social policies for immigrants have often reinforced tendencies to segregation. For instance, the 'dual strategy' pursued in German education (see Chapter 8) led to special classes for foreign children, causing social isolation and poor educational performance. Housing policies in Britain are intended to be non-discriminatory, yet they have sometimes led to the emergence of 'black' and 'white' housing estates. In the Netherlands, critics of the Minorities Policy argued that culturally specific social measures may actually increase

TABLE 9.1 Foreign resident population in France, the Netherlands, Sweden and Switzerland (thousands)

Country of origin	France 1990	Netherlands 1995	Sweden 1995	Switzerland 1995
Italy	252.8	17.5	4.0	358.9
Portugal	649.7	9.2	-	134.8
Spain	216.0	16.8	2.9	101.4
UK	–	43.0	11.2	18.4
Finland	–	–	104.9	–
Poland	47.1	–	16.0	4.8
Former Yugoslavia	52.5	29.6	38.4	294.2
Algeria	614.2	–	–	–
Morocco	572.7	158.7	–	–
Tunisia	206.3	2.1	–	–
Turkey	197.7	182.1	20.3	78.6
Others	787.6	298.1	334.1	339.5
Total	3 596.6	757.1	531.8	1 330.6
Of which: EC/EU	1 311.9	193.1	n.a.	824.9

n.a. = not available.
Notes: A blank indicates that a certain country of origin is not among the main sources of immigrants for a given receiving country. Smaller groups are aggregated under 'others'.
Source: OECD (1997): Table B1.

socioeconomic marginalisation. On the other hand, in Sweden, immigrant children have the right to instruction in mother-tongue classes. The official view is that these do not lead to separation, but encourage 'active bilingualism', which makes it easier for immigrant children to succeed at school and work (Lithman, 1987). Australian 'Access and Equity' policy is designed to ensure that government services are delivered in 'culturally-appropriate' ways, so that all groups have equal access to them.

Again it is possible to suggest a rough classification of social policy responses. Australia, Canada, Sweden and the Netherlands have pursued active social policies, linked to broader models of multiculturalism (or minorities policy in the case of the Netherlands). The basic assumption has been that special social policies do not lead to separatism but, on the contrary, form the precondition for successful integration. This is because the situation of immigrants and ethnic minorities is seen as the result both of cultural and social difference, and of barriers to participation based on institutional and informal discrimination. However, as will be discussed below, multicultural policies have become controversial in all these countries in the 1990s. A second group of countries reject special social policies for immigrants. US authorities oppose special social policies for immigrants because they are seen as unnecessary government intervention. None the less, equal opportunities, anti-discrimination and affirmative action measures deriving from civil rights laws have benefited immigrants. Special social and educational measures are to be found at the local level. French governments have rejected special social policies on the principle that immigrants should become citizens, and that any special treatment would hinder that. Yet despite this there have been a number of special social policies, as already described. Britain has also developed a range of social policies in response to the urban crisis, racist violence and youth riots, despite the ideological rejection of such measures by the Conservative Government from 1979 to 97. Indeed, British policies concerning education and youth are in many respects akin to multiculturalism.

The third group of countries is, again, the former 'guestworker' recruiters. Germany has pursued contradictory and changeable polices concerning the access of immigrants to the highly-developed welfare system. In the early years, the government delegated the provision of special social services to charitable organisations linked to the churches and the labour movement. Although foreign workers were guaranteed equal rights to work-related health and pension benefits, they were excluded from some welfare rights. For example, application for social security payments on the grounds of long-term unemployment or disability could lead to deportation.

In the meantime, settlement and family reunion have made it necessary for family and youth services, education, health and care of the aged to take account of the needs of immigrants. Anti-discrimination legislation or affirmative action programmes have little place in either Germany or Switzerland: many laws specifically provide for preferential treatment of nationals over foreigners, while restrictive naturalisation rules make it hard for foreign residents to become citizens. Yet the racist violence of the early 1990s has caused German authorities to seek ways of overcoming social exclusion of immigrants, which is seen as a major factor encouraging attacks by the extreme right. On the other hand, the high costs of the 'social wage' in countries such as Germany motivates governments to exclude immigrants who may need support. 'Welfare-chauvinism' is now seen as a factor encouraging restrictive immigration policies.

EXHIBIT 9.5

Minorities in the Netherlands

In 1995, there were 757 000 foreign residents in the Netherlands: 5 per cent of the total Dutch population of 15.4 million (see Table 9.1). However, many immigrants have become citizens. The foreign-born population was 1.4 million in 1995, of whom 57 per cent were Dutch citizens. The top five countries of origin of the foreign-born were Surinam (181 000), Indonesia (180 000), Turkey (182 000), Morocco (159 000) and Germany (131 000).

In the 1960s, Mediterranean, Surinamese and Antillean workers became concentrated in unskilled jobs in manufacturing and the services. In the period of economic restructuring, they bore the brunt of unemployment. By 1994, the unemployment rate stood at 19 per cent for the foreign-born, compared with 6.4 per cent for the Netherlands-born. Certain minority groups had extremely high rates: 30 per cent for Antilleans, 31 per cent for Moroccans and 36 per cent for Turks. The ethnic minority population became overwhelmingly concentrated in urban areas, where they often live in distinct neighbourhoods. In 1990, 38 per cent of Turks, 49 per cent of Moroccans, 52 per cent of Surinamese and 27 per cent of Antilleans lived in the four biggest cities, (Amsterdam, Rotterdam, The Hague and Utrecht).

The revised Constitution of 1983 introduced municipal voting rights for resident non-citizens. The 1983 Minorities Policy was based on multicultural principles, declaring the need for social policies to integrate minorities as ethnic groups rather than as individuals. The Minorities Policy covered Mediterranean workers and their families, people of Surinamese and Antillean origins, Moluccans, refugees (but not asylum seekers), gypsies and caravan dwellers. These groups were estimated to

$\longrightarrow$

Racism and minorities

Three categories of settlers may be distinguished in immigration countries. First, some settlers have merged into the general population and do not constitute separate ethnic groups. These are generally people who are culturally and socioeconomically similar to the majority of the receiving population: for instance, British settlers in Australia, French in Switzerland and Austrians in Germany.

Second, some settlers form ethnic communities: they tend to live in certain neighbourhoods and to maintain their original languages and cultures although they are not excluded from citizenship, political participation and opportunities for economic and social mobility. The ethnic community may have developed partly due to initial discrimination, but the principal reasons for membership today are

> →

add up to 876 385 people in 1990. However, by the end of the 1980s, the Minorities Policy was being criticised on the grounds that it did little to overcome unemployment, poor educational performance and social disadvantage.

In 1994, a new Integration Policy was introduced, covering persons of Turkish, Moroccan, Surinamese and Antillean descent, as well as refugees. The new policy aims at reducing social and economic deprivation, and has two elements: a 'newcomers' or 'reception policy', and an 'integration policy'. The newcomers policy consists of Dutch language courses, social orientation and vocational training, plus individual case-management to secure entry into further education or the labour market. Immigrants who fail to participate may be deprived of social security benefits. Integration policy is concerned with improving the educational and labour market position of minority youth, and ameliorating the safety and the living conditions of neighbourhoods.

Citizenship is fairly easy to obtain, with a five-year qualification period. Dual nationality has been accepted since 1991, which led to a sharp rise in the number of naturalisations. The Netherlands has laws which prohibit racial defamation, incitement to racial hatred, discrimination and violence, and discrimination at work or in public places. Organisations which call for racial discrimination can be forbidden. None the less racism and racist violence are still problems in the Netherlands. Extreme-right anti-immigrant groups, which blame unemployment on immigrants and carry out campaigns for repatriation, have been able to secure representation in Parliament.

Sources: Entzinger (1985); European Parliament (1985); Hira (1991); Muus (1991, 1995); OECD (1997): 131–6.

cultural and psychological. Examples are Italians in Australia, Canada or the USA; the Irish in Britain; and people of Southern European background in France or the Netherlands.

Third, some settlers form ethnic minorities. Like the ethnic communities they tend to live in certain neighbourhoods and to maintain their languages and cultures of origin. But, in addition, they usually share a disadvantaged socioeconomic position and are partially excluded from the wider society by such factors as weak legal status, refusal of citizenship, denial of political and social rights, ethnic or racial discrimination, racist violence and harassment. Examples are Asian immigrants in Australia, Canada or the USA; Hispanics in the USA; Afro-Caribbeans and Asians in Britain; North Africans and Turks in most Western European countries; and asylum seekers of non-European background just about everywhere.

All the countries examined have all three categories, but our concern here is with the second and third categories. It is important to examine why some immigrants take on the character of ethnic communities, while others become ethnic minorities. A further important question is why a far larger proportion of immigrants take on minority status in some countries than in others. Two groups of factors appear relevant: those connected with characteristics of the settlers themselves, and those connected with the social structures, cultural practices and ideologies of the receiving societies.

Looking at the settlers, it is inescapable that phenotypical difference (skin-colour, racial appearance) is the main marker for minority status. A survey carried out on behalf of the Commission of the European Community in all member countries in 1989 indicated widespread acceptance of fellow Europeans. However, there were strong feelings of distance and hostility towards non-Europeans, particularly Arabs, Africans and Asians. Overall one European in three believed that there were too many people of another nationality or race in his or her country, with such feelings being most marked in Belgium and Germany (Commission of the European Communities, 1989). This emphasis on phenotypical difference applies even more if non-immigrant minorities, such as aboriginal peoples in the USA, Canada and Australia, or African-Americans in the USA, are included. They, together with non-European immigrants, make up the most marginalised ethnic groups in all the countries.

There are four possible explanations for this: phenotypical difference may coincide with recent arrival, with cultural distance, with socio-economic position, or, finally, it may serve as a target for racism.

The first explanation is partly correct: in many cases, black, Asian or Hispanic settlers are among the more recently arrived groups. Historical studies reveal examples of racism and discrimination against white immigrants quite as virulent as against non-whites today (see Chapter 3 above). It may be that recent arrival makes a group appear more threatening to the majority population. New groups may also tend to compete more with local low-income groups for entry-level jobs and cheap housing. But recent arrival cannot explain why aboriginal populations are victims of exclusionary practices, or why African-Americans and other long-standing minorities are discriminated against. Neither can it explain why racism against white immigrant groups tends to disappear in time, while that against non-whites continues over generations.

What about cultural distance? Its significance depends partly on how culture is defined. Many non-European settlers come from rural areas with pre-industrial cultures, and may find it hard to adapt to industrial or post-industrial cultures. But the same applied to most post-1945 Southern European migrants to industrial countries. Today many Asian settlers in North America and Australia are of urban background and highly educated. This does not protect them from racism and discrimination. If culture is defined in terms of language, religion and values, then some non-European migrants are clearly different from the receiving populations. The largest non-European groups are often of Islamic background. Fear of Islam has a tradition going back to the mediaeval crusades. In recent years, fears of fundamentalism and loss of modernity and secularity have played a major role. But it could be argued that such fears are based on racist ideologies rather than social realities. The strengthening of Muslim affiliations is often a protective reaction of discriminated groups, so that fundamentalism is something of a self-fulfilling prophecy. In any case, some non-European migrants, such as Afro-Caribbeans in Britain, share the language and many of the cultural values of the immigration countries. Again this has proved no protection from discrimination or racism.

As for the third explanation, phenotypical difference does indeed frequently coincide with socioeconomic status. Some immigrants from less-developed countries do lack the education and vocational training necessary for upward mobility in industrial economies. But even highly-skilled immigrants may encounter hostility and discrimination. Many immigrants discover that they can only enter the labour market at the bottom, and that it is hard to move upwards subsequently. Thus low socioeconomic status is as much a result of processes of marginalisation as it is a cause of minority status.

We may therefore conclude that recentness of arrival is only a partial and temporary explanation of minority status, and that cultural difference and socioeconomic status are not adequate explanations on their own. The most significant explanation of minority formation lies in practices of exclusion by the majority populations and the states of the immigration countries. We refer to these practices as *racism* and to their results as the *racialisation* of minorities (see Chapter 2). Traditions and cultures of racism are strong in all European countries and former European settler colonies. The increased salience of racism and racist violence since the late 1970s is linked to growing insecurity for many people resulting from rapid economic and social change.

EXHIBIT 9.6

Minorities in Switzerland

In 1995, the 1.3 million foreign residents made up 19 per cent of the total population of Switzerland, the highest immigrant quota in Europe (except for Luxembourg: see Table 9.1). In 1995, there were 734 000 foreign resident workers, compared with 670 000 in 1990. However the number of seasonal workers declined from 121 700 in 1990 to 53 700 in 1995. The number of daily cross-frontier commuters declined from 181 300 in 1990 to 151 000 in 1995.

Foreign workers make up 26 per cent of the Swiss labour force. Workers from the Mediterranean basin have become concentrated in manual employment, while Swiss workers, and also immigrants from Germany, Austria and France, generally have white-collar and supervisory positions. Unemployment for workers from the Mediterranean countries is above the Swiss average, although very low compared with rates in other countries. Foreign residents have become concentrated in certain housing areas, but there are no areas of extreme social disadvantage.

The Swiss authorities still declare that Switzerland is not a country of immigration, although most immigrants have been in the country for many years. All foreign residents are denied political rights, in particular the right to vote, and foreigners are kept under surveillance by the *Fremdenpolizei* (foreigners' police). Employers and landlords have to report changes of job or residence to the authorities. Citizenship is extremely hard to obtain. The waiting period is twelve years, which must have been spent in the same canton: very high fees are charged in some cantons: and the authorities carry out rigorous examinations to ensure that an applicant is 'sufficiently assimilated'. Children of immigrants born in Switzerland have no automatic right to citizenship and can be deported.

In accordance with the Swiss *laissez-faire* tradition of leaving social issues to market forces and self-regulation, there are no special social policies for immigrants. Provision of support in emergency situations is left largely to voluntary efforts. Anti-racist and anti-discrimination legislation or affirmative action programmes have no place in the Swiss model.

Latent racism is widespread, forming the basis for institutional and informal discrimination. One expression of hostility towards immigrants has been a series of referenda, starting in 1965, designed to combat *Überfremdung* (foreign penetration) by limiting immigration and the number of foreign residents. In 1982, a new Aliens Law which would have led to minor improvements in the legal status of foreign residents was narrowly defeated in a referendum. In 1992, Swiss voters rejected joining the European Economic Area (linking EU and EFTA countries) which would have meant free movement of citizens of member countries.

Sources: Castles, Booth and Wallace (1984); Hoffmann-Nowotny (1985); OECD (1992, 1997).

Racism and racist violence

German reunification in 1990 was followed by an outburst of racist violence. Neo-Nazi groups attacked refugee hostels and foreigners on the streets, sometimes to the applause of bystanders. At first the violence was worst in the area of the former GDR, but in 1992 and 1993 several Turkish immigrants were killed in arson attacks in West Germany. Altogether 2600 racially-motivated acts of violence were officially recorded in 1992, leading to 17 deaths (Baringhorst, 1995: 225). But such incidents are neither new nor confined to Germany: racist harassment and attacks have become major issues in all the countries of immigration.

In Britain, racist violence led by the National Front and the British Movement became a problem from the 1970s. In London 2179 racial incidents were reported to the police in 1987, including 270 cases of serious assault, 397 of minor assault, 483 of criminal damage, 47 of arson and 725 of abusive behaviour. A survey in Glasgow found that 49 per cent of Pakistanis and 55 per cent of Indians had experienced damage to their property, 80 per cent of both groups had experienced racial abuse, and 18 per cent of Pakistanis and 22 per cent of Indians had experienced physical attack (Home Office, 1989). Only a small proportion of attacks ever get reported to the police, partly because many black people have experienced racist treatment by the police (Gordon, 1986; Institute of Race Relations, 1987).

In France, there was a series of murders of North Africans in 1973. In the 1980s and 1990s, the extreme-right FN was able to mobilise resentments caused by unemployment and urban decline, and to crystallise them around the issues of immigration and cultural difference. Although the FN does not openly advocate violence, it calls for immigration control, blames immigrants for crime and social problems, and creates an atmosphere conducive to racist attacks.

The USA has a long history of white violence against African-Americans. Despite the anti-racist laws secured by the civil rights movement, the Ku Klux Klan is still a powerful force. Asians, Arabs and other minorities are also frequent targets (Anti-Defamation League, or ADL, 1988). Police violence against minorities is common. The Los Angeles riots of May 1992 were provoked by police brutality towards a black motorist, which went unpunished by the courts.

Even countries which pride themselves on their tolerance, like Canada, Sweden and the Netherlands, report a growing incidence of racist attacks. In the mid-1980s, the European Parliament's Committee

---

EXHIBIT 9.7

Minorities in Sweden

Until 1945 Sweden was a fairly homogeneous country, with only a small aboriginal minority: the Sami or Lapps (about 10 000 people today). After 1945, labour migration was encouraged. Foreign worker recruitment was stopped in 1972, but family reunion and refugee entries continued. In 1995, the 532 000 foreign residents made up 5.2 per cent of Sweden's population (see Table 9.1). In fact 936 000 persons had been born abroad, but over half had acquired Swedish citizenship. Including children born in Sweden to at least one immigrant parent, the population of immigrant origin is 1.6 million, or about 15 per cent of the population! A third of the foreign population are non-Europeans (mainly refugees from the Middle East, Africa and Latin America).

Immigrant workers are overrepresented in manufacturing, and in lower-skilled services occupations. They are underrepresented in agriculture, health care and social work, administrative and clerical work, and commerce. In 1993, unemployment in Sweden reached a historical peak of 8 per cent. The rate for foreigners was 21 per cent, while for non-Europeans it reached 37 per cent. Immigrants have mainly settled in the cities, and people of the same nationality cluster in certain neighbourhoods, allowing linguistic and cultural maintenance.

The waiting period for naturalisation is two years for Scandinavians and five years for everybody else, while children born to foreign resident parents can obtain Swedish citizenship upon application. In 1975, Parliament set out an immigrant policy with three basic objectives: *equality*, which refers to giving immigrants the same living standards as Swedes; *freedom of choice*, which means giving members of ethnic minorities a

---

of Inquiry into Fascism and Racism in Europe found that 'immigrant communities . . . are daily subject to displays of distrust and hostility, to continuous discrimination . . . and in many cases, to racial violence, including murder' (European Parliament, 1985). A decade later, such aggressions had become so commonplace that they barely made the headlines. According to a study of racist violence in Europe: 'By the early 1990s, many groups of people have had to face racist violence and harassment as a threatening part of everyday life' (Björgo and Witte, 1993: 1). These groups included immigrants and asylum seekers, but also long-standing minorities such as Jews and gypsies.

The escalation of racist violence has not gone unchallenged. In Germany the violence of the early 1990s led to mass candle-light protest marches (known as *Lichterketten*), as well as to media campaigns and statements by public figures (Baringhorst, 1995). Anti-racist

→

choice between retaining their own cultural identities or assuming Swedish cultural identity; and *partnership,* which implies that minority groups and Swedes benefit from working together. Since 1975, foreign residents have had the right to vote and stand for election in local and regional elections. It was planned to extend such rights to national elections, but it proved impossible to get the parliamentary majority required for a change in the constitution.

In 1986, an Act Against Ethnic Discrimination came into force, and an Ombudsman Against Ethnic Discrimination was appointed. A new anti-discrimination law was passed by Parliament in 1994. Immigrants enjoy the benefits of Sweden's highly-developed welfare state, as well as a number of special services. New immigrants have the right to 400 hours of Swedish instruction with financial assistance. Children of immigrants can receive pre-school and school instruction in their own language, within the normal curriculum. Other measures include translator and interpreter services, information services, grants to immigrant organisations and special consultative bodies.

The increase in asylum-seeker entry in the late 1980s led to strains in housing and other areas. The extreme-right *Sverigepartiet* (SP, or the Sweden Party) started anti-immigrant campaigns in 1986. In 1988, a referendum in the small town of Sjöbo decided to keep refugees out. This was followed by an increase in racist violence, including arson and bomb attacks on refugee centres. From 1989, the government introduced a series of measures to restrict the entry of asylum seekers. In 1992 the inflow – particularly from former Yugoslavia – peaked at 84 000, but had declined to 9000 by 1995.

Sources: Hammar (1985b); Lithman (1987); Nobel (1988); Ålund and Schierup (1991); Larsson (1991); OECD (1995, 1997).

movements developed in most countries quite early in the settlement process, often based on coalitions between minority organisations, trade unions, left-wing parties, churches and welfare organisations. Anti-racist organisations have influenced government policies, often helping to bring about equal opportunities and anti-discrimination legislation, as well as policies and agencies designed to curb violence. However, the anti-racist movement was not effective in preventing the increase in racist violence in the early 1990s, though it may have prevented matters getting even worse. One reason for the limited success is that politicians often pay lip-service to anti-racism, while at the same time supporting discourses which put the blame for social evils on ethnic minorities.

The political implications of anti-immigrant campaigns and of the varying responses by members of ethnic minorities and by other groups will be discussed in Chapter 10. Racist campaigns, harassment and violence are important factors in the process of ethnic minority formation. By isolating minorities and forcing them into defensive strategies, racism may lead to various types of self-organisation and separatism, and even encourage religious fundamentalism. Conversely, anti-racist action may help overcome the isolation of minorities, and facilitate their social and political incorporation into mainstream society.

Minorities and citizenship

Why do some countries turn most of their settlers into ethnic minorities, while others marginalise only far more limited groups? The answer does not lie primarily in the characteristics of the migrants, but rather in the histories, ideologies and structures of the societies concerned. Varying models of the nation-state lead to different concepts of citizenship (see Chapter 2). Some countries of immigration make it very difficult for immigrants to become citizens, others grant citizenship but only at the price of cultural assimilation, while a third group makes it possible for immigrants to become citizens while maintaining distinct cultural identities.

Citizenship is more than just formal status, as demonstrated by possession of a passport. It is important to consider the contents of citizenship, in terms of civil, political and social rights. Moreover possession of citizenship is not an either/or question. With increasing length of residence, immigrants sometime acquire forms of 'quasi-citizenship', which confer some, but not all, rights of citizenship. One important form of quasi-citizenship is the citizenship of the EU, introduced through the 1991 Maastricht Treaty. The rules for becoming a citizen in various countries are complex and have undergone considerable change in recent years (see the excellent overviews provided by Çinar, 1994; Guimezanes, 1995).

Laws on citizenship or nationality derive from two competing principles: *ius sanguinis* which is based on descent from a national of the country concerned, and *ius soli* which is based on birth in the territory of the country. *Ius sanguinis* is often linked to an ethnic or folk model of the nation-state (typical of Germany and Austria, for instance), while *ius soli* generally relates to a nation-state built through incorporation of diverse groups on a single territory (such as the UK), or through immigration (USA, Canada, Australia, Latin American countries). In practice, all modern states have citizenship rules based on a combination of *ius sanguinis* and *ius soli*, although one or the other may be clearly predominant.

Naturalisation of immigrants

Table 9.2 shows the number of naturalisations and the 'naturalisation rate' (naturalisations per thousand foreign residents) in various countries.

Table 9.2 shows a clear trend towards increasing naturalisation of foreign residents: numbers and rates were higher in all countries (except the UK) in 1995 compared with 1988. The absolute number of naturalisations in both years was highest in the classical immigration

TABLE 9.2   Naturalisations in selected countries, 1988 and 1995

Country	Number of naturalisations 1988	Naturalisation rate 1988	Number of naturalisations 1995	Naturalisation rate 1995
Australia	81 218	57	114 757	74
Belgium	8 366	10	26 109	29
Canada	58 810	n.a.	227 720	n.a.
France	46 351	13	59 988	17
Germany (FRG)	16 660	4	31 888	5
Japan	5 767	6	14 104	10
Netherlands	9 110	14	71 440	98
Sweden	17 966	43	31 993	60
Switzerland	11 356	11	16 795	12
UK	64 600	35	40 500	19
USA	242 063	n.a.	445 853	n.a.

n.a. = not available.
Notes: The naturalisation rate is defined as the number of naturalisations per thousand foreign residents. The calculated naturalisation rate for Australia is based on an estimate for foreign resident population, assuming that 60 per cent of overseas-born persons are Australian citizens. The naturalisation rates for France is calculated using the foreign resident population figure for 1990. The German naturalisation figure excludes naturalisation based on legal entitlement, which applies mainly to 'ethnic Germans' from Eastern Europe. The comparison has only indicative value, as definitions and procedures vary from country to country.
Sources: Australian Census 1996 preliminary figures; OECD (1997): Table III.1, Tables A.1, B3, and C5.

countries of Australia, Canada and the USA. Australia's naturalisation rate is very high. It has not been possible to calculate rates for the USA and Canada, due to lack of data on the foreign resident population. However, the very large numbers of naturalisations make it reasonable to assume high rates in these countries too. In several European countries, notably Sweden and the Netherlands, naturalisation rates have increased sharply, so that there are now as many naturalised immigrants as foreign citizens present. This represents changes in rules (such as acceptance of dual citizenship in the Netherlands) and conscious efforts to encourage immigrants to become citizens. However, naturalisation rates remain very low in Germany, Japan and Switzerland, and fairly low in Belgium, the UK and France.

A very important criterion for naturalisation is whether an applicant can become a dual citizen. This has become a major political issue in Germany (see Chapter 8). People cling to their original affiliation for both practical and emotional reasons. Renouncing it may block return upon retirement, or lead to loss of rights to land ownership. Dual citizenship seems an appropriate way of managing the multiple identities which arise from globalisation. The principle of singular citizenship is in fact being eroded everywhere by mixed marriages. In many countries, the nationality of a child born abroad used only to be transmitted through the father. Such rules were changed to achieve equality of the sexes in the 1970s and 1980s. Once mothers obtain the same right to transmit their nationality as fathers, bi-national marriages automatically lead to dual citizenship.

Austria, Denmark, Finland, Germany, Japan, Luxembourg, Norway and Sweden legally require renunciation of the former nationality upon naturalisation, while other OECD countries, including Australia, Canada, France, the UK and the USA, permit dual citizenship (Guimezanes, 1995: 165). However, law and actual practice are often at odds: Sweden, for instance, generally accepts dual citizenship in practice. According to Çinar (1994: 62), 'the availability of dual citizenship has now become a matter of course in Western Europe'. This represents a major shift since 1963, when most European countries signed the Strasbourg Convention on the Reduction of Cases of Multiple Nationality. The burgeoning of multiple citizenships is a challenge to the traditional nation-state model.

Legal requirements for naturalisation (such as 'good character', regular employment, language proficiency, evidence of integration) seem quite similar in various countries, but actual practices are very different. Germany and Switzerland impose long waiting periods and complex bureaucratic practices, and make it clear to applicants that naturalisation is an act of grace by the state. At the other end of the spectrum, classical immigration countries encourage newcomers to become citizens. The Australian Government declared a Year of Citizenship in 1989, while Vice-President Gore launched a *Citizenship USA* drive in April 1995. About 1.2 million persons were naturalised in financial year 1996, more than twice as many as in the previous year (*Migration News*, 3:10, October 1996). In Texas, 10 000 new citizens were sworn in at once through mass ceremonies at the Dallas Cowboys' football stadium and 6000 at the Houston convention centre (*Guardian Weekly*, 22 September 1996). The act of becoming American (or Australian or Canadian) is seen as an occasion for celebration and part of the national myth. In contrast, to be German (or Austrian or Swiss) means to have been born so, and naturalisation is still an exception.

Status of the second generation

The transmission of citizenship to the second generation (the children of the original immigrants) and subsequent generations is the key issue for the future. National variations parallel those found with regard to naturalisation. In principle, *ius soli* countries confer citizenship on all children born in their territory. *Ius sanguinis* countries confer citizenship only on children of existing citizens. However, most countries actually apply models based on a mixture of the two principles. Increasingly entitlement to citizenship grows out of long-term residence in the country: the *ius domicili*.

Ius soli is applied most consistently in Australia, Canada, New Zealand, the USA, the UK and Ireland. A child born to immigrant parents in the USA becomes a US citizen, even if the parents are visitors or illegal residents. In Australia, Canada and the UK, the child obtains citizenship if at least one of the parents is a citizen or a legal permanent resident. Such countries only use the *ius sanguinis* principle to confer citizenship on children born to their citizens while abroad (Çinar, 1994: 58–60; Guimezanes, 1995: 159).

A combination of *ius soli* and *ius domicili* has emerged in France, Italy, Belgium and the Netherlands. Children born to foreign parents in the territory obtain citizenship, providing they have been resident for a certain period, and fulfil other conditions. Until 1993, France automatically conferred citizenship upon children born to foreign parents in France provided they had lived there for at least five years before reaching the age of 18. The 1993 *Loi Pasqua* changed this rule. Now young foreigners born in France have to declare their wish for citizenship at the age of 18, and it can be rejected on grounds of criminal convictions or prior deportation orders. Also removed in 1993 was the right of foreign parents to apply for naturalisation of their children born in France, even if they did not themselves wish to be naturalised. This created an insecure situation for some young immigrants, who could be forced to leave France if their parents depart (Çinar, 1994: 60). None the less, in all these countries, the great majority of the second generation do become citizens.

France, Belgium and the Netherlands also apply the so-called 'double *ius soli*': children born to foreign parents, at least one of whom was also born in the country acquire citizenship at birth. This means that members of the 'third generation' automatically become citizens, unless they specifically renounce this right upon reaching the age of majority (Çinar, 1994: 61).

Ius sanguinis is still the dominant legal principle in most European countries as well as in Japan (Guimezanes, 1995: 159). However, in Western Europe, only Austria and Switzerland still apply the principle strictly: children born in these countries to foreign parents have no entitlement to citizenship, even if they have lived there all their lives (Çinar, 1994: 68–9). Other *ius sanguinis* countries have taken cautious steps towards *ius domicili*. This means giving an *option* of facilitated naturalisation to young people of immigrant origin. Foreigners who have been resident in Sweden for five years before reaching the age of 16, and who have lived there since that age, can become citizens by declaration between the ages of 21 and 23. The 1990 German Foreigners Law gave an entitlement to naturalisation to young foreigners who apply between the ages of 16 and 23, have been resident in the country for at least eight years, have completed six years of schooling in Germany, and have not incurred any serious convictions. However, the value of this reform was undermined by prohibition of dual citizenship, even though many exceptions are made. Similar rules also exist in Belgium (Çinar, 1994: 61; Guimezanes, 1995: 178).

Overall, the distinction between *ius sanguinis* and *ius soli* countries remains significant. In the former, children who have been born and grow up in the country may be denied not only security of residence, but also a clear national identity. They are formally citizens of a country they may have never seen, and can even be deported there in certain circumstances. In countries with *ius soli* the second generation still generally have multiple cultural identities, but they have a secure legal basis on which to make decisions about their life perspectives. Dual citizenship seems the best solution, as it would avoid decisions which can be extremely difficult for many individuals.

Linguistic and cultural rights

Maintenance of language and culture is seen as a need and a right by most settler groups. Many of the associations set up in the processes of ethnic community formation are concerned with language and culture: they teach the mother tongue to the second generation, organise festivals and carry out rituals. Language and culture not only serve as means of communication, but take on a symbolic meaning which is central to ethnic group cohesion. In most cases, language maintenance applies in the first two to three generations, after which there is a rapid decline. The significance of cultural symbols and rituals may last much longer.

Many members of the majority see cultural difference as a threat to a supposed cultural homogeneity and to national identity. Migrant languages and cultures become symbols of otherness and markers for discrimination. Giving them up is seen as essential for success and integration in the country of immigration. Failure to do so is regarded as indicative of a desire for separatism. Hostility to different languages and cultures is rationalised with the assertion that the official language is essential for economic success, and that migrant cultures are inadequate for a modern secular society. The alternative view is that migrant communities need their own languages and cultures to develop identity and self-esteem. Cultural maintenance helps create a secure basis which assists group integration into the wider society, while bilingualism brings benefits in learning and intellectual development.

Policies and attitudes on cultural and linguistic maintenance vary considerably. Some countries have histories of multilingualism. Canada's policy of bilingualism is based on two 'official languages', English and French. Multicultural policies have led to limited recognition of – and support for – immigrant languages, but they have hardly penetrated into mainstream contexts, such as broadcasting. Switzerland has a multilingual policy for its founding languages, but does not recognise immigrant languages, and neither does it provide much in the way of language services (Belgium is similar). Australia and Sweden both accept the principle of linguistic and cultural maintenance. They provide a wide range of language services (interpreting, translating, mother-tongue classes) and support for ethnic community cultural organisations. Both countries have multicultural education policies. Australia has a 'national policy on languages', concerned with both community languages and languages of economic significance. Multicultural radio and television are funded by the government.

In the USA, language has become a contentious issue. The tradition of monolingualism is being eroded by the growth of the Hispanic community: in major cities like Los Angeles and Miami, the number of Spanish speakers is overtaking that of English speakers. This led to a backlash in the late 1980s, in the form of 'the US English movement' which called for a constitutional amendment to declare English the official language. Several states passed referenda to introduce this measure, but it proved extremely hard to implement, and public agencies and private companies continued to provide multilingual information material and services. Monolingualism is also the basic principle in France, Britain, Germany and the Netherlands. None the less, all these countries have been forced to introduce language services to take account of migrant needs in communicating with courts, bureaucracies and health services. The multilingual character of inner-city school classes has also led to special measures for integration of immigrant children, and to a gradual shift towards multicultural education policies in some areas.

Minorities and nation

On the basis of the preceding comparisons, it is possible roughly to divide the immigration countries into three categories (see Castles, 1995).

The differential exclusionary model

Differential exclusion is to be found in countries in which the dominant definition of the nation is that of a community of birth and descent (referred to as the 'folk or ethnic model' in Chapter 2). The dominant group is unwilling to accept immigrants and their children as members of the nation. This unwillingness is expressed through exclusionary immigration policies (especially limitation of family reunion and refusal to grant secure residence status), restrictive naturalisation rules and the ideology of not being countries of immigration. Differential exclusion means that immigrants are incorporated into certain areas of society (above all the labour market) but denied access to others (such as welfare systems, citizenship and political participation). Immigrants become ethnic minorities, which are part of civil society (as workers, consumers, parents, and so on) but are excluded from full participation in economic, social, cultural and political relations. Since such ethnic minorities are usually socioeconomically disadvantaged, there is a strong and continuing link between class and ethnic background.

The differential exclusion model applies to former 'guestworker' recruiting countries in Western Europe, such as Germany and Austria. It also fits some newer immigration countries, such as the Gulf oil states, Japan and several NICs in Asia (see Chapter 6). A variant is to be found in countries such as Switzerland, which have developed as nations with more than one 'founding group'. The historical arrangements developed to deal with this have led to delicate balances that make it hard to incorporate new groups.

The assimilationist model

Assimilation may be defined as the policy of incorporating migrants into society through a one-sided process of adaptation: immigrants are expected to give up their distinctive linguistic, cultural or social characteristics and become indistinguishable from the majority population. The role of the state is to create conditions favourable to this process, through insistence on use of the dominant language and attendance at normal schools for migrant children. In most cases, explicit assimilation policies have been abandoned over time, and replaced with 'integration policies'. This happened in the 1960s in Australia, Canada and Britain as it became clear that immigrants were becoming concentrated into particular occupations and residential areas, and were forming ethnic communities. Integration strategies stress that adaptation is a gradual process in which group cohesion plays an important part. None the less, the final goal is still absorption into the dominant culture, so that integration policies are often simply a slower and gentler form of assimilation.

Essentially the assimilationist model permits people who have become members of civil society to join the nation and the state at the price of cultural assimilation. The assimilationist model has been applied in all highly developed immigration countries to some extent. In some countries there has been an evolution, starting with differential exclusion, progressing to assimilationism, moving on to ideas of gradual integration, and finally leading to pluralist models (Australia is a case in point). Today, of all the highly developed immigration countries, France probably comes closest to the assimilation model (see below). Some European immigration countries are ambivalent: policies of assimilation in some areas (such as labour market or social policy) may coexist with pluralism in other sectors (for instance, education and cultural policy). To make matters even more complicated, policies may differ for varying categories of immigration (based on origins, characteristics of immigrants, and so on).

In some cases, assimilationism seems to derive from a merging of what we referred to as the 'imperial model' and the 'republican model' in Chapter 2. The countries concerned, France, Britain and the Netherlands, all have aspects of both models, albeit in different respects. All three were imperial powers, which turned colonial subjects into citizens. France introduced the notion of citizenship as a political community after the 1789 Revolution, yet its policies towards colonised peoples maintained elements of the 'imperial model'. Britain and the Netherlands have moved away from the 'imperial model' as their empires have crumbled after 1945. Introduction of a more modern form of citizenship, based on membership of the political community, often meant depriving former colonial subjects of citizenship. The ambiguity of the situation of minorities reflects the contradictory and transitional nature of these post-imperial states.

A closer look at the republican model in France shows some of its contradictions. The essence of the republican model is to be found in the first report of the official *Haut Conseil à L'Intégration* (High Council for Integration, or HCI) which was established in 1990:

> French conceptions of integration should obey a logic of equality and not a logic of minorities. The principles of identity and equality which go back to the Revolution and the Declaration of Rights of Man and of Citizens impregnate our conception, thus founded on the equality of individuals before the law, whatever their origin, race, religion . . . to the exclusion of an institutional recognition of minorities. (HCI, 1991: 10, quoted here from Lloyd, 1991: 65)

The central idea is that immigrants can (and should) become integrated into the political community as French citizens, and that this will bring about cultural integration. There is therefore no room for long-term cultural or ethnic diversity. Exponents of the model see France as temporarily multi-ethnic, but not as permanently multi-cultural. According to Weil (1991b), citizenship is essentially a political relationship, most simply expressed by the statement: *'Celui qui vote est français et citoyen'* ('a person who votes is French and a citizen'). Any granting of rights (such as local voting rights) to non-citizens means watering down this principle, and could lead to new identifications, not only by migrants but also by French people, on the basis of 'origins, blood, race or culture'. In this view, rights for minorities lead directly to racism. Despite the emphasis on political integration, the implication of cultural homogenisation is very strong. Weil argues that naturalisation presupposes a form of 'socialisation' leading to 'a collection of social roles based on cultural dispositions adequate to permit an understanding for the state and of civic matters'. He goes on to lament that the 'great Republican institutions' have become too weak to carry out this socialisation function and to produce national identity (Weil, 1991b: 300–2; see also Schnapper, 1994).

It is obvious that the republican model is unlike the German model of citizenship based on ethnicity. But it is also quite distinct from the US model, in which nation building has been based on immigration. France embodies a paradox: on the one hand it represents the model of the 'completed nation'[3] (on the basis of antiquity of its formation, the homogeneity of its population, and the rigidity of its political frameworks) but, on the other hand, it has been obliged to resort to massive immigration, which has transformed the composition of its original population (Noiriel, 1988: 334–6). This implies a certain instability in the French model, since it is based on the absurdity of believing that immigrants who become French citizens lose their distinct ethnic or cultural characteristics by virtue of this fact.

The relationship between citizenship and cultural difference has become an area of struggle. In the 1980s, immigration organisations called for municipal voting rights, which were seen as a form of quasi-citizenship. The demand was rejected by the state, because it was seen as a threat to the supposedly unitary and egalitarian nature of citizenship (compare Costa-Lascoux, 1989: 115–44). By the 1990s, new movements had developed out of struggles by second-generation immigrants against racism and for improvements in housing, education and vocational training (Poinsot, 1993).

Their critique of the republican model had two aspects. First, they pointed out that the concept of *citoyen* proclaimed by the 1789 Revolution was based purely on residence on French territory, had nothing to do with culture and was granted even to non-nationals (Bouamama, 1988; Bouamama, Cordeiro and Roux, 1992; compare also Wihtol de Wenden, 1987: 44). *Citoyenneté* and *nationalité* were almost antithetical concepts.[4] Citizenship should therefore be automatically granted to all permanent immigrants, and dual citizenship should be accepted. Second, they argued that the ideal of equality of rights embodied in citizenship is a dead letter for people who are socioeconomically marginalised and victims of racism. It is unrealistic to expect members of ethnic minorities to become culturally assimilated when they need their communities for protection and as a political basis. The new demand is for a notion of citizenship based not on cultural belonging but on actual participation in society (Wihtol de Wenden, 1995).

The multicultural model

The final category is multiculturalism (or pluralism), which implies that immigrants should be granted equal rights in all spheres of society, without being expected to give up their diversity, although usually with an expectation of conformity to certain key values.[5] In a multicultural country, membership of civil society, initiated through permission to immigrate, should lead to full participation in the state and the nation. There are two main variants. In the laissez-faire approach typical of the USA, cultural difference and the existence of ethnic communities are accepted, but it is not seen as the role of the state to ensure social justice or to support the maintenance of ethnic cultures. The second variant is multiculturalism as a government policy, as in Canada, Australia and Sweden. Here, multiculturalism implies both the willingness of the majority group to accept cultural difference, and state action to secure equal rights for minorities. As already noted, other immigration countries have taken multicultural approaches in some areas of society.

For the classical countries of immigration (Australia, Canada and the USA) multiculturalism appears as the best way of rapidly incorporating large groups of culturally diverse immigrants into society. Moreover the imperative of making immigrants into citizens reinforces the pressure for a multicultural policy: if immigrants become voters, ethnic groups can gain political clout. Sweden, by contrast, appears as an anomaly: it is a society which was unusually homogeneous until recently. Yet it has had large-scale settlement, and adopted multicultural policies very similar to those of Australia and Canada. The reason seems to lie in the strongly state interventionist model of Swedish social democracy, which has used the same approaches to integrating immigrants into civil society and the state as were used earlier to integrate the working class and reduce class conflict.

A closer look at current debates in Sweden helps illustrate some of the dilemmas of multiculturalism. The Swedish model, introduced in 1975 (see Exhibit 9.7) was based on the expectation of long-term integration into society and culture, even though this might take some generations. Public policies towards immigrants fall into two categories: indirect policies, concerned with guaranteeing access to general social programmes, and direct policies, which relate to immigrants' special needs. Indirect policies include measures to ensure that immigrants have equal rights to employment, social services, housing and education. This can involve use of anti-discrimination regulations, or the provision of interpreter and translator services. Direct policies include voting rights for resident non-citizens, mother-tongue classes at school, information services for immigrants, state grants to immigrant central organisations, participation in official consultative bodies such as the Immigrants' Council, and multilingual services provided by trade unions.

Despite the rhetoric of free choice, the Swedish model involves a high degree of social control. The relatively liberal policies towards settlers are based on strict control of new immigration (Hammar, 1985b: 28–32). Non-Scandinavian citizens require work permits and residence permits, and can only obtain social benefits if they are registered with the authorities. The system of grants to immigrant associations allows government to select bodies considered worthy of funding, and thus to influence their activities. Schierup (1991: 140) speaks of 'the Swedish experience of "prescribed multiculturalism"', whereby immigrant and ethnic organisations are co-opted into the corporatist state where they end up politically marginalised'.

Since the late 1980s, the Swedish model has faced increasing difficulties: economic constraints have made it harder to finance generous social policies, while public support for admission of refugees has declined. Anti-immigrant groups and racist violence have increased. In response, the government has cut refugee admissions, and adopted measures to stop illegal entry and to facilitate deportation of foreigners convicted of criminal offences (OECD, 1995: 119–22). Ålund and Schierup (1991) argue that Sweden is being influenced by the development of a 'fortress Europe' mentality, in which there are strong fears of economic influxes disguised as political refugees from the impoverished South. Islam is increasingly being seen as a threat to Swedish culture and values. Trends have emerged for regarding Eastern Europe as a future labour reserve, and reorienting refugee policy away from humanitarian criteria towards considerations of economic usefulness. Ålund and Schierup conclude:

> The moral compact on which Swedish immigrant policy is built is gradually disintegrating, giving way to a culturalist construction of new discriminatory boundaries . . . The hidden logic of a new commonsense cultural racism . . . finds . . . its way into the language and practices of public servants, professionals and into the everyday commonsense discourses of ordinary people. (1991: 10)

There are similar conflicts elsewhere. Multiculturalism has always been controversial: even in Australia and Canada, there has been a continual debate, with a substantial group calling for a return to assimilationism. To many members of the dominant ethnic group, multiculturalism appears as a threat to their culture and identity. Others criticise multiculturalism for leading to a superficial acceptance of cultural difference, without bringing about real institutional change (see Vasta, 1996). Indeed the trend of the 1990s has been away from multiculturalism. In Canada, the emphasis has shifted to 'heritage and citizenship'. In Australia, the centre-right government elected in 1996 is curtailing multicultural programmes and services, and is highly ambivalent about using the concept. The Netherlands Minorities Policy was modified after strong criticism of its multicultural aspects. However, it is too early to say that multiculturalism is being abandoned: growing ethnic diversity generates pressure for measures to recognise cultural rights and to prevent social exclusion, whatever the label given to such policies. Debates on such issues play an important role in virtually all immigration countries, as the difficulties of exclusionary and assimilationist models become apparent.

Conclusion

The comparison of the situation in various immigration countries can be summed up by saying that ethnic group formation takes place everywhere, but the conditions under which this happens vary considerably. This leads to different outcomes: in some countries ethnic groups become marginalised and excluded minorities, whereas in others they take the form of ethnic communities which are accepted as part of a pluralist society. Exclusion is most severe in former 'guestworker' countries such as Germany and Switzerland. Multicultural models are to be found in countries with explicit policies of permanent settlement and pluralism: above all Australia, Canada and Sweden. The USA comes close to the multicultural model, but with a lower level of state intervention. Between the extremes of exclusion or multiculturalism are countries such as France, the Netherlands and Britain, which recognise the reality of permanent settlement, but are unwilling to accept long-term pluralism. However there are important differences between these countries, particularly with regard to the role of the state in managing cultural difference.

The reality in each country is much more complex and contradictory than our brief account can show. None the less these general trends are significant, and provide some useful pointers for new immigration countries. The first is that temporary migrant labour recruitment is likely to lead to permanent settlement of at least a proportion of the migrants; settlement leads in turn to formation of ethnic groups. The second is that the character of these future ethnic groups will, to a large measure, be determined by what the state does in the early stages of migration. Policies which deny the reality of immigration by tacitly tolerating large-scale illegal movements lead to social marginalisation, minority formation and racism. Third, the ethnic groups arising from immigration need their own associations and social networks, as well as their own languages and cultures. Policies which deny legitimacy to these lead to isolation and separatism. A fourth conclusion is that the best way to prevent marginalisation and social conflicts is to grant permanent immigrants full rights in all social spheres. This means making citizenship easily available, even if this leads to dual citizenship.

This last point has far-reaching consequences: removing the link between citizenship and ethnic origin means changing the defining principle of the nation-state. This applies particularly to nations based on the ethnic model. The rapid shift away from ideas of ethnic homogeneity in Sweden shows that such changes can be carried out fairly smoothly. The principles of citizenship also need redefining in countries with post-imperialist or republican models, such as France, Britain and the Netherlands. The classical countries of immigration – Australia, Canada and the USA – have already moved towards citizenship based on territoriality and are capable of incorporating newcomers of varying origins.

Migration both to developed countries and to NICs is likely to continue in the years ahead, so the presence of ethnic communities will be an inescapable part of society. The most direct impact will be felt in 'global cities' such as Los Angeles, Paris, Berlin, Sydney, Singapore and Hong Kong. The formation of ethnic groups and the spatial restructuring of the city which this helps to bring about are powerful forces for change, which may give rise to conflicts and violence, but can also be a great source of energy and innovation.

Globalisation is leading to multiple identities and transnational belonging. Exclusionary models of immigrant rights and nationhood are questionable, because they lead to divided societies. Similarly, assimilationist models are not likely to succeed, because they fail to take account of the cultural and social situation of settlers. Policies and ideologies which lead to the emergence of ethnic minorities denied full participation in political, economic, social and cultural life must be destabilising for state and society. The multicultural model is a combination of a set of social policies to respond to the needs of settlers, and a statement about openness of the nation to cultural diversity. Multicultural citizenship appears to be the most viable solution to the problem of defining membership of a nation-state in an increasingly mobile world.

10 Immigrant Politics

As international migration reshapes societies, it inevitably and often profoundly affects political life. Yet, paradoxically, international migration is frequently viewed as a socioeconomic phenomenon largely devoid of political significance. This viewpoint is part and parcel of the temporary worker idea examined earlier. Relatively few people foresaw that the decision to recruit foreign labour in the wake of the Second World War would one day affect the political landscape of Western Europe. But immigration did lead to a significantly altered political environment: one that now includes Islamic fundamentalist parties and political movements comprised mainly of immigrants, as well as extreme-right, anti-immigrant parties.

The most lasting significance of international migration may well be its effects upon politics. This is not inevitably the case. Much depends on how immigrants are treated by governments, and on the origins, timing, nature and context of a particular migratory flow. It makes a difference whether migrants were legally admitted and permitted to naturalise or whether their entry (legal or illegal) was seen as merely temporary but they then stayed on permanently. On the one hand, immigrants can quickly become citizens without a discernible political effect, save for the addition of additional voters. On the other hand, international migration may lead to an accretion of politically disenfranchised persons whose political marginality is compounded by various socioeconomic problems.

The universe of possible political effects of international migration is vast and characteristically intertwines the political systems of two states: the homeland and the receiving society. The political significance of international migration can be active or passive. Immigrants can become political actors in their own right or manifest apoliticism, which itself can be important to maintenance of the status quo. On the other hand, immigrants often become the object of politics: allies for some and foes for others. Chapter 9 has already dealt with one key political issue: the extent to which immigrants and their descendants can become citizens with full rights of political participation. This chapter cannot hope to do justice to all the other facets of immigration-related politics. Only a few themes can be considered. The emphasis is on emergent forces that have rendered politics within and between states more complex and volatile.

Immigrants as political actors in Western Europe

By 1970, the immigrant presence in Western Europe had become so substantial that scholars and governments began to ask about its political ramifications. The answers were not clear-cut. The fact that many immigrant workers and their families were not entitled to vote because of their alien status probably helped conservative parties, as working-class voters often support parties of the left. However, not all immigrants support left-wing parties. Within Germany's Turkish community, for example, there was considerable support for right-wing Turkish parties. Many immigrants were uninterested in the politics of Western Europe. Their principal political concern continued to be politics in their homelands. Political extremism in Turkish politics spilled over to Turkish communities in Western Europe which, at times, became veritable battlegrounds. German government statistics on known political extremists included large numbers of aliens, both left-wing and right-wing (M. J. Miller, 1981).

That immigrant communities in Western Europe would become key areas for, say, Algerian or Turkish politics is scarcely surprising. After all, it is not unusual for 10 per cent of some emigration countries' populations to reside abroad. Immigrants are often freer to express themselves politically as aliens in Western European democracies than they were back home. Immigrant communities became the object of competition – occasionally violent – between pro-status quo and anti-status quo homeland political forces. Governments of emigration countries were acutely aware of the stakes involved and characteristically sought to influence the 'hearts and minds' of their citizens or subjects abroad through the nurturing of pro-governmental organisations and through diplomatic and consular services.

The *Amicale des Algeriens en Europe* (AAE) epitomised such efforts. The AAE was the overseas branch of the ruling National Liberation Front in Algeria. The head of the AAE was usually also a high-ranking official of the National Liberation Front and of the Algerian government. The AAE enjoyed a quasi-diplomatic status in France. It represented the interests of Algerian emigrants in Algerian policy-making circles as well as *vis-à-vis* the French government. Throughout the 1960s and 1970s, the AAE virtually monopolised the representation of Algerians in France, although it was opposed by rival groups, like the outlawed Movement of Arab Workers, a revolutionary communist organisation with ties to radical Palestinian factions, which played a key role in organising protests against attacks on Algerians and other North Africans in 1973 (M. J. Miller, 1981: 89–104). The AAE opposed the French governments decision in 1981 to grant aliens the right to form associations (Weil, 1991b: 99–114). Prior to 1981, associations of foreigners required government authorisation in order to operate, which condemned anti-Algerian regime parties to clandestinity. The 1981 reform undercut the virtual AAE monopoly, and open opposition to the Algerian regime soon flourished.

The Algerian government was particularly concerned by the ability of Muslim fundamentalist groups, such as the Islamic Salvation Front, to operate openly in France, which they could not do in Algeria. This concern was shared with other non-Islamic governments in predominantly Muslim societies such as Turkey and Tunisia. Political dissidence expressed on French soil presaged the fundamentalist victory in the December 1991 elections, although many Algerians who voted for the Islamic Salvation Front were not so much voting for an Islamic republic as protesting against National Liberation Front rule. The influence of French policies with regard to aliens' associations illustrates how international migration binds together the politics of two societies.

Foreign workers and their dependants in Western Europe benefited from diplomatic representation, and bilateral labour agreements regulated most major foreign labour flows. These agreements, along with certain international instruments, had some influence on Western European policies towards migrants. Generally, however, diplomatic representation of migrant interests was insufficient. Homeland governments did not want to appear to be meddling in the sovereign affairs of other states. Moreover, their stake in a continuing homeward flow of foreign worker remittances often made them reluctant to criticise treatment of their citizens abroad. The asymmetrical power of homelands and immigrant-receiving states was clearly demonstrated when one Western European state after the other abruptly and unilaterally curbed foreign worker recruitment in the 1970s.

The Algerian decision to suspend labour emigration in 1973, in the face of mounting attacks on Algerians in France, constituted a significant exception to the general pattern. Still Western European governments found it much harder to force out unwanted migrants that they had in the 1930s (Ponty, 1988). The French government did not want to renew the permits of several hundred thousand Algerians in the second half of the 1970s. But a combination of legal constraints and pro-immigrant political pressure forced the government to accept the principle of voluntary repatriation. In other words, the French government could not force out legally admitted foreign residents against their will (Weil, 1991b).

The inadequacy of diplomatic representation of foreign residents was one reason for the emergence of distinctive channels of political participation and representation. The key difference between most Western European countries and the classic lands of immigration like the USA, Canada and Australia is the difficulty of acquisition of citizenship in the former (see Chapter 9). The classic immigration lands expect immigrant admission to lead eventually to naturalisation and political participation. Most foreign workers admitted to Western Europe were not expected to stay on and to become citizens, and immigrant participation in politics is not regarded as fully legitimate. Yet participate immigrants do, both as non-citizens and, increasingly, as citizens.

Indeed there is reason to believe that nascent immigrant participation in Western European politics contributed to the decisions to curb foreign worker recruitment. By the early 1970s, supposedly politically quiescent aliens had become involved in a number of significant industrial strikes and protest movements. In some instances, extreme leftist groups succeeded in mobilising foreigners. Largely foreign worker strikes in French and German car plants (see Chapter 7) demonstrated the disruptive potential of foreign labour and constrained trade unions to do more to represent foreign workers. Generally speaking, foreigners were poorly integrated into unions in 1970. By 1980, significant strides had been made towards integration. This was reflected in growing unionisation rates among foreign workers and the election of foreign workers to works councils and union leadership positions.

Immigrants also sought participation and representation in local government. In several countries advisory councils were instituted to give immigrants a voice in local government. Experiences with these advisory councils varied and some were discontinued. Some people contested them as efforts to coopt aliens, while others saw them as illegitimate interference by aliens in the politics of the host society. In certain countries, aliens were accorded a right to vote in local and regional elections. Sweden was the pacesetter in this regard, but alien participation in Swedish local and regional elections declined over time.

The Netherlands was the second country to accord qualified aliens voting rights. However, the results of alien voting there have also been somewhat disappointing (Rath, 1988: 25–35). This has not prevented the granting of voting rights to aliens from becoming a significant political issue in many Western European countries.

Successive French governments have argued that it would be unconstitutional to accord aliens local voting rights. The German Federal Constitutional Court reached a similar conclusion in 1990, when the state government of Schleswig-Holstein sought to grant foreign residents voting rights. None the less the French Socialist Party included municipal voting rights for foreign residents in its party platform when it won the presidential and legislative elections of 1981. When Foreign Minister Cheysson endorsed the concept during a visit to Algiers in 1982, there was a storm of criticism both within and outside the Socialist Party. In 1983, the government printed pamphlets explaining the policy, but these pamphlets were never distributed for fear that they would increase support for the nascent FN, which was already a rapidly growing anti-immigrant political party. In 1988, President Mitterrand once again pledged to back municipal voting rights for certain resident aliens. By June of 1990, however, the minority government of Prime Minister Michel Rocard felt constrained to renounce this policy as a precondition for the traditional opposition parties joining in a national dialogue over immigration (Sole, 1990: 8).

This issue illustrates how questions of migrant rights came to the forefront of politics in many Western European states in the 1980s. Aliens could participate in politics through a variety of channels, ranging from membership in trade unions, to voting for representatives on municipal advisory councils, to joining political parties and demonstrating in the streets. By the 1980s, the stakes involved in the granting of voting rights were quite high in many Western democracies. Aliens were often spatially concentrated in major cities and certain neighbourhoods. Enfranchising them would dramatically affect political outcomes in many local elections. Supporters of the granting of municipal voting rights generally regarded it as a way to foster integration and as a counterweight to the growing influence of parties like the FN in France. However, many immigrants were already politically enfranchised, particularly in the United Kingdom. This did not prevent the eruption of riots involving immigrants and their British-born children in the mid-1980s. The granting of local voting rights was thus not in itself a panacea for the severe problems facing immigrants in Western Europe.

Since the 1970s, immigrants have increasingly articulated political concerns, participated in politics and sought representation. Immigrant protest movements became part of the tapestry of Western European politics and frequently affected policies. Persistent hunger strikes by undocumented immigrants and their supporters, for example, brought pressure to bear on French and Dutch authorities to liberalise rules regarding legalisation. There was great variation in patterns of alien political participation and representation from country to country, with some countries, like Sweden, succeeding in institutionalising much of it.

Mobilisation of immigrants and ethnic minorities outside the normal channels of political representation is often linked to experience of exclusion, either through racist violence or institutional discrimination. For instance, members of ethnic minorities often feel that the police are more concerned with social control than with protecting them from racist violence. In Britain, Afro-Caribbean and Asian youth have organised self-protection groups against racist attacks. Sub-cultures of resistance developed around reggae music and rastafarianism for the West Indians, and Islam and other religions for the Asians (Gilroy, 1987). The reaction by government and the media was to see ethnic minority youth as a problem of public order: a 'social time bomb' on the verge of explosion. There was widespread panic about the alleged high rates of street crime ('mugging') by black youth and a tendency to see black people as an 'enemy within' who threatened British society (Centre for Contemporary Cultural Studies, or CCCS, 1982).

Black youth discontent exploded into uprisings in many inner-city areas in 1981 and 1985 (Sivanandan, 1982; Benyon, 1986). In 1991, there were new disturbances, in which 'joy riders' stole cars and publicly raced them to destruction in inner-city streets, to the acclaim of crowds of onlookers. After the riots, the initial official response was to insist that the central issue was one of crime and to lament the breakdown of parental control (Solomos, 1988). Newspapers blamed the problems on 'crazed Left-wing extremists' and 'streetfighting experts trained in Moscow and Libya'. The disturbances were generally labelled as 'black youth riots'. But, in fact, there was a high degree of white youth involvement (Benyon, 1986).

The riots were caused by a number of interrelated factors. Deteriorating community relations and lack of political leadership against racism were major causes of alienation of black youth. There were concentrations of disadvantaged people (both white and black) in inner-city areas, marked by high unemployment, poor housing, environmental decay, high crime rates, drug abuse and racist attacks. As Benyon (1986: 268) points out, the areas where riots took place were politically disadvantaged: they lacked the institutions, opportunities and resources for putting pressure on those with political power. Finally these areas had suffered repressive forms of policing, experienced by young people as racism and deliberate harassment. The riots may be seen as defensive movements of minority youth, connected with protection of their communities as well as assertion of identity and culture (Gilroy, 1987; Gilroy and Lawrence, 1988).

Similar urban uprisings have taken place in France, where a second generation has emerged of young people of mainly Arab descent who feel French, but find themselves excluded by discrimination and racism. In the 1981 'hot summer' of Lyons, youth riots in public housing estates protested against heavy-handed policing, racism and unemployment (Lapeyronnie *et al.*, 1990: 65). They were to be repeated in Lyons, Paris and elsewhere in the following years (Lloyd, 1991: 63; Weil, 1991b: 262–3).

Fear of further unrest has led to a multifaceted response by governments. Some of the French and British measures were mentioned in Chapter 9. However, it is doubtful whether such policies can effectively combat the powerful economic, social and political forces which marginalise ethnic minority youth. Moreover, the capacity and willingness of Western European governments to carry out social policy measures in favour of immigrants has in many cases declined in the 1990s, resulting in situations of severe and persistent social exclusion.

New issues and new political forces: Islam in Western Europe

While France has long had a significant Islamic minority, the number of Muslims grew significantly after 1947. By 1970, Islam was the second religion of France. By 1990, it was the second religion of the French. There were 9–10 million Muslims in Western Europe in 1996, including over 3 million in France. None the less, as late as 1970, Islam was largely invisible in France. According to Kepel and Leveau (1987), the affirmation of Islam since then was part and parcel of the settlement of foreign workers, the progression of the migratory chain. It was manifested primarily through construction of mosques and prayer-rooms and through formation of Islamic associations. In turn, the reaction to Islamic affirmation, manifested above all through the emergence of the FN, has undermined governmental integration policies. By 1990, immigration had become one of the key political issues in France and the politicisation of immigration issues at times appeared to threaten the stability of French democratic institutions. The paradox was that this was largely unforeseen.

This politicisation became apparent around 1970 (Wihtol de Wenden, 1988: 209–19), when extreme-right student groups began to demonstrate against *immigration sauvage*, or illegal migration. Counterdemonstrations took place and violence erupted. By 1972, the extremist groups principally involved in this violence – the Trotskyist Communist League and the neo-fascist New Order – were banned. Leftist groups continued to mobilise immigrants in various struggles such as the long rent strike in the SONACOTRA housing for foreign workers (M. J. Miller, 1978). Elements of the extreme right, however, began to mobilise on anti-immigration themes. Françoise Gaspard (1990) has related how the FN began to campaign in local elections in the Dreux area near Paris. The FN gradually increased its share of the vote before scoring a dramatic breakthrough in 1983, when it obtained 16.7 per cent of the vote. In 1989, an FN candidate in a by-election in Dreux won a seat in the Chamber of Deputies, with 61.3 per cent of the vote. In the space of 11 years, the number of FN voters increased from 307 to 4716 (Gaspard, 1990: 205). By 1997, the FN dominated municipal governments in four southern cities, including Toulon, and was supported by about 15 per cent of the national electorate. Nearly 4 million French citizens voted for FN candidates in the first round of the 1997 legislative elections. Something fundamental had changed, and the emergence of Islam had much to do with it.

The French reaction to Islam was irrational but grounded in concrete immigration-related problems. The irrational dimension stemmed from the trauma of the Algerian war and the association of Islam and terrorism. In 1982, following a series of crippling strikes in major car plants in the Paris region which principally involved North African workers (see Chapter 7), Prime Minister Mauroy insinuated that Iran was trying to destabilise French politics by backing Islamic fundamentalist groups (*Le Monde*, 1 February 1983). While no evidence of an Iranian involvement was produced, it was clear that Islamic groups were heavily involved, with the French Communist Party and its trade union affiliate, the CGT, desperately trying to regain control of the strike movement (M. J. Miller, 1986: 361–82). Islam was seen by many as incompatible with democracy because it made no distinction between church and state. France's Muslims were portrayed as heavily influenced by Islamic fundamentalism when, in fact, only a small minority of them considered themselves fundamentalists and these were divided into multiple and often competing organisations (Kepel and Leveau, 1987). The integration problems affecting France's Islamic minority were perhaps more central to the politicisation of immigration issues. Gaspard (1990) recounts how tensions over housing exacerbated French–immigrant relations in Dreux. Immigrants, particularly those of North African origin, disproportionately lived in inadequate housing. As settlement and family reunification proceeded, more and more immigrants applied for subsidised governmental housing, causing severe friction when their numbers grew while non-immigrant residents diminished. Before long, entire buildings came to be viewed as immigrants' quarters. The physical isolation of many immigrants in substandard housing, along with the educational problems faced by disproportionally high numbers of immigrant children, contributed to a malaise on which the FN fed. By the 1980s, primarily North African Muslim-origin youths, most of whom were French citizens, became involved in urban unrest that was deeply unsettling to the French.

The French Socialist Party sought to galvanise support by appealing to North African-origin voters. The pro-immigrant *SOS-racisme* organisation was largely an initiative of the Socialist Party. The party clearly appealed to voters as a bulwark against the FN. Yet support for the Socialists had plunged dramatically by 1992 and they were booed at pro-immigrant rallies. The Socialist message of integration of resident aliens and curbing illegal immigration was viewed as pro-immigrant by the extreme right and as anti-immigrant by the extreme left.

Illustrative of the broader issue was the question of the *foulards* or Islamic headscarves worn by some young girls to school in the late 1980s. In a country where the tradition of the separation of church and state is deeply rooted and politically salient, wearing of the headscarves appeared to many people as incompatible with the very principles of the French Republic, which prohibited the wearing of religious articles. On the other side of the debate was the claim that the choice of wearing a headscarf was an individual's prerogative, a private matter of no consequence to public authorities. In the end, French authorities ruled in favour of the girls, but not before the question had become a *cause célèbre*. Should school cafeterias serve *halal* food (that is, food prepared in accordance with Islamic ritual prescriptions)? Should Muslims be granted representation in French politics, as Catholics are through governmental consultations with the bishops and Jews are through the consistory? Should factories honour Islamic holidays in addition to Catholic feast days? As Islam was affirmed, a host of long latent issues came to the fore, with major consequences for the French political system. Paradoxically the French government had encouraged the creation of Islamic mosques and prayer-rooms back in the 1960s and 1970s. Islam was seen by some businesses and public authorities as a means of social control. Prayer-rooms were constructed in factories in the hope that North African workers would be less likely to join left-wing trade unions. Moreover, supporting Islam was part of a policy of cultural maintenance, designed to encourage the eventual repatriation of migrant workers and their families. Saudi Arabia and Libya financed the construction of mosques across Western Europe, hoping to influence the emerging Islam of Western Europe (Kepel and Leveau, 1987). Despite the separation of church and state in France, many local governments supported the construction of mosques as part of integration policy. The building of mosques was often violently opposed, and several were bombed. Other Western European governments also fostered Islam through policies which brought Islamic teachers to Western Europe. These policies usually stemmed from provisions of bilateral labour agreements which granted homeland governments a role in educating migrant children. Many Koran schools in Germany were controlled by Islamic fundamentalists. Such institutionalisation of Islam in Western Europe has probably progressed the furthest in Belgium.

Most of Western Europe's Muslims saw their religion as a private matter. The Rushdie affair made Islamic identity more of a political problem than, say, Catholicism or Protestantism. Salman Rushdie is an Indian-born Muslim citizen of the UK, who scandalised many Muslims with his book *The Satanic Verses* and was condemned to death by Iran's Ayatollah Khomeini. Much-publicised anti-Rushdie demonstrations by Muslims in England, France and Belgium confirmed the incompatibility of Islam with Western institutions in the eyes of some people. Rushdie denounced the hypocrisy of Western European governments in their dealings with Iran. He alleged that trade considerations mattered more than human rights principles: too little was done diplomatically to retaliate for the *fatwa* or to get it rescinded.

The crisis over the Iraqi occupation of Kuwait in 1990 also prompted fear of Islamic subversion. Muslims in France were more supportive of Iraq than was French society as a whole (Perotti and Thepaut, 1991: 76–9). But many Muslims opposed the Iraqi invasion, and the Gulf

War did not produce the terrorism and mass unrest in Western Europe that some had predicted. None the less it was clear that French governmental support for the war effort alienated it from France's Islamic community. Tensions between Muslims and non-Muslims reached new heights, prompting rumours of thousands of Tunisians in the South of France returning home out of a feeling of insecurity (Perotti and Thepaut, 1991: 70–1). Similarly in Australia, incidents of abuse and harassment against Muslims, particularly women, increased during the Gulf crisis, prompting government action to improve community relations.

While the vast majority of Muslim immigrants eschewed fundamentalism, Western Europe certainly was affected by the upsurge in religious fervour that swept the Muslim world in the 1980s. Fundamentalism often had the greatest appeal amongst groups affected by various forms of social exclusion. Across Western Europe, Muslims are affected by disproportionately high unemployment rates. In areas where unemployment is compounded by educational and housing problems, and these underlying socioeconomic tensions are overlaid with highly politicised religious identity issues, the ingredients for sociopolitical explosions are strong. All it takes is an incident, usually a violent encounter between a Muslim youth and the police, for violence to erupt. This was the pattern behind urban unrest in France in the 1980s and 1990s. The profound problems facing Western Europe's Muslims are one reason why integration will remain the top immigration policy priority for Western European governments and for the EU for the foreseeable future (Commission of the European Communities, 1990).

Immigrants as objects of politics: the growth of anti-immigrant extremism

The French were not alone in finding it difficult to come to grips with the emergent Islamic reality in their midst. Belgium became the scene of urban unrest in 1991, when largely Moroccan-origin youths clashed with police following a rumour that an anti-immigrant political party, the Flemish *Vlaams Blok,* was going to organise a political rally in an area heavily populated with immigrants (*The Bulletin,* 1991: 20). Partly as a result of this violence, support for the *Vlaams Blok* increased sharply in the 1991 Belgian elections.

Similarly, in the 1991 Austrian municipal and regional elections, the anti-immigrant Freedom Party scored an important breakthrough by increasing its share of the vote to almost one-quarter. By 1996, the Freedom Party's support was so great that it challenged the political dominance of the Austrian Socialist Party and the Catholic-oriented People's Party, which had controlled Austria since the 1950s. In Italy, a backlash against immigration figured importantly in the political convulsions of the early 1990s. The Northern Leagues, *Forza Italia* and the neo-fascist National Alliance expressed frustration over immigration to varying degrees. Meanwhile, the politically influential Catholic clergy and the Pope himself voiced support for humanitarian initiatives such as legalisation. Many Italian voters supported right-wing parties and protested against the deeply-embedded corruption of the Christian Democrats and the Socialists. Protest voting against a discredited *partitocrazia* was far more prevalent than anti-immigrant voting.

Certainly support for anti-immigrant parties involved an element of protest voting. While 15 per cent of the electorate voted for the FN in France and one-third of all voters sympathised with FN positions on immigration (Weil, 1991a: 82), it also was clear that the FN was picking up part of the protest vote traditionally received by the French Communist Party. The FN did particularly well in areas with concentrations of *Pieds-Noirs*, Europeans repatriated from Algeria in 1962 and their offspring. FN opposition to the Single European Market was also a major point of attraction to some of its electorate (Marcus, 1995).

In 1997, it was estimated that the FN candidates would be strong contenders in 200 of France's 577 legislative districts. However, in most French elections, if one candidate does not win a seat outright with 50 per cent + 1 of the vote, there is a second run-off election. After the first round of the 1997 elections, 133 NF candidates became eligible for the second round by garnering more than 12.5 per cent of the vote. Candidates from parties which have fashioned national electoral alliances – generally there is one for left-leaning and one for right-leaning parties – are favoured in second-round voting. The FN has encountered difficulty forging such electoral pacts outside the Marseilles area and therefore stands little chance of winning seats in the National Assembly. It won only one seat in the 1997 election. The major exception to this pattern occurred in the 1986 elections when the FN won 35 seats in the National Assembly. This election was conducted according to modified proportional representative rules, unlike other national legislative elections during the Fifth Republic (Tiersky, 1994: 111–12).

By the 1990s, anti-immigrant political movements had developed virtually across Western Europe. Many of these movements had historical precedents. Part of the hardcore support for the FN, for example, came from quarters traditionally identified with the anti-republican right. These political forces had been discredited by the Second World War and their programmes and policies were generally viewed as illegitimate until the anti-immigrant reaction of the 1980s. Immigration issues have served as an entrée for extreme right-wing parties into mainstream politics across Western Europe.

It would be mistaken to dismiss the upsurge in voting for anti-immigrant parties as simply an expression of racism and intolerance. As pointed out in Chapter 2, support for extreme-right groups is often the result of bewilderment in the face of rapid economic and social change. The erosion in organisational and ideological strength of labour organisations due to changes in occupational structures is important as well. Extreme-right parties also attract support as a result of public dissatisfaction with certain policies, such as those concerning asylum seekers and illegal immigration. Other extremist parties have fared less well. The National Front in the United Kingdom, for example, appeared to be gaining strength in the mid-1970s before the Conservative Party under Margaret Thatcher pre-empted it by adopting key parts of its programme (Layton-Henry and Rich, 1986: 74–5). Great Britain's two party system and its 'first past the post' electoral law make it very difficult for any new party to win seats in the House of Commons.

Some scholars have suggested that the emergence of right-wing parties has had anti-immigrant effects across the political spectrum (Messina, 1989). It has been argued, for example, that French socialist stands on immigration shifted to the right as support for the FN increased. However it is difficult to reconcile the Socialist Party's celebration of its anti-racism with such a thesis. As Patrick Weil observed, 'immigration can appear as the ideal arena for differentiating politics of the Left from the Right. The Socialist Party, first and foremost François Mitterrand, has found in immigration and antiracism a privileged domain for political intervention' (Weil, 1991a: 95).

The French Communist Party (PCF) has been accused of exploiting anti-immigrant feelings for electoral ends. There were cases in the 1980s of communist mayors leading bulldozers in to demolish housing illegally constructed by immigrants. Much of the frustration that led to such widely-publicised incidents was rooted in efforts by communist municipal governments to get housing for immigrants constructed elsewhere in addition to the communist suburbs. When confronted by often illegal housing, they sometimes took ill-considered steps to dramatise their opposition to the immigrant housing situation, which were roundly criticised by friend and foe alike. The PCF was consistently critical of governmental *laissez-faire* immigration policies in the 1950s and 1960s, but it has staunchly supported equal rights for immigrants and militantly opposed racism. The electoral collapse of the PCF in the 1980s, from 20 per cent of the electorate to less than 10 per cent, created a void which the FN deftly filled.

In addition to immigrants becoming the object of political party programmes, they have also become the object of violence in Western Europe, some of which is politically inspired (see Chapter 9). The roots of anti-immigrant violence in France can be traced back to the nineteenth century (Lequin, 1988: 389–410). During the latter stages of the Algerian war, there was horrific violence against Algerian Muslims residing on the mainland (Belloula, 1965: 84–102). The toll in lives and injuries to immigrants as a result of racial attacks has been high and steady since the early 1970s (Bernard and Chemin, 1991).

In 1970, few political parties in Western Europe gave any thought to immigration issues. By 1990, many parties had hired immigration specialists as advisers and had detailed immigration programmes. The FN issued a 50-point immigration programme (Sole, 1991). Critics denounced the programme as racist and as seeking to establish apartheid *à la française*. The essence of the FN programme was to turn back the clock on immigrant rights, much as the French extreme right in the 1930s wanted to turn the clock back on the rights acquired by Jews since 1789. Indeed there is much that is anachronistic in the new politics of immigration in Western Europe in the 1980s and 1990s. Although FN spokespersons attempted to play down the radicalness of the 50 propositions and to emphasise their similarity to the position of the traditional conservative parties in France, it was no exaggeration to regard them as incompatible with the founding principles of the French Republic. Clearly further growth in support for the FN would endanger French political stability.

Migrants and ethnic voting blocs

The most extreme example of international migration transforming politics is the case of Palestine and Israel. From 1920 to 1939, British-authorised immigration increased the Jewish share of the population in the British mandate of Palestine from roughly 10 per cent to one-third, despite fierce Palestinian Arab opposition including strikes, riots and revolts. The goal of the mainstream Zionists was the creation of a Jewish homeland, which did not necessarily connote the creation of a Jewish state. A minority Zionist current – the so-called Revisionists, led by Vladimir Jabotinsky – proclaimed the creation of a Jewish state on all the territory of the Palestine Mandate, including the East Bank of the Jordan, as the goal of Zionism (Laqueur, 1972). During the Holocaust and the Second World War, the Zionist movement was radicalised and the creation of a Jewish state in Palestine became the paramount goal of the movement. Palestinians and other Arabs had long opposed the Zionist project because they feared it would displace the Palestinian Arabs or reduce them from majority to minority status. Fighting broke out in 1947 and the worst fears of the Arabs were realised.

The politics of the Jewish state of Israel, created in 1948, remain heavily influenced by immigration. As a result of the inflow of Oriental or Sephardic Jews primarily from largely Muslim societies during the 1950s and 1960s, the Sephardic-origin Jewish population surpassed that of European-origin Ashkenazi Jews in the mid-1970s. This demographic shift benefited the modern-day followers of Jabotinsky and the Revisionists: the Likud bloc led by Menachem Begin, who was elected prime minister in 1977 with the support of Sephardic-origin Jews. In 1990, a new wave of Soviet Jewish immigration began, again affecting the balance between Ashkenazi and Sephardic Jews as well as the Arabs. Nearly 600 000 Soviet Jews arrived in Israel in the first half of the 1990s. As Jewish immigrants quickly became Israeli citizens according to the Law of Return, one of the key questions during the general election of 1992 concerned the voting patterns of recent Soviet immigrants who by then comprised about one-tenth of the electorate. Given the rough parity between the two principal Israeli political party alliances – Labour and the Likud – Russian immigrant votes decisively affected the 1992 election by giving Labor a narrow edge. In 1996, the Soviet immigrant voting pattern changed as many supported an immigrant party led by the former Soviet dissident, Natan Sharansky. The party won seven seats in the new Knesset and joined in the coalition government dominated by the Likud.

The Israeli case illustrates in the extreme the potential impact of an immigrant voting bloc upon electoral outcomes. Immigrants generally are not such an important factor as in Israel and immigrants do not necessarily vote in ethnic blocs. Yet immigration clearly is affecting electoral politics across Western democracies as growing numbers of aliens naturalise, and as immigrant-origin populations are mobilised to vote. In the 1996 referendum over the future of Quebec and the Canadian Federation, Quebec's immigrant voters overwhelmingly voted against the referendum and for maintenance of the status quo. They decisively affected the outcome, prompting angry anti-immigration remarks by Quebecois leaders.

The growing mass of immigrant voters has made many political parties and their leaders more sensitive to multicultural concerns and issues. In some instances, immigration policy debates have been influenced by electoral calculations. In general, political parties on the left side of the political spectrum appear to take the lead in appealing to immigrant voters and are rewarded for their efforts. Conservative parties often benefit electorally from anti-immigrant backlash. And a number of conservative parties have begun to compete in earnest for the immigrant-origin electorate, particularly in Great Britain and the USA. Following the 1996 US elections, some Republicans felt that President Clinton and the Democrats had outmanoeuvred the Republicans by encouraging a naturalisation campaign while several Republican presidential candidates embraced anti-immigrant positions. The endorsement of multiculturalism by the conservative coalition which was in power in Australia from 1975 to 1982 also seemed to be connected with concern about the 'ethnic vote' (Castles *et al.*, 1992c). In several countries, new ethnic voting blocs have come into existence. This is seen as normal in some democracies, but as a problem in others.

The history of American parties vying for immigrant votes is well known. While anti-immigrant sentiment was a boon to the Know-Nothing party in the 1840s and 1850s, the Democratic Party benefited from the support of immigrant groups like the Irish whose overwhelming identification with the Democratic Party remains one of the fixtures of American politics. In the 1920s, anti-immigrant sentiment was a factor in fairly widespread support for the Ku Klux Klan which was a significant political force in many states. Indeed, at the apogee of the Ku Klux Klan's influence, it controlled state governments even in quite populous non-Southern states like Indiana. It was during the 1920s and 1930s that the enduring identification of recent immigrant groups such as the Italians and Poles with the Democratic Party was forged (Archdeacon, 1983). Voting blocs based on ethnicity became part of the fabric of American politics, especially in major urban areas, where party tickets were often tailored to maximise appeal to ethnic voters.

Immigrant politics largely concerned European-origin voters until the 1965 amendments to immigration law, which opened the door to entries from around the world (see Chapter 4). The seemingly inevitable outcome of the changed composition of legal immigration to the USA has been the emergence of new constituencies appealed to, in part, on an ethnic basis. Much attention has focused on Hispanic and Asian voters, whose numbers increased sharply in the 1980s and 1990s. Indeed European-origin Americans are being outnumbered by so-called minorities in a number of key states, including California, and in several major cities, including New York City. Obviously, not all persons enumerated as minorities are of recent immigrant origin. The ancestors of most Afro-Americans and many Hispanics were established on the territory of the present-day USA long before the ancestors of many European-origin Americans. None the less the largely immigration-driven evolution of the American population may profoundly affect the future of politics. The question is: will the current wave of immigrants, the Mexicans and the Filipinos, be like the waves that preceded them? For all the alarm raised by the mass arrival of Irish Catholics in the nineteenth century, they ended up becoming Americans. The tendency is to believe that the outcome will be the same for immigrants of Latin American and Asian origin, but such results are not foreordained and the emerging debate over multiculturalism may affect the ultimate outcome.

Immigration figured prominently in the 1996 US election, which came just after an upsurge in naturalisations, in part due to a citizenship campaign but also to legal changes which threatened to strip benefits from legally resident aliens but not from citizens. New voters affected electoral outcomes in many districts and Democrats generally benefited. One defeated congressman alleged that ineligible immigrant voters helped defeat his re-election bid. To expedite naturalisation and new citizens voter registration, certain organisations were empowered to process applications. Republicans claimed there were irregularities, including voting by non-citizens and invalid naturalisation of ineligible aliens.

Immigrants from various countries and regions evince quite variable rates of naturalisation, with key Hispanic nationalities like the Mexicans lagging far behind the average rate for all foreign-born. Harry Pachon has pointed out that the issue of Hispanic naturalisation dates from the cession of nearly a third of Mexico to the USA after the US victory in the war of 1848, a war precipitated by a revolt by white settlers in Texas. The treaty ending the war gave US citizenship to Mexicans in the territory lost by Mexico, but access to US citizenship by post-1848 immigrants was unclear. Federal law restricted naturalisation to 'free white aliens' before extending it to 'aliens of African nativity or descent' in 1870. An 1897 court case concluded that Mexican immigrants were eligible to naturalise on the basis of the 1848 treaty. But it was not until 1940 that Congress formally extended naturalisation rights to aliens indigenous to the western hemisphere (Pachon, 1987: 299–310).

This historical background may help account for the lagging Mexican naturalisation rate in the USA, briefly discussed in Chapter 1. Other factors have also been cited, such as the proximity of such countries as Mexico and various provisions of immigration law with regard to family entry. A major factor in the case of Mexican immigrants was the constitutional restriction against foreigners owning land in Mexico. As many Mexican immigrants in the USA own small plots of land, this discouraged naturalisation in the US. Proposed changes to the Mexican constitution in 1996 facilitating dual citizenship were expected to increase naturalisation of Mexicans legally resident in the USA. Immigrants in other Western democracies also have variable rates of naturalisation. Groups comprising large numbers of refugees (such as Vietnamese and Cubans in the USA) almost always demonstrate the highest rates of naturalisation (see Chapter 9).

Many naturalised immigrants do not exercise their voting rights. Abstention rates are very high among Asian-American voters despite voter registration and participation drives aimed specifically at them. In 1992, only 350 000 of the estimated 2.9 million Asian-Americans living in California were registered to vote (Choo, 1992). The 33rd US Congressional district in California, downtown Los Angeles, was thought to be one of the districts with the highest number of non-citizens: 225 116 out of the 384 158 adults resident in 1992. Only 13 per cent of the adult population voted in the 1992 election. Twenty-eight per cent did not exercise their voting rights and 59 per cent were ineligible as non-citizens. This compared to a national average of 52 per cent of adults voting, 44 per cent not voting and 4 per cent ineligible to vote due to non-citizenship (*Washington Post*, 22 May, 1994). Abstention rates are also high for French citizens of immigrant background. In the first round of the 1997 legislative elections 32.1 per cent of the electorate abstained and 3.3 per cent cast blank ballots.

Abstention rates were especially high in the St Denis district which is heavily immigrant. In Sweden, participation by non-citizens in local and regional elections has declined since it was first introduced in 1975. The immigration trends of the last several decades have significantly affected electoral politics in many Western democracies. In the USA, Hispanics and Asian-Americans have emerged as significant ethnic voting blocs since the 1970s. Hispanic voters, in particular, have become a focus of inter-party competition as Democrats and Republicans attempt to woo them. The inroads made by the conservative Republic Party into an ethnic clientele traditionally viewed as predisposed towards the Democrats have affected electoral outcomes in several areas with large concentrations of Hispanic voters. A large segment of the Hispanic community of Florida, for instance, is comprised of Cubans to whom the Republicans appeal through a stridently anti-communist, anti-Castro rhetoric. Homeland politics are of concern for virtually all immigrant voters, a factor that interjects issues pertaining to US foreign policy towards their homelands into campaigns. While such concerns generally are not enough to alter the traditional focus of US electoral campaigns on domestic issues, candidates often adopt foreign policy positions favoured by immigrant groups in the quest for campaign donations and the electoral support of the group.

Immigrant groups can also have some influence on domestic issues. An illustration of the growing significance of Hispanic voters in the USA came during the 1984 campaign for the Democratic nomination for the presidency. All three of the major Democratic candidates voiced their opposition to pending legislation that would enact sanctions against illegal employment of aliens. Their stated reason for opposing employer sanctions was the fear that they would cause additional employment discrimination against minorities. However, such principled positions were probably influenced by a perception that Hispanics were strongly opposed to employer sanctions. The most strident opposition to employer sanctions came from Hispanic groups like the Mexican-American Legal Defense Fund. Nationally, however, Hispanics were about evenly split on the wisdom of employer sanctions, whereas the general US population was strongly supportive of the concept.

Prior to the 1996 elections, a nationwide campaign to register recently naturalised immigrants was undertaken. It was alleged by Republicans that the INS drive to naturalise aliens was politically motivated. In California, large numbers of citizenship applications were determined to have been inadequately scrutinised, especially for disqualifying criminal records. This registration effort appears to have borne fruit as Hispanic voters turned out massively in the 1996 election thereby helping many candidates of the Democratic Party (*New York Times*, 10 November, 1996). Some observers termed the Hispanic vote a watershed event.

The size of the Asian-American community in the USA roughly doubled over the 1980s to number over 7 million by 1990. A 1992 report by the Federal Civil Rights Commission found that Asian-Americans faced extensive discrimination and that 'there has been a widespread failure of government at all levels and of the nation's public schools to provide for the needs of immigrant Asian-Americans' (Dagger, 1992). The extent to which issues of concern to Asian-American and Hispanic voters influenced the agendas and platforms of the two major political parties was unclear. The 1992 presidential primary, for instance, was marked by 'Japan bashing' that perhaps contributed to an upsurge in attacks on Asians. Asian-Americans have been less successful than the far more numerous Hispanic-Americans in winning public office. But their growing propensity to donate money to candidates has become a factor of some influence (Choo, 1992). The 1996 election witnessed a number of questionable donations by Asian-Americans which were feared to reflect efforts by foreign nations to influence US policies.

The 1996 contest for the Republican presidential nomination featured several anti-immigrant candidates as well as at least one (Jack Kemp) pro-immigrant candidate. California Governor Pete Wilson launched his candidacy with a speech about the need for immigration control in New York City, but quickly dropped out of the race. The eventual Republican nominee Robert Dole never effectively exploited the immigration issue, despite periodic efforts to do so. Adoption of the welfare and immigration laws of 1996 by Congress potentially could have confronted the incumbent President Clinton with serious difficulties, but he chose to sign the two into law and thereby defused the issue, albeit at considerable cost to legally resident aliens. Republican divisions over immigration policy prevented Congress from reducing admission levels, as had been recommended by the Commission on Immigration Reform. Meanwhile, the restrictionist-minded Federation for American Immigration Reform had championed an immigration moratorium. But this radical measure elicited scant support. The Clinton Administration embraced a middle-of-the-road position supporting stepped-up enforcement of laws against illegal migration, opposing expanded temporary foreign worker policy and upholding legal immigration.

The ability of legal immigrants to naturalise, and eventually to vote, constitutes a major concern for any democracy. That immigrant political participation is viewed as legitimate and as an anticipated outcome demarcates the USA, Australian and Canadian experiences from those of many Western European nations. Political exclusion is inherent in the concept of temporary worker policy. That is one reason why it is commonplace in authoritarian and undemocratic settings, such as in the Arab monarchies of the Gulf. Post-Second World War Western European guestworker policies created a conundrum when unplanned, unforeseen mass settlement occurred. The guestworkers and their families could not be excluded from Western European democracies without grievous damage to the fabric of democracy.

The United Kingdom constitutes an exception to the Western European pattern in that most post-1945 immigrants – those from the Commonwealth up to 1971, and the Irish – entered with citizenship and voting rights. However, as previously suggested, this seemed to have little effect upon the socioeconomic position of immigrants which was quite similar to that of guestworkers on the continent. Immigration became an object of political debate as early as 1958 when there were race riots in Notting Hill in London and other areas. In 1962, British immigration law was tightened up, setting a precedent for even more restrictive measures in the future. In the late 1960s, right-wing politicians such as Enoch Powell warned of looming racial conflict, of 'rivers of blood' on the horizon. Immigration became increasingly politicised in the mid-1970s. The National Front, a descendant of Sir Oswald Mosley's British Union of Fascists of the 1930s, played a key role in provoking immigration-related violence. British neo-fascists and leftists battled over immigration in much the same way that French neo-fascists and left-wing, pro-immigrant groups had confronted one another several years earlier (Reed, 1977).

The frequently violent clashes, which then were regarded as uncharacteristic of normally civil British politics, combined with the mounting numbers of immigrants to make immigration a key issue in the 1979 general election. Margaret Thatcher, the Conservative leader, adroitly capitalised on the immigration backlash to deflate support for the National Front and to score a victory over the Labour Party, which was supported by most immigrant voters. A 1975 pamphlet published by the Community Relations Commission underscored the growing electoral significance of immigrant ethnic minorities, and even the

Conservative Party began efforts to recruit ethnic minority members as a result (Layton-Henry, 1981).

In the 1983 and 1987 general elections and in local elections, black and Asian Briton participation became more conspicuous. In 1987, four black Britons were elected to Parliament and three of them joined a black member of the House of Lords to form a black parliamentary caucus styled upon the 24 member strong US Congressional black caucus. Hundreds of black and Asian Britons were elected to positions in local government. In the industrial city of Birmingham, for example, the first Muslim municipal councillor (like most immigrant-origin elected officials a Labourite) was elected in 1982. In 1983, two more Muslim Labourites were elected. By January 1987, there were 14 municipal councillors of immigrant origin, including six Muslims. Within the Birmingham Labour Party, in the Sparkbrook area, 600 of the 800 local party members were Muslims (Joly, 1988: 177–8). But, Studlar and Layton-Henry argue, this growing black and Asian participation and representation in British politics generally has not resulted in greater attention being paid to immigrant issues and grievances:

> Aside from a small number of race-conscious liberal politicians and activists, the discovery of non-white problems has never really generated optimism about the capacity of the British polity to cope with them. Both political decision makers and the public have more commonly simply wanted the problems to go away without government or public commitment to alter them. Serious and active consideration of race-related problems is rare and is even harder to maintain. (Studlar and Layton-Henry, 1990: 288)

Part of the difficulty faced by immigrants in getting their concerns on the Labour Party agenda stems from the necessity of defining group issues in terms of class. However formation of an alternative immigrants' party is not a viable option. Hence, even in a Western European country where most immigrants are enfranchised, their participation and representation remains problematic. Immigrant-origin voters can significantly affect electoral outcomes in 30–60 of Great Britain's 650 parliamentary constituencies. These are located in cities.

The weight of immigrant voters is generally far less on the continent. Sweden, France and Austria have significant foreign-born or immigrant-origin citizen populations, but an immigrant vote appears to be openly counted only in France, where the Socialist Party has appealed with mixed results to the growing electorate of North and sub-Saharan African background. US-style ethnic voter campaigning, however, would violate the Jacobin rules of the game that govern French politics and tend to exacerbate a political backlash against immigrants manifest in the growing electoral appeal of the FN, headed by Jean-Marie Le Pen.

Even in the USA, politicians and parties had to weigh the expected benefits of appealing to immigrant voters, say Hispanics or Asian-Americans, against a possible backlash. The right-wing Republican presidential hopeful Patrick Buchanan, as well as the Louisiana gubernatorial and later US presidential candidate David Duke (who was a Ku Klux Klan leader) both made anti-immigrant themes key elements of their electoral campaigns in 1991 and 1992. Buchanan renewed and amplified this theme in his 1996 presidential bid.

In Australia, there has been considerable debate on the impact of post-war immigration on politics. Most observers argue that the effects have been very limited (Jupp, York and McRobbie, 1989: 51). McAllister states that post-war immigration 'has not resulted in any discernible change in the overall pattern of voting behaviour. Despite large-scale immigration, social class, not birthplace, has remained the basis for divisions between political parties' (1988: 919). A study of the role of Italo-Australians in political life found that they did not have a high profile, and argued that this was typical for immigrants in Australia (Castles *et al.,* 1992c). Italians have not established their own political parties or trade unions, and neither have they gained significant representation in Parliament. On the other hand, there are a large number of local councillors and some mayors of Italian origin. Yet even at this level of government Italo-Australians are under-represented in comparison to their share in the population. Despite this, the 'ethnic vote' appears to be an issue which influences the behaviour of Australian political leaders. Not only do they make efforts to approach ethnic associations to mobilise electoral support, they also make concessions to ethnic needs and interests in their policies.

The explanation for this combination of a low political profile with fairly successful interest articulation seems to lie in the relative openness of the Australian political system for immigrant groups, at least at a superficial level. As a reaction to mass immigration since 1947, governments and trade unions combined to guarantee orderly industrial relations, which would not threaten the conditions of local workers. The policy of assimilation from the 1940s to the early 1970s provided civil rights and citizenship, which laid the groundwork for political integration. Multicultural policies after 1972 accepted the legitimacy of representation of special interests through ethnic community associations. Their leaderships were granted a recognised, if limited, political role in government consultative bodies. Thus immigrant groups obtained some political influence in ethnic affairs and welfare policies. Yet they were still far from gaining significant influence in central political and economic decision-making processes. The question is whether this situation will change as the mainly poorly educated migrant generation leaves the centre stage and is replaced by a new self-confident second generation, which has passed through the Australian educational system (Castles *et al.*, 1992a: 125–39).

Migration and security

The duality of international migrants as political actors and as targets of politics is perhaps most vivid when broaching the increasingly important topic of migration and security, and particularly political terrorism. Involvement of a minority of immigrants in political violence contributed to international migration's new salience on post-Cold War security agendas. What largely passed unnoticed was the disproportionate victimisation of immigrants by perpetrators of terrorism. Skewed and insufficiently informed discussion of immigration and terrorism was par for the course in the post-Cold War period and new measures and laws against terrorism eroded the legal status of aliens in several Western democracies, most notably Germany and the USA. Three cases can be summarised to elucidate why migration and security concerns have become so important.

It has long been known that Turks of Kurdish background were over-represented in the ranks of Turkish emigrants. However, during the mass recruitment period, this seemed to be of little political consequence. In the 1980s Kurdish aspirations for independence or autonomy from Turkey galvanised (see Exhibit 5.1). The PKK, or Kurdish Workers Party, emerged as an important force and began an armed insurrection against the Turkish Republic.

It is estimated that one-quarter to one-third of the over 2 million Turkish citizens resident in Germany are of Kurdish origin. Perhaps 50 000 of these sympathise with the PKK and up to 10 000 are active members of the party or its front organisations. As argued above, it is not unusual for migrants to be actively engaged in homeland-oriented political parties. What is unsettling to German and Turkish authorities is that the PKK transformed Germany into a second front in its struggle and frequently struck at Turkish consulates, airlines and businesses in Germany and elsewhere in Western Europe. Moreover, Turkish repression of the PKK-led insurgency, which has taken tens of thousands of lives, has seriously complicated its diplomatic ties with EU member states. Turkish counter-insurgency measures have included mysterious death squads and the uprooting and forced relocation of millions of Kurdish civilians. This backdrop renders the PKK activities on German soil and German and Turkish countermeasures highly emotive and significant. Indeed, the PKK became one of the primary German national security concerns by the mid-1990s, particularly after the PKK leader Ocalan threatened to send Hamas-style suicide bombers against German targets in retaliation for German cooperation with Turkey in its war against the PKK.

Despite the decision to outlaw the PKK and its front organisations, the PKK possesses an extensive organisational infrastructure in Germany and nearby European states. PKK tactics have featured protest marches and hunger strikes. In recent years, German authorities have routinely banned street demonstrations on Kurdish and Turkish issues. None the less, many have been staged and they frequently result in violent clashes. Until recently, participation in such events was legally a minor offence and resident aliens apprehended at them did not become subject to deportation. In 1996, the German government sought to strengthen its ban on PKK street protests by making participation in banned events a major offence. Several Kurdish protesters were subsequently apprehended and slated for deportation at a time when hunger strikes in Turkish prisons had cost the lives of numerous prisoners, and torture and ill-treatment of prisoners appeared commonplace. Hence, deportation of Kurdish activists raised important legal and human rights issues which polarised German public opinion.

Meanwhile, across the Rhine, French authorities grappled with the spillover of the fundamentalist insurgency in Algeria to French soil. An offshoot of the Islamic Salvation Front, the Armed Islamic Group, pursued an insurgency against the Algerian government, which is dominated by the military. Tens of thousands have died in a merciless war of terrorism and counterterrorism. France has given military and economic support to the beleaguered Algerian government. This became the pretext for the extension of Armed Islamic Group operations to French soil. A network of militants waged a bombing campaign, principally in the Paris region in 1995, before being dismantled. In late 1996, the Armed Islamic Group was thought to have planted another fatal bomb, although no group took responsibility for the attack.

French authorities undertook numerous steps to prevent bombings and to capture the bombers. Persons of North African appearance were routinely subjected to identity checks. These checks were accepted by most French citizens and resident aliens of North African background as a necessary inconvenience. Indeed, information supplied by such individuals greatly aided in the dismantling of the group, several of whom were killed in shootouts with French police. From time to time, French police have rounded up scores of suspected sympathisers with the Armed Islamic Group.

Several guerrillas involved in attacks against hotels in Morocco, designed to disrupt the economically important tourism industry so despised by some Islamic militants, were French citizens of North African background. They had been recruited into a fundamentalist network in the Parisian suburbs and their involvement was deeply disturbing to the French population, inclusive of the great bulk of the Islamic community. All available evidence suggests that mobilisation of North African-origin citizens and permanent residents of France into violence-prone Islamicist organisations is extremely rare, but this incident stoked concern over the potential for that to happen more frequently.

The USA has also received millions of Islamic immigrants. Most have entered legally, while others have come illegally or as asylum applicants. Islam is the fastest growing religion in the USA. The Iranian-origin immigrant population, for instance, is estimated to number over 1 million persons by one Iranian-American organisation (*New York Times*, 28 June, 1995). Major influxes of Palestinians have occurred since 1967 which were connected to the turmoil and difficult living conditions faced by Palestinians in the Middle East.

In the 1990s, several major acts of terrorism were perpetrated by groups linked to Islamic fundamentalism and comprised mainly of immigrants and asylum seekers. Israeli authorities complained that the USA had become a key base of operations for Hamas, an Islamic fundamentalist Palestinian political movement which emerged during the period of the Palestinian Intifada. Hamas has violently opposed the Palestinian-Israeli peace agreement and rejects Palestinian recognition of Israel as well as renunciation of armed struggle against Israel by the Fatah-dominated Palestinian Authority presided over by Yasser Arafat. Hamas sponsored a campaign of violent attacks against Israeli targets in the mid-1990s which seriously jeopardised the peace process and undoubtedly contributed to the narrow victory of the Likud in the 1996 Israeli elections. The attacks also caused the Israeli government to seal off Gaza and the West Bank, preventing tens of thousands of Palestinians from going to work in Israel (see Chapter 5).

The approximate coincidence of the attacks in Israel with those in the USA prompted adoption of a counterterrorism law in the USA in 1996, with significant implications for the rights of immigrants. The new law empowered the government to expedite detention and removal of aliens without customary judicial review. Fund-raising activities by terrorist organisations and their fronts were also targeted. It was unclear whether the new powers given to authorities would stymie fund-raising by groups like Hamas as it is very difficult to distinguish between legitimate humanitarian fund-raising – say, to provide schools or welfare for Palestinians in the area under the control of the Palestinian Authority and in militarily occupied Palestinian areas – and fund-raising that aids and abets perpetuation of terrorism.

These three cases illustrate why migration increasingly is viewed as germane to national security policies in the transatlantic area. However, as Myron Weiner in particular has demonstrated, concern over the security implications of international migration has been a significant factor around the world (Weiner, 1993). The common thread in transatlantic regional responses to immigrant violence has been increased repression and erosion of the legal status of resident aliens. Too often, there has been conflation of immigration with terrorism when, in fact, very few immigrants have been involved in it.

Organised, politically motivated violence against immigrants and foreign-born populations is distressingly commonplace. This is why Turkey, for instance, declares the security of its citizens abroad to be a top foreign policy objective. The vulnerability of migrants to political violence appears to have grown in the post-Cold War period, although the history of anti-immigrant violence in France, as noted above, is longstanding. Yet discussions of political terrorism and counterterrorism strategy pays little heed to anti-immigrant violence.

The risk of overreaction to violence by a handful of immigrants appears quite high. Without minimising the importance of the integration barriers faced by Islamic-origin immigrants in Western democracies, the overall pattern is one of integration and incorporation. The results of several surveys of France's Muslim population, citizen and non-citizen, confirm this (Tribalat, 1995). The most important survey found that persons of Algerian Muslim background are quite secular in orientation. The Moroccan-origin population is considerably more religiously oriented. However, like Catholics, Protestants and Jews in France, only a minority practise their faith regularly. There is considerable dating and socialising with non-Muslims, and intermarriage is not uncommon. The surveys confirm the importance of unemployment and educational problems faced by France's Muslims, but the unmistakable overall thrust of the findings is that integration is occurring.

Integration, of course, provides security for immigrants and the host population. It is the decisive long-term factor affecting migration and security. The risk run in measures like the 1996 counterterrorism legislation is that they will adversely affect integration without appreciably enhancing deterrence of terrorism. As argued elsewhere in this book, policies that exclude immigrants by denying them equal rights risk generating conflict over the long run. Hence, the inescapable conclusion is that democracies have a vital security interest in immigrant rights.

The growing, if belated, interest in migration and security involves a paradox. Many states have a profoundly important security interest in effective implementation of their immigration laws and regulations. Yet, all too often, insufficient appropriations are made or too few personnel engaged to enforce laws and regulations effectively. Stated or proclaimed policies often are undermined by funding or staffing decisions or undercut by political pressure to protect certain constituents, clients or (especially in the USA), contributors to election campaigns. One result is a credibility gap which potentially endangers legally-admitted aliens, who have an extraordinary stake in well-managed policies which ensure that immigration and settlement are consented to and legitimate.

Thus far, there is little evidence that racism and violence against immigrants have provoked violent countermeasures by immigrants. However, the potential for racism and anti-immigrant violence begetting terrorism in response should not be underestimated, once again underscoring everyone's stake in vigilance against violent opponents of immigrants.

Conclusion

International migration has played a major role in fostering multi-cultural politics. Migration can dramatically affect electorates, as witnessed in the Israeli case, and immigrants can influence politics through non-electoral means as well. Immigrants have fostered transnational politics linking homeland and host society political systems in fundamental ways. Migrants and minorities are both subjects and objects of politics. An anti-immigrant backlash has strengthened the appeal of right-wing parties in Western Europe. One way in which migration has fundamentally altered the Western European political landscape is through the constitution of increasingly vocal Islamic organisations, which present a dilemma for democratic political systems: refusal to accept their role would violate democratic principles, yet many people see their aims and methods as intrinsically antidemocratic. International migration has fostered new constituencies, new parties and new issues. Many of Western Europe's newly emerging political parties, such as the FN in France, feature anti-immigrant themes. Violence against immigrants has also grown everywhere, and is a factor in ethnic minority formation and political mobilisation.

In the USA, Canada and Australia immigrant political participation and representation is less of a problem, partly because of the preponderance of family-based legal immigration. However, disenfranchisement of legally resident aliens and illegally resident aliens in major US cities increasingly troubles authorities. Much of New York's population cannot vote, either because they are not naturalised or they are illegally resident. Virtually everywhere international migration renders politics more complex. Ethnic mobilisation and the ethnic vote are becoming important issues in many countries. Another new issue may be seen in the politics of naturalisation. One or two decades ago, virtually no one knew naturalisation law or considered it important. The changing nature of international migration and its politicisation has changed that. Most democracies now face a long-term problem stemming from growing populations of resident aliens who are unable or unwilling to naturalise; hence there is a heightened concern cver dual nationality.

Immigrant politics are in a continual state of flux, because of the rapid changes in migratory flows as well as the broader transformations in political patterns which are taking place in many Western societies. As migratory movements mature – moving through the stages of immigration, settlement and minority formation – the character of political mobilisation and participation changes. There is a shift from concern with homeland politics to mobilisation around the interests of ethnic groups in the immigration country. If political participation is denied through refusal of citizenship and failure to provide channels of representation, immigrant politics is likely to take on militant forms. This applies particularly to the children of immigrants born in the countries of immigration. If they are excluded from political life through non-citizenship, social marginalisation or racism, they are likely to present a major challenge to existing political structures in the future.

11 Conclusion: Migration in the New World Disorder

This book has argued that international migration is a constant, not an aberration, in human history. Population movements have always accompanied demographic growth, technological change, political conflict and warfare. Over the last five centuries mass migrations have played a major role in colonialism, industrialisation, the emergence of nation-states and the development of the capitalist world market. However, international migration has never been as pervasive, or as socioeconomically and politically significant, as it is today. Never before have statesmen accorded such priority to migration concerns. Never before has international migration seemed so pertinent to national security and so connected to conflict and disorder on a global scale.

The hallmark of the age of migration is the global character of international migration: the way it affects more and more countries and regions, and its linkages with complex processes affecting the entire world. This book has endeavoured to elucidate the principal causes, processes and effects of international migration. Contemporary patterns, as discussed in Chapters 4, 5 and 6, are rooted in historical relationships and shaped by a multitude of political, demographic, socioeconomic, geographical and cultural factors. These flows result in greater ethnic diversity within countries and deepening transnational linkages between states and societies. International migrations are greatly affected by governmental policies and may, in fact, be started by decisions to recruit foreign workers or to admit refugees.

Yet international migrations may also possess a relative autonomy and be more or less impervious to governmental policies. As we have seen, official policies often fail to achieve their objectives, or even bring about the opposite of what is intended. People as well as governments shape international migration. Decisions made by individuals, families and communities – often with imperfect information and constrained options – play a vital role in determining migration and settlement. The social networks which arise through the migratory process help shape long-term outcomes. The agents and brokers who make up the burgeoning 'migration industry' may have their own interests and aims. Despite the growth in migratory movements, and the strength of the factors which cause them, resistance to migration is also of growing importance. Large sections of the populations of receiving countries may oppose immigration. Governments sometimes react by adopting strategies of denial, hoping that the problems will go away if they are ignored. In other instances, mass deportations and repatriations have been carried out. Governments vary greatly in their capacities to regulate international migration and in the credibility of their efforts to regulate unauthorised migration.

In Chapter 2 we provided some theoretical perspectives on the reasons why international migrations take place and discussed how they almost inevitably lead to permanent settlement and the formation of distinct ethnic groups in the receiving societies. We suggested that the migratory process needs to be understood in its totality as a complex system of social interactions with a wide range of institutional structures and informal networks in both sending and receiving countries, and at the international level. In subsequent chapters it was shown that the model of a four-stage migratory process fits better in some cases than others. In a democratic setting, however, legal admission of migrants will almost always result in some settlement, even when migrants are admitted temporarily.

The comparison of two very different immigration countries – Australia and Germany – in Chapter 8 showed how the migratory process takes on its own dynamics, sometimes leading to consequences unforeseen and unwanted by policy-makers. Acceptance of the seeming inevitability of permanent settlement and formation of ethnic groups is the necessary starting-point for any meaningful consideration of desirable public policies. Serious discussion requires an elementary measure of realism; something not found, for instance, in the time-worn slogan that 'Germany is not a country of immigration'. The key to adaptive policy-making in this realm (as in others) is understanding of the causes and dynamics of international migration. Policies based on misunderstanding or mere wishful thinking are virtually condemned to fail. Hence, if governments decide to admit foreign workers, they should from the outset make provision for the legal settlement of that proportion of the entrants that is almost sure to remain permanently: a consideration that needs to be taken to heart by the governments of countries as diverse as Japan, Malaysia, Italy and Greece at present.

Today the governments and peoples of immigration countries have to face up to some very serious dilemmas. The answers they choose will help shape the future of their societies, as well as their relations with the poorer countries of the South. Central issues include:

• regulating legal immigration and integrating settlers
• policies to cope with illegal migration
• finding 'durable solutions' to emigration pressure through improved international relations
• the role of ethnic diversity in social and cultural change, and the consequences for the nation-state.

Legal migration and integration

Virtually all democratic states, and many not so democratic states as well, have growing foreign populations. As shown in Chapters 4, 5 and 6, the presence of these immigrants is generally due to conscious labour recruitment or immigration policies, or to the existence of various linkages between sending and receiving countries. In some cases (notably the USA, Canada and Australia) policies of large-scale immigration still exist. Invariably they are selective: economic migrants, family members and refugees are admitted according to certain quotas which are politically determined. In other countries (particularly in Western Europe), past labour recruitment policies have been suspended, and governments try to limit entries of workers, family members or refugees. None the less most countries welcome one group of migrants – highly-skilled temporary workers – and have policies which allow at least some entries on humanitarian grounds. Finally, countries with labour shortages admit workers, either in an overt and controlled way (as in the Arab oil countries, Taiwan or Singapore) or by tacitly permitting illegal entries (as in Italy, Korea and Japan).

There is considerable evidence that planned and controlled entries are conducive to acceptable social conditions for migrants as well as to relative social peace between migrants and local people. Countries with immigration quota systems generally decide on them through political processes which permit public discussion and the balancing of the interests of different social groups. Participation in decision-making increases the acceptability of immigration programmes. At the same time this approach facilitates the introduction of measures to prevent discrimination and exploitation of immigrants, and to provide social services to support successful settlement. There is therefore a strong case for advocating that all countries which actually continue to have immigration should move towards planned immigration policies. This would apply to much of Western and Southern Europe, and to many new immigration countries in Asia.

As Chapter 9 showed, governmental obligations towards immigrant populations are shaped by the nature of the political system in the host society, as well as the mode of entry of the newcomers. Governments possess an internationally recognised right to regulate entry of aliens, a right that may be voluntarily limited through governmental signature of bilateral or multilateral agreements (for example, in the case of refugees). Clearly it makes a difference whether an alien has arrived on a territory through legal means of entry or not. In principle, the proper course for action with regard to legally admitted foreign residents in a democracy is straightforward. They should be rapidly afforded equality of socioeconomic rights and a large measure of political freedom, for their status would otherwise diminish the quality of democratic life in the society. However, this principle is frequently ignored in practice. As Chapters 7 and 10 showed, unauthorised immigration and employment makes immigrants especially vulnerable to exploitation. The perceived illegitimacy of their presence can foster conflict and anti-immigrant violence.

Guestworker policy-style restrictions on the employment and residential mobility of legally admitted aliens appear anachronistic and, in the long run, administratively unfeasible. They are difficult to reconcile with prevailing market principles, to say nothing of democratic norms. The same goes for restrictions on political rights. Freedom of speech, association and assembly should be unquestionable. Under normal circumstances of international cooperation, there is no reason to restrict recent immigrants' ability to participate in their homelands' political system. The only restriction on the rights of legally admitted aliens which seems compatible with democratic principles is the reservation of the right to vote and to stand for public office to citizens. This is only justifiable if resident aliens are given the real opportunity of naturalisation, without daunting procedures or high fees. But, even then, some foreign residents are likely to decide not to become citizens for various reasons. A democratic system needs to secure their political participation too. This can mean setting up special representative bodies for resident non-citizens, or extending voting rights to non-citizens who fulfil certain criteria of length of stay (as in Sweden and the Netherlands).

The global character of international migration results in the intermingling and cohabitation of people from increasingly different physical and cultural settings. The severity of integration problems is highly variable. In some instances, public authorities may regard it as unnecessary to devise policies to facilitate integration. In most cases, however, specific and selective measures are necessary in order to forestall the development of socioeconomic, cultural or political cleavages which can be conflictual. Here the multicultural models developed in Australia, Sweden and Canada deserve careful scrutiny. Their common thread is an acceptance of the cultural diversity and social changes wrought by immigration. Immigrants are not forced to conform to a dominant cultural or linguistic model but instead can maintain their native languages and cultural life if they choose to do so. The diversity produced by immigration is seen as an enrichment rather than as a threat to the predominant culture.

A multicultural approach enhances democratic life in that it allows for choice. It can mean a redefinition of citizenship to include cultural rights, along with the widely accepted civil, political and social rights. With the passage of time, it is expected that most immigrants and their offspring will reconcile their cultural heritage with the prevailing culture, and the latter will be somewhat altered, and most likely richer, for that. Conflict will have been minimised. None the less multicultural models have their contradictions and are often the subject of heated debate and renegotiation. For instance, multiculturalism may proclaim the right to use of an immigrant's mother tongue, but those who do not learn the dominant language can find themselves disadvantaged in the labour market. Maintenance of some cultural norms may be a form of discriminatory social control, particularly for women and youth. The dividing line between real participation of ethnic leaderships in decision-making and their cooption through the patronage of government agencies can be very thin.

Many people argue that an explicitly multicultural approach to immigrant integration may not be appropriate for all societies. This applies particularly in states like the USA and France, with established traditions of immigrant incorporation and assimilation. In these countries it is believed that political integration through citizenship provides the essential precondition for social and cultural integration. Special cultural or social policies for immigrants are thought to perpetuate distinctions and lead to formation of ghettoes and separatist groups. Thus the basic principle of the US model is a policy of benign (but not unthinking) neglect in the public sphere and a reliance on the integrative potential of the private sphere: families, neighbourhoods, ethnic solidarity organisations and so on. Yet the formation of racial or ethnic

ghettoes in the USA and the growth of ethnic conflict in France present
a challenge to such approaches at the present time. Recent changes,
such as the 1996 restriction of welfare rights for immigrants in the USA
and the 1993 *Loi Pasqua* limiting automatic citizenship for children of
immigrants in France, may reflect a questioning of the assimilationist
model.

However, whether the choice is made for benign neglect or for more
explicitly multicultural policies, certain preconditions must be met if
marginalisation and isolation of minorities are to be avoided. The state
needs to take measures to ensure that there is no long-term link
between ethnic origin and socioeconomic disadvantage. This requires
legal measures to combat discrimination, social policies to alleviate
existing disadvantage and educational measures to ensure equal opportunities and to provide the chance of upward mobility. The state
also has the task of eliminating racism, combating racial violence and
above all of dealing with organised racist groups. As pointed out in
Chapter 9, racist discrimination and violence are major factors leading
to formation of ethnic minorities in all the countries of immigration
examined. There is clearly a great need for action in this area.

What seem counterproductive to the long-range goal of integration
are policies that assume cultural conformity or that seek to impose it.
Former 'guestworker' countries like Germany or Switzerland are
beginning to move away from their previous exclusionary policies,
which were based on the illusion that immigrants were just temporary
foreign workers. But often the price they demand of immigrants in
return for the right to settle is assimilation. As other countries of
immigration have learnt, processes of adaptation and integration take
time, and complete assimilation requires many generations. Policies
requiring conformity of immigrants do not take this into account and
thereby can increase the risk of conflict latent in immigration.

Regulating 'unwanted' immigration

Prospects are slim for significantly increased legal immigration flows to
Western democracies over the short to medium term. In Germany and
similar countries some observers have suggested a need for increased
immigration to compensate for low birth-rates and an ageing population: foreign workers might provide the labour for age-care and other
services as well as the construction industry. The rather anachronistic
resurgence of domestic labour in the USA, Europe and parts of Asia

and Latin America is based on the feminisation of labour migration. But immigration cannot effectively counteract the demographic ageing of Western societies unless it is substantially increased. Political constraints will not permit this. There will be some room for highly skilled labour, family reunification and refugees, but not for a resumption of massive recruitment of foreign labour for low-level jobs. Most industrial democracies will have to struggle to provide adequate employment for existing populations of low-skilled citizen and resident alien workers. The generally adverse labour market situation will make any recruitment of foreign labour politically controversial.

One of the most pressing challenges for many countries today is therefore to find ways of coping with 'unwanted' migratory flows. 'Unwanted immigration' is a somewhat vague blanket term, which embraces:

- illegal border-crossers
- legal entrants who overstay their entry visas or who work without permission
- family members of migrant workers, prevented from entering legally by restrictions on family reunion
- asylum seekers not regarded as genuine refugees

Most such migrants come from poor countries and seek employment, but generally lack work qualifications. They compete with disadvantaged local people for unskilled jobs, and for housing and social amenities. Many regions throughout the world have had an enormous increase in such 'unwanted immigration' in the last twenty years or so. Of course, the migration is not always as 'unwanted' as is made out, employers often benefit from cheap workers who lack rights, and some governments tacitly permit such movements. 'Unwanted immigration' is often seen as being at the bottom of public fears of mass influxes. It is therefore a catalyst for racism and is at the centre of extreme-right agitation.

Stopping 'unwanted immigration' is increasingly regarded by governments as essential for safeguarding social peace. In Western Europe, the result has been a series of agreements designed to secure international cooperation in stopping illegal entries, and to speed up the processing of applications for asylum (see Chapters 4 and 5). But the European experience is that such agreements are hard to introduce and even harder to implement. However, governmental and intergovernmental control measures seem to have contributed to the decline in

East–West migration and the reduction in the number of asylum seekers in the early 1990s.

In the USA, Canada and Australia, measures have also been taken to improve border control and to speed up refugee determination. The USA, in particular, has moved towards sanctions against employers of undocumented workers. Several African and Asian countries have carried out quite draconian measures, such as mass expulsions of foreign workers (for example, Nigeria, Libya, Malaysia), building fences and walls along borders (South Africa, Israel, Malaysia), severe punishments for illegal entrants (corporal punishment in Singapore; imprisonment or a bar on future admission in many countries) and sanctions against employers (South Africa, Japan and other countries). In addition, non-official punishments such as beatings by police are routinely meted out in Italy, some Arab countries and elsewhere. The effectiveness of these measures is hard to assess; however, unauthorised migration clearly remains a concern almost everywhere.

The difficulty in achieving effective control is not hard to understand. Barriers to mobility contradict the powerful forces which are leading towards greater economic and cultural interchange. In an increasingly international economy, it is difficult to open borders for movements of information, commodities and capital and yet close them to people. Global circulation of investment and know-how always means movements of people too. Moreover, as shown in Chapters 5 and 6, flows of highly-skilled personnel tend to encourage flows of less-skilled workers too. The instruments of border surveillance cannot be sufficiently fine-tuned to let through all those whose presence is wanted, but to stop all those who are not.

The matter is further complicated by a number of factors: the eagerness of employers to hire foreign workers (whether documented or not) for menial jobs, when nationals are unwilling to take such positions; the difficulty of adjudicating asylum claims and of distinguishing economically motivated migrants from those deserving of refugee status; and the inadequacies or insufficiencies of immigration law. The weakening of organised labour and declining trade union membership in many Western democracies has also tended to increase unauthorised foreign employment. Similarly, policies aimed at reducing labour market rigidities and enhancing competitiveness may result in expanded employer hiring of unauthorised foreign workers. Social welfare policies also have unintended consequences, making employment of unauthorised alien workers more propitious.

Thus, despite the claimed desire of governments to stop illegal migration, many of the causes are to be found in the political and social structures of the immigration countries, and their relations with less-developed areas. This has led to the call for 'durable solutions' to address the root causes of mass migration. But such measures are not likely to bring a quick reduction in 'unwanted immigration'. There are many reasons to expect that the number of individuals worldwide desiring to migrate will continue to expand in coming decades, perhaps exponentially. In the current political climate there is no doubt that receiving countries will continue to regulate migration and attempt to curb illegal immigration. This will require investing more personnel and budgetary resources into enforcement of employer sanctions and adjudication of asylum claims than in the past. Enforcement of immigration laws will probably be accorded higher priority in the future, if only because of growing apprehension over the possible political consequences of continuing illegal migration. How successful such measures can be remains to be seen.

Durable solutions and international relations

Clearly international migration is not the solution to the North–South gap. Migration will not resolve North Africa's unemployment problem, or appreciably reduce the income and wage gap between the USA and Mexico, or make a significant impact on rural poverty in India. The only realistic long-term hope for reduction of international migration is broad-based, sustainable development in the less-developed countries, enabling economic growth to keep pace with growth in the population and labour force. Growing realisation in the highly-developed countries that border control alone cannot stop 'unwanted immigration' has led to a discussion on 'durable solutions', to achieve a long-term reduction of migration pressures. Such measures are wide-ranging and closely linked to the debate on development strategies for the countries of the South. They include trade policy, development assistance, regional integration and international relations.

Reform of trade policies could help encourage economic growth in the less-developed countries. The most important issue is the level of prices for primary commodities as compared with industrial products. This is linked to constraints on world trade through tariffs and subsidies. The conclusion of the GATT Uruguay Round and the formation of the WTO in 1994–5 may help to improve the trade perspectives of less-developed countries, though it is hard to be certain as the USA, Japan and the EU insisted on safeguards for their own primary producers. Reform of the European Common Agricultural Policy could bring important benefits for less-developed countries. But trade policies generally operate within tight political constraints: few politicians are willing to confront their own farmers, workers or industrialists, particularly in times of economic recession. Reforms favourable to the economies of the less-developed countries will only come gradually, if at all.

Development assistance is a second strategy which might help to reduce 'unwanted' migration over the long term. Some states have good records in this respect, but international assistance generally has not been at a level sufficient to make a real impression on problems of underdevelopment. Indeed, the balance of nearly four decades of development policies is not a positive one. Although some countries have managed to achieve substantial growth, in general the gap between the poor and rich countries has grown. Income distribution within the countries of the South has also become more inequitable, increasing the gulf between the wealthy elites and the impoverished masses. The problems of rapid demographic growth, economic stagnation, ecological degradation, weak states and abuse of human rights still affect many countries of Africa, Asia and Latin America. Development assistance became a political instrument in the Cold War, leading to 'aid' in the form of weapons, and the fighting of surrogate wars on behalf of the great powers. The result was political instability, increased poverty and outflows of refugees. Moreover, control of world finance by bodies such as the International Monetary Fund and the World Bank led to credit policies which increased the dependency and instability of many countries of the South. Yet the end of the Cold War and the loss of the bipolar organising principle for world politics seems to have led to even greater disorder and conflict.

Regional integration – the creation of free-trade areas and regional political communities – is sometimes seen as a way of diminishing 'unwanted' migration by reducing trade barriers and spurring economic growth, as well as by legalising international movement of labour. But regional integration usually takes place between states which share political and cultural values and which resemble one another economically. Italy's membership in the EC contributed to the dramatic lessening of Italian emigration and it has become a significant country of immigration. However a more pertinent reference is to Turkey's application to join the EC. In this case, EC apprehension over increased Turkish immigration if Turkey were to be accorded full membership played a decisive role in the 1989 decision to deny that country membership. Another example is the NAFTA between Mexicc, the USA and Canada. In the NAFTA negotiations, labour mobility was specifically excluded from the free-trade agreement. Generally the development gap is too profound to enable extension of freedom of labour mobility between developed and less-developed societies to be viewed as desirable. There is little evidence that regional trade agreements have done much to reduce labour migration.

Policies designed to limit immigration are likely to play a growing role in international relations. Some of the first cooperative agreements between Western Europe and the new states of Eastern Europe concerned arrangements for limiting migration. There are many conceivable situations in which bold and imaginative foreign policy holds out a genuine prospect for substantial reduction in refugee flows and economic migrant movement. In this respect, the UN decision to intervene in Iraq's Kurdish area in 1991, to prevent a further outflow of refugees to Turkey and to enable their repatriation, set a significant precedent. The US-led UN intervention in Haiti in 1994 was also designed to prevent refugee flows. Yet the collapse of the UN action in Iraqi Kurdistan in 1996, when one of the rival Kurdish factions called in support from Iraq, showed the precarious nature of such actions in volatile regions.

Perhaps the end of the Cold War could provide the resources and the current fear of migrant influxes could provide the motivation to achieve real change through international cooperation. This would mean restricting the international weapons trade, altering the terms of trade between the North and the South, and changing world financial systems so that they encourage a real transfer of resources from the rich to the poor countries, rather than the other way round, as at present. It would also mean basing development assistance programmes on criteria of human rights, environmental protection, ecological sustainability and social equity. Worker migration could be linked to development policies through training and investment measures, designed to help returning migrants contribute to growth in their home countries.

Yet however successful such policies might be – and sadly they seem fairly utopian in the light of the current world disorder – they will not bring about substantial reductions of international migration in the short term. As shown in Chapters 3, 5 and 6, the initial effect of development and integration into the world market is to increase migration from less-developed countries. This is because the early stages of development lead to rural–urban migration, and to acquisition by many people of the financial and cultural resources needed for international migration. The 'migration transition' – through which emigration ceases, and is eventually replaced by immigration – requires specific demographic and economic conditions, which may take generations to develop. Neither restrictive measures nor development strategies can totally curb international migration, at least in the short term, because there are such powerful forces stimulating population movement. These include the increasing pervasiveness of a global culture and the growth of cross-border movements of ideas, capital, commodities and people. The world community will have to learn to live with mass population movements for the foreseeable future.

Ethnic diversity, social change and the nation-state

The age of migration has already changed the world and many of its societies. Most highly-developed countries and many less-developed ones have become far more culturally diverse than they were even a generation ago. A large proportion, indeed the majority, of nation-states must face up to the reality of ethnic pluralism. In fact few modern nations have ever been ethnically homogeneous. However, the nationalism of the last two centuries strove to create myths of homogeneity. In its extreme forms, nationalism even tried to bring about such homogeneity through expulsion of minorities and genocide. The appalling spectacle of 'ethnic cleansing' in the ruins of former Yugoslavia shows that such tendencies still exist. But the reality for most countries today is that they have to contend with a new type of pluralism, and that – even if migration were to stop tomorrow – this will affect their societies for generations. Moreover, as this book has documented, although migration may change in character and composition, overall it shows few signs of ceasing, and is indeed more likely to grow in volume as we move into the twenty-first century.

One reason why immigration and the emergence of new ethnic groups have had such an impact in most highly-developed countries is that these trends have coincided with the crisis of modernity and the transition to post-industrial societies. The labour migration of the pre-1973 period appeared at the time to be reinforcing the economic dominance of the old industrial nations. Today we can interpret it as part of a process of capital accumulation which preceded a seminal change in the world economy. Growing international mobility of capital, the electronic revolution, the decline of old industrial areas and the rise of new ones are all factors which have led to rapid economic change in Western Europe, North America and Australia. The erosion of the old blue-collar working class and the increased polarisation of the labour force have led to a social crisis in which immigrants find themselves doubly at risk: many of them suffer unemployment and social marginalisation, yet at the same time they are often portrayed as the cause of the problems. That is why the emergence of the 'two-thirds society' is everywhere accompanied by ghettoisation of the disadvantaged and the rise of racism.

Nowhere is this more evident than in the global cities of the late twentieth century. Los Angeles, Toronto, Paris, London, Berlin and Sydney – to name just a few – are crucibles of social change, political conflict and cultural innovation. They are marked by enormous gulfs: between the corporate elite and the informal sector workers who service them, between rich, well-guarded suburbs and decaying and crime-ridden inner cities, between citizens of democratic states and illegal non-citizens, between dominant cultures and minority cultures. The gulf may be summed up as that between inclusion and exclusion. The included are those who fit into the self-image of a prosperous, technologically innovative and democratic society. The excluded are the shadow side: those who are necessary for the reproduction of society, but who do not fit into the ideology of the model.

Both groups include nationals and immigrants, though the immigrants are more likely to belong to the excluded. But the groups are more closely bound together than they might like to think: the corporate elite need the illegal immigrants, the prosperous suburbanites need the slum-dwellers they find so threatening. It is out of this contradictory and multilayered character of the post-modern city that its enormous energy, its cultural dynamism and its innovative capability emerge. But these coexist with potential for social breakdown, conflict, repression and violence. It is here that the complex social and cultural interaction between different ethnic groups may in future give birth to new peoples and provide the basis for new forms of society.

The new ethnic diversity affects societies in many ways. Amongst the most important are issues of political participation, cultural pluralism and national identity. As Chapter 10 showed, immigration and formation of ethnic groups have already had major effects on politics in most developed countries. These effects are potentially destabilising. The only resolution appears to lie in broadening political participation to embrace immigrant groups, which in turn may mean rethinking the form and content of citizenship, and decoupling it from ideas of ethnic homogeneity or cultural assimilation. This leads on to the issue of cultural pluralism. Processes of marginalisation and isolation of ethnic groups have gone so far in many countries that culture has become a marker for exclusion on the part of some sections of the majority population, and a mechanism of resistance by the minorities. Even if serious attempts were made to end all forms of discrimination and racism, cultural and linguistic difference will persist for generations, especially if new immigration takes place. That means that majority populations will have to learn to live with cultural pluralism, even if it means modifying their own expectations of acceptable standards of behaviour and social conformity.

This move towards cultural pluralism corresponds with the emergence of a global culture, which is fed by travel, mass media and commodification of cultural symbols, as well as by migration. This global culture is anything but homogeneous, but the universe of variations which it permits has a new meaning compared with traditional ethnic cultures: difference need no longer be a marker for strangeness and separation, but rather an opportunity for informed choice among a myriad of possibilities. The new global culture is therefore passionately syncretistic, permitting endless combinations of elements with diverse origins and meanings. The major obstacle to the spread of the global culture is that it coincides with a political, economic and social crisis in many regions. Where change is fast and threatening, narrow traditional cultures seem to offer a measure of defence. Hence the resurgence of exclusionary nationalism in areas like the former Soviet Union and Yugoslavia, which have been cut off so long from global influences that change, now that it has come, is experienced as a cataclysm. And hence the resurgence of racism in highly-developed societies amongst those groups who find themselves the main victims of economic and social restructuring.

Clearly trends towards political inclusion of minorities and cultural pluralism can threaten national identity, especially in countries in which it has been constructed in exclusionary forms. If ideas of belonging to a nation have been based on myths of ethnic purity or of cultural superiority, then they really are threatened by the growth of ethnic diversity. Whether the community of the nation has been based on belonging to a *Volk* (as in Germany) or on a unitary culture (as in France), ethnic diversity inevitably requires major political and psychological adjustments. The shift is far smaller for countries that have seen themselves as nations of immigrants, for their political structures and models of citizenship are geared to incorporating newcomers. However, these countries too have historical traditions of racial exclusion and cultural homogenisation which still need to be worked through. Assimilation of immigrants, as epitomised in the American Dream, seems less viable in view of continuing population movements and strong trends towards cultural and linguistic maintenance by ethnic communities.

That means that all countries of immigration are going to have to re-examine their understanding of what it means to belong to their societies. Monocultural and assimilationist models of national identity may no longer be adequate for the new situation. Immigrants may be able to make a special contribution to the development of new forms of identity. It is part of the migrant condition to develop multiple identities, which are linked to the cultures both of the homeland and of the country of origin. Such personal identities possess complex new transcultural elements.

Immigrants are not unique in this; multiple identities are becoming an almost general characteristic of the people of post-modern societies. But it is above all migrants who are compelled by their situation to have multi-layered sociocultural identities, which are constantly in a state of transition and renegotiation. Moreover, migrants frequently develop a consciousness of their transcultural position, which is reflected not only in their artistic and cultural work, but also in social and political action. Despite current conflicts about the effects of ethnic diversity on national cultures and identity, immigration does offer perspectives for change. The hope must be that new principles of identity can emerge, which will be neither exclusionary nor discriminatory, and which will provide the basis for better intergroup cooperation. Moreover, multilingual capabilities and intercultural understanding are beginning to be seen as important economic assets in the context of international trade and investment.

Inevitably transcultural identities will affect our fundamental political structures. The democratic nation-state is a fairly young political form, which came into being with the American and French revolutions and achieved global dominance in the nineteenth century. It is characterised by principles charaterising the relationship between people and government which are mediated through the institution of citizenship. The nation-state was an innovative and progressive force at its birth, because it was inclusive and defined the citizens as free political subjects, linked together through democratic structures. But the later nationalism of the nineteenth and twentieth centuries turned citizenship on its head by equating it with membership of a dominant ethnic group, defined on biological or cultural lines. In many cases the nation-state became an instrument of exclusion and repression.

National states, for better or worse, are likely to endure. But global economic and cultural integration and the establishment of regional agreements on economic and political cooperation are undermining the exclusiveness of national loyalties. The age of migration could be marked by the erosion of nationalism and the weakening of divisions between peoples. Admittedly there are countervailing tendencies, such as racism, the 'fortress Europe' mentality, or the resurgence of nationalism in certain areas. The decline of national divisions is likely to be uneven, and setbacks are possible, especially in the event of economic or political crises. But the inescapable central trends are the increasing ethnic and cultural diversity of most countries, the emergence of transnational networks which link the societies of emigration and immigration countries and the growth of cultural interchange. The globalisation of migration provides grounds for optimism, because it does give some hope of increased unity in dealing with the pressing problems which beset our small planet.

Notes

2 The Migratory Process and the Formation of Ethnic Minorities

1. Migration can even transcend death: members of some migrant groups have been known to pay money into burial societies, which, after death, transport their bodies back for burial in their native soil. In a recent survey, Tribalat (1995: 109–11) found that large numbers of immigrants in France plan to have their bodies returned to their native countries for burial. This applies to 10 per cent of Spaniards and a third of Portuguese, while about half of all Muslim immigrants plan to re-migrate after death.
2. The visible markers of a phenotype (skin colour, features, hair colour, and so on) correspond to what is popularly understood as 'race'. We avoid using the term 'race' as far as possible, since there is increasing agreement among biologists and social scientists that there are no measurable characteristics among human populations that allow classification into 'races'. Genetic variance within any one population is greater than alleged differences between different populations. 'Race' is thus a social construction produced by the process we refer to as racism.
3. We lay no claim to originality with regard to this definition and discussion of racism. It is oriented towards current sociological debates, which have generated a large body of literature. See, for example, CCCS (1982); Rex and Mason (1986); Cohen and Bains (1988); Miles (1989); Wieviorka (1991, 1992); Solomos (1993). There is no unanimity among social scientists about the correct definition and explanations of racism, but we have no space for a more detailed discussion of these matters here.

4 Migration to Highly Developed Countries since 1945

1. A detailed review of the literature is not possible here. For Europe the account is based mainly on our own works: Castles and Kosack (1973); M. J. Miller (1981); Castles, Booth and Wallace (1984); Castles (1986); Castles (1989). For the USA, we recommend Briggs (1984); Portes and Rumbaut (1990). For Australia, see Collins (1991). For useful overviews, see Kritz, Keely and Tomasi (1983); Cohen (1987); *International Migration Review*, (1989). Precise references will only be given where absolutely necessary.
2. Post-1945 refugee movements were most significant in the case of Germany, as will be discussed in Chapter 8.
3. Another case worth mentioning is that of Italy, in which migration from the underdeveloped south was crucial to the economic take-off of the northern industrial triangle between Milan, Turin and Genoa in the 1960s: this was internal migration, but very similar in its economic and social character to foreign worker movements in other European countries.

4. Including Pakistan, which subsequently left the Commonwealth.
5. The exception is the roughly 32 000 Moluccans, who wanted to return to their homeland if it could achieve independence from Indonesia. They remained segregated in camps, and rejected integration into Dutch society. In the late 1970s, their disaffection led to several violent incidents.
6. For more detail and sources on Australia, see Castles *et al.* (1992b); Collins, (1991).
7. See Castles and Kosack (1973: Chapter 9) and Castles, Booth and Walace (1984: Chapter 2) for more discussion of these issues.
8. The use of the terms South–North and East–West is Eurocentric, but will be retained here because it has become part of general usage. It is important to understand that these concepts refer not primarily to geographical locations but to economic, social and cultural divisions.
9. The total fertility rate is the average number of births per woman during her lifetime, assuming constant fertility. The rate needed to maintain a constant population is just over two children per woman.

5 The Next Waves: The Globalisation of International Migration

1. We use the term 'the Arab region' to include not only the Arab countries of North Africa and Western Asia, but also the non-Arab states of Turkey, Iran and Israel. The term refers to a geographical, rather than a political or ethnic, area. The term 'the Arab region' is not entirely satisfactory, but seems better than the possible alternatives: the term 'Middle East' is Eurocentric, and excludes North Africa; the term 'Western Asia' also excludes North Africa.
2. The situation of Algerians in France is discussed in more detail in Chapters 7, 9 and 10.

6 New Migrations in the Asia-Pacific Region

1. Strictly speaking, Asia includes the Middle East and Turkey. However, these countries have already been dealt with, so that this section will be concerned mainly with South Asia (the Indian sub-continent), East Asia and South-east Asia.
2. One exception to this was the recruitment of 400 000 Korean workers by Japan between 1921 and 1941. Many settled, to form a permanently discriminated against minority. Japan also made extensive use of forced labour during the Second World War.
3. There were also some smaller movements, as of people from Goa, Macau and East Timor to Portugal.
4. A further movement, which will not be discussed here for reasons of space, was that of Vietnamese workers to the Soviet Union and the German Democratic Republic. Although often disguised as trainees, these migrants shared many of the characteristics of other contract workers.
5. These figures are world-wide remittances, but the largest component is remittances from the Middle East.

6. In addition, about 10 million Bengalis sought asylum in India at the time of the Bangladesh independence struggle in 1971. They were able to return home the following year (UNHCR, 1991).

7 Migrants and Minorities in the Labour Force

1. It should be noted that in Australia, Aboriginal men and women are hardly integrated into mainstream labour markets at all; their situation is characterised by extremely high rates of unemployment, insecure low-skilled jobs, and low wages.
2. France does not have unions organised on the basis of a single union for each industry or trade. Rather there are a number of competing trade union federations, which try to organise in each industry. The federations have different political and ideological characters. The most important are the communist *Confédération Générale du Travail* (CGT), the militant-reformist *Confédération Française Démocratique du Travail*, the more moderate *Force Ouvrière* and the employer-dominated *Confédération des Syndicats Libres* (CSL). For accounts of the policy of the different unions towards foreign workers see Gani (1972); Castles and Kosack (1973); M. J. Miller (1981).

8 The Migratory Process: A Comparison of Australia and Germany

1. For convenience we use the name 'Germany' to refer to the Federal Republic of Germany (FRG) in this text. Where confusion with the former German Democratic Republic (GDR) is possible, we will use the full names or their abbreviations.
2. Kreuzberg was a backwater with low property values because it was cut off from Berlin's old centre by the Wall. After the demolition of the Wall in 1989, prices soared, and minority groups were displaced, though not without resistance.
3. That is why we have to use *birthplace figures* to show the immigrant population in Australia, while we use *foreign resident* figures for Germany, where few immigrants have obtained citizenship.
4. The notion of *Verfassungspatriotismus* was originally put forward by Jürgen Habermas, although his understanding of the principle differs somewhat from Oberndörfer's. The latter stresses individual assimilation of immigrants into the civic culture, while Habermas (1994) draws attention to the need for recognition of collective cultural and social differences, and points out that this may lead to considerable institutional change in receiving societies.
5. For a definition of racism, see Chapter 2.

9 New Ethnic Minorities and Society

1. This passage is based on one of the authors' personal experience as a member of a community group in Frankfurt in the early 1980s.

2. This phrase was coined by the 'Chicago school' of sociology in the early part of this century.
3. Noiriel's phrase is *le modèle achevé de la nation*.
4. The British and Americans use citizenship and nationality as almost identical terms. For the French they have almost opposite meanings: *citoyenneté* refers to political belonging to the nation-state, *nationalité* refers to belonging to a cultural community, which could be called the nation, or indeed the ethnic group. The French generally refer to *groupes ethniques* only in an ethnological context. The term *communitaire* is not to be confused with the English term 'community'. It refers to affiliations on the basis of a relatively closed group, and should be translated as 'ethnic', in sociological usage as Gemeinschaft. *Mouvement communitaire* (local community or ethnic community-based movement) is often used as the opposite of *mouvement social* (class-based or interest group-based movement).
5. The term multiculturalism sometimes leads to confusion due to its varying usages. In the USA it mainly refers to demands for rethinking history and culture to include the role of minorities, and may thus even include women's studies. In Western Europe, multiculturalism is often used pejoratively to refer to a policy of ethnic separatism (in the sense of a 'nation of tribes'). In Canada, Australia and Sweden, multiculturalism usually denotes a certain type of government policy, combining cultural rights and social equality for minorities. It might be more appropriate to use a more neutral term, such as 'pluralism', or 'inclusionary citizenship', but multiculturalism has become too well established in public debates to be easily displaced.

Further Reading

1 Introduction

Important information on all aspects of international migration is provided by a large number of specialised journals, of which only a few can be mentioned here. *International Migration Review* (published by the Center for Migration Studies, New York) was established in 1964 and provides excellent comparative information. *International Migration*, published by the IOM, Geneva, is also a valuable comparative source. *Social Identities* started publication in 1995 and is concerned with the 'study of race, nation and culture'. *Diaspora*, published in the USA, is dedicated to 'transnational studies'. Journals with a European focus include *New Community* (edited in Utrecht by the European Research Centre on Migration and Ethnic Relations, or ERCOMER; this journal is to be renamed *Journal of Ethnic and Migration Studies* from 1998); *Migration* (Berlin: Edition Parabolis, in English and German) and the *Revue Européenne des Migrations Internationales* (Paris, in French and English). Britain has several journals including *Race and Class* (London: Institute for Race Relations), *Ethnic and Racial Studies* (Routledge). In Australia there is the *Journal of Intercultural Studies* (Melbourne: Monash University). The *Asian and Pacific Migration Journal* (Quezon City, Philippines: Scalabrini Migration Center) provides information and analyses movements in the world's most populous region.

There are also many publications with a 'magazine' format which provide up-to-date information and shorter commentaries, such as *Asian Migrant* (also published by the Scalabrini Migration Center in Quezon City) and *Hommes et Migrations* in Paris. A very valuable resource is the monthly *Migration News,* published by the University of California at Davis and available as hard copy, e-mail or on the Internet.

Several international organisations provide comparative information on migrations. The most useful is the OECD's annual *Trends in International Migration* (Paris: OECD), which until 1991 was known as OECD SOPEMI *Continuous Reporting System on Migration*. This provides comprehensive statistics on most OECD countries of immigration, as well as some data on countries of emigration. Cohen's massive *Survey of World Migration* (1995) is a valuable reference work with contributions on all aspects of our theme.

There are many Internet sites concerned with issues of migration and ethnic diversity. A few of the most significant are listed here. Since they are hyperlinked with many others, this should provide a starting-point for further exploration:

ERCOMER:	http:www.ercomer.org
Migration News:	http//migration.ucdavis.edu/
Scalabrini Migration Center:	http:www.sequel.net/~smc/

Asia Pacific Migration
Research Network
(APMRN):   http://www.uow.edu.au/arts/cms/apmrn.html
Department of Immigration   http://www.immi.gov.au/
and Multicultural Affairs,
Australia:

2 The Migratory Process and the Formation of Ethnic Minorities

Zolberg (1989) provides a useful overview of theories of migration, while Boyd
(1989) is good on migration networks. Several other articles in the same special
issue of *International Migration Review* (1989, 23:3) are also valuable. Kritz,
Lin and Zlotnik (1992) is an excellent collection on migration systems theory.
Morokvasic (1984), Phizacklea (1983) and Lutz, Phoenix and Yuval-Davis
(1995) have edited useful collections on the relationship between migration and
gender. Sassen (1988) gives an original perspective on the political economy of
migration, while Borjas (1990) presents the neo-classical view. Rex and Mason
(1986) is a very useful collection of theoretical approaches to race and ethnic
relations. Mosse (1985), Miles (1989), Cohen and Bains (1988), Balibar and
Wallerstein (1991) and Essed (1991) are good on racism. For those who can
read French, Wieviorka (1991, 1992) has carried out important work. Wieviorka (1995) is now available in English. Anderson (1983) and Gellner (1983)
provide stimulating analyses of nationalism, while A. D. Smith (1986, 1991)
discusses the relationship between ethnicity and nation. Bauböck (1991, 1994)
gives a useful summary of citizenship issues, while Soysal (1994), Kymlicka
(1995), Schnapper (1994) and Gutmann (1994) present varying perspectives on
the topic.

3 International Migration before 1945

Cohen (1987) provides a valuable overview of migrant labour in the international division of labour, while Potts (1980) presents a history of migration
which leads from slavery and indentured labour up to modern guestworker
systems. Blackburn (1988) and Fox-Genovese and Genovese (1983) analyse
slavery and its role in capitalist development. Archdeacon (1983) examines
immigration in US history, showing how successive waves of entrants have
'become American'. For German readers, Dohse (1981) gives an interesting
historical analysis of the role of the state in controlling migrant labour in
Germany. Cross gives a detailed account of the role of migrant workers in
French industrialisation, de Lepervanche (1975) shows how ethnic divisions
played a central role in the formation of the Australian working class, while
Homze (1967) describes the extreme exploitation of migrant labour practised
by the Nazi war machine. Moch (1992) is good on earlier European migration
experiences, while many contributions in Cohen (1995) are on the history of
migration.

4 Migration to Highly Developed Countries since 1945

Castles and Kosack (1973 and 1985) is a comparative study of immigrant
workers in France, Germany, Switzerland and Britain during the phase of mass

labour recruitment from 1945 to 1973. Castles, Booth and Wallace (1984) continue the story for the period following the ending of recruitment in 1973–4. Portes and Rumbaut (1990) give a detailed analysis of recent immigrant settlement in the USA, while Collins (1991) provides a valuable account for Australia. Hammar (1985a) provides a comparative study of the position of immigrants in Western European countries. The *International Migration Review* Special Issues 23:3 (1989) and 26:2 (1992) also provide comparative material. The OECD reports (mentioned in Further Reading for Chapter 1) give useful data on migratory movements and immigrant populations. Harris (1996) gives a popular overview of global migration, while Stalker (1994) presents a global picture and provides very useful tables and charts. Zolberg, Suhrke and Aguayo (1989) examine global refugee movements, while UNHCR (1995) provides more recent comprehensive information. Regulation issues are discussed in Teitelbaum and Weiner (1995).

5 The Next Waves: The Globalisation of International Migration

Appleyard (1988, 1991), Stahl (1988) and Stichter (1985) provide global perspectives on international migrations. The *International Migration Review* Special Issue 26:2 (1992) gives an overview of East–West movements within Europe. Kerr and Yassin (1982) and Semyonov and Lewin-Epstein (1987) provide information on labour migrations concerning Arab countries and Israel. Ricca (1990) gives an overview of international migration in Africa.

6 New Migrations in the Asia-Pacific Region

Fawcett and Cariño (1987) and various issues of the *Asian and Pacific Migration Journal* examine migratory patterns within and from Asia. Skeldon (1994) presents an interesting study of Hong Kong migration.

7 Migrants and Minorities in the Labour Force

Böhning (1984) and OECD (1987) provide comparative perspectives on migrants in the labour market. Sassen's work (1988) is significant for this topic too. Borjas (1990) and Portes and Rumbaut (1990) examine the US situation. Piore's earlier work (1979) is still useful. Collins (1991) and Lever-Tracy and Quinlan give good analyses for Australia. Waldinger *et al.* (1990) is excellent on ethnic small business, while Phizacklea (1990) looks at the links between gender, racism and class, through a case-study of the fashion industry.

8 The Migratory Process: A Comparison of Australia and Germany

Details of migration and ethnic group formation in Australia are to be found in Wilton and Bosworth (1984), Collins (1991), Collins *et al.* (1995), Lever-Tracy and Quinlan (1988), Castles *et al.* (1992a) and Castles *et al.* (1992b). For

Germany see Martin (1991b), Castles and Kosack (1973 and 1985) and Castles, Booth and Wallace (1984). German readers will also find Hoffmann (1990), Leggewie (1990), Tichy (1990), Funcke (1991), Nirumand (1992), Bade (1994), and Cohn-Bendit and Schmid (1993) useful.

9   New Ethnic Priorities and Society

Feagin (1989) gives a good overview of ethnic relations, with special emphasis on the USA. Breton *et al.* (1990) present a thorough empirical study on ethnic identity and class in Canada. Stasiulis and Yuval-Davis (1995) give an interesting comparison of ethnic relations in settler societies. Björgo and Witte (1993) and Hargreaves and Leaman (1995) look at racism and responses to it in Europe. Solomos (1993), Solomos and Back (1995), Cohen and Bains (1988) and Layton-Henry and Rich (1986) describe and analyse racism and political reactions to it in Britain. Gilroy's work (1987) has led to considerable debate on the significance of culture and community, especially for second generation migrants. Hammar's comparative study (1985a) is valuable here too. Ålund and Schierup (1991) provide a sceptical account of Swedish multiculturalism, with important theoretical insights. Davis's (1990) book on Los Angeles is a fascinating case study of the 'post-modern' city and the role of minorities within it. Comparative urban sociological studies are also to be found in Cross and Keith (1993) and Mingione (1996). For those who read French, the books of Wihtol de Wenden (1988), Noiriel (1988), Weil (1991b) and Dubet and Lapeyronnie (1992) are highly recommended.

10   Immigrant Politics

Miller (1981) provides one of the first comparative studies on the political role of migrant workers. Layton-Henry (1990) looks at the political rights of migrant workers in Western Europe. The *International Migration Review* Special Issue 19:3 (1985) gives information on the political situation in several countries. The comparative studies on citizenship by Hammar (1990) and Brubaker (1989) are of great value. Solomos and Wrench (1993) examine racism and migration in several European counties, while Layton-Henry and Rich (1986) focus on Britain. Shain (1989) looks at the consequences of refugee movements for the nation-state.

Bibliography

Abella, M. I. (1995) 'Asian migrant and contract workers in the Middle East', in R. Cohen (ed.), *The Cambridge Survey of World Migration* (Cambridge: Cambridge University Press).

ABS (1989) *Overseas Born Australians: A Statistical Profile* (Canberra: Australian Government Publishing Service).

ABS (1993) *Australia in Profile* (Canberra: Australian Government Publishing Service).

Ackland, R. and Williams, L. (1992) *Immigrants and the Australian Labour Market: The Experience of Three Recessions* (Canberra: Australian Government Publishing Service).

ADL (1988) *Hate Groups in America* (New York: ADL of B'nai B'rith).

Alcorso, C., Popoli, C. and Rando, G. (1992) 'Community networks and institutions', in S. Castles, C. Alcorso, G. Rando and E. Vasta (eds), *Australia's Italians: Culture and Community in a Changing Society* (Sydney: Allen & Unwin).

Ålund, A. and Schierup, C.-U. (1991) *Paradoxes of Multiculturalism* (Aldershot: Avebury).

Amjad, R. (1996) 'Philippines and Indonesia: on the way to a migration transition', *Asian and Pacific Migration Journal* 5:2–3.

Andepoju, A. (1988) 'Links between internal and international migration: the African situation', in C. Stahl (ed.), *International Migration Today*, vol. 2 (UNESCO/University of Western Australia).

Anderson, B. (1983) *Imagined Communities* (London: Verso).

Anthias, F. and Yuval-Davis, N. (1983) 'Contextualising feminism: gender, ethnic and class divisions', *Feminist Review*, no. 15.

Anthias, F. and Yuval-Davis, N. (1989) 'Introduction', in N. Yuval-Davis and F. Anthias (eds), *Woman–Nation–State* (London: Macmillan).

Appleyard, R. T. (ed.) (1988) *International Migration Today: Trends and Prospects* (Paris: UNESCO).

Appleyard, R. T. (1989) 'International migration and developing countries' in R. T. Appleyard (ed.), *The Impact of International Migration on Developing Countries* (Paris: OECD).

Appleyard, R. T. (1991) *International Migration: Challenge for the Nineties* (Geneva: IOM).

Archdeacon, T. (1983) *Becoming American: An Ethnic History* (New York: The Free Press).

Arnold, F., Minocha, U. and Fawcett, J. T. (1987) 'The changing face of Asian immigration to the United States', in J. T. Fawcett and B. V. Cariño (eds), *Pacific Bridges: The New Immigration from Asia and the Pacific Islands* (New York: Center for Migration Studies).

Aronson, G. (1990) *Israel, Palestinians and the Intifada: Creating Facts on the West Bank* (Washington, DC: Institute for Palestine Studies).

Asian and Pacific Migration Journal (1992) 1:1.

Bade, K. J. (ed.) (1994) *Das Manifest der 60: Deutschland und die Einwanderung* (Munich: Beck).

Baker, M. and Wooden, M. (1992) *Immigrant Workers in the Communication Industry* (BIR, Canberra: Australian Government Publishing Service).

Balibar, E. (1991) 'Racism and nationalism' in E. Balibar and I. Wallerstein (eds) *Race, Nation, Class: Ambiguous Identities* (London: Verso).

Balibar, E. and Wallerstein, I. (eds) (1991) *Race, Nation, Class: Ambiguous Identities* (London: Verso).

Banton, M. (1985) *Promoting Racial Harmony* (Cambridge: Cambridge University Press).

Baringhorst, S. (1995) 'Symbolic highlights or political enlightenment? Strategies for fighting racism in Germany', in A. Hargreaves and J. Leaman, *Racism, Ethnicity and Politics in Contemporary Europe* (Aldershot: Edward Elgar).

Barlán, J. (1988) *A System Approach for Understanding International Population Movement: The Role of Policies and Migrant Community in the Southern Cone*, IUSSP Seminar, Genting Highlands, Malaysia, September.

Basch, L., Glick-Schiller, N. and Blanc, C. S. (1994) *Nations Unbound: Transnational Projects, Post-Colonial Predicaments and Deterritorialized Nation-States* (New York: Gordon & Breach).

Battistella, G. and Paganoni, A. (eds) (1992) *Philippine Labor Migration: Impact and Policy* (Quezon City: Scalabrini Migration Center).

Bauböck, R. (1991) 'Migration and citizenship', *New Community* 18:1.

Bauböck, R. (1994) 'Changing the Boundaries of Citizenship: the Inclusion of Immigrants in Democratic Polities', in R. Bauböck (ed.), *From Aliens to Citizens* (Aldershot: Avebury).

Beauftragte der Bundesregierung für die Belange der Ausländer (1993) *Das Einbürgerungs- und Staatsangehörigkeitsrecht der Bundesrepublik Deutschland* (Bonn: Beauftragte der Bundesregierung für die Belange der Ausländer).

Bell, D. (1975) 'Ethnicity and social change', in N. Glazer and D. P. Moynihan (eds), *Ethnicity – Theory and Experience* (Cambridge, MA: Harvard University Press).

Belloula, T. (1965) *Les Algériens en France* (Algiers: Éditions nationales algériennes).

Bernard, P. (1993) *L'immigration* (Paris: Le Monde Éditions).

Bernard, P. and Chemin, A. (1991) 'Les faux-semblants de la délinquance étrangère', *Le Monde*, 6 December.

Benyon, J. (1986) 'Spiral of decline: race and policing', in Z. Layton-Henry and P. B. Rich (eds), *Race, Government and Politics in Britain* (London: Macmillan).

BIMPR (1996) *Australia's Population Trends and Prospects 1995* (Canberra: Australian Government Publishing Service).

Binur, Y. (1990) *My Enemy, Myself* (New York: Penguin).

BIR (1991) *Immigration Update June Quarter* (Melbourne: BIR).

Birks, J. S., Sinclair, C. A. and Seccombe, I. J. (1986) 'Migrant Workers in the Arab Gulf: The Impact of Declining Oil Revenues', *International Migration Review* 20:4.

Björgo, T. and Witte, R. (eds) (1993) *Racist Violence in Europe* (London: Macmillan).

Blackburn, R. (1988) *The Overthrow of Colonial Slavery 1776–1848* (London and New York: Verso).

Böhning, W. R. (1984) *Studies in International Labour Migration* (London: Macmillan; New York: St Martin's).

• Böhning, W. R. (1991a) 'Integration and immigration pressures, in western Europe', *International Labour Review*.

Böhning, W. R. (1991b) 'International Migration to Western Europe: What to Do?', paper presented to the *Seminar on International Security* (Geneva: Graduate Institute of International Studies), 15-20 July.

Borjas, G. J. (1989) 'Economic theory and international migration', *International Migration Review*, Special Silver Anniversary Issue, 23:3.

Borjas, G. J. (1990) *Friends or Strangers: The Impact of Immigration on the US Economy* (New York: Basic Books).

Bouamama, S. (1988) 'De l'anti-racisme à la citoyenneté', IM'média 8.

Bouamama, S., Cordeiro, A. and Roux, M. (1992) *La Citoyenneté dans tous ses États* (Paris: CIEMI/L'Harmattan).

Boudahrain, A. (1985) *Nouvel Ordre Social International et Migrations* (Paris: L'Harmattan/CIEMI).

Bourdieu, P. and Wacquant, L. (1992) *An Invitation to Reflexive Sociology* (Chicago: University of Chicago Press).

Boyd, M. (1989) 'Family and Personal Networks in Migration', *International Migration Review*, Special Silver Anniversary Issue, 23:3.

Brah, A. (1991) 'Difference, Diversity, Differentiation', in J. Donald and A. Rattansi (eds), *'Race', Culture and Difference* (London, Newbury Park, New Delhi: Sage).

Breton, R., Isajiw, W. W., Kalbach, W. E. and Reitz, J. G. (1990) *Ethnic Identity and Equality* (Toronto: University of Toronto Press).

Briggs, V. M., Jr. (1984) *Immigration Policy and the American Labor Force* (Baltimore, MD, and London: Johns Hopkins University Press).

Brubaker, W. R. (ed.) (1989) *Immigration and the Politics of Citizenship in Europe and North America* (Lanham, MD: University Press of America).

Bureau of the Census (1991) 'Census Bureau Releases 1990 Census Counts on Specific Racial Groups', *Commerce News* (Washington, DC: US Department of Commerce), 12 June.

Cahill, D. (1990) *Intermarriages in International Contexts* (Quezon City: Scalabrini Migration Center).

Callovi, G. (1992) 'Regulation of immigration in 1993. Pieces of the European Community Jig-Saw Puzzle', *International Migration Review*, Special Issue on the New Europe and International Migration, 26:2.

Castells, M. (1983) *The City and the Grassroots* (London: Edward Arnold).

Castles, S. (1985) 'The guests who stayed – the debate on "foreigners policy" in the German Federal Republic', *International Migration Review*, 19:3.

Castles, S. (1986) 'The guest-worker in western Europe: an obituary', *International Migration Review*, 20:4.

Castles, S. (1989) *Migrant Workers and the Transformation of Western Societies* (Ithaca, NY: Cornell University).

Castles, S. (1995) 'How nation-states respond to immigration and ethnic diversity', *New Community* 21:3.

Castles, S. and Kosack, G. (1973 and 1985) *Immigrant Workers and Class Structure in Western Europe* (Oxford: Oxford University Press).

Castles, S., Alcorso, C., Rando, G. and Vasta, E. (eds) (1992a) *Australia's Italians: Culture and Community in a Changing Society* (Sydney: Allen & Unwin).

Castles, S., Booth, H. and Wallace, T. (1984) *Here for Good: Western Europe's New Ethnic Minorities* (London: Pluto Press).

Castles, S., Collins, J., Gibson, K., Tait, D. and Alcorso, C. (1991) *The Global Milkbar and the Local Sweatshop: Ethnic Small Business and the Restructuring of Sydney* (Wollongong: Centre for Multicultural Studies for the Office of Multicultural Affairs, Working Papers on Multiculturalism).

Castles, S., Cope, B., Kalantzis, M. and Morrissey, M. (1992b) *Mistaken Identity – Multiculturalism and the Demise of Nationalism in Australia*, 3rd ed (Sydney: Pluto Press).

Castles, S., Rando, G. and Vasta, E. (1992c) 'Italo-Australians and Politics', in S. Castles, C. Alcorso, G. Rando and E. Vasta (eds), *Australia's Italians: Culture and Community in a Changing Society* (Sydney: Allen & Unwin).

CCCS (1982) *The Empire Strikes Back* (London: Hutchinson).

Chazan, N. (1994) 'Engaging the state: associational life in Sub-Saharan Africa', *State Power and Social Forces* (Cambridge: Cambridge University Press).

Choo, A. L. (1992) 'Asian-American political clout grows stronger', *Wall Street Journal*, 21 February.

Cinanni, P. (1968) *Emigrazione e Imperialismo* (Rome: Riuniti).

Çinar, D. (1994) 'From aliens to citizens: a comparative analysis of rules of transition', in R. Bauböck (ed.), *From Aliens to Citizens* (Aldershot: Avebury).

Coffey, J. F. (1987) 'Race training in the United States: an overview', in J. W. Shaw, R. M. Nordlie and M. Shapiro (eds), *Strategies for Improving Race Relations: The Anglo-American Experience* (Manchester: Manchester University Press).

Cohen, P. and Bains, H. S. (eds) (1988) *Multi-Racist Britain* (London: Macmillan).

Cohen, R. (1987) *The New Helots: Migrants in the International Division of Labour* (Aldershot: Avebury).

Cohen, R. (1991) 'East-West and European migration in a global context', *New Community* 18:1.

Cohen, R. (1995) 'Asian indentured and colonial migration' in R. Cohen (ed.), *The Cambridge Survey of World Migration* (Cambridge: Cambridge: University Press).

Cohn-Bendit, D. and Schmid, T. (1993) *Heimat Babylon: Das Wagnis der multikulturellen Demokratie* (Hamburg: Hoffmann & Campe).

Collins, J. (1978) 'Fragmentation of the working class', in E. L. Wheelwright and K. Buckley (eds), *Essays in the Political Economy of Australian Capitalism* 3 (Sydney: ANZ Books).

Collins, J. (1991) *Migrant Hands in a Distant Land: Australia's Post-War Immigration*, 2nd ed (Sydney: Pluto Press).

Collins, J. and Castles, S. (1991) 'Restructuring, migrant labour markets and small business in Australia', *Migration*, 10.

Collins, J., Gibson, K., Alcorso, C., Castles, S. and Tait, D. (1995) *A Shop Full of Dreams: Ethnic Small Business in Australia* (Sydney: Pluto Press).

Commission of the European Communities (1989) *Eurobarometer: Public Opinion in the European Community, Special: Racism and Xenophobia* (Brussels: Commission of the European Community).

Commission of the European Communities (1990) *Policies on Immigration and the Social Integration of Migrants in the European Community* (Brussels: Commission of the European Community).

Cornelius, W., Martin, P. and Hollifield, J. (1994) *Controlling Immigration: A Global Perspective* (Stanford, CA: Stanford University Press).

Costa-Lascoux, J. (1983) 'L'immigration algérienne en France et la nationalité des enfants algériens', in Larbi Talha (ed.) *Maghrebins en France: Emigrés ou immigrés* (Paris: Édition du CNRS).

Costa-Lascoux, J. (1989) *De l'Immigré au Citoyen* (Paris: La Documentation Française).

Croissandeau J. M. (1984) 'La formation alternative au chomage?', *Le Monde de l'Education*, February.

Cross, G. S. (1983) *Immigrant Workers in Industrial France: The Making of a New Laboring Class* (Philadelphia: Temple University Press).

Cross, M. (1995) 'Race, class formation and political interests: a comparison of Amsterdam and London', in A. Hargreaves and J. Leaman, *Racism, Ethnicity and Politics in Contemporary Europe* (Aldershot: Edward Elgar).

Cross, M. and Keith, M. (eds) (1993) *Racism, the City and the State* (London: Routledge).

CSIMCED (1990) *Unauthorized Migration: An Economic Development Response* (Washington, DC: US Government Printing Office).

Dagger, C. W. (1992) 'Study says Asian-Americans face widespread discrimination', *New York Times*, 29 February.

Davis, M. (1990) *City of Quartz: Excavating the Future in Los Angeles* (London: Verso).

de Lattes, A. and de Lattes, Z. (1991) 'International migration in Latin America: patterns, implications and policies', *Informal Expert Group Meeting on International Migration* (Geneva: UN Economic Commission for Europe/UNPF paper).

de Lepervanche, M. (1975) 'Australian immigrants 1788–1940', in E. L. Wheelwright and K. Buckley (eds), *Essays in the Political Economy of Australian Capitalism*, Vol. 1 (Sydney: ANZ Books).

Decloîtres, R. (1967) *The Foreign Worker* (Paris: OECD).

DIMA (1996) *Fact Sheet 2: Migration and Humanitarian Programs* (Canberra: DIMA).

Dohse, K. (1981) *Ausländische Arbeiter und bürgerliche Staat* (Konistein/Taunus: Hain).

Dubet, F. and Lapeyronnie, D. (1992) *Les Quartiers d'Exil* (Paris: Seuil).

Engels, F. (1962) 'The Condition of the Working Class in England', in *Marx, Engels on Britain* (Moscow: Foreign Languages Publishing House).

Entzinger, H. B. (1985) 'The Netherlands', in T. Hammar (ed.) *European*

Immigration Policy: A Comparative Study (Cambridge: Cambridge University Press).

Esman, M. (1992) 'The political fallout of international migration', *Diaspora* 2:1.

Esman, M. J. (1994) *Ethnic Politics* (Ithaca, NY, and London: Cornell University Press).

Essed, P. (1991) *Understanding Everyday Racism* (London, and Newbury Park New Delhi: Sage).

European Parliament (1985) *Committee of Inquiry into the Rise of Fascism and Racism in Europe: Report on the Findings of the Inquiry* (Strasbourg: European Parliament).

Ewald, (1983) *L'Ecole des Esclaves* (Paris: Editions de la Table Ronde).

Fadil, M. A. (1985) 'Les effets de l'émigration de main d'oeuvre sur la distribution des revenus et les modèles de consommation dans l'économie égyptienne', *Revue Tiers Monde* 26:103.

Faist, T. (1993) 'From school to work: public policy and underclass formation among young Turks in Germany during the 1980s', *International Migration Review* 27:2.

Falchi, N. (1995) *International Migration Pressures* (Geneva: IOM).

Fawcett, J. T. (1989) 'Networks, linkages, and migration systems', *International Migration Review,* Special Silver Anniversary Issue, 23:3.

Fawcett, J. T. and Arnold, F. (1987) 'Explaining diversity: Asian and Pacific immigration systems' in J. T. Fawcett and B. V. Cariño (eds), *Pacific Bridges: The New Immigration from Asia and the Pacific Islands* (New York: Center for Migration Studies).

Fawcett, J. T. and Cariño B. V., (eds) (1987) *Pacific Bridges: The New Immigration from Asia and the Pacific Islands* (New York: Center for Migration Studies).

Feagin, J. R. (1989) *Racial and Ethnic Relations* (Englewood Cliffs, NJ: Prentice-Hall).

Fergany, N. (1985) 'Migrations inter-arabes et développement', *Revue Tiers Monde* 26:103.

Ferguson, E. (1997) 'Drowned in a sea of apathy', *Guardian Weekly,* 26 January 1997.

Findlay, A. M. (1995) 'Skilled transients: the invisible phenomenon', in R. Cohen (ed.), *The Cambridge Survey of World Migration* (Cambridge: Cambridge University Press).

Fishman, J. A. (1985) *The Rise and Fall of the Ethnic Revival: Perspectives on Language and Ethnicity* (Berlin, New York and Amsterdam: Mouton).

Fix, M. and Passel, J. S. (1994) *Immigration and Immigrants: Setting the Record Straight* (Washington, DC: The Urban Institute).

Foot, P. (1965) *Immigration and Race in British Politics* (Harmondsworth: Penguin).

Fox-Genovese, E. and Genovese, E. D. (1983) *Fruits of Merchant Capital: Slavery and Bourgeois Property in the Rise and Expansion of Capitalism* (New York and Oxford: Oxford University Press).

French, H. W. (1990) 'Sugar Harvest's Bitter Side: Some Call It Slavery', *New York Times,* 27 April.

French, H. W. (1991) 'Haitians Expelled by Santo Domingo', *New York Times,* 11 August.

Frey, M. and Mammey, U. (1996) *Impact of Migration in the Receiving Countries: Germany* (Geneva: IOM).

Fritscher, F. (1989) 'Sauve-qui-peut au Sahel', *Le Monde,* 3 May.

Funcke, L. (1991) *Bericht der Beauftragten der Bundesregierung für die Integration der ausländischen Arbeitnehmer und ihrer familienangehörigen* (Bonn: German Government).

Gallagher, D. and Diller, J. M. (1990) 'At the crossroads between uprooted people and development in Central America', *Commission for the Study of International Migration and Cooperative Economic Development,* working paper no. 27, Washington DC.

Gani, L. (1972) *Syndicats et Travailleurs Immigrés* (Paris: Éditions Sociales).

Gardner, R. W. (1992) 'Asian immigration: the view from the United States', *Asian and Pacific Migration Journal* 1:1.

Garrard, J. A. (1971) *The English and Immigration: A Comparative Study of the Jewish Influx 1880–1910* (Oxford: Oxford University Press).

Gaspard, F. (1990) *Une petite Ville en France* (Paris: Gallimard).

Geertz, C. (1963) *Old Societies and New States – The Quest for Modernity in Asia and Africa* (Glencoe, II: Free Press).

Gellner, E. (1983) *Nations and Nationalism* (Oxford: Blackwell).

Gilroy, P. (1987) *There Ain't no Black in the Union Jack* (London: Hutchinson).

Gilroy, P. and Lawrence, E. (1988) 'Two-tone Britain: white and black youth and the politics of anti-racism', in P. Cohen and H. S. Bains, (eds), *Multi-Racist Britain* (London: Macmillan).

Glazer, N. and Moynihan, D. P. (1975) 'Introduction', in N. Glazer and D. P. Moynihan (eds), *Ethnicity: Theory and Experience* (Cambridge, MA: Harvard University Press).

Gordon, M. (1978) *Human Nature, Class, and Ethnicity* (New York: Oxford University Press).

Gordon, P. (1986) *Racial Violence and Harassment* (London: Runnymede Trust).

Guimezanes, N. (1995) 'Acquisition of nationality in OECD countries', in OECD (ed.), *Trends in International Migration: Annual Report* (Paris: OECD).

Gurr, T. R. and Harf, B. (1994) *Ethnic Conflict in World Politics* (Boulder, CO: Westview).

Gutmann, A. (ed.) (1994) *Multiculturalism: Examining the Politics of Recognition* (Princeton, NJ: Princeton University Press).

Habermas, J. (1994) 'Struggles for recognition in the democratic constitutional state', in A. Gutmann (ed.), *Multiculturalism: Examining the Politics of Recognition* (Princeton, NJ: Princeton University Press).

Halliday, F. (1985) 'Migrations de main d'oeuvre dans le monde arabe: l'envers du nouvel ordre économique', *Revue Tiers Monde* 26:103.

Hammar, T. (ed.) (1985a) *European Immigration Policy: A Comparative Study* (Cambridge: Cambridge University Press).

Hammar, T. (1985b) 'Sweden', in T. Hammar (ed.), *European Immigration Policy: A Comparative Study* (Cambridge: Cambridge University Press).

Hammar, T. (1990) *Democracy and the Nation-State: Aliens, Denizens and Citizens in a World of International Migration* (Aldershot: Avebury).

Hargreaves, A. and Leaman, J. (1995) *Racism, Ethnicity and Politics in Contemporary Europe* (Aldershot: Edward Elgar).

Harris, N. (1996) *The New Untouchables: Immigration and the New World Worker* (Harmondsworth: Penguin).

Häussermann, H. and Kazepov, Y. (1996) 'Urban poverty in Germany', in E. Mingione (ed.) *Urban Poverty and the Underclass* (Oxford: Blackwell).

HCI (1991) *Journal Official, Assemblée Nationale* (Paris: French Government), 7 June.

Hira, S. (1991) 'Holland: the bare facts', *Race and Class* 32:3.

Hoffmann, L. (1990) *Die unvollendete Republik* (Cologne: Pappy Rossa Verlag).

Hoffmann-Nowotny, H.-J. (1985) 'Switzerland' in T. Hammar (ed.), *European Immigration Policy: A Comparative Study* (Cambridge: Cambridge University Press).

Home Office (1981) *Racial Attacks: Report of a Home Office Study* (London: Home Office).

Home Office (1989) *The Response to Racial Attacks and Harassment: Guidance for the Statutory Authorities – Report of the Inter-Departmental Racial Attacks Group* (London: Home Office).

Homze, E. L. (1967) *Foreign Labor in Nazi Germany* (Englewood Cliffs, NJ: Princeton University Press).

Houstoun, M. F., Kramer, R. G. and Barrett, J. M. (1984) 'Female Predominance in Immigration to the United States Since 1930: A First Look', *International Migration Review* 18:4.

HREOC (Human Rights and Equal Opportunity Commission) (1991) *Racist Violence: Report of the National Inquiry into Racist Violence in Australia* (Canberra: Australian Government Publishing Service).

Hugo, G. (1986) *Australia's Changing Population: Trends and Implications* (Melbourne: Oxford University Press).

Hugo, G. (1990) 'Recent international migration trends in Asia', paper presented to the Fifth Conference of the Australian Population Association, Melbourne.

Hugo, G. (1993) *The Economic Implications of Emigration from Australia* (Canberra: Australian Government Publishing Service).

Hugo, G. (1994) *Migration and the Family*, Vienna: United Nations, Occasional Papers Series for the International Year of the Family, no. 12.

Huguet, J.W. (1995) 'Data on international migration in Asia: 1990–94', *Asian and Pacific Migration Journal* 4:4.

ILO (1991) *Report of the Director-General: Third Supplementary Report* (Geneva: ILO).

Immigration Canada (1991) *Annual Report to Parliament: Immigration Plan for 1991–1995 Year Two* (Ottawa: Canadian Government).

Institute of Race Relations (1987) *Policing Against Black People* (London: Institute of Race Relations).

International Centre for Migration Policy Development (1996) Newsletter on Bosnia and Herzegovina, Number 3, February.

International Migration Review (1984) Special Issue on Women in Migration, 18:3.

International Migration Review (1985) Special Issue on Civil Rights and the Sociopolitical Participation of Migrants, 19:3.

International Migration Review (1989) Special Silver Anniversary Issue, 23:3.

Ireland, P. (1997) 'Socialism, Unification Policy and the Rise of Racism in Eastern Germany', *International Migration Review* Vol. 31 (Fall).

Jackson, J. A. (1963) *The Irish in Britain* (London: Routledge & Kegan Paul).

Jackson, J. A. (ed.) (1969) *Migration* (Cambridge: Cambridge University Press).

Jakubowicz, A. (1989) 'The state and the welfare of immigrants in Australia', *Ethnic and Racial Studies* 12:1.

Jarreau, P. (1983) 'Cher Mustapha' *Le Monde*, 13–14 March.

Joly, D. (1988) 'Les musulmans à Birmingham', in R. Leveau and G. Kepel (eds), *Les Musulmans dans la Société Française* (Paris: Presse de la Fondation Nationale des Sciences Politiques).

Jupp, J., York, B. and McRobbie, A. (1989) *The Political Participation of Ethnic Minorities in Australia* (Canberra: Australian Government Publishing Service).

Kang, S. D. (1996) 'Typology and conditions of migrant workers in Korea', *Asian and Pacific Migration Journal* 5:2–3.

Kay, D. and Miles, R. (1992) *Refugees or Migrant Workers? European Volunteer Workers in Britain 1946–1951* (London: Routledge).

Kepel, G. and Leveau, R. (1987) *Les Banlieues d'Islam* (Paris: Seuil).

Kerr, M. and Yassin, E. S. (1982) *Rich and Poor States in the Middle East: Egypt and the New Arab Order* (Boulder, CO: Westview Press).

Kindleberger, C. P. (1967) *Europe's Postwar Growth – The Role of Labor Supply* (Cambridge, MA.: Harvard University Press).

Kiser, G. and Kiser, M. (eds) (1979) *Mexican Workers in the United States* (Albuquerque: University of New Mexico Press).

Klug, F. (1989) '"Oh to be in England": the British case study' in N. Yuval-Davis and F. Anthias (eds), *Woman–Nation–State* (London: Macmillan).

Kratochwil, H. K. (1995) 'Cross-border population movements and regional economic integration in Latin America', *IOM Latin America Migration Journal* 13:2.

Kritz, M. M., Keely, C. B. and Tomasi, S. M. (eds) (1983) *Global Trends in Migration* (New York: Center for Migration Studies).

Kritz, M. M., Lin, L. L. and Zlotnik, H. (eds) (1992) *International Migration Systems: A Global Approach* (Oxford: Clarendon Press).

Kubat, D. (1987) 'Asian Immigrants to Canada', in J. T. Fawcett and B. V. Cariño (eds), *Pacific Bridges: The new Immigration from Asia and the Pacific Islands* (New York: Center for Migration Studies).

Kwong, P. (1992) 'The first multicultural riots', *Voice*, New York, 9 June.

Kymlicka, W. (1995) *Multicultural Citizenship* (Oxford: Clarendon Press).

Lapeyronnie, D., Frybes, M., Couper, K. and Joly, D. (1990) *L'Intégration des Minorités Immigrées, Étude Comparative: France – Grande Bretagne* (Paris: Agence pour le Développement des Relations Interculturelles).

Laqueur, W. (1972) *A History of Zionism* (New York: Holt, Rinehart & Winston).

Larsson, S. (1991) 'Swedish racism: the democratic way', *Race and Class* 32:3.

Layton-Henry, Z. (1981) *A Report on British Immigration Policy since 1945* (Coventry: University of Warwick).

Layton-Henry, Z. (1986) 'Race and the Thatcher Government', in Z. Layton-Henry and P. B. Rich (eds), *Race, Government and Politics in Britain* (London: Macmillan).

Layton-Henry, Z. (ed.) (1990) *The Political Rights of Migrant Workers in Western Europe* (London: Sage).

Layton-Henry, Z. and Rich, P. B. (eds) (1986) *Race, Government and Politics in Britain* (London: Macmillan).

Le Monde Dossiers et Documents (1983), 102.

Lebon, A. (1995) *Migrations et Nationalité en France en 1994* (Paris: Ministère de l'Amenagement du territoire, de la Ville et de l'Intégration).

Lebon, A. (1996) *Immigration et presence étrangère en France 1995–1996* (Paris: Direction de la Population et des Migrations).

Lee, J. S. and Wang, S.-W. (1996) 'Recruiting and managing of foreign workers in Taiwan' *Asian and Pacific Migration Journal* 5:2–3.

Leggewie, C. (1990) *Multi Kulti: Spielregeln für die Vielvölkerrepublik* (Berlin: Rotbuch).

Lequin, Y. (ed.), (1988) *La Mosaïque France* (Paris: Larousse).

Leveau, R. and Kepel, G. (eds), (1988) *Les Musulmans dans la Société Française* (Paris: Presse de la Fondation Nationale des Sciences Politiques).

Lever-Tracy, C. and Quinlan, M. (1988) *A Divided Working Class* (London: Routledge).

Lever-Tracy, C., Ip, D., Kitay, J., Phillips, I. and Tracy, N. (1991) *Asian Entrepreneurs in Australia* (Canberra: Australian Government Publishing Service).

Levine, M., McLenna, P. and Pearce, J. (1992) *Immigrant Workers in the Automotive Industry* (Canberra: Australian Government Publishing Service).

Lidgard, J. M. (1996) *East Asian Migration to Aotearoa/New Zealand: Perspectives of Some New Arrivals*, Hamilton: University of Waikato Population Studies Centre Discussion Papers, no. 12.

Light, I. and Bonacich, E. (1988) *Immigrant Entrepreneurs* (Berkeley, CA: University of California Press).

Lim, L. L. (1996) 'The migration transition in Malaysia', *Asian and Pacific Migration Journal* 5:2–3.

Lim, L. L. and Oishi, N. (1996) 'International labor migration of Asian women', *Asian and Pacific Migration Journal* 5:1.

Lithman, E. L. (1987) *Immigration and Immigrant Policy in Sweden* (Stockholm: Swedish Institute).

Lloyd, C. (1991) 'Concepts, models and anti-racist strategies in Britain and France', *New Community* 18:1.

Lohrmann, R. (1987) 'Irregular Migration: A Rising Issue in Developing Countries' *International Migration* 25:3.

Loutete-Dangui, N. (1988) 'L'immigration étrangère au Congo', in Association Internationale des Démographes de Langue Française, *Les Migrations Internationales* (Paris: Edition de l'INED).

Lucassen, J. (1995) 'Emigration to the Dutch colonies and the USA', in R. Cohen (ed.), *The Cambridge Survey of World Migration* (Cambridge: Cambridge University Press).

Lutz, H., Phoenix, A. and Yuval-Davis, N. (1995) 'Introduction: nationalism, racism and gender', in H. Lutz, A. Phoenix and N. Yuval-Davis (eds),

Crossfires: Nationalism, Racism and Gender in Europe (London: Pluto Press).

MacMaster, N. (1991) 'The "seuil de tolérance": the uses of a "scientific" racist concept', in M. Silverman (ed.), *Race, Discourse and Power in France* (Aldershot: Avebury).

Maguid, A. (1993) 'The importance of systematizing migration information for making policy: recent initiatives and possibilities for Latin America and the Caribbean', *IOM Latin America Migration Journal* 11:3.

Manfrass, K. (1992) 'Süd-Nord oder Ost-West Wanderung', *International Migration Review*, Special Issue on the New Europe and International Migration 26:2.

Mann, J. A. (1979) 'For Millions in Colombia, Venezuela is El Dorado', 23 December.

Marcus, J. (1995) *The National Front and French Politics* (New York: New York University Press).

Marshall, T. H. (1964) 'Citizenship and Social Class', in *Class, Citizenship and Social Development: Essays by T. H. Marshall* (New York: Anchor Books).

Martin, P. (1996) 'Labor contractors: a conceptual overview', *Asian and Pacific Migration Journal* 5:2–3.

Martin, P., Mason, A. and Nagayama, T. (1996) 'Introduction to special issue on the dynamics of labor migration in Asia', *Asian and Pacific Migration Journal* 5:2–3.

Martin, P. L. (1991a) 'Labor migration in Asia: conference report', *International Migration Review*, 25:1.

Martin, P. L. (1991b) *The Unfinished Story: Turkish Labour Migration to Western Europe* (Geneva: ILO).

Martin, P. L. (1992) 'Trade, Aid and Migration', *International Migration Review* 26: 1.

Martinez, J. N. (1989) 'Social Effects of Labour Migration: The Colombian Experience', *International Migration* 27:2.

Martiniello, M. (1994) 'Citizenship of the European Union: a critical view', in R. Bauböck (ed.), *From Aliens to Citizens* (Aldershot: Avebury).

Massey, D. S., Alarcón, R., Durand, J. and González (1987) *Return to Aztlan: The Social Process of International Migration from Western Mexico* (Berkeley: University of California Press).

Massey, D. S., Arango, J., Hugo, G. and Taylor, J. E. (1993) 'Theories of international migration: a review and appraisal', *Population and Development Review*, 19.

Massey, D. S., Arango, J., Hugo, G. and Taylor, J. E. (1994) 'An evaluation of international migration theory: the North American case', *Population and Development Review*, 20.

McAllister, I. (1988) 'Political attitudes and electoral behaviour', in J. Jupp, (ed.) *The Australian People: An Encyclopedia of the Nation, its People and their Origins* (Sydney: Angus & Robertson).

Mehideb, J. (1973) 'Usines Renault Billancourt: le tiers monde à l'usine', *Croissance des Jeunes Nations*, June.

Meissner, D., Papademetriou, D. and North, D. (1987) *Legalization of Undocumented Aliens: Lessons from Other Countries* (Washington, DC: Carnegie Endowment for International Peace).

Messina, A. M. (1989) 'Anti-immigrant illiberalism and the "new" ethnic and racial minorities in Western Europe', *Patterns of Prejudice* 23:3.

Messina, A.M. (1996) 'The not so silent revlolution: Postwar Migration to Western Europe,' *World Politics*, 49.

Miles, R. (1989) *Racism* (London: Routledge).

Miller, J. (1985) 'Wave of Arab Migration Ending with Oil Boom', *New York Times*, 6 October.

Miller, J. (1991) 'Egyptians now replace other Arabs in Saudi jobs', *New York Times*, 4 February.

Miller, M. and Martin, P. (1996) 'Prospects for cooperative management of international migration in the 21st century', *Asian and Pacific Migration Journal* 5:2–3.

Miller, M. J. (1978) *The Problem of Foreign Worker Participation and Representation in France, Switzerland and the Federal Republic of Germany* (Madison, WI: University of Wisconsin).

Miller, M. J. (1979) 'Reluctant Partnership: Foreign Workers in Franco-Algerian Relations, 1962–1979', in R. O. Matthews, A. G. Rubinoff and J. Gross Stein (eds), *International Conflict and Conflict Management* (Scarborough, Canada: Prentice-Hall).

Miller, M. J. (1981) *Foreign Workers in Western Europe: An Emerging Political Force* (New York: Praeger).

Miller, M. J. (1984) 'Industrial policy and the rights of labor: the case of foreign workers in the French automobile assembly industry', *Michigan Yearbook of International Legal Studies*, vol. vi.

Miller, M. J. (1986) 'Policy ad-hocracy: The Paucity of Coordinated Perspectives and Policies', *Annals*, 485.

Miller, M. J. (1991) 'La nouvelle loi américaine sur l'immigration: vers un modèle d'après-guerre froide', *Revue Européenne des Migrations Internationales* 7:3.

Miller, M. J. (1994) 'Towards understanding state capacity to prevent unwanted migration: Employer sancions enforcement in France, 1975–1990', *Western European Politics*, 17:2.

Mingione, E. (1996) *Urban Poverty and the Underclass* (Oxford: Blackwell).

Mitchell, C. (1989) 'International migration, international relations and foreign policy', *International Migration Review*, Special Silver Anniversary Issue, 23:3.

Moch, L. P. (1992) *Moving Europeans: Migration in Western Europe since 1650* (Bloomington, IN: Indiana University Press).

Moch, L. P. (1995) 'Moving Europeans: historical migration practices in Western Europe', in R. Cohen (ed.), *The Cambridge Survey of World Migration* (Cambridge: Cambridge University Press).

Mori, H. (1995) 'Foreign migrant workers in Japan: trends and policies' *Asian and Pacific Migration Journal* 4: 2–3.

Morokvasic, M. (1984) 'Birds of passage are also women', *International Migration Review* 18:4.

Moss, I. (Federal Race Discrimination Commissioner) (1993) *State of the Nation: A Report on People of Non-English Speaking Backgrounds* (Canberra: Australian Government Publishing Service).

Mosse, G. C. (1985) *Towards the Final Solution* (University of Wisconsin Press).

Münz, R. (1996) 'A continent of migration: European mass migration in the twentieth century', *New Community* 22:2.

Muus, P. J. (1991) *Migration, Minorities and Policy in the Netherlands: Recent Trends and Developments – Report for SOPEMI* (Amsterdam: University of Amsterdam, Department of Human Geography).

Muus, P. J. (1995) *Migration, Immigrants and Policy in the Netherlands – Report for SOPEMI 1995* (Amsterdam: Centre for Migration Research).

Naidoo, J. C. (1989) *Canada's Response to Racism: Visible Minorities in Ontario,* background paper, Third International Symposium on the World Refugee Crisis, Oxford.

(National Population Council (1991) *Refugee Review* (Canberra: National Population Council).

Nirumand, B. (ed.) (1992) *Angst vor den Deutschen: Terror gegen Ausländer und der Zerfall des Rechtstaates* (Reinbek bei Hamburg: Rowohlt).

Nobel, P. (1988) *Human Rights of Aliens – Experience and Practice of the Ombudsman* (Stockholm: Ombudsman Against Ethnic Discrimination).

Noble, K. B. (1991) 'Congo Expelling Zairian Citizens', *New York Times,* 11 December.

Noiriel, G. (1988) *Le creuset français: Histoire de l'immigration XIXe–XXe siècles* (Paris: Seuil).

Oberndörfer, D. (1993) *Der Wahn des Nationalen* (Freiburg: Herder).

OECD (1987) *The Future of Migration* (Paris: OECD).

OECD (1990) *OECD Continuous Reporting System on Migration (SOPEMI), Report 1989* (Paris: OECD).

OECD (1992) *Trends in International Migration: Annual Report 1991* (Paris: OECD).

OECD (1994) *Trends in International Migration: Annual Report 1993* (Paris: OECD).

OECD (1995) *Trends in International Migration: Annual Report 1994* (Paris: OECD).

OECD (1997) *Trends in International Migration: Annual Report 1996* (Paris: OECD).

Oishi, N. (1995) 'Training or employment? Japanese immigration policy in dilemma', *Asian and Pacific Migration Journal* 4:2–3.

Okunishi, Y. (1996) 'Labor contracting in international migration: the Japanese case and implications for Asia', *Asian and Pacific Migration Journal* 5:2–3.

Pachon, H. P. (1987) 'An overview of citizenship in the Hispanic community', *International Migration Review* 21:2.

Pascoe, R. (1992) 'Place and community: the construction of Italo-Australian space', in S. Castles, C. Alcorso, G. Rando and E. Vasta (eds), *Australia's Italians: Culture and Community in a Changing Society* (Sydney: Allen & Unwin).

Pe-Pua, R., Mitchell, C., Iredale, R. and Castles, S. (1996) *Astronaut Families and Parachute Children: The Cycle of Migration from Hong Kong* (Canberra: AGPS).

Péan, L. (1982) 'L'alliance hégémonique insulaire', *Le Monde Diplomatique,* August.

Pelligrino, A. (1984) 'Illegal Immigration from Colombia', *International Migration Review* 18:3.

Perotti, A. and Thepaut, F. (1991) 'Les répercussions de la guerre du golfe sur les arabes et les juifs de France', *Migrations Société* 3:14.

Pfahlmann, H. (1968) *Fremdarbeiter und Kriegsgefangene in der deutschen Kriegswirtschaft 1939–45* (Darmstadt: Wehr & Wissen).

Phizacklea, A. (ed.) (1983) *One Way Ticket? Migration and Female Labour* (London: Routledge & Kegan Paul).

Phizacklea, A. (1990) *Unpacking the Fashion Industry: Gender, Racism and Class in Production* (London: Routledge).

Picquet, M., Pelligrino, A. and Papail, J. (1986) 'L'immigration au Venezuela', *Revue Européenne des Migrations Internationales* 2:2.

Piore, M. J. (1979) *Birds of Passage: Migrant Labor and Industrial Societies* (Cambridge: Cambridge University Press).

Poinsot, M. (1993) 'Competition for political legitimacy at local and national levels among young North Africans in France', *New Community* 20:1.

Ponty, J. (1988) 'Les rapatriements des travailleurs polonais dans les années trente', *Hommes et Migrations* 1115.

Pool, I. and Bedford, R. (1996) *Macro Social Change in New Zealand: Historical and International Contexts,* Hamilton: University of Waikato Population Studies Centre Discussion Papers no. 18.

Portes, A. and Böröcz, J. (1989) 'Contemporary immigration: theoretical perspectives on its determinants and modes of incorporation', *International Migration Review* 23:83.

Portes, A. and Rumbaut, R. G. (1990) *Immigrant America: A Portrait* (Los Angeles: University of California Press).

Potts, L. (1990) *The World Labour Market: A History of Migration* (London: Zed Books).

Price, C. (1963) *Southern Europeans in Australia* (Melbourne: Oxford University Press).

Prost, A. (1966) 'L'immigration en France depuis cent ans', *Esprit* 34:348.

Purcell, J. N. Jr. (1995) 'Forward' in N. Falchi *International Migration Pressures* (Geneva: IOM).

Rajaee, B. (1996) The Evolution of Iran's Post-Revolutionary Refugee Policy unpublished paper University of Delaware.

Rath, J. (1988) 'La participation des immigrés aux élections locales aux Pays-Bas' *Revue Européenne des Migrations Internationales* 4:3.

Ravenstein, E. G. (1885) 'The laws of migration', *Journal of the Statistical Society,* vol. 48.

Ravenstein, E. G. (1889) 'The laws of migration', *Journal of the Statistical Society,* vol. 52.

Rawls, J. (1985) 'Justice as fairness: political not metaphysical', *Philosophy and Public Affairs* 14:3.

Reed, R. (1977) 'National Front: British threat', *New York Times,* 18 August.

Research Perspectives on Migration (1997) (Washington, DC: The Urban Institute and the Carnegie Endowment for International Peace), 1:2.

Rex. J. (1986) *Race and Ethnicity* (Milton Keynes: Open University Press).

Rex, J. and Mason, D. (eds) (1986) *Theories of Race and Ethnic Relations* (Cambridge: Cambridge University Press).

Ricca, S. (1990) *Migrations internationales en Afrique* (Paris: L'Harmattan).

Rogers, R. (1992) 'The future of refugee flows and policies', *International Migration Review* 26:4.

Roussillon, A. (1985) 'Migrations de main-d'oeuvre et unité arabe: Les enjeux unitaires du modèle irakien', *Revue Tiers Monde* 10.

Ruddock, P. (Minister for Immigration and Multicultural Affairs) (1996) *Media Release: MPS 28/96 Humanitarian Program* (Canberra).

Rudolph, H. (1996) 'The new G*astarbeiter* system in Germany', *New Community* 22:2.

Rutten, T. (1992) 'Why LA burned', *New York Review of Books,* reprinted in *The Independent Monthly,* June.

Salt, J. (1989) 'A comparative overview of international trends and types', *International Migration Review,* Special Silver Anniversary Issue, 23:3.

Sanz, L. C. (1989) 'The Impact of Chilean Migration on Employment in Patagonia', *International Migration* 27:2.

Sassen, S. (1988) *The Mobility of Labour and Capital* (Cambridge: Cambridge University Press).

Schierup, C.-U. (1991) 'The puzzle of trans-ethnic society', in A. Ålund and C.-U. Schierup, *Paradoxes of Multiculturalism* (Aldershot: Avebury).

Schierup, C.-U. and Ålund, A. (1987) *Will they still be Dancing? Integration and Ethnic Transformation among Yugoslav Immigrants in Scandinavia* (Stockholm: Almquist & Wiksell International).

Schnapper, D. (1991) 'A host country of immigrants that does not know itself', *Diaspora* 1:3.

Schnapper, D. (1994) *La Communauté des Citoyens* (Paris: Gallimard).

Seccombe, I. J. (1986) 'Immigrant Workers in an Emigrant Economy', *International Migration* 24:2.

Seccombe, I. J. and Lawless, R. I. (1986) 'Foreign Worker Dependence in the Gulf and International Oil Companies', *International Migration Review* 20:3.

Segal, A. (1993) *An Atlas of International Migration* (London: Hans Zell Publishers).

Seifert, W. (1996) 'Occupational and social integration of immigrant groups in Germany' *New Community* 22:3.

Sekine, M. (1990) *Guest Workers in Japan* (Wollongong: Centre for Multicultural Studies), Occasional Paper no. 21.

Semyonov, M. and Lewin-Epstein, N. (1987) *Hewers of Wood and Drawers of Water* (Ithaca, NY: ILR Press).

Seton-Watson, H. (1977) *Nations and States* (London: Methuen).

Shain, Y. (1989) *Frontier of Loyalty: Political Exiles in the Age of the Nation-State* (Middletown CT: Wesleyan University Press).

Shevstova, L. (1992) 'Soviet Emigration Today and Tomorrow', *International Migration Review,* Special Issue on the New Europe and International Migration, 26:2.

Shimpo, M. (1995) 'Indentured migrants from Japan', in R. Cohen, (ed.) *The Cambridge Survey of World Migration* (Cambridge: Cambridge University Press).

Simon, G. (ed.) (1990) *Les effets des migrations internationales sur les pays d'origine: le cas du Maghreb* (Paris: SEDES).

Simon, J. (1989) *The Economic Consequences of Immigration* (Oxford: Blackwell).

Singaby, T. E. (1985) 'Migrations et capitalisation de la campagne en Egypte: La reconversion de la famille paysanne', *Revue Tiers Monde,* 26:103.

Sivanandan, A. (1982) *A Different Hunger* (London: Pluto Press).

Skeldon, R. (1992) 'International migration within and from the East and Southeast Asian region: a review essay', *Asian and Pacific Migration Journal* 1:1.

Skeldon, R. (ed.) (1994) *Reluctant Exiles? Migration from Hong Kong and the New Overseas Chinese* (Hong Kong: Hong Kong University Press).

Smith, A. D. (1986) *The Ethnic Origins of Nations* (Oxford: Blackwell).

Smith, A. D. (1991) *National Identity* (Harmondsworth: Penguin).

Smith, S. (1989) *The Politics of 'Race' and Residence* (Cambridge: Polity).

Sole, R. (1990) 'Obsédante immigration', *Le Monde,* 22 May.

Sole, R. (1991) 'Le Front National présente cinquante mesures pour régler le problème de l'immigration', *Le Monde,* 19 November.

Solomos, J. (1988) 'Institutionalised racism: policies of marginalisation in education and training', in P. Cohen and H. S. Bains (eds), *Multi-Racist Britain* (London: Macmillan).

Solomos, J. (1993) *Race and Racism in Contemporary Britain,* 2 edn (London: Macmillan).

Solomos, J. and Back, L. (1995) *Race, Politics and Social Change* (London: Routledge).

Solomos, J. and Wrench, J. (1993) *Racism and Migration in Europe* (Oxford and New York: Berg).

Soysal, Y. N. (1994) *Limits of Citizenship: Migrants and Postnational Membership in Europe* (Chicago and London: University of Chicago Press).

Stahl, C. (ed.) (1988) *International Migration Today: Emerging Issues* (Paris: UNESCO).

Stahl, C. W. (1990) 'South North migration in the Asian-Pacific region', paper presented to the IOM Conference on South-North Migration Geneva.

Stahl, C. (1993) 'Explaining international migration', in C. Stahl, R. Ball, C. Inglis and P. Gutman (eds), *Global Population Movements and their Implications for Australia* (Canberra: Australian Government Publishing Service).

Stalker, P. (1994) *The Work of Strangers: A Survey of International Labour Migration* (Geneva: ILO).

Stark, O. (1991) *The Migration of Labour* (Oxford: Blackwell).

Stasiulis, D. K. (1988) 'The symbolic mosaic reaffirmed: multiculturalism policy', in K. A. Graham (ed.), *How Ottawa Spends, 1988/89* (Ottawa: Carleton University Press).

Stasiulis, D. and Jhappan, R. (1995) 'The fractious politics of a settler society: Canada', in D. Stasiulis and N. Yuval-Davis (eds), *Unsettling Settler Societies* (London: Sage).

Stasiulis, D. and Yuval-Davis, N. (eds) (1995) *Unsettling Settler Societies* (London: Sage).

Statistics Canada (1996) *Selected Ethnic Origins, 1991,* WWW Site, Catalogue no. 93-315.

Steinberg, S. (1981) *The Ethnic Myth: Race, Ethnicity and Class in America* (Boston, MA: Beacon Press).

Stichter, S. (1985) *Migrant Labourers* (Cambridge: Cambridge University Press).

Stirn, H. (1964) *Ausländische Arbeiter im Betrieb* (Frechen/Cologne: Bartmann).

Stola, D. (1992) 'Forced Migrations in Central European History', *International Migration Review*, Special Issue on the New Europe and International Migration, 26:2.

Studlar, D. T. and Layton-Henry, Z. (1990) 'Non-white minority access to the political agenda in Britain', *Policy Studies Review* 9:2 (Winter).

Suhrke, A. and Klink, F. (1987) 'Contrasting patterns of Asian refugee movements: the Vietnamese and Afghan syndromes', in J. T. Fawcett and B. V. Cariño (eds), *Pacific Bridges: The New Immigration from Asia and the Pacific Islands* (New York: Center for Migration Studies).

Suzuki, H. (1988) 'A new policy for foreign workers in Japan? Current debate and perspective', *Waseda Business and Economic Studies*, no. 24.

Szoke, L. (1992) 'Hungarian Perspectives on Emigration and Immigration in the New European Architecture', *International Migration Review*, Special Issue on the New Europe and International Migration, 26:2.

Taifel, H. (1982) 'The social psychology of minorities', in C. Husband (ed.), *'Race' in Britain* (London: Hutchinson).

Tamas, K. (1997) 'The Immigration Control Politics of Hungary', conference paper presented at the New School for Social Research, June.

Tapinos, G. (1993) *Regional Economic Integration and the Effects on Employment and Migration* (Paris: OECD).

Teitelbaum, M. S. and Weiner, M. (1995) *Threatened Peoples, Threatened Borders: World Migration and US Policy* (New York and London: Norton).

Thränhardt, D. (1996) 'European Migration from East to West: present patterns and future directions', *New Community*, 22.2.

Tichy, R. (1990) *Ausländer rein! Warum es kein 'Ausländerproblem' gibt* (Munich: Piper).

Tiersky, R. (1994) *France in the new Europe: Changing yet Steadfast* (Belmont, CA: Woodsworth).

Toth, J. (1992) 'Changing refugee policy in Hungary', *Migration World Magazine* 20:2.

Tribalat, M. (1992) 'Chronique de l'immigration', *Population* 47:1.

Tribalat, M. (1995) *Faire France: Une Enquête sur les Immigrés et leurs Enfants* (Paris: La Découverte).

Trlin, A. D. (1987) 'New Zealand's Admission of Asians and Pacific Islanders', in J. T. Fawcett and B. V. Cariño (eds), *Pacific Bridges: The New Immigration from Asia and the Pacific Islands* (New York: Center for Migration Studies).

UN Economic Commission for Europe (1995) *International Migration Bulletin* No. 7 (November).

UNHCR (United Nations High Commissioner for Refugees – Italian Office) (1991) *For Forty Years, UNHCR Alongside Refugees* (Rome: Vita Italiana).

UNHCR (United Nations High Commissioner for Refugees) (1995) *The State of the World's Refugees* (Oxford: Oxford University Press).

US Census Bureau (1996) *The Foreign-Born Population 1994,* US Census Bureau, WWW Site, 22 August 1996.

US Committee for Refugees (1996) *World Refuge Survey 1996* (Washington, DC: Immigration and Refugee Services of America).

US Department of Justice (1994) *Statistical Yearbook of the Immigration and Naturalization Service* (Washington: US Government).

US Department of Labor (1989) *The Effects of Immigration on the US Economy and Labor Market* (Washington, DC: US Government Document).

Vasileva, D. (1992) 'Bulgarian Turkish Emigration and Return', *International Migration Review,* Special Issue on the New Europe and International Migration, 26:2.

Vasta, E. (1990) 'Gender, class and ethnic relations: the domestic and work experiences of Italian migrant women in Australia', *Migration,* no. 7.

Vasta, E. (1991) 'Australia's Post-War Immigration: Power Identity and Resistance' (University of Queensland, PhD thesis).

Vasta, E. (1992) 'The second generation', in S. Castles, C. Alcorso, G. Rando and E. Vasta (eds), *Australia's Italians: Culture and Community in a Changing Society* (Sydney: Allen & Unwin).

Vasta, E. (1996) 'Dialectics of domination: racism and multiculturalism' in E. Vasta and S. Castles (eds), *The Teeth are Smiling: The Persistence of Racism in Multicultural Australia* (Sydney: Allen & Unwin).

Vasta, E. and Castles, S. (eds) (1996) *The Teeth are Smiling: The Persistence of Racism in Multicultural Australia* (Sydney: Allen & Unwin).

Vasta, E., Rando, G., Castles, S. and Alcorso, C. (1992) 'The Italo-Australian community on the Pacific rim', in S. Castles, C. Alcorso, G. Rando and E. Vasta (eds), *Australia's Italians: Culture and Community in a Changing Society* (Sydney: Allen & Unwin).

Verbunt, G. (1985) 'France', in T. Hammar (ed.) *European Immigration Policy: A Comparative Study* (Cambridge: Cambridge University Press).

Vuddamalay, V. (1990) 'Tendances nouvelles dans le commerce étranger en France', *Migrations et Société* 2:11.

Waldinger, R., Aldrich, H., Ward, R. and Associates (1990) *Ethnic Entrepreneurs Immigrant Business in Industrial Societies* (Newbury Park, London, New Delhi: Sage).

Wallerstein, I. (1991) 'The ideological tensions of capitalism: universalism versus racism and sexism' in E. Balibar and I. Wallerstein (eds), *Race, Nation, Class: Ambiguous Identities* (London: Verso).

Wallman, S. (1986) 'Ethnicity and boundary processes', in J. Rex and D. Mason, (eds), *Theories of Race and Ethnic Relations* (Cambridge: Cambridge University Press).

Weber, M. (1968) *Economy and Society,* G. Roth, and C. Wittich, (New York: Bedminister Press).

Weil, P. (1991a) 'Immigration and the rise of racism in France: The contradictions of Mitterrand's policies', *French Society and Politics,* 9:3–4.

Weil, P. (1991b) *La France et ses Étrangers* (Paris: Calmann-Levy).

Weiner, M. (ed.) 1993 *International Migration and Security* (Boulder, Co: Westview Press).

Weintraub, S. (1996) 'NAFTA benefits flow back and forth across the Rio Grande', *The Wall Street Journal,* 10 May, A11.

Werner, H. (1992) 'Labour market trends and migration from the perspective of the Single European Market', in L. Tomasi (ed.), *In Defense of the Alien* (New York: Center for Migration Studies).

Widgren, J. (1987) 'International Migration: New Challenge to Europe', *Migration News* 2:3–35.

Widgren, J. (1989) 'Asylum-seekers in Europe in the context of South–North movements', *International Migration Review*, Special Silver Anniversary Issue 23:3.

Wieviorka, M. (1991) *L'Espace du Racisme* (Paris: Seuil).

Wieviorka, M. (1992) *La France Raciste* (Paris: Seuil).

Wieviorka, M. (1995) *The Arena of Racism* (London: Sage).

Wihtol de Wenden, C. (1987) *Citoyenneté, Nationalité et Immigration* (Paris: Arcantère Éditions).

Wihtol de Wenden, C. (1988) *Les Immigrés et la Politique* (Paris: Presses de la Fondation Nationale des Sciences Politiques).

Wihtol de Wenden, C. (1995) 'Generational change and political participation in French suburbs', *New Community* 21:1.

Willard, J. C. (1984) 'Conditions d'emploi et salaires de la main d'oeuvre étrangère', *Economie et Statistique*, January.

Wilton, J. and Bosworth, R. (1984) *Old Worlds and New Australia* (Ringwood, Vic.: Penguin).

Wong, D. (1996) 'Foreign domestic workers in Singapore', *Asian and Pacific Migration Journal* 5:1.

Zolberg, A. R. (1983) 'The formation of new states as a refugee generating process', *The Annals of the American Academy of Political and Social Science*, 467.

Zolberg, A. R. (1989) 'The next waves: migration theory for a changing world', *International Migration Review* 23:3.

Zolberg, A. R., Suhrke, A. and Aguao, S. (1989) *Escape from Violence* (New York: Oxford University Press).

Index

Note: page numbers in **bold** type indicate references to exhibits.